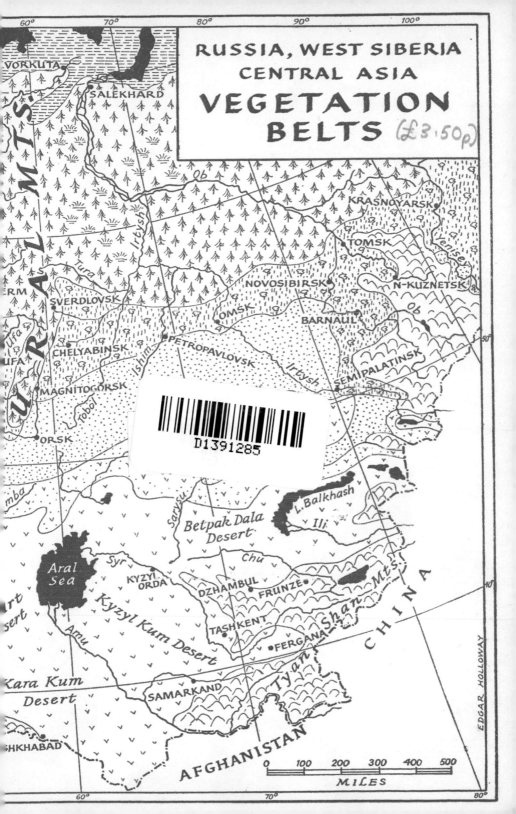

RUSSIA, WEST SIBERIA CENTRAL ASIA VEGETATION BELTS (£3·50p)

EDGAR HOLLOWAY

AN HISTORICAL GEOGRAPHY OF RUSSIA

AN HISTORICAL GEOGRAPHY OF RUSSIA

W. H. PARKER M.A. B.SC. D.PHIL. (OXON.)
Lecturer in the Geography of the U.S.S.R.
in the University of Oxford

UNIVERSITY OF LONDON PRESS LTD

SBN 340 06940 6

University of London Press Ltd
St Paul's House, Warwick Lane, London EC4

Maps and diagrams drawn by Edgar Holloway

Printed and bound in Great Britain by
C. Tinling and Co. Ltd, Liverpool, London and Prescot

PREFACE

There are two traditional views of historical geography which have some weight of authority behind them. One is commonly held by historians and is concerned with geographical factors in history, especially as they affect the rise and fall, and the expansion and contraction of states. Position with regard to other states, and the international relationships consequent upon it, loom large among the geographical factors considered. The approach is chronological and might better be called geographical history than historical geography. It is sometimes dubbed 'history plus maps' by geographers; but it could be argued that history with maps is better than history without them, and that history that needs cartographic illustration —or benefits from it—has some geographical content.

Until recently, geographers concerned themselves less than historians with historical geography, but in so far as there is a geographer's tradition, it may be said to involve the reconstruction of past geographies. This tradition goes back to Clüver's *Germania Antiqua* (1616), and had the support of Kant, Ritter, Hettner and Mackinder. Probably no one has made a more thorough study of the sum of geographical writing than Richard Hartshorne, who wrote in 1939: 'That historical geography is to be considered simply as the geography of past periods is a view on which there is perhaps more agreement among geographers than on almost any other question of definition in our field' (*The Nature of Geography*, p. 185). When these past geographies are reconstructed for times of historical and cultural significance, they are especially valuable, both in illuminating the historical event or cultural phase to which they provide the background, and also in comparison one with another.

Since the war there has been an attempt by a few geographers to introduce a third subject into historical geography. This is defined as 'geographical change through time': it aims to be a history of landscape change but more often turns out to be economic history. Unlike the historian's historical geography, which also deals with evolution through time, it has no authority or tradition to justify a claim to be historical geography. It should be given its true name, i.e. 'the history of landscape' or 'economic history'.

The present book attempts to combine the historical geography of the historian with that of the geographer. Reconstructions of past economic and social geographies are linked by 'geographical histories' of the intervening periods of time. As I regard Russia's position in relation to Europe as the key geographical factor in her history, I have emphasized this aspect of her historical geography throughout. In so far as the book has a theme, it is to be found in the consequences of the juxtaposition of Europe and Russia.

I wish to thank all who have helped me in one way or another in writing this book: my wife, Marjorie, and my sons, William and Richard; Mr J. A. Cragg, Professor E. W. Gilbert, Professor D. J. M. Hooson and Mr J. Simmons; the staffs of the Slavonic Studies Reading Room and the Map Room of the Bodleian Library, of the Oxford School of Geography, of the British Museum Reading Room and Map Room, and of the Shropshire County Library. The Nuffield Foundation and the University of Oxford assisted me with travel grants. I am particularly indebted to Mr L. M. H. Timmermans of University of London Press Ltd for his patient understanding of the problems involved in this work and to Mr Pendleton Campbell, for his care of the book during its production.

Christ Church
Oxford, February 1967   W.H.P.

CONTENTS

MAPS AND DIAGRAMS

PLATES

To E. W. Gilbert

CHAPTER ONE
GEOGRAPHICAL FACTORS AND RUSSIAN HISTORY

The most striking feature of Russia's geographical position is its continentality. The peninsularity which marks the western extremities of the great Eurasian land mass is absent, and the country is almost wholly bounded by land or frozen sea. The expansion of old Russia into the modern U.S.S.R. has changed this surprisingly little. Where Russia does have connections with non-freezing or 'warm-water' seas, these links have been tenuous and easily broken. Russian external policy has, therefore, from early times been influenced by the desire to secure better access to the sea. Since such access has usually been liable to interference from other peoples, this policy has resulted in a long history of conflict. The early Russia, centred around Kiev, struggled to maintain its Black Sea communications with Byzantium or Constantinople across the nomad-ridden steppes. Muscovy fought to retain its precarious foothold on the Gulf of Finland. The new Russian Empire of the tsars exhausted itself in repeated wars for improved outlets on the Baltic, Black, Mediterranean and Caspian Seas, not to mention the Pacific Ocean.[1]

The Soviet Union has tried to adapt itself to this continentality rather than struggle against it as did Russian rulers in the past. The Stalinist determination to achieve economic self-sufficiency, and the development of vast industrial complexes in the heart of the country, have lessened the significance of maritime outlets and the importance of seaports. This is exemplified by the decline in the relative importance of Odessa, built by Catherine the Great as a Black Sea outlet for Russian produce. In 1897 it was third in population among Russian towns; in 1959 it was fourteenth among Soviet cities. On the other hand, Novosibirsk, in the continental heartland of the U.S.S.R., has risen from nothing to a population of a million in seventy years, thus becoming the twentieth century's fastest growing town.[2]

Russia's continentality is emphasized by her isolation from maritime influences—isolation not only by distance, but by mountain, marsh and ice (fig. 1). This is true both of the original Russia and of her extension

[1] *The explanation of the expansion of Russia in terms of a conscious 'urge to the sea' or 'a desire for warm water ports' is dubbed a 'fallacious generalization' by Morrison (1952), p. 1,169. His arguments are not entirely convincing. On the other hand, Kerner (1946) called his work,* The Urge to the Sea; the Course of Russian History. *The view implicit in this title was that of Klyuchevskiy (1956), vol. 1, p. 65, and many other eminent historians of Russia*

[2] *For an illuminating account of the development of continental interior of the U.S.S.R., see D. J. M. Hooson (1964)*

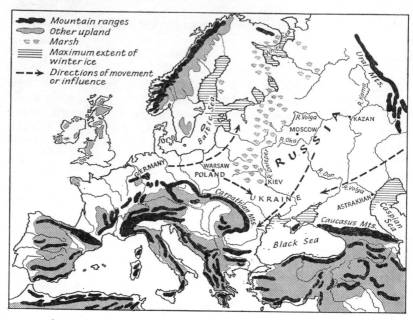

figure 1   Russia and Europe: the physiographical contrast. Note the mountain barriers enclosing Russia and the importance of gaps in these barriers.

beyond the Urals and the Caspian. The marshes on Russia's western borders, particularly the Pripyat marshes, by making movement difficult between Poland and Russia, helped to keep Russia apart from Europe. In the south-west the Carpathians and the Balkan mountains formed an obstacle between Russia on the one hand and southern Europe and the Mediterranean on the other. Between the Russian lowland and the West Siberian plain, the Urals form a range of worn hills which seldom have a really mountainous aspect, although dropping steeply to the east. Nevertheless their forested slopes for long formed a barrier to Russian eastward expansion, just as the Appalachians held up the European advance westward in North America. The ancient empire of Novgorod had reached the Urals by the year 1200 but it was not until about 1600 that the Russians began to cross the barrier in significant numbers. With modern communications, the Urals have ceased to form any kind of barrier. For the greater Russia which has expanded far beyond them, the immense and tangled girdle of high mountain chains which rim its territory to the south-east, south and south-west, are more important. These mountain masses have divided the Russian Empire from the lands of south-east Asia far more thoroughly than the Alps have separated northern and southern Europe. Because of them, the contrast between the human geography of northern and southern Asia is complete.

The geographical position of Canada in North America resembles that

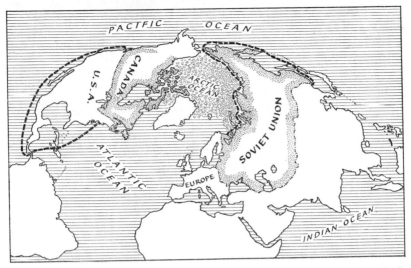

figure 2 The Arctic Sea Route of the Soviet Union compared with the Panama Canal Route between the east and west coasts of North America.

of the U.S.S.R. in Eurasia. But, in North America, the southern limits of Canada are merely political boundaries crossing a continent whose physical grain runs north and south: they leave that country open to American influence. In Eurasia on the other hand, the southern boundary of the U.S.S.R. follows the dictates of physical geography. Russia's position in northern Eurasia also differs from Canada's in northern North America because of the dissimilar configuration of the two continents. The narrowing of North America southwards to the isthmus of Panama has facilitated sea communication between its east and west coasts. But Russia's intercoastal seaway has to follow the Arctic coast and is only feasible because of modern techniques in ice mapping and ice breaking, and then only for a few weeks each year (fig. 2).

While the location of a country remains constant, the various influences impinging upon or emanating from it are unlikely to do so over a long period. Russia's continental position, landlocked within Eurasia, laid her open to influences from north, south, east and west in turn (fig. 3). But it has also enabled her to affect her neighbours. During the eighth, ninth and tenth centuries Russia was penetrated and conquered from Scandinavia. For many centuries, from well before to well after the period of Scandinavian domination, Kievan Russia was culturally overshadowed by Byzantium whence, in the tenth century, she received the Greek form of Christianity. Then, in the thirteenth century, the Tartar conquest imposed a strong Mongol influence upon the growing Muscovite state which succeeded Kiev as the leading Russian power. This oriental influence outlasted the period of actual Tartar overlordship and, according to

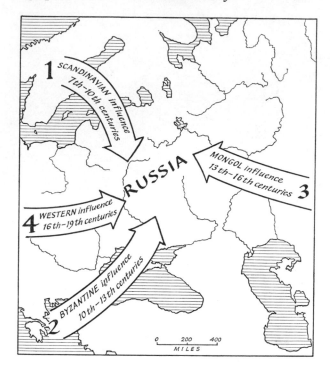

figure 3   Before becoming herself a powerful source of influence, Russia was successively subjected to influences from various directions.

Karamzin, marked indelibly the character of the nation.[1] During the seventeenth century, impulses from Europe, previously weak and intermittent, made a significant impact upon Russia, while the reign of Peter I (1684-1725) was one of active and enforced westernization. From then on until the twentieth century, Russia was regarded as part of the European system.

The Revolution of 1917 witnessed the birth of a new Russia which, besides receiving ideas and influences from without, began itself to influence the countries around, firstly through its political, social and economic doctrines (1917-39), secondly by its military successes over Nazi Germany (1941-5), thirdly by its rapid industrial recovery and progress after the war (1945-57), and finally by its achievements in rocketry and space research after 1957.

Despite her continental position, a comparison can be made between Russia and insular Britain. Both are marginal to Europe. Both throughout their histories have stood, to varying degrees, apart from the continent and its affairs; and both expanded territorially and imperially away from its

[1] *Karamzin (1820), V, pp. 447-9*

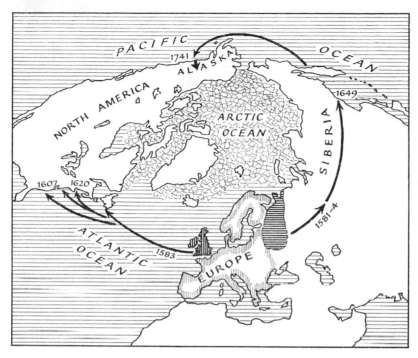

figure 4 The simultaneous expansion of Russia landward and of England seaward from the margins of Europe.

confines into distant regions: Russia overland and Britain overseas. It is indeed a remarkable coincidence that at the same time as English coloniza-tion of North America began, the Russians first penetrated Siberia (fig. 4). In both countries there were a surplus population and adventurers willing to probe the unknown. In 1581 the Cossack Yermak penetrated Siberia, and the conquest and settlement of that region by Russians began; in 1583 Sir Humphrey Gilbert carried the first group of English colonists to Newfoundland. During the seventeenth century, while the English sailed west across the Atlantic, Russian fur traders crossed northern Asia by canoe and portage. Whereas the English colonists—and other West Europeans—were delayed by the Appalachian barrier, no obstacle pre-vented the Russians, already across the Urals, from reaching the Pacific. In the eighteenth century they went still farther, crossing the Bering Strait and entering North America at the Alaskan end. Had this approach been easier, North America might well have been peopled by Russians before the Europeans spread beyond the Appalachians. Instead, Russian North America atrophied owing to the unattractiveness of Alaska and the intensification of serfdom, which made it increasingly difficult for peasants to leave old Russia. When Alaska was purchased by the United States in 1867, Russia lost her feeble foothold on the North American continent.

A geographical factor of the utmost importance in the history of the Russian people has been the sheer size of the land it was destined to control. To the east of the East Slavs lay the largest extent of land on the earth's surface, but because of its physical geography it remained but sparsely populated by isolated and backward tribes. Hence, all the time the Russians and associated nations were prolific and resourceful enough to take advantage of it, opportunity for expansion was always present in the frontier zone:

> *Throughout Russian history one dominating theme has been the frontier; the theme of the struggle for the mastering of the natural resources of an untamed country, expanded into a continent by the ever-shifting movement of the Russian people, and their conquest of and intermingling with other peoples.*[1]

The 'frontier', a mere century-long episode in American history, has been a dominating influence in Russian history since the birth of the nation a thousand years and more ago; it remains a strong factor in the present evolution of the Soviet state, and is likely to persist as such for centuries. It was the reason for the extension and prolongation of serfdom, since landlords in the old-settled areas had to try to keep their labour from migrating to new lands. It gave Russian agriculture a characteristic it still retains today, i.e. a preference for increasing production by extending the sown area rather than improving the yield from existing farmland.

The contrast with the United States can be carried further. While engaged in pushing her own frontier westwards to the Pacific, the United States was almost completely free from outside interference, having the ocean as her eastern limit. Such wars as she fought were with the weaker peoples who stood in the way of her 'manifest destiny'—even the 1812 war with Britain was fought against the Canadians. Only when she no longer had a frontier within her own territory, were the surplus energies of a vigorous nation deployed in European and Asian wars. Russia, on the other hand, has never been able to devote herself entirely to her eastern frontier, having repeatedly to deal with problems created by a land boundary with Europe. Not the least of these has been the need to repel a series of European invasions: by Lithuanians, Poles, Swedes, French, British and Germans. But this has been a question for governments rather than the Russian people. Although compelled from time to time to fight in the west, their natural bent has been to colonize in the east.

Another great geographical factor that has formed a powerful influence in Russia's historical development, is uniformity. From her simplicity of geological structure (fig. 5) have been derived a uniformity of relief and a monotony of landscape over large areas in which historians have seen a main cause of political unity and centralized authority.[2] In Europe, a complex structure is reflected in broken and varied relief; this favoured the formation of small autonomous political units with individualistic

---

[1] *Sumner (1944), p. 9*
[2] *Platonov (1929), p. 9; Clarkson (1962), p. 9*

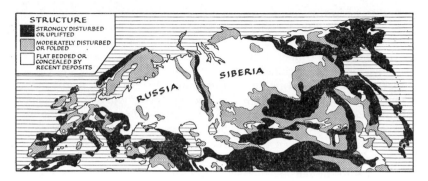

figure 5 Russia and Siberia are large areas of relatively uniform structure and relief, surrounded by regions of disturbed structure and pronounced relief (based, with permission, on a map in the Oxford Atlas).

customs, cultures and languages. A centralizing monarch found his way opposed by physical obstacles which often lent themselves to defiant fortification against him. In Russia, not only were such obstacles few, but the great riverways facilitated the swift passage of large armies over large distances. European physical diversity fostered a regional separatism which provided popular support for those who wished to resist unification. Thus Russia, despite her vast size, proved easier to hold down than many a European state of much smaller extent.

The uniformity of the Russian lowland is surpassed by that of the West Siberian plain to the east. Here, the largest extent of flat land in the world, with width and length over 1,200 miles, does not rise above 700 feet. Again, the level nature of this plain, combined with the length and number of rivers which it favoured, facilitated the Russian conquest of Siberia.

A very important consequence of relative uniformity of relief and structure has been the evolution of a system of long navigable rivers. The importance of these to Russian history is immense, especially before the spread of railways. The rivers enabled the Russians to travel more extensively and expeditiously than the more advanced peoples of Europe, with their bad roads and lock-ridden canals. In this respect Russians rather resembled the North American Indians to whom rivers had given the freedom of a whole continent. Rivers offered swift communication in all directions and the trellis pattern of their drainage systems gave the greatest possible accessibility to all parts of the country. They passed through forest and swamp alike, depriving these obstacles of much of their difficulty. Until the end of the sixteenth century Russian armies were often moved by water and the courses of the rivers determined the strategy of the rulers. Not only metropolitan Russia, but all Siberia to the east was easily penetrable in all directions by way of its rivers. And, as an early seventeenth-century English merchant wrote: 'the many rivers that are found to be in this country, doth much further trading in general'.[1] This ease of accessibility did much to counteract the disadvantage of sheer size.

In general, the course of the great Russian and Siberian rivers is north-south. This is an advantage because the great belts of differing climate, vegetation and soil, stripe the continent from east to west: the rivers link them together and thus they favoured the evolution of a north-south aligned state running athwart the climatic belts. But, although the main courses run north-south, their tributaries run east and west, giving good water communication in these directions also, with the aid of portages. So, although the great Siberian rivers cross the country from the southern mountains to the northern ocean, the fur-trading explorers of the seventeenth and eighteenth centuries were able to establish water routes from the Urals to Okhotsk on the Pacific, a distance of over 5,000 miles.

Long navigable rivers and the absence of pronounced uplands meant that the easiest route between northern and southern Europe lay across the Russian lowland. Peninsular Europe, by contrast, is crossed by mountain ranges: even the Rhine leads up to mountain peaks, whereas the great Russian streams lead up to each other.

The fact that the rivers of Russia, instead of originating in a mountain mass, rise from a central area of no great relief, endows that central area with unique advantages. Although the part of the country farthest from the sea, it has excellent water communications with seas in four directions: with the Baltic by the Volkhov, Narva and West Dvina; with the White Sea by the North Dvina; with the Black Sea by the Don and Dnieper; and by the Volga with the Caspian. Inevitably the power which gained control of these riverheads came to dominate the whole country, each river offering a direction for expansion.[2] Normally great rivers originate in high mountain masses from which they flow to the sea; but mountain masses are not propitious as cradles for growing states. Dispersal of mighty streams from a habitable zone occurs only in central Russia, and thus the conditions favouring the rise and expansion of Muscovy were unique. Its growth would be unintelligible without reference to the river system.

The rivers led eventually to the seas, and the Russians could not be content, if only for commercial reasons, until they had reached these seas, however distant they were. Geography made it extremely probable that the state holding the central river heads would eventually be fighting to wrest the river mouths from those who held them. The resulting state would be large because the rivers were long and the seas they led to far apart.

The general uniformity which characterizes the structure and relief of Russia is again found in the climate. In fact, the absence of pronounced relief is one of the causes of climatic similarity over wide areas. Climatic uniformity is even more extensive than that of relief, as it applies to almost

[1] *Roberts (1638), II, p. 159*
[2] *Klyuchevskiy (1956), I, p. 65*

the whole Soviet Union. The Urals do not form a real climatic divide.[1]
Over a vast area the climate is continental, and marked by extreme
ranges of temperature, cold winters which become severe eastwards, warm
summers which become hot southwards, and moderate summer rainfall
followed by winter snow. An essential feature is the contrast between
summer and winter. These characteristics distinguish the climate of almost
the whole Soviet Union from the predominantly oceanic climates to the
west, the mountain climates to the south, and the monsoon climate to the
south-east. There are indeed differences within the area but they are
usually differences of degree rather than of kind. The real exceptions are
marginal. The Far North has no real summer; the lowlands of Central
Asia suffer from extreme aridity; sheltered parts of the Black Sea coast
have a mild Mediterranean-type winter.

For centuries the lack of water in the trans-Caspian deserts was as much
an obstacle to Russian expansion in that direction as the resistance of the
nomadic inhabitants. The distinct climates of the Black Sea coast and
adjoining Caucasus are not without historical interest. When the Anglo-
French forces attacked Russia in the Crimean peninsula in the war of
1854-6, they were doing so in a region where 'General Winter' could not
aid the Russians. As this was one of the few stretches of Russian coastline
unimpeded by ice, the allies, with their open sea route, benefited; but
winter's severity farther north hindered the supply of the Russian armies.
One may escape the rigours of a Russian winter by a stay on the Black
Sea Riviera at such resorts as Yalta or Sochi, sometimes with important
consequences. The fact that Trotsky was on this coast in 1924 when Lenin
died and was not present at the funeral, helped Stalin in the struggle for
the succession. The Yalta Conference of 1945, where Stalin outmanoeuvred
Roosevelt and where such fateful decisions were taken, was held in the
Crimea partly because it made so much pleasanter a venue than Moscow
in February. Khrushchev was removed from power while on holiday by
the Black Sea.

The Russian winter freezes not only the rivers but the surrounding
seas, depriving Russian ports of their function in winter. But the Murmansk shore of the Arctic, west of the White Sea, is kept relatively free
from ice by the warmer waters of the North Atlantic drift and is navigable
with ice-breakers in all but the worst winters. For this reason it became
the most important gateway into Russia for allied supplies in both the
1914-17 and 1941-5 wars. During the former conflict a railway was built
to link the new port of Murmansk with Petrograd (fig. 6). A supply
route across Persia from the Gulf was also used during the latter.

Because of climatic extremes, Russian settlement in Siberia followed a
narrow belt instead of diffusing over a wide area. This belt lies between
two zones where agricultural activities are difficult or impossible owing to
climatic controls. There is a great northern tract, the largest wilderness in
the world, where not only are the summers too cool and brief for farming,

[1] *Kendrew (1953), p. 260*

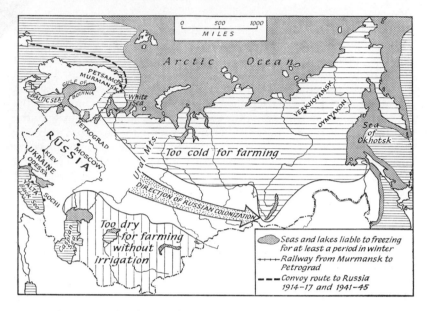

figure 6   The climatic factor.

but the subsoil is permanently frozen over much of the area. And on the south side, a series of deserts and semi-deserts runs eastward from the Caspian Sea. Between these two inhospitable zones, Russian colonization pushed eastwards to the Pacific (fig. 6). However, under the Soviet régime, the simplicity of this pattern has been disturbed. Mining and military settlements expand in the cold north, and irrigation canals water the southern deserts.

Natural vegetation and soils (front endpapers)

Lacking the diversification produced in Europe by a mosaic-like relief pattern, the natural vegetation of Russia—and indeed of the whole Soviet Union—is disposed in broad tracts, each dominated by a particular vegetation type. These zones run from west to east and, being a response to changing climatic conditions, are not sharply demarcated. The distribution of soil types follows a similar pattern.

The northernmost belt, the *tundra*, is the least significant and occupies very little territory in Russia proper. In recent years mining, military activities, biological and meteorological research, the Northern Sea route and some experimental agriculture have increased its population.

Southwards the tundra is replaced by the *tayga*, a vast zone of coniferous forest, interspersed with swamps and peat bogs, which stretches from Finland to Kamchatka. Infertile soils and short cool summers long prevented the Russian tayga from harbouring an agricultural population;

instead it supported only a sprinkling of primitive Finns and Ugrians who could offer little resistance to the infiltration of Russian traders and colonists from the south-west. Hence early Russian territorial expansion took place most rapidly in a north-easterly direction, the line of least resistance.

Furs were the attraction which caused the traders of medieval Novgorod to penetrate far north-east into the tayga until the Urals were reached. Actual colonization was slower, but monasteries were active in pioneering settlement in the forest in the fourteenth century; the new inhabitants lived by lumbering, growing flax and rye in forest clearings, and keeping cattle. The coming of English traders to the White Sea in 1553 led to the opening up of the Moscow-Archangel route; this stimulated economic progress, particularly as there was now an overseas market for the timber, flax and hemp of the region. The construction of railways, beginning with that from Vologda to Archangel in 1908 and followed by that to Vorkuta, has led to further development in the twentieth century.

The great tayga belt, the world's largest timber reserve, has enabled Russia to earn foreign currency with which to finance her imports for four centuries. At first it was the valuable furs that made possible the acquisition of goods from Europe and, therefore, the westernization of the upper classes. Later timber became important: massive exports of this commodity enabled Stalin to acquire essentials from the West in the critical period of the first Five Year Plan. Timber was almost all Russia had to offer, and the combination of the immense tayga forests, plentiful slave labour and great rivers for transport, enabled Stalin to satisfy his foreign customers.

Southwards from latitude 58°/55° N succeeds the next natural vegetation zone, that of the *mixed forest*, made up of both needle-leaved conifers and broad-leaved deciduous trees, with oak, spruce and pine the leading species. Deciduous trees become more numerous southwards until along the southern margins a wholly deciduous woodland is found. In shape the mixed forest is roughly triangular: it has a broad western side, fronting on Poland and the shores of the Baltic, and at its broadest reaches south to Kiev; the belt narrows eastwards to the Urals which it approaches as a narrow strip.

Soils are often podzols with the upper layer lacking body and deficient in plant food, since the mineral salts and finer clayey particles have been washed down below the reach of normal ploughing. This enforced a measure of communal agriculture upon the early Slav colonists of these forests and their successors: only a multiple team of horses or oxen could plough deep enough to bring up the latent fertility of the soil, moderate though that was. During the Nazi occupation, the Germans were compelled to admit that the Stalinist collectivization of agriculture was economically necessary in this region, since the individual peasant with his single horse could not plough as deeply as the podzol required.[1] Even

[1] *Leimbach* (*1950*), *p. 139*

with deep ploughing the soils of the mixed forest are generally poor: they lack humus, and are deficient in lime and other mineral constituents. This poverty of soil, combined with forest cover, and with a climate in which most of the rain falls in the late summer—the ripening and harvesting period for wheat—handicapped the region in the production of bread grains.

Difficult though not impossible for agriculture, the mixed forest zone had some definite advantages that led to its sheltering the heart of the Muscovite state. Although its clearing caused great hardship and exacted immense toil, this eventually developed strength of muscle in the Russians, which stood them in good stead when fighting their many enemies. On the other hand, living in the forest appears to have caused fear and superstition to develop in the minds of the early pioneers. The dense forest limited visibility and made the inhabitants feel insecure: they peopled it with many enemies and dangers, real or imaginary, natural or supernatural, as Russian folk and fairy tales tell.

The forest provided abundant wood for fuel, building and utensils. All the chief Russian rivers rose within its confines, taking their various ways to seas hundreds of miles distant, giving the forested heartland an invaluable strategic position for commercial and industrial development and for military and political expansion. The forest offered protection from the steppe nomads, who constituted the chief scourge of the Russian peoples for a thousand years: horsemen whose natural habitat was the open dry grassland were ill at ease in the dark dank forest. They preferred to move with speed and take by surprise, detesting the ambushes afforded by the woods and the pitched battles demanded by the river lines. For this reason, despite its lack of agricultural wealth, refugees early flocked into this centrally-placed region: not only from the south (from Tartars), but from the north-west (from Germans and Swedes) and from the west (from Lithuanians and Poles).

The central mixed forest area—its soils and climate unsuited to successful agriculture and its population expanding from natural increase and immigration—needed to find other occupations for its surplus people. This was a factor in its early industrialization. Domestic handicraft industries, important even before the thirteenth-century Mongol conquest, flourished again with Muscovite independence. Surplus population also made possible the recruitment of armies for the military campaigns which, like industry, benefited from a central location and radiating water routes.

The industries that developed here—linen, leather, woollen cloth, woodworking and iron-smelting—were based upon locally available raw materials. The rapid growth of factory industry that took place after 1870 was made possible by the building of railways and the liberation of serfs, both of which events made labour more mobile. It was aided by the existence in the central parts of the mixed forest region of a numerous artisan population with industrial traditions.

In an area west of Vladimir, where an island of superior black-earth soils displaces the normal podzol, and where, therefore, agriculture flourished, domestic industry did not evolve as it did in the surrounding districts. In fact, Vladimir early rose to importance as the leading town of the mixed forest region because of the existence of this fertile district— about 80 miles long and 30 miles wide—which fostered a numerous and prosperous farming population in the middle of inhospitable forests. Moscow took its place as capital because it was far less vulnerable to attack, being surrounded by these same almost impenetrable forests.

The Russian central mixed forest zone may be compared, surprisingly, with New England. Both regions had to support a fast-expanding refugee influx and a virile natural increase, within a forested environment, on poor podzol soils under a cool damp climate. Both turned to domestic manufacture and later to specialized factory industry. But, whereas New Englanders also turned to the sea, becoming merchant seamen, fishermen and whalers, the surplus Muscovites served in the tsar's armies, settled as colonists in conquered and depopulated territory, or went fur trading into the tayga.

For 1,600 miles from the Carpathians, the *wooded steppe* belt trends north-eastwards to the forested Urals; thence it continues eastwards to the river Ob. Wooded steppe is not an open grassland studded with scattered and isolated individual trees, but a mixture of steppe grassland and islands of deciduous woodland; these islands were often extensive and, along the northern margins of the belt, almost continuous. Today, the woodland has been almost wholly cleared away and amounts to only about 5 per cent of the area. Soils are richer and more alkaline than the forest podzols to the north, and are often black and fertile chernozems. Originally extremely fertile, they have degenerated from centuries of overcropping.

In early times, when nomadic peoples held the steppe area peacefully, the wooded steppe, better suited to arable farming than the steppes because of its higher rainfall, was cultivated by subject peoples who supplied them with grain and hemp. The Slavs appear to have stood in this position relative to the Scythians and the Khazars. But in times of instability, when a new wave of hostile invaders flooded in from the east, the region became uninhabitable for settled farmers. This was so from the great invasion of the Mongols in the thirteenth century until the sixteenth century when part of the wooded steppe became a frontier region between Muscovy and the Tartars. The Russian rulers settled people of divers origin, including renegade Tartars, in these borderlands, to defend Muscovy from attack. They were liberally granted both land and peasants so that serfdom became particularly widespread here.

After the need for defence from the Tartars had passed, the landowners of the wooded steppe, aided by serf labour, grew grain for the densely populated mixed forest region to the north. They continued to do this until two blows were struck at their cereal-based economy. One was the liberation of the serfs (1861) and the other was the spread of railways which, followed by cultivation of the steppe proper, meant the opening up of virgin wheat lands with which the older wooded steppe region, its soils now depleted, could not compete. The new peasants, cultivating portions of the great estates, could scarcely exist on their narrow strips of land, so that the wooded steppe was notorious for its exhausted soils and impoverished peasants. A million people left the region in the twenty years before the Revolution. The towns were little better off, being too close to the manufacturing centres of the Moscow district to be able to develop industry.

Between the wooded steppe and the Black Sea lies the *steppe* proper, for centuries a grassland which stretched not only eastwards to the Ob river, but westwards into Hungary. For thousands of years the steppe was grazing ground, partly because it is natural grassland and partly because it was too open to periodic attack by horsemen from the east to offer security to sedentary farmers. Early Russian attempts to push their agricultural state from the wooded steppe of the Dnieper region southwards failed for this reason, and it was not until after the Volga line to the east was held and fortified, in the sixteenth century, that the settlement of the steppe to the west could seriously begin.

The steppes eastward from the Volga, with a drier climate and less productive soils, have only recently been ploughed up in an effort to increase grain production so that the growing population of the Soviet Union may be fed. Droughts have imperilled the success of this experiment, much as they caused distress in America after the ploughing up of the drier grasslands of the Great Plains in the late 1880s and 1930s.

As climate becomes still drier south-eastwards, the steppes of southern Russia merge, along the lower Volga, into a *desert steppe* in which the vegetation cover is not continuous and, finally, into *desert*, in which the surface consists mainly of bare rock, baked clay or sand. These arid zones widen to cover the whole area of Soviet Central Asia. In much of this region there is enough grass or foliage to permit of shepherd nomadism and, since the Revolution, Soviet irrigation projects have converted ribbons of this land into one of the main cotton-growing regions of the world.

Just as the cold forested tayga, by supporting only a sparse population of primitive people, made the extension of Russian control easy in the north-east, the dry deserts and semi-deserts offered little obstacle to Russian penetration up to the mountain rim. The lack of water did, however, prove an embarrassment to Russian armies accustomed to campaigning in more humid conditions. But the main eastward movement of Russian colonization, later bound together by the Trans-Siberian railway, took a middle course between the tayga and the arid lands, following the wooded steppe and steppe. These vegetation types, although discontinuous beyond the Ob, were nonetheless present sufficiently to encourage a chain of settlements leading to the Amur valley and thence to the Pacific.

Is Russia in Europe? The geographical viewpoint

There can be but one answer to the question whether Russia should be included in Europe on purely geographical grounds, and it has been forcibly expressed by the Swiss historian Reynold: *'Russia does not belong to Europe . . . Russia is the geographical antithesis of Europe. This premise is fundamental: the Russia-Europe antithesis is found at every level.'*[1] The Polish historian Halecki implies a similar answer when he writes that Europe is distinguished by its

> *extraordinary variety of particular regions within the narrow limits of that peninsula attached to the huge Asiatic continent. Whatever is colossal and uniform is definitely un-European.*[2]

And the great Russian historian, Klyuchevskiy, after stating that

> *two geographical peculiarities distinguish Europe from other parts of the earth and especially from Asia: first, the varied form of the surface, and second, the extraordinarily tenuous outline of its seacoasts,*

points out that

> *Russia . . . does not share these favourable natural characteristics with Europe, or to be more precise, shares them only in the same degree as Asia. . . . Monotony is the chief characteristic of her surface: one form of relief dominates almost her whole extent. . . . Even in Asia, our plain would not take last place: the Persian plateau, for instance, is almost half its size. To complete its geographical affinity with Asia, this plain merges southwards into the vast waterless and woodless steppe for tens of thousands of square miles. In its geological structure this steppe is exactly like the steppes of Central Asia, of which, geographically, it constitutes a direct and uninterrupted prolongation. Temperate in all things, western Europe does not know such exhausting summer droughts and such terrible winter snowstorms as are common on this steppe plain; these come from and are sustained by Asia.*[3]

This last sentence recalls Samuel Purchas's eulogy of Europe, which would have made no sense if Russia had been included:

> *In Europe neither watery fens, nor unstable bogs, nor inland seas, nor unwholesome airs, nor wild woods, with their wilder savage inhabitants, nor snow covered hills, nor stifling frosts, nor long long nights, nor craggy rocks, nor barren sands, nor any other angry effect of nature.*[4]

For Russia, to quote the nineteenth-century French geographer, Elisée Reclus, *'is half Asiatic in its extreme climate, in the landscape of its monotonous countryside and limitless steppes'.*[5] And a more recent French

[1] *Reynold (1950), VI, p. 25*
[2] *Halecki (1950), pp. 87-90*
[3] *Klyuchevskiy (1956), I, pp. 46-7*
[4] *Purchas (1613), p. 248*
[5] *Reclus (1875), I, p. 13*

geographer, Raoul Blanchard, writes: '*In Europe all is variety. . . . Europe is a mosaic made up of countless cells*'; but he is compelled to except Russia because '*it weighs upon the continent with all its Asiatic mass*'.[1]

The fundamental division between Europe and the rest of Eurasia lies in the low-lying ill-drained zone between the Baltic and Black Seas. To the west is an area which an eventful geological history has endowed with a very complex structure and a lithological mosaic; these are reflected in a highly fragmented and individualistic relief. But eastwards there stretches the monolithic mass of the Russian structural platform. The climatic frontier between the maritime and continental climates, however imprecise it may be, must fall in this very same zone. It is here that Köppen's formulae produce the dividing line between his temperate 'C' climates and those of the severe-winter 'D' type. Another climatologist, Kendrew, who found it convenient to include all Russia with Asia, wrote:

> *at the Vistula the climate has become definitely continental. That river forms a convenient if arbitrary boundary between the relatively maritime climates of western and central Europe and the essentially continental type of practically all the Russian territory.*[2]

The great east-west trending vegetation and soil belts, themselves a product of physiographic and climatic uniformity, come to a halt in this zone to give way, westwards, to a fine-grained pattern in which, everywhere, local variations in bedrock, drift, aspect, slope and height are reflected in vegetation and soil.

So clear and obvious is the frontier nature of this Baltic-Black Sea zone that any political boundary between Russia and the West that falls within it, must constitute, on an irresistible combination of physical and political grounds, the eastern boundary of Europe.[3] Historians have recognized this fact more so than geographers, who have wandered all over Russia, and even into Siberia, looking for the 'natural' limit. At various times they have used the following Russian rivers as part of such a boundary: Dnieper, Don, Dvina, Irtysh, Kama, Kuban, Kuma, Manych, Medveditsa, Ob, Pechora, Sura, Terek, Tobol, Ural, Volga and Yenisey, and doubtless others, not to mention the Caspian and Aral Seas. Many geographers have earned Toynbee's scathing reference to their being reduced to

> *dissecting the living body politic of Russia into an imaginary 'Russia in Europe' and 'Russia in Asia' along the unconvincing line of the Ural river and the Ural Mountains.*

> *. . . thereafter the geographers belatedly discovered that the Ural Mountains which they had made into a household word were not more noticeable a feature in the physical landscape than the Chiltern Hills, and that this vaunted physical barrier between Europe and Asia was*

---

[1] *Blanchard (1936), pp. 1-2*
[2] *Kendrew (1953), pp. 260-1*
[3] *The question of Europe's eastern boundary, with special reference to the inclusion of Russia, is fully discussed in Parker (1960), pp. 278-97*

not strongly enough pronounced even to serve as a boundary between one local province of the Russian Empire and another.[1]
As Cressey pertinently wrote: *'the crest of the Urals supplies no more of a boundary than the Appalachians. Would anyone divide the United States into two continents?'*[2]

To exclude Russia from Europe is not necessarily to place her in Asia. Rather should she form a subcontinental division in her own right. The simple division of the great Eurasian continent into two very unequal halves, called Europe and Asia, has no sound geographical basis. It is much more reasonable to divide Eurasia into several subcontinents without violating the integrity of the Soviet Union. This was Mackinder's verdict. He too saw the 'world island' as consisting of a Eurasian 'heartland' around which there were four appendages: peninsular Europe, south-west Asia, China and India.[3]

[1] *Toynbee (1954), VIII, p. 713*
[2] *Cressey (1951), p. 175*
[3] *Mackinder (1904), pp. 424-31*

EARLIEST TIMES

Fifteen thousand years ago, the last of the great ice sheets which spread from Lapland over northern Europe was melting away. Arctic and sub-arctic climates, comparable to those now found in northernmost Canada and Siberia, lay to the south of the shrinking glacier, and the shores of the Baltic experienced conditions now found on those of the Arctic Ocean. This harsh environment was none the less the home of man.

The Stone Age

Men of the Palaeolithic or Old Stone Age followed in the wake of the retreating ice. For, despite the severe climate, the tundra zone which spread out southwards from the ice sheet was exceedingly rich in animal life—fish, waterfowl and herds of reindeer—and well suited to tribes living by hunting and fishing.[1] They have left behind reindeer antlers fashioned for various uses, as well as stone weapons for spearing fish and hunting seal. In the great forests that developed to the south of this post-glacial tundra, hunters and fishers moved along the rivers, leaving traces of their presence in the valleys and on the sea shores (fig. 7). Here an abundance of large animals—mammoth, woolly rhinoceros, cave lion, wild horse and wild ox—favoured hunting by large communities whose combined efforts in killing these large beasts were rewarded by an ample food supply. With the greatest ingenuity they satisfied their basic needs of food and shelter from the unpromising environment, living in caves and hollows roofed with logs or animal skins.

With the departure of the ice, new belts of natural vegetation gradually colonized the ice or tundra-covered lands of the glacial epoch. This transitional period (13,000-5000 B.C.) witnessed the spread of the culture of Mesolithic or Middle Stone Age man. The changes of climate and vegetation reduced the size and variety of animal life and impoverished hunting resources, although this was offset to some extent by improved techniques such as the invention of the bow and arrow. But a smaller and sparser wild life meant smaller and more nomadic communities. The tundra and tundra-tayga zones remained richer in animals than the more southerly regions, and population, therefore, tended to move northwards, following the ice.[2]

The new belts of vegetation were those of today (front endpaper map): open tundra, snow-covered for most of the year, followed southwards by zones of coniferous forest or tayga, mixed coniferous-deciduous

[1] *Rybakov (1966), I, p. 24*
[2] *Rybakov (1966), I, pp. 35-6*

figure 7   Palaeolithic Russia.

woodland, wooded steppe and steppe grassland. The grassland extended to the Black Sea but, south-castwards towards the Caspian, it gave way to arid semi-desert and, eventually, the deserts of Central Asia. This new natural vegetation resulted, in the Neolithic period (5000-3000 B.C.) in a pronounced differentiation in culture between the forested northern and central area and the grassland south, a distinction that was for long to divide the inhabitants of the Russian plain.[1] With the introduction of live-stock breeding and primitive agriculture, the south, with its forest-free rich black soil and long warm summer, gained an immense advantage. Its culture advanced more rapidly, especially in pottery and metal working. But in the north, where the basis of existence remained hunting and

[1] *Rybakov (1966), I, p. 41*

figure 8   Hunters on skis (Neolithic rock engraving).

fishing, progress continued to be made in the older way of life—stone implements were perfected and boat-building developed.[1]

In the north, New Stone Age settlements have been found on the shores of lakes Ladoga and Onega and by the banks of rivers. In winter, these people hunted on skis and used sledges, and in summer they moved by river through the forest in dug-out canoes. Along the Baltic coast they worked amber, while on the shores of Lake Onega there grew up an industry in which masses of green slate, originally brought into the region by the ice sheet, were worked into tools and ornaments.[2] These objects were traded by way of the Baltic Sea.

The Bronze Age

During the Bronze Age (3000-700 B.C.), objects of metal took their place alongside those of stone, but owing to the lack of readily accessible copper deposits in the Russian lowland, most bronze had to be imported. The chief sources were the Carpathians and the Caucasus area, the latter being one of the chief cradles of Bronze Age culture. Man had now learned to domesticate animals and practise agriculture, and the steppe grass-

[1] *Rybakov (1966), I. p. 40*
[2] *Clark (1952), pp. 245-6*

figure 9   Reconstruction of a Neolithic dwelling on piles.

land, more suited to these pursuits than to the hunting and fishing of the Neolithic Age, was well settled at its western end. The Tripolyan culture, disclosed by archaeology, flourished from about 3000 to 1000 B.C. between the Dnieper and the Pruth. Here tribes who had lived originally by herding livestock and harvesting wild grass seed, adopted agriculture, growing wheat and millet for food. They used implements of both stone and bronze and made a distinctive form of pottery. They lived in villages, the houses of which were now built above ground with walls and roofs of wood and clay. Buildings were often large and divided into compartments, each with its stove and quern. Tripolyan settlements contained as many as fifty and sometimes up to two hundred dwellings. The great advance in culture had obviously led to a significant increase in the density of population.[1]

The Early Iron Age

THE STEPPE

Later in the Bronze Age, from about 1000 to about 700 B.C., the Cimmerians extended livestock herding and grain growing across the Black Sea steppes to the Caucasus, but about the year 700 B.C. they were replaced as rulers of the steppe by the nomadic Scythians. The Scythians were the forerunners of a series of nomadic invaders—Sarmatians, Huns, Avars, Magyars, Khazars, Pechenegs, Polovtsy, Turks and Tartars—who, for whatever cause, whether drought, pressure of overpopulation, or hostile neighbours, swept across the steppe plains of southern Russia from the east. Although these migrations were spaced over a period of some two

[1] *Lyashchenko (1956), I, p. 33; Clark (1952), p. 143; Grekov (1949), pp. 33-4; Rybakov (1966), I, pp. 90-5*

B

thousand years, the nomadic peoples had much in common. They were all highly mobile, moving swiftly on horseback and conveying their few possessions in covered waggons. They drank mare's milk in bowls fashioned from the skulls of their foes. They lived by keeping cattle and spoiling their enemies. Having fastened their yoke upon the peoples of the steppe and the neighbouring woodlands, they flourished upon the tribute they levied and the trade they taxed. They all fought as mounted cavalry. Even the Goths, who came from the north on foot, became horsemen when in the steppes, and it was their cavalry which defeated the Romans at Adrianople (A.D. 378). This description of the Scythians by Herodotus would have applied also to most of their successors:

> *they have established neither cities nor walled places, but all carry their houses about with them, riding on horses and shooting with the bow, and their sustenance is not from ploughing but from their herds, and their dwellings are on waggons.*[1]

Proximity to the metalliferous Caucasus was an advantageous factor in the development of the culture of the pastoral nomads. Mountain miners and smiths worked iron, copper, gold and silver, supplying the horsemen with weapons, utensils and ornaments. The Scythians did not exterminate the agricultural peoples already in possession of the wooded steppe and steppe, but left them to grow food for their conquerors. Herodotus, writing in the fifth century B.C., refers to some of the tribes who lived in the woods beyond the steppe. There were the Budini who '*are a great and mighty people; all have wondrous blue eyes and red hair. And there is a city among them builded of wood . . . and their houses and temples are of wood also*'; and the Geloni, who '*till the earth and eat corn and possess gardens*'.[2] Some of these tributary tribes may have been Slavs.[3]

Soon after the Scythians had conquered the Black Sea steppes, the Greeks began to found colonies on the Black Sea coast. Tyras, at the mouth of the Dniester, Olbia, near the mouth of the Bug, Chersonese (Kherson) and Theodosia in the Crimea, were among the more important on the north shore. Because of their favourable position for trade by land and sea in many directions, they grew rapidly into important trading cities. Their marts received timber, furs, wax, honey and grain from the distant forests and nearer wooded steppe; cattle, hides and yet more grain from their steppe hinterland; luxury goods, textiles, wines and olive oil from the Mediterranean. They also maintained slave markets and were themselves centres of varied handicraft industries. They suffered severely from the later nomadic invasions and, partly because of these and partly because of their mercantile character, they came to have very mixed populations.

The Scythians gave way in turn to the Sarmatians who ruled southern Russia for four centuries from about 200 B.C. to A.D. 200. All three steppe régimes—those of the Cimmerians, Scythians and Sarmatians—based

---

[1] *Herodotus (1949), I, pp. 290-1*
[2] *Herodotus (1949), I, p. 314*
[3] *Vernadsky (1959), p. 62*

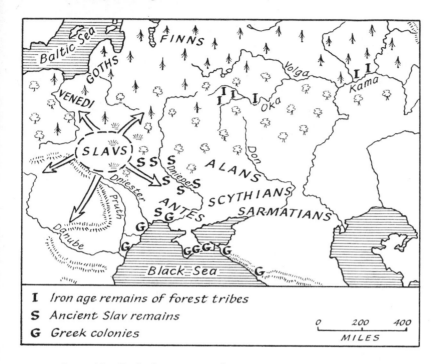

I   *Iron age remains of forest tribes*
S   *Ancient Slav remains*
G   *Greek colonies*

0   200   400
MILES

figure 10   Early Iron Age settlement and remains.

their wealth and power not only on their military prowess as horsemen and the subjection of agricultural tribes, but on the rich commerce borne by the steppe trade routes which linked the eastern and western worlds.

THE FOREST

In the forests of central and northern Russia, out of reach of the nomadic masters of the steppe, a sparse population of hunters and fishers lived on throughout the Neolithic Age. In the Bronze Age, those of the upper Volga region had begun to keep cattle in clearings, and during the Early Iron Age—from the seventh century B.C.—primitive agriculture began among them. This advance in culture was found in the valleys of the Kama and the Oka, and probably thus early, these two valleys, joined by the Volga, were part of an important trade route (fig. 10). According to archaeological evidence, the Kazan people traded furs for precious metals.

These early Iron Age forest dwellers, who sowed grain and kept cattle in forest clearings, and who built wooden villages and used iron, may have been Slavs. According to Vernadsky, 'the westward migration of the Slavs seems to have started in the Scythian era. By about 550 B.C. a number of Slavic tribes must have penetrated into the area of present-day Ukraine.'[1]

[1] *Vernadsky (1959), p. 9*

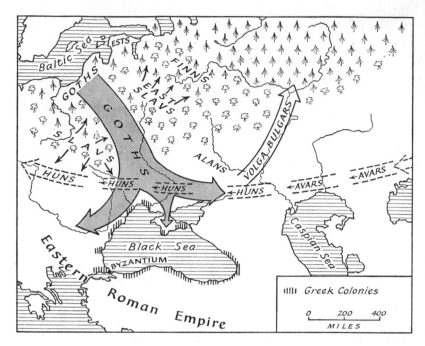

figure 11   Russia in the third to sixth centuries A.D.: *Slavs, Goths, Huns and Bulgars.*

But, historically, the Slavs are first discovered in the first century A.D., living in the Vistula basin and eastwards towards the upper Dnieper. Pliny and Tacitus call them Veneti or Venedi (Wends), and these Slav peoples, who lived to the east of the Germans, are contrasted with the nomads of the steppe. They are described as settled in their abode and as going about on foot, '*unlike the Sarmatians who live in waggons and on horseback.*'[1]

GOTHS, HUNS AND KHAZARS

There were also agricultural Slavic and related peoples (Slovenes, Alans and Antes) in the wooded steppe and bordering steppe area between the Pruth and the Dnieper, when the Goths invaded it in the third century A.D., and they may have been the descendants of tribes described by Herodotus as subject to the Scythians. But there was also a migration of Slavs into this area from the Danube early in the second century A.D. as a result of Roman pressure.[2] The Goths came from the Baltic area and ruled an empire which ran from the Gulf of Danzig to the Crimea (fig. 11). Later in the fourth century the Huns broke the power of the Goths and,

[1] *Tacitus, 46, 3*
[2] *Lyashchenko (1956), I, p. 46*

figure 12 Russia in the seventh and eighth centuries.

with this barrier removed, the Slavs began a vigorous movement of colonization eastwards into the forest, the wooded steppe, and the bordering steppe. The Slavs who took part in this eastward movement are known henceforth as East Slavs to distinguish them from the West Slavs of the Vistula basin and the South Slavs who penetrated into the Balkans.

Although the Huns soon disappeared from off the steppe, a remnant of them followed the Volga up to its confluence with the Kama and settled there, probably in the sixth century. The strong agricultural, commercial and military state which they founded at this strategic position lasted until the thirteenth century, when it was destroyed by the Mongol invaders. According to the Arabic writer Ibn Rusta (*c.* A.D. 920), they were '*a people engaged in cultivation and tillage; they sow all grains: wheat, barley and millet, and others besides.*'[1]

In the sixth century A.D. it was the turn of the Avars to invade and terrorize the steppe, but their power there was short-lived. The seventh century witnessed the establishment of the powerful Khazar state which, like its Scythian and Sarmatian predecessors, grew rich from control of the steppe trade routes (fig. 12). Although originally nomadic horsemen, the Khazars became increasingly sedentary and commercial, trading with the peoples around them, including the Volga Bulgars, the Slavs and the Greeks. Their capital, Itil, was thronged with merchants from many parts: Moslems, Jews, Christians and Slavs. Like their predecessors, the Khazars levied tribute on the tribes dwelling amidst the woods and in the forests adjacent to the steppes, many of whom were Slavs. The Russian chronicle relates how '*the Khazars came upon them as they lived in the hills and forests, and demanded tribute from them*'. This amounted to '*a white squirrel skin from each hearth*'.[2] The Khazars also dominated the Alans and Magyars of the western steppes. Alans, Magyars and Slavs supplied auxiliary troops to the Khazar army.[3]

The East Slavs in the Ninth Century

By the ninth century, as a result of the north-eastward expansion already referred to, tribes of East Slavs inhabited a broad zone of territory extending from the Carpathians to lakes Ladoga and Onega. The shape of this territory becomes more intelligible if it is compared with the vegetation map (front end paper). It corresponds closely to the area occupied by deciduous forest, mixed forest and wooded steppe. The swampy sandy Baltic lands were left to primitive Ests and Lithuanians who, though backward culturally, were extremely warlike. The northern coniferous forest, useless agriculturally, was thinly peopled by Finns, Chuds and Pechors. The open steppe was held by the strong Khazars.

Population was doubtless densest in the wooded steppe zone from the Carpathians to the upper Oka, and particularly in the river valleys. Here the Volynians, Ulichians and Tivertsy had their homes along the Dniester and the Bug. According to the Russian Primary Chronicle, '*there was a multitude of them, for they inhabited the banks of the Dniester almost down to the east*'. The Polyanians were '*settled on the Dnieper*' and their city of Kiev was on that river. The Severyans '*had their homes along the Desna, the Sem and the Sula*' and their chief town of Chernigov lay on the Desna. The Vyatichians dwelt in the basin of the upper Oka. There is a remarkable

---

[1] *Macartney (1930), p. 193*
[2] *Cross & Sherbowitz-Wetzor (1953), pp. 58-9*
[3] *Vernadsky (1959), pp. 92-3*

figure 13 Russia in the ninth century. East Slav tribes numbered as follows: 1 Volynians; 2 Tivertsy; 3 Ulichians; 4 Polyanians; 5 Severyans; 6 Vyatichians; 7 Drevlyans; 8 Radimichians; 9 Krivichians; 10 Ilmensky Slavs.

confirmation by place-name evidence of these locations of the tribes as given by the Chronicle, apart from some minor discrepancies.[1] All these tribes had rich black-earth soils as well as access to woods in which they could hunt fur-bearing animals and keep bees. Against these advantages, their position exposed them to the steppe nomads, and by the ninth century most of them were paying tribute to the Khazars (fig. 13).

The other tribes lived in isolated forest clearings on soils greatly inferior to the black earths farther south. There were the Drevlyans among the Pripyat marshes, the Radimichians along the Dnieper, and the Krivichians who lived 'at the headwaters of the Volga, the Dvina and the Dnieper'. Farthest north of all were the Illmensky Slavs who lived among the swamps and forests surrounding lake Ilmen and whose city was Novgorod.[2]

[1] Barsov (1885), p. 124 ff
[2] Cross & Sherbowitz-Wetzor (1953), pp. 53-6

In the lands which they occupied, the East Slavs intermingled with the aborigines, especially the Chuds, the Ves, the Mers and the Muroms. Klyuchevskiy attributed certain non-European traits in the Great Russian physiognomy to Chud admixture.[1] The fact that the initial colonization had to take place in small and scattered clearings, isolated from each other by tracts of forest, swamp and sandy ground, influenced the social organization of the East Slavs. The large tribes and consanguineous clans that had entered the country were broken up and dispersed into smaller territorial communes living among the clearings and along the river banks. But the economic unit, though small and isolated, had to remain communal because the soils were such that they could only be worked by large teams.

Scarcely able to support themselves from their poor soils alone, the forest-dwelling Slavs exploited the rivers by fishing and the woods by hunting and bee-keeping. They were fortunate that their forest products— animal fur, honey and beeswax—were in great demand in many parts of the world, both near and far, so that trade was, from the beginning, prominent in their economy. Situated as they were athwart routes between north and south and between east and west, they were well placed for trade, both transit and direct. Their commercial intercourse was with the Volga Bulgars, the Khazars, Byzantium and the Baltic lands, and a wide range of oriental products—silk, precious metals, spices, salt, luxury goods such as perfume—entered into this trade.

As a result of this commercial intercourse, some idea of the East Slavs and of the country they lived in penetrated to the Arabic world. Such ideas were often imprecise but usually contained an element of truth:

> The country of Slavia is a flat country and full of trees, and they dwell there, and they have no vines or fields. They have a kind of large jar made of wood used as nests for their bees and their honey. They are a people who keep pigs like sheep. (Ibn Rusta, c. 920)

> Their wine is made of honey. . . . None has a horse except the distinguished man. (Ibn Rusta)

> In this country the cold is very severe, and it reaches such severity that a man there digs himself in like a wild animal under the earth and then makes himself a roof of wood like that of a church. Then he heaps earth on to it, and the man enters with his family and brings some firewood and stones, and kindles a fire there until it gets warm and becomes red, and when it becomes very hot he sprinkles water on it, so that the vapour rises in that place and the house is warmed, and they remain in that house until the spring. (Ibn Rusta)

> They have a custom of making a fortress: everybody comes together and they make a fortress because the Magyars constantly come and raid and plunder them. When the Magyars come, the Slavs go into

[1] *Klyuchevskiy (1956), I, p. 297*

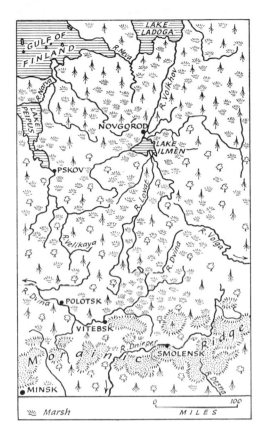

figure 14   The position of Novgorod and Smolensk.

that fortress which they have made and most of their dwellings in
winter are castles and fortresses, and in summer among the trees.
(Gardezi)[1]
The Magyars, as vassals of the Khazars, dominated the Dnieper-Bug
section of the steppe until the late ninth century when they migrated into
Hungary.

The East Slavs had only narrow and precariously held outlets on to
both the Baltic and the Black Seas, yet the existence of these outlets made
possible the development within their territory of a north-south trading
route by water. Before the days of surfaced roads and railways, land
transport was difficult, dangerous, slow and expensive; water carriage was
much more expeditious, much less costly, and relatively easy and safe;
it also permitted the moving of larger consignments. The remarkable fact
that Russia's great rivers rise from a watershed that is low and easily

[1] *Macartney (1930), pp. 210-12*

B*

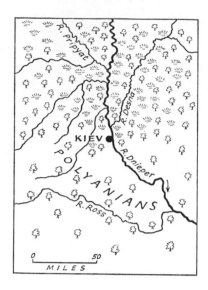

figure 15   The position of Kiev.

crossed, means that those rivers have gentle gradients and are easily navigable; it also means that the headwaters of the rivers are mutually accessible by portages. As this geographical knowledge spread, so trade between northern and southern Europe, potentially large because of their widely differing needs and products, tended to move eastwards and flow between Baltic ports and Constantinople, rather than take the stormy Atlantic sea route or the slow and perilous journey across western or central Europe. The main waterway route was from the Gulf of Finland via the Neva, Volkhov, Lovat and Dnieper rivers to the Black Sea, and the Slavs knew it as the way *'from the Varangians [Scandinavians] to the Greeks'*.[1] Several tributary routes joined it, and it was also linked with the great Volga waterway which connected with the main trade routes from the east. Important Slavic merchant towns grew up on these waterways, notably Novgorod, Smolensk and Kiev.

Novgorod lay on the main Baltic-Black Sea waterway and numerous other river routes converged upon it (fig. 14). Smolensk lay on the Dnieper where it makes its way through the hilly terminal moraine dumped by the last ice sheet of the Ice Age, on its retreat. This moraine provided a high and dry road from west to east across ill-drained country, so that Smolensk grew up where a main east-west land route crossed a main north-south river-and-portage route. Kiev was built high on the western bank of the Dnieper, defensible against attackers from the east, and where the swampy forested zone gives way to the wooded steppe (fig. 15). It was well placed to draw upon the agricultural produce of the rich black

[1] *Cross & Sherbowitz-Wetzor (1953), p. 53*

earth soils to the south, and the different products of the forest which came down to it by the Dnieper, the Pripyat and the Desna.

Settlement in isolated clearings militated against political unification, and the fortified towns which grew up at strategic points on the waterways were probably in the hands of powerful chieftains, who sailed up the rivers and then scoured the forests in search of inhabited clearings where they could seize slaves, furs, honey and wax for their merchants to sell to the Varangians, Byzantines, Bulgars or Khazars.

The Slavic chieftains and the merchants of their towns were not allowed to exploit the forest economy undisturbed. The Scandinavian Vikings or Varangians as the Slavs called them, began to make the rivers their own, to seize the towns, to monopolize the trade, and increasingly to raid and plunder the Slavs. This development, which probably began in the eighth century, was in full spate during the ninth and tenth.

The Varangians did not confine their attention to the Slavs. Byzantine records refer to their activities in the Black Sea area and to attacks on Constantinople itself. There is much Arabic, Khazar and Persian evidence that, during the late ninth and early tenth centuries, they swept down the Volga and raided the shores of the Caspian Sea. In these accounts the raiders are known as Russes. Such incursions were made sometimes with the connivance of the Khazars and sometimes in spite of them. In one raid, reference is made to the Alans, Slavs and others as participants. The Russes still fought in the manner of Scandinavian vikings, relying on swift movement by water and sudden appearance on the shore to surprise their victims. One oriental writer pointed out that '*if they had horses and were riders, they would be a great scourge to mankind*'.[1]

These Caspian ventures had no permanent success and often ended in catastrophe. On one occasion the Russes were weakened by an epidemic caused by eating too much unaccustomed fruit, for '*theirs is an exceedingly cold country, where no tree grows, and the little fruit which they have is imported from distant regions*'.[2]

---

[1] *Chadwick (1946), pp. 50-9; Kendrick (1930), p. 162*
[2] *Chadwick (1946), p. 53*

CHAPTER THREE
RUSSIA BEFORE THE MONGOL CONQUEST

The Scandinavian Conquest, 862-82

During the ninth century, Scandinavian Norsemen succeeded in establishing a large state in Russia. This, at its maximum extent, stretched from the Gulf of Finland and lake Ladoga in the north, to the middle reaches of the Dnieper river, and at times even as far as the Black Sea shore. The invaders were known to the Slavs as Varangians and to the Greeks, Arabs and Persians as Russes. The land they controlled took the name of Rus. This was apparently first applied to Novgorod (*'On account of the Varangians, the district of Novgorod became known as the land of Rus'*), but was later extended to the middle Dnieper region round Kiev.[1]

The inhospitable Scandinavian peninsulas and islands, glaciated and forested, bred a race of men whose only resource was to take to the sea for adventure and plunder. Iceland and Ireland, England and Scotland, France and Germany, all felt their impact and suffered varying degrees of Viking penetration and occupation, but in Russia their enterprise was on a vaster scale. The country they founded and organized covered a greater area than any other in Europe. This achievement was favoured by relatively uniform relief and by the pervasive Russian river network which enabled these axe-bearing boatmen to cover large distances swiftly.

If adventure and rapine brought the Varangians into Russia, it was trade that kept them there. There were already two great river trading routes in use: the Baltic-Black Sea link by way of the Volkhov and the Dnieper, and the Baltic-Caspian connection via the Volga (fig. 13). The former led to Constantinople, the latter to Persia, the Arab world and the Orient. The importance of these routes was enhanced by the confusion prevailing in western Europe during the Dark Ages, and by Arabian control of the Mediterranean. Trade was, in fact, to be the basis of the strength and prosperity of early Russia during its golden age, a period when '*the volume and scope of Russian foreign commerce was far above the west European standard of the period*'.[2] In view of the compelling mutual desire among the peoples of northern and southern Europe for each other's products, it was no mere coincidence that trade flourished most along these eastern lines of communication when trade in western Europe was at a low ebb.

To the commercial exploitation of the natural trade routes, the Varangians soon added the political organization of the territory through which the westernmost of the two Russian waterways ran. They were unable to do this for the Volga route because the strong nation of Bulgars, firmly entrenched on the middle course of the river, blocked their way. These Volga Bulgars flourished because of their intermediary position

[1] *Cross & Sherbowitz-Wetzor (1953), pp. 59-60*
[2] *Vernadsky (1948), p. 31*

between the Russes and Slavs to the north-west and the Khazars to the south-east:

> *the Khazars trade with them and buy and sell to them and also the Russes come to them with their merchandise, and all of them on the two sides of the river have different kinds of merchandise, such as sable and ermine and grey squirrel.* (Ibn Rusta, c. 920)[1]

The Varangians had found the Slavs with only a rudimentary social organization and with even less political organization. There were the wooden fortress towns from which chiefs dominated the surrounding country and in which dwelled the merchants, and there were the rural communities of primitive farmers. The Norsemen quartered themselves on the towns and plundered the countryside for women and food. Where necessary they built further wooden forts of their own to hold down the country and collect tribute. At first, individual bands operated from separate centres, but by the second half of the ninth century they had all been brought under the control of one family. In 862, Rurik, founder of the dynasty, ruled a northern state with his headquarters at Novgorod. '*The present inhabitants of Novgorod are descended from the Varangian race*', says the Chronicle, '*but aforetime they were Slavs.*'[2] It is probable that the Arabic writer Ibn Rusta (writing c. 920, but using earlier information) is referring to Novgorod—at the southern end of lake Ilmen and surrounded by marshes, in the following passage:

> *Rus is an island around which is a lake, and the island in which they dwell is a three days' journey through forests and swamps covered with trees, and it is a damp morass, such that when a man puts his foot to the ground it quakes owing to the moisture.*[3]

Rurik soon extended his power over the whole of the northern East Slavic territory as far east as Rostov and Murom.

From the very beginning of the Scandinavian conquest, men from the conquered tribes, Slav and non-Slav, served together with the Norsemen. In 880 Oleg, Rurik's successor,

> *set forth, taking with him many warriors from among the Varangians, the Chuds, the Slavs, the Merians and the Krivichians. He thus arrived with his Krivichians before Smolensk, took the city, and set up a garrison.*[4]

Possession of Novgorod had given control of the northern part of the waterway trade artery. Smolensk stood in the central watershed area where the Dnieper pierces the great glacial terminal moraine that sweeps in a giant arc from Germany across Poland far into Russia; to it led not only the Volkhov-Lovat water route via Novgorod, but also the Narva-lake Peipus route via Pskov, and the West Dvina route via Polotsk (fig. 14).

In 882 Oleg '*set himself up as prince in Kiev* . . . *Varangians and Slavs*

---

[1] *Macartney (1930), p. 192*
[2] *Cross & Sherbowitz-Wetzor (1953), p. 60*
[3] *Macartney (1930), p. 213*
[4] *Cross (1930), p. 146*

accompanied him, and his retainers were called Russes'.[1] With Kiev in his hands, Oleg held the three great towns of the waterway, northern, central and southern. Originally the Varangians kept to the water and did not own or cultivate land, as the following quotations from Arabic sources testify:

> *their raids are not made riding, but their raids and fights are only in ships.* (Gardezi)

> *they have no cultivated lands; they eat only what they carry off from the land of Slavia.* (Ibn Rusta)

> *they have no landed property nor villages nor cultivated land; their only occupation is trading in sables and grey squirrel and other furs, and in these they trade, and they take as the price, gold and silver and secure it in their belts.* (Ibn Rusta)[2]

Soon, however, the leaders were allocating lands along the river banks to members of their retinues, lands peopled by Slavs. The Scandinavians thus settled among and intermarried with Slavs, and so came to lose their separate identity and their Swedish language.

The rapid Viking progress southward, taken together with the independent existence of a Norse-Slav state on the Sea of Azov, meant Varangian control of the waterway route from the Baltic to the Black Sea. Thus, for a time, the north-south fluvial lineaments of the Russian lowland prevailed over the east-west trending Eurasian vegetation zones. For a time there was to be a north-south aligned state, originating in alien rule over the Slav population and in the promotion of trade between Scandinavia and the eastern part of the Roman Empire (fig. 16).

Their greater energy, better weapons, superior organization and leadership enabled the Scandinavians to extend their sway over the tribes which bordered the rivers. The initial plundering raids soon developed into regular tribute-taking expeditions whereby foodstuffs, furs, honey, wax and slaves were extorted. Later, local officials were given the responsibility of levying the tribute, which became a regular tax. The foodstuffs went to feed the towns, but the furs, honey, wax and slaves were traded southwards for precious metals. Some of the female captives became the concubines of the ruling Russes. Before becoming a Christian, Vladimir I of Kiev had—if the Chronicle is to be believed—eight hundred women for his pleasure.[3]

There are references to Russ raids and tribute-taking expeditions against the Slavs in both Greek and Arabic sources:

> *In winter the harsh mode of life of the Russes is thus: at the beginning of November their chiefs go out without delay from Kiev with their retainers 'on polyudye', which means 'on their rounds', among the*

[1] *Cross (1930), p. 146*
[2] *Macartney (1930), p. 213*
[3] *Cross & Sherbowtiz-Wetzor (1953), p. 94*

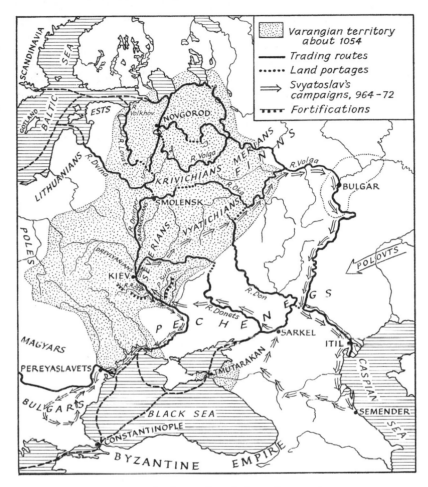

figure 16   Russia in the tenth and eleventh centuries.

Slavic settlements of the Drevlyanians, the Dregovichians, the Krivichians and the Severyans and the other Slavs who are tributary to the Russes.[1]

They make raids on the Slavs, coming to them in boats, seizing their people and carrying them off to Khozeran and to the Bulgars to be sold.[2] Throughout the ninth and tenth centuries, this Varangian control over the East Slavic and other tribes was strengthened and extended, the occasional revolt being severely suppressed. Rurik of Novgorod built forts in the territory of the Krivichians and Merians to overawe them and protect

[1] *Moravcsik (1949), p. 62*
[2] *Lyashchenko (1956), I, p. 97*

the waterways. Oleg of Kiev compelled or persuaded the Severyans and Radimichians to transfer their tribute from the Khazars to himself. His successor, Igor, had to put down a revolt of the Drevlyanians, who soon retaliated by killing him. For this they were punished and driven back into subjection by his widow, the regent Olga. Vladimir I (977-1015) had to discipline the Vyatichians and Radimichians. In this way the Varangian state was hammered into shape. But from the beginning, the ruling class of 'Russes' probably included high-born Slavs as well as Varangians, and expeditionary forces continued to be mixed. The Norsemen, as in France, and like the Normans in England after the Conquest, were absorbed by the much more numerous native peoples: it was from them they took their wives, and it was a Slavonic language and not a Scandinavian tongue that prevailed in Russia.

The Dnieper Route in the Tenth Century

There is a vivid account of the way in which the tenth-century Russes traded with Constantinople in the *De Administrando Imperio*, a book compiled in the name of the Emperor Constantine VII (Porphyrogenitus) for the benefit of his son Romanus, about 950. It tells how, in spring, as soon as the rivers were free of ice, boats were made by the Slavs from hollowed-out tree trunks. These boats came from Novgorod, Smolensk, Lyubech and Vyshgorod, and were assembled at Kiev, where the Russes spent the month of May fitting them out.

> *And in June they go down the river to Vitichev, a town tributary to the Russes. They wait here for two or three days until all the boats have arrived, and then move off down the river.*[1]

Of all the great Russian rivers, the Dnieper alone had a serious impediment to navigation in the forty-mile stretch of rapids between the present towns of Dnepropetrovsk and Zaporozhe, where the river crosses a series of granite ridges, now drowned by the reservoir for the Zaporozhe power station (fig. 17). The writer in Constantine's book gives what must be an eye-witness description of how the boatmen pass seven successive turbulent stretches of rapids caused by the granite obstructions. The first of these

> *is so narrow that it is no wider than the* tzykanisterion [*the polo ground at Constantinople*]; *in the middle there are high and dangerous rocks which stick out like islands. The water rushes up and over them, plunging down the other side with a great and terrifying roar. The Russes do not therefore dare to pass through them; they put in*

[1] *Moravcsik (1949), p. 58. This account of the Dnieper traffic is in Chapter 9 of the* De Administrando. *It should be read with the commentary by D. Obolensky, a work of great scholarship which throws light on almost every aspect of the original's fascinating description. See Jenkins (1962) and also Sorlin (1965)*

figure 17   The Dnieper rapids.

at the bank, landing some of the men, and leaving the goods in the boats; they try out the way with their bare feet lest they strike a rock. While some at the prow and others in the middle do this, those in the stern propel with poles, and so, with the greatest care they get past this first obstruction, keeping in close to the river bank. When they

have got through, they take on those whom they had set down, and
come down to the second obstruction.[1]

Here the boats 'are again guided by the men who are landed', and so also
at the third obstruction. At the fourth,

some lead the chained slaves along the bank for six miles until they
have passed the obstruction. Meanwhile, some dragging the boats along
and others carrying them on their shoulders, they pass by the rapids;
and so they return to the river with their goods, and push off from
the bank.[2]

Having passed the fifth, sixth and seventh rapids, they came to the
Krarion ford, an important crossing place on the river used by merchants
from western Russia who were making for the Crimea by a direct overland
route.

The island of Khortitsa marked the end of the rapids and here the Russ
boatmen made sacrifices to their gods for their safe passage. They then had
an uneventful four-day passage down the river to its mouth, where they
landed on another island (Berezan) to rest and refit their boats for the sea-
going journey along the western shores of the Black Sea; rudders, masts
and sails were added. They put in at the Dniester mouth and sailed on to
the Danube delta, after which they skirted the Bulgarian coast, eventually
reaching Constantinople.

Besides natural hazards, the Russ merchants were often in danger from
the Pecheneg nomads. As the *De Administrando Imperio* says:

The Russes cannot come to this Imperial City of the Romans [Con-
stantinople], whether for war or trade, unless they are at peace with
the Pechenegs. For when the Russes come to the obstructions in the
river with their boats, and cannot pass unless they take their boats
out of the water and carry them on their shoulders, men of the Pecheneg
race attack them, and easily rout them and slay them, since they
[the Russes] cannot do two things at once.[3]

Once past the Danube delta they came under the protection of the Eastern
Empire and had no more to fear from the steppe nomads.

When the lower Dnieper, which crossed the open steppe and was
dangerously exposed to nomadic raids, was too unsafe, a more direct course
was taken to the Black Sea across the Bug to the Dniester, through land
well settled by Slavs.[4] Early in the eleventh century, the main Dnieper way
was to some extent abandoned for a route up the Seym from Chernigov
and down the Donets and Don to the Sea of Azov (fig. 18). This temporary
shift of traffic may have been due to Pecheneg activity on the Dnieper or
to closer trade relations with the Azov state of Tmutarakan.[5] But the
Dnieper route was preferred in normal times, despite its formidable rapids,

[1] *Moravcsik (1949), p. 58*
[2] *Moravcsik (1949), p. 60*
[3] *Moravcsik (1949), p. 50*
[4] *Beazley (1949), III, p. 409*
[5] *Vernadsky (1948), p. 77*

since it did not involve extensive laborious land portages but offered a continuous waterway.

It is not clear how the Russes returned from Constantinople to Kiev. The *De Administrando* says that they equipped their new dug-outs in spring at Kiev with oars, rowlocks and other necessities dismantled from their old boats, from which it would appear that these were brought back to Kiev.

Inevitably, the state controlling the river routes between the Baltic and Black Seas had much to do with Byzantium, capital of the eastern section of the Roman Empire, and which, as Constantinople, survived the fall of Rome for a thousand years. The relationship was limited to commerce for well over a century, although the Varangian-Slav barbarians had several times to resort to force to secure the trading privileges they coveted. As early as 839, Scandinavian ambassadors had appeared at the court of the Emperor Theophilus, while in 860, 907 and 944, large and well-organized raids were made on Constantinople to obtain favourable trade treaties. The 945 treaty stated that

> the great prince of Rus and his boyars shall send to Greece to the great Greek Emperor as many ships as they desire with their agents and their merchants, according to the prevailing usage.

But the Russians had to underake not to winter at the Dnieper mouth, to respect the rights of the fishermen of the Greek city of Kherson, and to protect them from the Bulgars.[1]

Svyatoslav and the Steppe Nomads, 962-72

Between Kiev and Byzantium, however, there lay not only the Black Sea, but the open steppe grassland, where the hold of the Russes was uncertain. The steppes were the natural habitat of mounted nomadic herders and marauders, and most of the energies and policies of the Varangian rulers were devoted to keeping the trade routes open across them. The Magyars, who had given trouble in Oleg's reign (882-913), had moved up the Danube into Hungary. They were driven off the Black Sea steppes by a new tide of nomads, this time the fearsome Pechenegs, who defeated them in 897 and first raided the Russian state in 915. But normally the Khazar empire was strong enough to hold them back.

The minimum requirement was to keep the Dnieper waterway, but, ideally, control of the Danube route leading westwards, and of the Sea of Azov-Don-Volga route to the east, was needed for a sure grasp of the commerce that thronged the Black Sea and converged upon Byzantium. There had long been a separate Russ commercial state by the Sea of Azov, centred on the port of Tmutarakan (fig. 16). This was in constant danger of isolation from the Kievan state by nomadic domination of the intervening steppe. Farther afield, Russ establishment on the lower Volga

[1] *Cross & Sherbowitz-Wetzor (1953), p. 74*

and the Caspian Sea was desirable, as it would bring in the Volga traffic, hitherto largely in the hands of Swedes, Bulgars and Arabs. An attempt to build a political and commercial empire of these dimensions was made by Grand Prince Svyatoslav (962-72).

He struck first at the Vyatichians, and next at the Finns, in 964 (fig. 16). Then the Volga Bulgars were crushed, the Khazars were attacked and their capital, Itil, sacked (965). After the Volga mouth had been secured, the Grand Prince of Kiev turned his attention to the Don mouth and the Azov area, which was subjugated by the storming of Sarkel, another Khazar stronghold. Svyatoslav next turned west and made a successful onslaught upon the Bulgars of the Danubian valley.

In his imperial ambitions in southern Russia, Svyatoslav anticipated those of Peter the Great in the north, especially in his desire to move his capital to the newly conquered territory so as to be closer to trade and civilization. He wrote:

> *I do not care to remain in Kiev, but should prefer to live in Pereyaslavets on the Danube . . . where all riches are concentrated: gold, silks, wines and various fruits from Greece, silver and horses from Hungary and Bohemia; and from Russia, furs, wax, honey and slaves.*[1]

What St Petersburg was to be to Moscow, Pereyaslavets would have been to Kiev.

But Svyatoslav had over-reached himself. The resources of the young Russian state were not sufficient for such a challenge to those east-west trending geographical forces which forbade, as yet, the building of a Russia from the northern forest to the mouths of the Danube and the Volga. The Prince had brought about his own undoing. His destruction of the Khazar empire removed the barrier which had hitherto kept back the main force of Pechenegs. In 968 they laid seige to Kiev and in 972 ambushed Svyatoslav at the Dnieper rapids. He was slain and '*the nomads took his head and made a cup out of his skull, overlaying it with gold, and they drank from it*'.[2] This incident shows how little the nomads had changed in their customs since the time of Herodotus, a space of fourteen hundred years:

> *the skulls . . . of their bitterest enemies they use thus. A man saweth away all the parts beneath the brows and cleanseth it. Then . . . if he be rich . . . gildeth it within; and he useth it for a drinking cup.*[3]

The Conversion to Christianity [989] and its Results

In 989, Grand Prince Vladimir was baptized, his subjects compelled to embrace Christianity, and the pagan idols thrown down in the temples. Throughout the known world at this time human civilization was making

[1] *Cross & Sherbowitz-Wetzor (1953), p. 86*
[2] *Cross & Sherbowitz-Wetzor (1953), p. 90*
[3] *Powell (1949), I. p. 297*

the advance from heathen adoration of concrete objects and personified deities to worship of an abstract spiritual God. Most of the states adjoining Russia had taken this step forward. The rulers of Poland and Hungary had recently been converted to Roman Christianity; the Khazars had accepted Judaism a century before; the Danubian Bulgars were Christian and those on the Volga, Moslems.

There was perhaps a possibility that Russia too might have embraced Judaism or Islam, but as relations were closest with Constantinople, it was the Byzantine influence that prevailed. The immediate occasion of the conversion was Vladimir's desire for a marriage alliance with the Byzantine Empire, but so strong were the cultural, commercial and military prestige and primacy of Byzantium that Russian barbarism and paganism were bound to succumb sooner or later. Many of the prince's subjects were already Christians, for Christianity had been established in Kiev since the ninth century.[1]

The immediate results of the conversion were cultural. Stone churches in the Byzantine style replaced wooden temples and these still give character to the townscape of many an old Russian town. Kiev in particular became a city of handsome churches and monasteries in the reign of Yaroslav (1019-54). The arts and crafts benefited, as in all Christian countries, for a considerable amount of wealth and talent was henceforth enlisted in the cause of ecclesiastical architecture, painting, embroidery, music and manuscript production. Literacy spread as the number of clergy grew. It has been said of Russia's cultural progress in the two centuries following the conversion that

> *this young Christian nation had made such progress in so short a time that it, in many ways, outstripped Western nations converted centuries before the Russians by Roman missionaries.*[2]

Certainly, the splendour of Kiev made a strong impression upon those Westerners who witnessed it.

Belonging to Christendom made possible closer relationships with all the countries of Christian Europe. Dynastic marriages took place in this period, not only with the Byzantines and Bulgarians, but with the royal houses of Germany, France, England, Norway, Sweden, Denmark, Hungary, Poland and Bohemia.[3] It is likely that, in 1090, Grand Prince Vsevolod of Kiev was related to more reigning houses than any other European monarch.[4] Cultural, especially literary, ties were established. Commercial exchanges with central Europe developed: '*the commercial route crossed Hungary towards the Danube, where Regensburg became the main clearing house for Kievan goods imported into the rest of Germany and into France*'. In fact, for a brief period, '*Russia was fully conscious of belonging to Europe*'.[5]

[1] *Ericsson (1966), pp. 78-121*
[2] *Dvornik (1949), p. 239*
[3] *Baumgarten (1927), p. 6*
[4] *Leib (1924), p. 143*
[5] *Dvornik (1949), pp. 248, 256*

Paradoxically, a more far-reaching result was to set Russia upon a different path from the rest of Europe and promote the split between what are now referred to, however unsatisfactorily, as 'West' and 'East'. The civilization of Ancient Greece was distinct from that which developed in Italy under Rome. When the Roman Empire grew to unwieldy proportions it was divided into two parts, western or Roman and eastern or Greek. The Christian Church also followed this division and in 1054 the two branches of the Church parted company. Before long they were vilifying each other, and the last of the crusades was fought, not against the infidel, but against Constantinople. After the destruction of the Eastern Empire by the Turks, Moscow inherited the position previously held by Constantinople. The theological, philosophical and intellectual movements known as Scholasticism, Renaissance, Reformation, Counter-Reformation, Reason and Enlightenment, the common heritage of countries which had drawn their Christianity from Rome, by-passed Russia, where orthodoxy and autocracy went hand in hand until the Bolshevik revolution. The division between western individualism and Russian collectivism, between western capitalism and eastern socialism, is in some respects the old ecclesiastical schism writ large.

Russia in the Eleventh and Twelfth Centuries

For a century and a half after the Conversion, the Kievan state was held together by capable rulers, despite intervening periods of anarchy and civil strife. Yet constant wars on all sides—with the Lithuanians, Ests and Finns, with the Bulgars on the Volga, with Poles and Hungarians, with the steppe nomads—gave no respite. It was from the latter that the chief danger came. Vladimir (980-1015) successfully organized the defence of Kiev again the Pechenegs. In the words of the Chronicle (988):

> Then Vladimir reflected that it was not good that there were so few towns round about Kiev. So he founded forts on the Desna, the Oster, the Trubezh, the Sula and the Stugna. He gathered together the best men of the Slavs, and Krivichians, the Chuds and the Vyatichians, and peopled these forts with them. For he was at war with the Pechenegs, and when he fought with them, he often overcame them.[1]

For a few decades there was relative peace on the steppe, but in 1061 the Polovtsy or Cumans invaded Rus *'for the first time'*.[2] From now on it was a desperate struggle for survival by the exposed principalities of the wooded steppe zone. 1093 was a black year for Kiev:

> Our own native land has fallen a prey to torment: some of our compatriots are led into servitude, others are slain, and some are even delivered up to vengeance and endure a bitter death. Some tremble as

[1] *Cross & Sherbowitz-Wetzor (1953), p. 119*
[2] *Cross & Sherbowitz-Wetzor (1953), p. 143*

they cast their eyes upon the slain, and others perish of hunger and thirst.[1]
The city was sacked, and the Polovtsy
> *divided the inhabitants, led them away among their tents to their
> relatives and kin. A multitude of Christian people were thus reduced
> to dire distress: sorrowing, tormented, weak with cold, their faces
> ravaged with hunger, thirst and misfortune, their bodies black with
> blows, as they made their painful way, naked and barefoot, upon
> feet torn with thorns, toward an unknown land and barbarous
> races.*[2]

Nevertheless, some Kievan princes intermarried with the Polovtsy while
others enlisted their help to fight their rivals.

Victories over the nomads in 1103 and 1107 gave the troubled region
security for a few more decades, but Kiev was now in decline. In 1157,
Prince Svyatoslav described the land round Chernigov as deserted except
for hunters and roaming Polovtsy.[3] Trade was badly affected by the raids.
The supremacy of the eastern waterway routes was passing. Western
alternatives, using the Mediterranean Sea, Alpine passes and the Rhine
river, were the chief beneficiaries. Commerical walled towns were now
arising in western Europe, as they had done in Russia centuries before.
Dynastic quarrels, aggravated by the jealousy of the various towns for
each other, also weakened the Kievan state. Yet, when its size is compared
with that of other contemporary European states, it seems remarkable
that Kievan Russia held together as long as it did.

This size was in itself a factor in the break-up of the old Russian
state. Soviet historians consider that it was big before its time. A large
unified state was not suited to a developing feudalism—boyars wanted
their prince's aid to be locally available and not to have to send to Kiev.
From the more distant parts, this might take weeks. In the new principalities, as they developed in the twelfth century, no place was more than
three days' journey from the prince's seat.[4]

One principality struggled, with some success, for independence from
Kiev, even during the latter's prime in the tenth and eleventh centuries.
This was Polotsk, which occupied a commanding position on the West
Dvina route to the Gulf of Riga, a rival branch to the main waterway to
the Baltic via Novgorod. But Polotsk had to fight on two fronts to maintain
and increase its trade: with Novgorod and Kiev on the east, and with
the warlike Lithuanian tribes to the west. For although the Dvina offers a
short cut to the Baltic, it was not, like the lake Ilmen—Novgorod—
Volkhov river route, wholly in Russian-controlled territory.[5]

The twelfth century witnessed a remarkable increase in the population
and power of the central mixed forest region between the upper Volga

[1] *Cross & Sherbowitz-Wetzor (1953), p. 178*
[2] *Cross & Sherbowitz-Wetzor (1953), p. 179*
[3] *Lyashchenko (1956), I, p. 152*
[4] *Rybakov (1966), I, pp. 574-6*
[5] *Rybakov (1966), I, pp. 598-601; Serodonin (1916), p. 240*

and Oka rivers, a region favoured by accessibility to routes leading in every direction. Many towns grew up here, of which Vladimir became the chief; others were Suzdal, Rostov, Yuryev, Moscow and Tver (fig. 18). Although the forest soils of the region are generally poor, the island of superior black earth soil west of Vladimir fostered a numerous farming population in the midst of the inhospitable forests. And it was partly into this region that refugees from Kiev and the rich lands of the harried Dnieper valley began to trek. Others migrated westwards to the Carpathians. The growing strength of the Volga-Oka region relative to the Dnieper valley found drastic illustration in the sacking of Kiev in 1169 by Andrey Bogolyubskiy of Suzdal, who then made Vladimir his capital.

While the Kievan state was degenerating into a group of warring principalities, with its centre of gravity shifting north-eastwards from Kiev to Vladimir, Novgorod continued to prosper. It threw off Kievan control early in the eleventh century. Isolated by marshes and protected from the covetousness of princes by its lack of productive and well-populated agricultural land, it was able to concentrate on its fur trade with Europe. It pushed its domination of the fur-bearing forests farther and farther to the north-east. The headwaters of the Sukhona river were reached during the tenth century, the Pechora and the Urals by the end of the eleventh.[1] In 1069 the Kievan chronicler tells of a journey made by a Novgorodian

> *to the Pechora, a people who pay tribute to Novgorod. . . . When he arrived among them, he went on among the Yugra. The latter are an alien people dwelling in the north with the Samoyedes. . . .*
>
> *. . . their language is unintelligible. They point, however, at iron objects, and make gestures as if to ask for them. If given a knife, or axe, they supply furs in return. The road to these mountains is impassable with precipices, snow and forests. Hence we do not always reach them, and they are also far to the north.*[2]

Despite its possession of commercial wealth and a vast territorial empire, Novgorod's geographical position contained fatal weaknesses. It was dependent on imported food supplies brought by way of the Volga from the more productive countryside to the south-east. When, in the twelfth century, this agricultural land fell into the hands of ambitious princes of Vladimir-Suzdal, like Yuriy Dolgorukiy and his son Andrey, they used their advantage to interfere with Novgorod's policies and to impose their nominees as its princes.[3]

Russia in A.D. 1200: Economic and Social Geography (fig. 18)

In 1200 the Russian territory stretched from the Carpathians in the southwest to the Urals in the north-east. Already this territory was known

[1] *Beazley (1949), II, pp. 38-9, III, pp. 493-4*
[2] *Cross & Sherbowitz-Wetzor (1953), p. 184*
[3] *Lantzeff (1947), pp. 4-8*

figure 18   Russia in 1200.

as the Russ land and the people as Russes. For half a century or more, Kiev had ceased to be supreme over one East Slav state, for Kievan Russia had broken up into a number of warring principalities, united only by a common language and religion, and by close family ties among the princes. Apart from this internecine strife, the western parts were involved in wars with the Poles while those in the south-east had been fatally weakened by Turkish raids. The north-eastern states were relatively free from foreign involvements, and here Novgorod had been able to extend its sway over an empire which reached the Arctic Ocean and the Urals, an empire which, though only thinly peopled by Finnish tribes, was none the less essential to the trade upon which the strength of the city state depended, since it was the source of valuable pelts. Vladimir-Suzdal was free to throw its energies into attempts to dominate the other Russian towns: its prince had sacked Kiev in 1169.

This Russian group of city states no longer reached to the Black Sea, for the Polovtsy, Turkish nomads, now dominated the steppes as far west as the Danube. The Kiev region was protected from them by lines of fortifications built by Vladimir I; these mainly utilized two tributaries of the Dnieper: the Ross and the Sula. Slavs and Finns from newly subdued tribes had originally been settled in the fortified towns to take the brunt of the Pecheneg attacks. One of these had grown into the large town of Pereyaslavl, capital of a principality in the march or frontier zone; this area was known as the *ukraina* or border, whence the name Ukraine. Now that the Pechenegs had been replaced by the Polovtsy, other Turks willing to defend the Russian state against them had also been settled along the frontier. Nevertheless, in 1203 the Polovtsy were to break through these defences and attack Kiev.

The Baltic Sea was still reached by Russian land, but only for the short distance where Novgorod's territory touched the southern shore of the Gulf of Finland. Here also, Russian interests were threatened. The various Baltic peoples, Lithuanians, Livonians and Letts, hitherto under the sway of Novgorod, Pskov and Polotsk, were now under serious pressure from the Germans, Danes and Swedes.

The Volga Bulgars still maintained an independent state on the middle course of the river, controlling from their fortress capital of Bulgar, the three important routes of the upper Volga, the Kama and the lower Volga. Malarial marshes separated their territory from that of the Russians, and they were for long a barrier to the progress of Russian settlement down the river.[1]

Driven back from the steppes, the Russians now inhabited a tree-covered land—great forests in the north interspersed with swamps, and a more open woodland in the south, but again with areas of swamp. The forest remained vital to the life of the people. Hunting and trapping provided sport for the aristocracy, food for the population, furs for trade and tribute, hides and skins for clothing and tanning. The bear, bison, boar, deer and elk are all mentioned as prey for the huntsman. Bees were still kept in the hollow trunks of trees, and in 1150 the Prince of Smolensk had presented a bishop with a '*beehive wood*'.[2] Fishing may have been even more important than in earlier times owing to the introduction of church fasts.

Useful though the forest was, its extent was decreasing as agricultural clearings widened outwards from the rivers, along which the foremost

[1] *Clarkson (1962), p. 44*
[2] *Vernadsky (1948), p. 106*

settlements had been made. Everywhere the axe was being wielded by strong arms intent on building, boat-making and wood-working of all kinds. In the larger towns the streets were often paved with logs, and portages likewise were made passable in this way. Fires, both accidental and those calculated to free and fertilize land for farming, were also agents aiding the diminution of the wooded area. In the south, along the zone of 'wooded steppe', where timber was relatively rare, man helped the steppe to encroach upon the woodland. This encroachment may have facilitated nomadic raids on Kiev and other Russian settlements in the south, as time went on.

Arable farming, along with Russian settlement and control, had been driven from the steppes, which now reverted to pasture for the horses and cattle of the Turks. But in the forested lands to the north agriculture expanded in area, in productivity and in variety of crops. As population grew it was no longer possible in the older settled areas to burn away the forest, cultivate the soil for a few years until fertility was gone, and then move on. There was no more virgin forest in these areas. Instead, systems using two or three fields had to be introduced. But, away from the river valleys and in the northern and western frontier areas, the old primitive methods survived.[1] Wheat and rye were the predominant cereals in the south, but the poorer soils and colder climate of the north limited the farmer to barley, oats and rye. Flax, hemp and vegetables of all kinds were now to be found in most parts of the country. Cattle, sheep, pigs and poultry were universally reared, and especially horses, for which the almost continual warfare created a great demand. There were, in the main, three types of farm: the large princely or baronial estate, worked by slaves and hired labourers; monastic farms tilled by the monks themselves; and peasant holdings of varying size. A large manorial estate or *votchina* would produce a wide range of goods in great abundance: grain, livestock, flax, wool, eggs, butter, fish, honey; in addition, further supplies of such products would be brought in by dependent peasants as dues in kind or *obrok*.

The primitive soil-scratching implements of early Slavic times had been by now almost everywhere superseded by the plough. There were two principal types in use: the *ralo*, a slow and cumbersome instrument, often needing several beasts to draw it through deep and heavy soils; and the *sokha*, a lighter plough better suited to the shallower boulder-strewn soils of the northerly glaciated districts.

Iron ore was Russia's only accessible metal, but nevertheless a most essential resource in an iron-using culture, enabling such necessities as tools, stoves, utensils and weapons to be made without costly imports. Hydrous oxide of iron or limonite occurs in swampy areas, and as the Russian lands had more than their share of these, this bog ore was widespread.[2] Much of it came from the northerly parts of Novgorod's

[1] *Lyashchenko (1956), I, p. 129*
[2] *Rybakov (1948), pp, 92, 123-5*

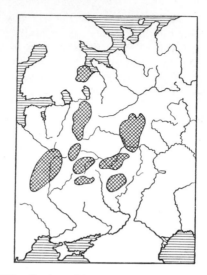

figure 19   Distribution of bog ore (after Rybakov).

empire and from the marshes of Volynia (fig. 19). Other metals had to be imported. Salt, extremely valuable in a country where a long severe winter necessitated the slaughter of cattle and salting of meat, was abundant in Galicia and was also derived from sea water on the Baltic and White Sea shores.

Metal working was probably the chief single industry, and iron production took place in many localities. But the skilled production of finished metallic articles seems to have been confined to the larger towns, especially Kiev and Novgorod. Gold and silver were worked into vessels and ornaments for the Church and for the wealthy; silver was also used for coinage. Copper was made into kettles and church bells. Lead and tin were used for roofing.

The textile industry had also developed rapidly with the growth of a wealthy class and the spread of Byzantine fashions of dress. Owing to the ability of many of the poorer soils to produce fair crops of flax and hemp, linen was the commonest cloth and these fibres also found uses as tent cloth for the soldiers, sailcloth and rope for the sailors and merchants, and nets for the fishermen. Woollen cloth manufacture was also on the increase. Leather-working was an essential industry which not only made boots for the upper classes, but shields and other equipment for the warriors.[1]

Woodworking was naturally widespread, though products were often crude and rough hewn, being shaped by the axe. But Novgorod was so famed as a centre for skilled carpentry that its inhabitants were sometimes referred to as 'the carpenters'. They came not only from the city itself

[1] *Lyashchenko (1956), p. 145*

but from the villages of the countryside, where the ill-drained marshes offered little scope for farming, and they travelled great distances in search of work. Boatbuilding was a speciality both of this town and of Kiev. Sawmills worked by water power were probably common, and there is mention in the Chronicle of one driven by the Ross river (1195).[1]

Generally speaking, Russia was an exporter of primary commodities, mainly the products of forest and farm, and an importer of manufactured goods and non-ferrous metals. Her wax, furs, honey and surplus grain went to Constantinople and eastward to the Arabs, Persians and Turks. They were often accompanied by slaves, particularly Finns from the north-eastern forest. From Constantinople were brought into Russia: icons, jewellery and glassware, gold and silver, and Mediterranean wines, olive oil and fruit. Copper and tin arrived from the Caucasus and Asia Minor. From the East, spices, precious stones, silk and satin were imported, and horses and cattle were purchased from the steppe nomads. Westwards to Europe, by way of Novgorod and Smolensk, went furs, flax, hemp, hides, skins, suet and tallow. In return came lead and salt; linen, woollen and silken cloth; glassware, tools and small metal objects like needles; fish, wines and beer. The recent development of a trade connection between Regensburg on the German Danube and Kiev had given the latter city a share in the trade with Central Europe.

The Dnieper was still the main commercial artery linking Kiev, Chernigov and Pereyaslavl with Constantinople across the Black Sea. Although subject to Polovts interference, which greatly lessened its usefulness, there were periods of peace with the Turks, during which it remained fairly safe. Most eastern trade still went through the Volga Bulgar territory.

Domestic trade had also grown in significance. This was largely due to the contrasts between the needs and produce of northern and southern Russia, and to the complementary economies of town and countryside. Each town had its large market square, where farm and forest produce were exchanged for the output of the craftsman and for imported goods.

The total population of Russia at this time has been estimated at 7½ million.[2] A high birth rate can be assumed for what was, by all accounts, a remarkably energetic, healthy and virile people, whose even more rapid increase was checked by the recurrence of famine, plague and warfare. The ability of the princes to indulge in such strife indicates that population was increasing faster than the land, despite clearing of the forest, could support.

This large population included, besides the handful of princes, a few thousand *boyars* or nobles. These had a dual origin. Some may have been descendants of the bodyguard companions who rowed with the first Viking invaders and who, when too old for active raiding and trading, had been given land along the river routeways. These lands, already peopled by

[1] *Vernadsky* (*1948*), *p. 300*
[2] *Vernadsky* (*1948*), *p. 104*

Slavs, they were expected to keep in order. Others were descended from the native Slavic aristocracy. But the two types were now indistinguishable, having intermarried, and all spoke the Slavonic tongue. There were perhaps several thousand merchants and rich traders in the towns, tens of thousands of urban artisans, and a numerous clergy. But the mass of the population consisted of *smerds* or free peasants, *zakups* (men bound to masters to whom they were indebted), and the paid labourers and slaves who worked the large estates of the boyars and princes.

Galicia, combining rich black-earth soils with a situation out-of-the-way as regards Polovtsy raids, was now probably the most densely peopled of the Russian lands. Many of its inhabitants had come from the middle Dnieper region, which most likely still held a large population, but from which large numbers were trekking on account of its insecurity. It was of this area that the chronicler wrote:

> *as soon as the* smerd *begins to plough, the Polovtsy will come, shoot with the arrow, and have his horse; and going into the village, they will have his wife, his children and all that he has.*[1]

It was none the less a region with marked advantages: large extents of unwooded land with rich black-earth soil, a long warm summer season, well frequented trading routes, and large cities.

But the fastest developing region was that lying between the upper Volga and the Oka. Already it was filled with young towns, each of which must have been surrounded by freshly cleared and recently colonized countryside. Even this region, despite its indifferent soils, severe climate and dense forest cover, had been inhabited since the Old Stone Age. No doubt freedom from the nomadic raids that weakened the south, and the absence of powerful hostile neighbours as in the west, were factors encouraging its progress, together with a situation accessible to all the main river routes of the country. (Fig. 18.)

Of the approximately three hundred towns, although most were probably very small, with perhaps just a few thousand inhabitants, some were very large and flourishing cities, and the urban population can hardly have been less than a million. The average town would have sheltered several kinds of people: if it was the capital of a principality, it would have housed those retainers who were habitually around the ruler. Many boyars had town houses. Merchants, both native and foreign, were the wealthiest and most influential class. Tradesmen and artisans of all sorts—carpenters, boot-makers, fullers, masons, potters, blacksmiths, silversmiths, goldsmiths, tailors, tanners, weavers, etc.—and labourers, made up the rest. Towns which were capitals of principalities were Kiev, Smolensk, Novgorod the Great, Polotsk, Turov, Chernigov, Pereyaslavl, Novgorod-on-Desna, Galich, Ryazan, Suzdalian Vladimir and Volynian Vladimir. (Fig. 18.)

Kiev, Smolensk and Novgorod the Great were undoubtedly very large towns. Kiev, though no longer so prosperous as a century before, and lying dangerously exposed to nomadic attack, was nevertheless still the capital of

[1] *Lyashchenko (1956), p. 134*

the rich densely populated black-earth region of the middle Dnieper basin, and distinguished by many fine churches built in the reign of Yaroslav (1019-54). Smolensk owed its greatness to a remarkable intersection of routes.

Novgorod's strength lay in its near monopoly of the supply of furs and in its membership of the Hanseatic League. German merchants and those from Visby in Gotland formed powerful guilds in its midst. Because of the infertility of the surrounding countryside, the large population of the town was dependent upon imported grain. Shortages elsewhere meant famine in Novgorod. This was so severe in 1230 that

> *some, as if they were common beasts, were cutting up and eating live human beings; others were dissecting and eating the dead flesh of corpses; yet others devoured the flesh of horses, dogs and cats; still others ate moss, pinewood the bark of linden, trees and the leaves of elms.*[1]

Moscow, first mentioned in 1147, and fortified in 1156, had become large enough to bury 24,000 corpses after the Mongol visitation of 1237-8.[2]

Because of the marshy nature of the Baltic coastal plain, commerce preferred the sea route from the ports of northern Europe, entering Russia by one of the river routes leading inland from the coast. The three main such routes were those using the rivers (or lakes) Neva-Ladoga-Volkhov, Narva-Peipus-Velikaya, and Dvina. On each a commercial city arose: Novgorod the Great, Pskov and Polotsk. Of these, Novgorod was by far the greatest. It alone had river-and-portage connections with the Volga basin as well as with the Dnieper. And it alone had the vast hinterland of fur-bearing coniferous forest stretching away to the north-east and constituting an empire as vast as the rest of Russia put together. (Fig. 18.)

Those leading Russian towns which had been in existence at the time of the Varangian incursions must have presented a vastly different picture in 1200. From being small collections of wooden huts built around a market place and surrounded by a palisade, they had become large and prosperous cities adorned with ornate churches, often in stone, and with the large houses of princes, nobles and merchants elaborated with wood carving. Fire, however, was an ever-present danger to these mainly wooden towns and doubtless some of them would have displayed quarters still charred from the latest conflagration.

This menace, as well as Byzantine influence and an increase in the number of skilled masons, encouraged use of stone and brick, although lack of places where stone could be quarried was a serious handicap. Both in the south, where thick deposits of fine-grained loess were widespread and in the north, where forest on clay predominated, building stone was not easily found. The river network did, however, make possible its transport over large distances. Although Kiev had long been outstanding for its stone buildings and masons, the mastery in this respect had, by the

---

[1] *Lyashchenko (1956), p. 130*
[2] *Lyashchenko (1956), p. 215*

year 1200, passed to Suzdalia, whose princes were proud builders and who had imported Byzantine and German architectural talent for the palaces and churches of their old and new capitals, Suzdal and Vladimir. Two large and impressive new cathedrals were built in Vladimir between 1150 and 1200. This was but one aspect of the transfer of power, prosperity and population from the Kievan south-west to the Suzdalian north-east.

The people of the countryside had almost certainly made very little cultural or material progress in the past four centuries, so that an immense gulf now separated them from the townspeople. Except for the aristocratic or boyar families and the wealthier landowners, the people still inhabited log huts if they lived in northern Russia and clay-walled wood-framed hovels if in the south. But the better-off farmer might well have a substantial three-roomed house with one room heated by the stove.

Similar contrasts would have been noticeable between the dress and diet of the urbanized upper classes and those of the rural peasants. Imported silks and home-woven linen in summer, woollens and dressed furs in winter, with leather boots, clothed the well-off, but coarser homespuns and sheepskins, with boots of bark or felt were the lot of the poorer classes. The towns were now supplied with a wide variety of food and drink: meat and game; eggs, dairy produce and vegetables; imported fruit; mead, and imported wines and beer. Rural food depended more on the locality itself, and would be basically rye bread in the south, supplemented by such meat and fish as were available. The common drink was *kvass*, a fermented liquor made from sour bread.

CHAPTER FOUR
RUSSIA, 1200-1400: THE MONGOL CONQUEST

While Kiev, entangled with the nomadic Polovtsy, was in slow decline, and while the newly dominant north-eastern principality of Suzdal-Vladimir was preparing to drive eastwards down the Volga, a formidable Mongolian empire was forming under the guidance of Chingis Khan. Its first victim was China, but soon after the fall of Peking in 1215 the Mongols moved westwards, and in 1219 they destroyed the prosperous and civilized agricultural and commercial state of Khoresm which flourished, with the help of irrigation, on the arid lands to the south and east of the Caspian and Aral Seas. In 1221 the Great Khan sent a reconnaissance force into

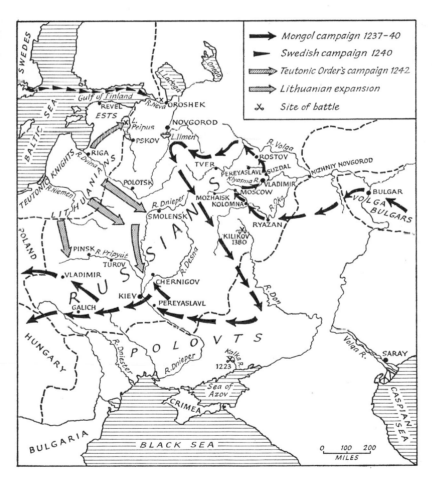

figure 20   Russia in the mid-thirteenth century.

C

the steppes of south Russia. The Polovtsy and the southern Russians united to resist this new and unexpected menace, but their combined armies were defeated on the Kalka river to the north of the Sea of Azov (fig. 20). The Tartars, as they came to be known in Russia and the West, then returned home.

Yuriy, Grand Prince of Vladimir, now closely allied with his brother Yaroslav of the great commercial centre of Novgorod, had just built the fortified trading post of Nizhniy Novgorod (Lower Novgorod, now Gorkiy) where the Oka joins the Volga. His object in this was to overawe the surrounding Finnish tribes and to threaten the Volga Bulgars. His plans were to be rudely interrupted. In 1237 the Tartars returned with a vast force of over a hundred thousand men. Aware of the decline of Kiev and the pre-eminence of Vladimir among the Russian states, they struck first at the middle Volga region, hitherto considered safe from nomadic attack.

More than any of their many predecessors on the steppe, the Mongols excelled in horsemanship and archery. They were superbly led and organized, and their cruelty was such that the terror of their deeds pre-ceeded their arrival and unnerved their victims: *'the slaughter of other people is accepted a matter of nothing with them'*.[1]

In the midst of winter, when they might have felt themselves safe, the Volga Bulgars were struck down. But winter held no terror for the Tartars, familiar with the extremes of the Mongolian and Siberian climates. For them the cold season was more of an advantage than a handicap, freezing the rivers and marshes and so facilitating their movement in the forested country. One after another the Russian towns were destroyed and their inhabitants slain or made captive. After sacking Ryazan, Kolomna, Moscow, Vladimir, Suzdal and Rostov, killing the Grand Prince and routing his army, they made for Novgorod. The great merchant city was saved by the approach of the spring of 1238: the Tartars dared not risk the thaw in this swampy region. They hurried back to the steppes where, gorged with loot, they rested awhile.

In 1239 it was the turn of south-west Russia: Chernigov, Pereyaslavl, Kiev, Galich and Volynian Vladimir suffered total destruction. Piano Carpini, sent by Pope Innocent VI as an envoy to the Tartars in 1246, gave this account of his visit to Kiev:

> *we found an innumerable multitude of dead men's skulls and bones lying upon the earth. For it was a very large and populous city, but it was now in a manner brought to nothing: for there do scarce remain two hundred houses, the inhabitants whereof are kept in extreme bondage.*[2]

The Mongol onslaught of 1237-9, although novel in its incursion into the forest region, was for the Russians of the wooded steppe and steppe zones, the violent culmination of a long series of nomadic raids which

[1] *Hakluyt (1598), p. 55*
[2] *Hakluyt (1598), p. 61; Painter (1965), p. 78*

had for a century or more led to migration from the area. This migration took two main directions. One was north-eastwards up the Desna valley into the forested region; the other was westwards into Volynia and Galicia and, when these lands became insecure, up into the Carpathians. Thus the Kievan Russians lost their unity: some became Great Russians tributary to the Mongols, while others became Ukrainians and subject to Lithuania, Poland and Austria.

After they had ravaged southern Russia, the Mongols entered Silesia and Hungary before returning to the steppe. Here the general in charge of these successful campaigns set up a south Russian khanate, known as the Golden Horde, with a new capital at Saray in the Volga delta area, not far from the ruins of the old Khazar capital of Itil. (Fig. 20.)

Although Novgorod and the other towns of the north-west escaped the Tartar ravages, the Baltic Germans and Swedes, both of whom hoped to control the Baltic shores and the trading cities of their hinterland, soon took advantage of the new situation. Teutonic and Scandinavian encroachment had been going on for nearly a century. Riga had been founded in 1201, and soon after, the Livonian Order of German knights had taken over control of the Latvian tribes from the Russian town of Polotsk. In 1219 Revel was founded, and from it the Ests were dominated. Now, in 1240, the Swedes, who had already established their rule in Finland to the north of the gulf, attempted to control its southern shores, held by Novgorod. Prince Alexander of that city beat them soundly on the river Neva and two years later, in defence of Pskov, defeated the German knights on the ice of lake Peipus. The Russian fortress of Oroshek was built in 1323 as a safeguard against any Swedish penetration eastwards to lake Ladoga.

Alexander Nevsky himself, despite his great Baltic victories over Swede and German, had, with all the other Russian princes, to journey to the Mongol capital to acknowledge the supremacy of his new overlord and receive from him authority to rule his lands. Again and again, for instance in 1280, 1313 and 1342, such humiliating pilgrimages were made. When, in 1252, the Grand Prince of Vladimir refused to go, his territory was devastated as punishment. The princes had also to agree that tribute, both in men and in goods, should be levied from their lands, and soon Mongol officials were supervising the extortion of whatever town and countryside had to offer. The Russian peasant in his forest clearing must henceforth labour that the Tartar on the steppe might live in ease, yet think himself fortunate if he was not carried off to serve in the Mongol army. In 1327 Tver was sacked in reprisal for an anti-Mongol rebellion. Princes or claimants to princely authority were executed by the Mongols in 1319, 1325 and 1328.

The impact of the Mongols not only brought immediate disaster, but also had lasting economic, social and political effects. The ravaged districts took up to a hundred years to recover. The surviving peasants, bowed down beneath the tribute, lost all hope of rising above bare subsistence. The destruction of the leading towns and the slaughter or captivity of their skilled artisans and handicraftsmen, reduced material life to a barbarous level compared with the civilization of Kievan Russia and of Europe to the west. To the deep spiritual divide between East and West, already existing because of the religious schism between the eastern and western branches of the Christian church, was now to be added a wide gulf in material culture.

Socially and politically, the weakening of the democratic or oligarchic forces represented by the urban artisan and merchant populations, facilitated the growth of autocracy. This was also helped by the Mongols who handed over to the princes the task of levying tribute. The tyranny and terror previously employed by the conquerors went with this power, and before long the Mongols were assisting the princes to suppress rebellions against its ruthless exercise. Eventually this absolute control over the resources of the state enabled the Russian grand princes to throw off the Tartar yoke. While the princes were elevated to a position of supreme authority, the middle classes shrank into insignificance, and the peasants were degraded to a brutish existence.

K. A. Wittfogel argues that oriental despotism, as introduced by the Mongols into Russia, arose in what he calls 'hydraulic' societies, i.e. populations established on the arid lands of Asia and dependent upon the efficient organization of irrigation by a powerful and centralized authority. Once this monopolistic state enterprise had been evolved, it spread to areas *'that had no comprehensive waterworks and, in some cases, not even small-scale irrigation.'*[1] The Mongols brought the machinery of absolutism into Russia, including the idea of taking censuses on which to base taxation and conscription. Such a census was taken in 1275.

The Expansion of Lithuania

A most serious effect of the Mongol onslaught was the division of Russia into two parts and the development of differences in the people as between Great, White and Little Russians. The subjugation of eastern and southern Russia by the Mongols left the western part of the country ill-defended against the aggressive Lithuanians. In the thirteenth century, the Lithuanian tribes, always fearsome warriors, but hitherto unorganized, were hammered into a coherent military force and political state by Teutonic pressure and able leaders. Even so, there can be little doubt that, but for the Tartar conquest, the Russians would have at least withstood Lithuanian encroachment. They might even have absorbed the Lithuanians, converted them to the eastern rite, and led them against the Germans. As it was, the princes and boyars of western Russia, isolated from their cousins to the east, and fearful of Mongol attack upon themselves, welcomed the security which absorption into a powerful Lithuania gave them.

[1] *Wittfogel (1956), p. 154*

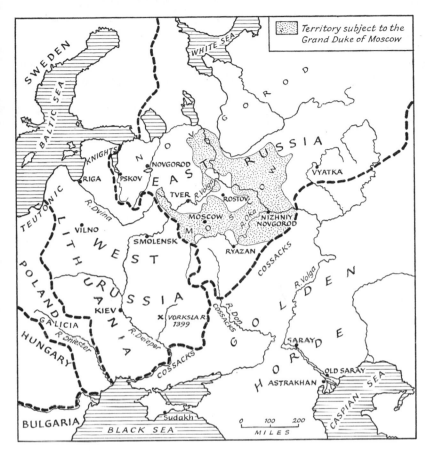

figure 21   Russia in 1400.

The first moves of Lithuanian expansion were advances up the Dvina
and Niemen, rivers in the lower valleys of which the Lithuanian tribes
had long dwelled. This meant the annexation of the Polotsk, Turov and
Pinsk territories, and was followed in the fourteenth century by a spreading
westwards into the land of Smolensk, and southwards into Volynia and
Galicia. The superior soils of these two provinces meant a great acquisition
of wealth and population. Holding Pinsk, the Lithuanians were now on
the Pripyat, which river led down to the Dnieper valley. Here the Kiev
territory was reconquered from the Mongols, and Lithuanian control
reached the Black Sea between the estuaries of the Dnieper and the
Dniester. Grand Duke Orgerd of Lithuania (1341-77) was not content
with western Russia, but repeatedly invaded the east. This he was able
to do because his territory now bestrode the great morainic ridge which
ran eastwards to Moscow, from which city he was twice driven off.
(Figs. 20, 21.)

The Expansion of the Grand Duchy of Moscow

While Lithuania was absorbing the west Russian lands, the principality of Moscow was likewise gathering under its wing the various lands of central Russia. Moscow in 1200 was a small fortified town in the principality of Suzdal-Vladimir, but its immediate environment and general situation held many advantages. Although sacked during the original Tartar campaign, it lay too deep in the forest to be easily reached; its site gave access to rivers leading in all directions; the surrounding region was one of active colonization and expanding population which aided recruitment. We read several times of the Moscow princes going north to beyond the Volga to recruit for their armies. Geographical causes apart, Moscow owed much to the cunning, cruelty and resourcefulness of its princes. In 1263 it became the centre of a very small appanage created for a member of the royal house. Its grand dukes, insignificant at first, took every advantage of its position to expand along the river valleys. Territory was acquired by many means: by force, treaty, marriage, murder, purchase, intrigue, colonization, and above all by keeping on good terms with the Mongol overlords and acting as their agents. Suffering, as a result, less from Tartar punitive expeditions than its less compliant neighbours, it was able to conserve its resources and gather strength.[1]

In 1301, Kolomna was seized from Ryazan, a stage in expansion down the Oka, and in 1303 the capture of Mozhaysk represented an advance up the Moskva. At the same time control was won of the Zaleski-Pereyaslavl appanage which reached to the upper Volga. In 1317, a Moscow prince, Yuriy, married a sister of the Khan, initiating a period of close cooperation with the Mongols. As a mark of favour, Yuriy was made Grand Duke of Vladimir. His younger brother, Ivan I, helped the Tartars suppress anti-Mongol revolts in Rostov in 1322 and in Tver in 1327: Tver, which might have rivalled Moscow for the leadership of eastern Russia, was so savagely dealt with that it ceased to matter. Ivan followed a policy of cordial subservience to the Tartars, efficiently collecting their tribute and at the same time stocking his own treasury, whence his name *Kalita* (money-bag). This he was able to do because the quiet conditions resulting from his policy led to relative prosperity in the Grand Duchy. Agriculture flourished, trade expanded, population grew. Attracted by this, no doubt, and by the security such a policy offered, the heads of the Russian Church, still known as 'metropolitans of Kiev and all Russia', came to reside in Moscow, giving it the prestige of being the religious capital of the country. For a time after the Mongol conquest they had lived amidst the ruins of Kiev. Then they had moved from place to place until finally settling in Moscow. Moscow's rulers benefited from the practical support they often received from the Church's leaders. And from this reign on, the Grand Princes of Vladimir and Moscow imitated the metropolitans and added the words '*and of all*

[1] *Platonov (1929), pp. 147-51*

Russia' to their own titles. Ivan's successors, Simeon and Ivan II, continued subservient to the Golden Horde.

Hitherto the khans, when confirming the princes of Moscow in the title of Grand Prince of Vladimir, had exempted the older parts of the principality, notably Suzdal and Rostov, from their jurisdiction. Dmitry (1359-89) asserted his authority over the whole Vladimir principality. This lay mainly along the Klyasma river, which itself is tributary to the Oka. He made extensive gains of territory on the Volga and beyond, areas in which colonization was proceeding apace. These lands, reaching northwards almost to lake Onega, threatened Novgorod's communications with her empire, and thus enabled Moscow to bring increasing pressure to bear on the imperial city state (fig. 21). But Nizhniy Novgorod, which had also been elevated to the status of a grand principality by the Tartars, blocked the way to the valuable strategic region of the Oka-Volga confluence.

In 1367 Dmitry replaced the wooden walls of the Moscow citadel or Kremlin with stone, a precaution which enabled the city to withstand Lithuanian and Mongol assaults on several occasions. It became clear that Dmitry meant to be his own master and to challenge the Tartar authority. His great victory over the Mongols at Kulikov-on-Don in 1380 made him a national hero. But Moscow was not yet ready for such defiance. Ivan I's policy of conserving resources had proved more suited to the times than Dmitry's dissipation of them, however glorious. Russian losses were heavy and in 1382 the Tartars came back to sack and burn Moscow. The various princes of eastern Russia hastened to renew their allegiance to the Khan who imposed a heavy tribute.

This situation was redressed by strife among the Mongols themselves and by the threat of a new Central Asian tyrant, Tamerlane the Great. In 1392 the Khan, desperate for support, turned to Moscow and allowed Grand Prince Basil I to annex the Grand Principality of Nizhniy Novgorod, which gave him the long-coveted control over the Volga-Oka confluence and brought the princes of Vladimir back to the point which they had reached when the Mongol storm first burst over them. In 1395 the Muscovites, thus strengthened, waited for Tamerlane on the Oka, but the nomad warrior chief decided to leave Russia alone.

By 1400, although there was a continual ebb and flow of fortune, the Russians had become stronger and more confident, the Mongols less so. And, whereas the Russians were becoming united under the centralizing tendencies of Moscow, the Mongols were increasingly plagued with internal strife. After 1360 there was a rapid decline in Tartar authority which the victories of 1382 only partially offset. It was already clear that Russia could not be held much longer in subjection. The damage done by Tamerlane to the Golden Horde in the 1390s placed this beyond doubt.

Russia in 1400

Russia was now partitioned between an eastern zone subject to Mongol authority, and a western which had been brought under the wing of the Grand Dukes of Lithuania (fig. 21). Although the peoples in both areas still regarded themselves as Russian and their country as Russia, and although they shared a common religion and held church services in the same language, they were becoming differentiated. Mongol-dominated Russia was open to Asiatic and oriental influences and was already set on the road to an autocratic form of government. Lithuanian Russia was exposed to Polish domination and western influences, notably that of Rome, especially after Roman Catholicism became the official religion of Lithuania in 1385. Here the aristocracy exerted much more political power. Linguistic variations were developing: the eastern Russians were speaking Great Russian; those of the Lithuanian west, White Russian; and those of the south-west, where there had always been a considerable amount of admixture with the peoples moving across the steppes to the Balkans, Little Russian or Ukrainian.[1]

East Russia was made up of many states and dukedoms, large and small. The chief were the two city states of Novgorod and Pskov, the former still mistress of a vast empire in the northern forest, and the grand duchies of Ryazan, Tver and Moscow. There had been a fourth grand duchy, that of Nizhniy Novgorod, but this, along with many smaller parcels of land, had been added to Moscow. A close relationship existed between Novgorod and Moscow. It was normal to have the Grand Duke of Vladimir (and Moscow) as Duke of Novgorod, but his powers in Novgorod were very limited. The two duchies were in some ways complementary. Novgorod, a large and prosperous mercantile state which had never been looted by the Tartars, had great wealth, some of which went to finance Moscow's enterprises; but she was dependent on Moscow for food supplies and for safe passage along the Volga. Another benefit to Moscow from this relationship arose from the fact that her chief rival for the control of the strategic upper Volga—Oka area, Tver, lay between the two allies and could the more easily be restrained by a common policy. This suited Novgorod too, for Tver constituted a threat as much to her own Volga traffic as to Moscow's plans for expansion. By 1400, Moscow had gathered together enough well-placed territory to ensure her supremacy over both Tver and Ryazan (fig. 21). Territorial acquisition by Moscow had already wrested from Tver its stranglehold on the upper Volga; Ryazan, though still controlling the Don routeway southwards, had seen its grip on the Oka seriously weakened. Pskov, to which Novgorod had granted independence in 1347, acted as a buffer between Novgorod and the Teutonic Knights, and still controlled the trade route

[1] *For the origin of the terms Great, White and Little Russian, see Vernadsky (1953), pp. 234-7*

from the Baltic via lake Peipus. The distant fur-trading post of Vyatka, once part of Novgorod's empire, had become an important centre of Russian colonization beyond the Volga, in land previously roamed by Finnish tribes.

Lithuania in 1400 was a Grand Duchy within the kingdom of Poland, but it was administered as a separate state. It consisted of a federation of Lithuanian and Russian principalities with whose internal administration the Grand Duke interfered little. Smolensk in particular was almost completely autonomous under its prince. Despite the defeat on the Vorksla river at the hands of the Tartars in 1399, Lithuania had kept the Mongols out of some Russian territory and driven them out of more. But although the population of the Grand Duchy was predominantly Russian, Lithuania was increasingly under Polish cultural and religious sway, while remaining virtually independent politically. The Roman faith had become, as in Poland, the official religion and a threat to the Orthodoxy of the Russian population. Poland exercised direct sovereignty over Russian land in Galicia.

The Mongol state known as the Golden Horde not only ruled the steppes, but was the recognized sovereign over all East Russia. The Russian princes admitted its authority and brought their quarrels to the Khan; to him they paid the tribute, though not with the regularity and punctuality of the immediate post-Conquest period. But the Tartar heyday was already past. Despite successful campaigns against the Grand Duke of Moscow in 1382 and against the Grand Duke of Lithuania in 1399, their real power had been undermined by internal rivalries and by the visitation of Tamerlane who had destroyed their prosperous lower Volga cities of Saray and Astrakhan. These, standing at the cross-roads where the Volga-Caspian waterway intersected the overland caravan route from the east, had brought them mercantile wealth; and they had depended upon the skill of their urban artisan populations for weapons.

Agricultural progress had been delayed by the Mongol invasion. The levying of men and material brought about a shortage of labour and capital, although there seems to have been some improvement in the type of implement used. But the area most advanced agriculturally in 1200, the wooded steppe, was that which had been most exposed to the Mongol scourge and therefore the most heavily ravaged. Except for the little farming done by the Cossacks, there had been a retreat of arable farming in the steppes which now, more than ever, were grazing land for the nomads. Horse-rearing remained important on the domains of the princes, owing to the continuing needs of their armies.

Iron ore was now mined, smelted and treated, though with primitive equipment, mainly in various parts of the Novgorod Empire: around Novgorod itself, on the White Sea shores, near Ustyug, and in the Yamsk, Koporsk and Ladoga districts. Silver also was now mined in the distant parts of the same Empire. The production of salt remained one of the chief aspects of the economy. Although everyone needed it, it could be obtained from only a few parts of the country whence it had to be transported. The more important producing areas were far from the main centres of population, e.g. along the northernmost coasts where the industry was organized by monasteries.[1]

The artisans and handicraftsmen of the two or three hundred towns of pre-Mongol Russia, who had produced buildings, paintings, textiles, pottery, tools, implements and weapons of a high standard, had either been killed or made captive by the Mongols: Piano Carpini had found a Russian goldsmith at the court of the Great Khan.[2] As a result, the Mongol capital of Saray came to be distinguished for its metal work, weaving and pottery; yet these crafts also had suffered destruction in their turn at the hands of Tamerlane. But Novgorod the Great, unscathed, continued as a centre of industry and was still famous for its wood carvers and stone masons, while Moscow and Tver shared the lead in the field of metal working. There is even evidence that Russian locks were exported to Bohemia and Hungary at the beginning of the fifteenth century.[3] But standards of workmanship could not be compared with those of Kievan Russia two centuries before. And whereas then the handicraftsmen of the towns were producing for the open market, with many customers from all classes, the industries of northern and central Russia now produced almost exclusively for a closed circle of princes and boyars. Some urban industry was already in the hands of foreigners, notably the new glass trade and some of the more advanced metal-working trades.[4]

In commerce, Novgorod continued to play the leading part in trade with Europe, which was carried on through the Baltic ports of the Hanseatic League and by direct overland routes. The German merchants of the Hanse enjoyed a privileged position in the city. Goods imported into Novgorod—woollens, metals, metal goods, wines and beer—were distributed to all parts of Muscovy, and her exports—furs, hemp and flax, fish and train oil—were likewise gathered from all over the country as well as from the distant recesses of her northern empire.

The Mongol conquest had come to benefit the trade of eastern Russia. It had removed the strong Bulgar state on the Volga which had previously blocked full Russian use of that river, and it had established a 'pax Mongolica' over the steppes. This ensured that the overland caravan routes with which the Volga and the Don were connected, were under a single authority; and this authority was exercised with a favourable eye to trade. There was an intensive concentration of trade routes on the sea of Azov at the mouth of the Don and along the adjacent Black Sea and Crimean coasts. Here Genoese merchants revived the pristine importance of the ancient Greek seaports. The rise of Moscow was intimately linked with these developments: she was advantageously placed with regard to the waterway routes which led down the Don and down the Volga.

---

[1] *Lyashchenko (1956), vol. 1, pp. 198-9*
[2] *Hakluyt (1598), p. 70*
[3] *Rybakov (1948), p. 600*
[4] *Lyashchenko (1956), vol. 1, p. 190*

Moscow thus came to rival Novgorod as the chief commercial city of the country, but her trade was more Asiatic and dealt with cottons and silks, precious stones and spices.[1] And Moscow had, at this time, begun to break into Novgorod's monopoly of the fur trade.

The population of East Russia in 1400 has been estimated at 10 million, compared with $7\frac{1}{2}$ million in 1200. Slaughter by the Mongols and in subsequent warfare had most likely been more than compensated for by active colonization of the remaining woodlands in the Volga-Oka region and in the forests north of the Volga. The population of this central area had also been swollen by refugees: those from the south in flight from the Tartars; those from the north-west seeking refuge from the Germans and Swedes; and those from the west, whose lands had been invaded by the Lithuanians and Poles. But the urban population was much less than in 1200, representing a possible decrease from 15 per cent of the total to under 5 per cent.[2] It was the towns that had suffered most from the Tartar terror, and although Novgorod had survived and some new towns had emerged, their increased population may only have been a fraction of that lost through the reduction of Kiev and other southern cities to the status of small towns.

Novgorod must have supported a very large population which can, however, only be guessed at. It has been put as high as 400,000.[3] Moscow also must have contained a considerable number of inhabitants by the year 1400. In 1382 its casualties in the great Tartar raid were said to be 35,000 slain and 25,000 taken away in captivity; and in 1446 its population was estimated at 100,000.[4] Perhaps the most noteworthy feature of Moscow's townscape in 1400 were the new stone walls of the Kremlin, for the other buildings, even the Grand Duke's palace, were all of wood.[5] It offered no comparison with the resplendent Kiev of three centuries before, and probably still bore the scars of the Mongol visitation of 1382. The nearest rivals to old Kiev in splendour would have been the Mongol towns of Saray and Astrakhan, with their Moslem mosques and Christian churches, had not Tamerlane left them in ruins (1395-6). The Black Sea merchant towns, such as Solkhat in the Crimea, where Khan Uzbeg had built an impressive mosque, survived, and their architecture presented the visiting Russian merchants with a striking contrast to the often crude wooden erections of their own towns.

The main function of the smaller towns was to act as markets in which the produce of the local handicraftsmen, mainly clothing and household utensils, and the goods brought in from the surrounding countryside, were offered for sale. The latter included a wide variety: cows, horses,

[1] *Mirsky (1952), pp. 100-1*
[2] *Vernadsky (1959B), p. 7*
[3] *Coxe (1784), vol. 1, p. 449*
[4] *Blum (1961), p. 62*
[5] *Vernadsky (1953), p. 252*

sheep, geese, ducks, fish, honey, wax, incense, wheat, rye, oats, flour, bread, salt, vegetables, flax, firewood, etc.[1]

The social stratification of Russia in 1400 consisted, as before, firstly of the princes and the leading boyar families. After them came a new class of growing importance, the lesser boyars, or *dvorians*, who often entered the personal service of the Grand Duke. The urban classes of resident merchants and artisans were no longer of great importance. Instead, the East Russian towns were often reduced to mere fortified princely residences frequented by visiting merchants from Novgorod and elsewhere and by Tartar horse-dealers. In West or Lithuanian Russia, the trade of the towns was becoming monopolized by Germans and Jews. A strong middle class no longer stood between prince and boyar on the one hand and the peasant on the other. Both in West and East Russia, landed estates rather than trading cities had become the basis of wealth and power; Novgorod was the outstanding exception, remaining as a city state empire with a local democratic city council (*veche*) somewhat like that of Kiev in the twelfth century. Here alone the princely powers were severely limited. Pskov and Vyatka, formerly subordinate to Novgorod, but now independent, were also governed by their *veches*.

Increasingly, the peasants found the land, on which they had once lived as free men, granted to landlords or monasteries for whom they had to do work and to whom they had to pay dues. Slaves continued to form a numerous element in society.

[1] *Lyashchenko (1956), vol. 1, p. 200*

CHAPTER FIVE
RUSSIA, 1400-1600: THE RISE OF MUSCOVY

During the 200 years from 1400 to 1600, the collection of East Russian lands under Mongolian suzerainty, of which Moscow had already become the chief, was transformed into the unified and sovereign state of Muscovy, whose rulers laid claim to all the Russian lands of old, whether now subject to Tartar, Lithuanian or Pole. They styled themselves *'sovereign* (gosudar) *of all Russia'*, and in dealing with the Holy Roman Emperor and other foreign monarchs, began to use the title of *'Tsar (Emperor) of All Russia'*.[1] This expansion of Muscovy took place in the reigns of Grand Dukes Basil II (1425-62), Ivan III (1462-1505), Basil III (1503-33) and Ivan IV (1533-84). The latter was succeeded by Theodore I (1584-98) and Boris Godunov (1598-1605).

Of the territorial gains made by Moscow in this period, the chief were the Grand Duchies of Ryazan and Tver, and the City States of Novgorod and Pskov. Ryazan, weakened by its exposed position, subordinated itself to Moscow in 1447 in return for help against the Tartars. In 1520 it was annexed by Basil III, its last grand duke fleeing to Lithuania. In 1485 Tver was conquered by Ivan III: its last grand duke also fled to Lithuania. The greatest prize of all was Novgorod, with its immense wealth and its great empire. (Fig. 22.)

Novgorod was unable to withstand Muscovite aggression for a variety of reasons. Owing to the poverty of the soil of its environs, it was dependent on Moscow-held land for food. Agricultural poverty also meant a thin population from which no great armies comparable to those of Moscow could be drawn. As it was, the resources of Novgorod were strained by the ever present threat of war with Lithuania, Sweden or the German Knights of Livonia. The city was torn by internal dissension arising from the mutual suspicions and jealousies of the land-owning boyars, the rich merchants, and the plebeian artisans and workers. The former tended to look to Lithuania for help in retaining independence; the latter, with less to lose, and more easily stirred emotionally by the appeals to Russian nationalism and unity made by Moscow, tended to favour that city. As help from Lithuania was not forthcoming, Novgorod could not resist effectively. After an attack on the city by Basil II in 1456 its liberties were curtailed. In 1471, Ivan III, helped by a long summer drought which had dried up the marshes so essential to Novgorod's defences, crushed her military strength, but allowed some semblance of independence to continue. This was short-lived. In 1478 complete surrender was insisted upon. The two remaining city states were likewise incorporated: Vyatka in 1489 and Pskov in 1510. Moscow was now supreme.

This 'gathering' of the lands of central and north-eastern Russia by Moscow was accompanied by extreme cruelty and ruthless terror of such

[1] *Bain (1908), p. 103 fn*

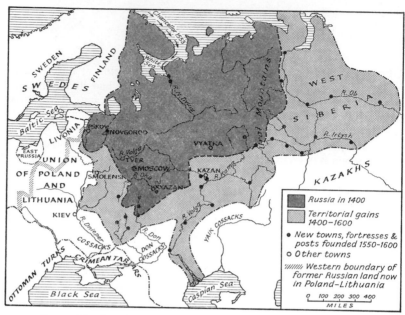

figure 22   Russia in 1600, showing expansion since 1400, and new fortress towns.

a kind that it is difficult to avoid the conclusion that the Mongol impact on Russia had a brutalizing effect. Baumgarten wrote of

> the extraordinary ferocity of the Muscovite princes towards their relations: two princes were blinded, five poisoned and two slain; two princesses were drowned, one starved to death, and eleven died in dungeons, often in irons.[1]

Annexation of the various lands was followed by executions and mass deportations; Muscovites were brought in to take the place of the inhabitants of the stricken towns. All this weakened the affected areas economically, while strengthening the relative position of the city of Moscow as the centre of trade and industry. During the reign of Ivan IV, the Terrible (1533-84), parts of Muscovy were systematically ravaged by the Tsar and his marauding bands. The most horrible of these expeditions was that made to Novgorod in 1569-70, when Ivan and his troops devastated the countryside, indulging without restraint in murder, arson, rape and robbery. An English contemporary, Sir Jerome Horsey, relates the sack of Novgorod in the following passage:

> he chargeth it with thirty thousand Tartars and ten thousand gunners of his guard, without any respect ravished all the women and maids, ransacked, robbed and spoiled all that were within it of their jewels, plate and treasure; murdered the people, young and old; burnt all

[1] *Baumgarten (1934), p. 6*

their household stuff, merchandises, and warehouses of wax, flax, tallow, hides, salt, wines, cloth and silks; set all on fire, with wax and tallow melted down the kennels in the streets, together with the blood of seven hundred thousand men, women and children, slain and murdered; so that with the blood that ran into the river, and of all other living creatures and cattle, their dead carcases did stop as it were the river Volkhov, being cast therein. No history maketh mention of so horrible a massacre.[1]

These horrors seem to have done little to affect the loyalty of the Muscovites to their ruler, but rather to have increased their admiration for him. The extent to which the autocrat, however cruel and ruthless, could rely upon massive support, providing he appeared to further the national aspirations of the Russian people, was to be a factor of immense weight in the future strength of Russia. When the Emperor Maximilian enquired of a Muscovite envoy why Russians served such tyrants so well, he was told: '*We Russians are devoted to our sovereigns whether they be merciful or cruel*'. In this respect the Muscovite expansion contrasted badly with the Lithuanian rule in West Russia.

The Muscovite claim to the whole of the old Russian territory inevitably meant continued conflict with Lithuania, and therefore with Poland, while at the same time the determination to consolidate an outlet on to the Baltic Sea meant trouble with Sweden and the Livonian Germans.

The expansion of a vigorous and virtually independent Lithuania continued on into the fifteenth century under Grand Duke Vitovt (1393-1430). After inflicting a shattering blow upon the Teutonic Knights at Tannenberg in 1410, he fortified the Dnieper against the Tartars from Kiev to the Black Sea. He exacted indemnities from Pskov and Novgorod in 1426-8, but died two years later when on the point of receiving a crown from the Holy Roman Emperor. This would have set the seal upon a strong and independent West Russian Lithuania. Its official style was for long the 'Grand Duchy of Lithuania and Russia' and its official language was at one time White Russian.[2]

Instead, Lithuania came more and more under Polish domination, thus losing its claim to be heir to Kievan Russia. For the Russian population, instead of supporting an independent Lithuania in its struggles against Germans to the north-west and Tartars to the south-east, had now to resist Polonization and defend their orthodoxy against Polish Jesuit pressure. So, in the latter part of the fifteenth century, several Russian princes transferred their allegiance to Moscow, and in 1494 and again in 1514, Lithuania had to recognize considerable Muscovite gains; these included the basins of the upper Oka, the upper Ugra, the upper Dnieper with Smolensk, and the upper Desna. In 1569 the Union of Lublin bound Lithuania closer to Poland. Lithuania was caught between the preponderant and bitterly hostile power of Moscow on the one hand, and a

[1] *Bond (1856), p. 162*
[2] *Mirsky (1952), p. 67*

vigorous Poland, which had already deprived her of the Ukrainian portion of her Russian lands, on the other. She had no alternative but to accept Polish protection if she were to survive.

Muscovy waged repeated campaigns, defensive and offensive, in Livonia and Estonia against the weakening Livonian Order and the land-hungry power of Sweden. Tartaric frontiersmen from the steppe were employed with the Russian armies and the utmost barbarity was used:

> O the lamentable outcries and cruel slaughters, drowning and burning, ravishing of women and maids, stripping them naked without mercy or regard of the frozen weather, tying and binding them by three and by four at their horses tails, dragging them, some alive, some dead, all bloodying the ways and streets, lying full of carcases of the aged men and women and infants.[1]

Yet there were no permanent Muscovite gains. Livonia became Polish, and the south shore of the Gulf of Finland, except for a precarious Russian foothold, became Swedish. Thus Muscovy attained only partial success in those aims which had involved her in perennial conflict with the Lithuanians, Poles, Baltic Germans and Swedes: recovery of ancient Russian land and an outlet to the Baltic.

In 1400 the future Muscovy was still part of the Mongol Empire and for a time this overlordship continued to be recognized. Tribute was no longer paid regularly but, after his capture in a Tartar raid in 1445, Basil II had to promise its resumption as a condition of his release. Nevertheless, times when the Horde was in this dominant position were now exceptional. The break-away of two separate independent khanates, those of the Crimea and of Kazan on the Volga, further weakened it.

During the early fifteenth century there was some recovery of grain-growing and settled population in the western parts of the steppe and wooded steppe. This was in some degree a result of the expansion of Polish-Lithuanian power to the Black Sea, and in part because the Tartars had come to allow trade in grain, fish and other products down the Russian rivers to the Genoese-controlled ports of the Crimea. The Tartars, of course, took their share of the profits from this commerce.

The conquest of Constantinople by the Ottoman Turks in 1453 destroyed this trade. The Turks soon found in Danubia their main source of grain but they had an insatiable market for slaves. The Crimean Tartars therefore began—after 1474—to substitute slave-raiding for grain-trading.[2] Ivan III wisely made an alliance with them (1480), and so diverted their slave-hunting raids into Lithuanian-held territory. Between 1474 and 1534 there were thirty-seven large-scale raids on Polish-Lithuanian territory. These depopulated the Lithuanian-held wooded steppe and steppe. Kiev, which had made slow progress since the disasters of the thirteenth century was again destroyed by the Crimeans in 1482. During the sixteenth century, the Polish-Lithuanian Ukraine became so ruined

---

[1] *Bond (1856), p. 160*
[2] *McNeill (1964), pp. 20-6*

that raids upon it became less frequent, but by 1575 it had recovered sufficiently for a Tartar expedition in that year to secure 50,000 captives.

Ivan III not only set the Crimean khan on to Lithuania but also against the Golden Horde itself: *'the two hordes began to war among themselves and thus God saved the Russian lands from the heathens'.*[1] The grand dukes also made increasing use of Tartaric enemies of and refugees from the Horde by settling them in the Oka frontier region, by employing them in their armies, and by setting up a vassal khanate of their own on the Oka, the Khanate of Kasimov.

Final Muscovite independence of the Golden Horde was declared in 1476 when Ivan III ceased to pay tribute and ignored a summons to Saray. The Khan Ahmed prepared a massive punitive expedition in 1480, in alliance with Lithuania, but he was unable to cross the Oka-Ugra line in face of Russian fire. His ally failed to join him and his army dispersed to ravage the countryside; so, with winter approaching, the great Khan decided to retreat. The following year, other Tartars, those of Nogay and Sibir, severely mauled the Golden Horde and killed the Khan. The final blow was administered by the Crimean Tartars in 1502, after which its place was taken by the relatively weak Khanate of Astrakhan.

After independence had been secured from Saray, the Muscovite princes were especially concerned with the Khanate of Kazan. It now controlled the Volga trade route, much as the Volga Bulgars had in the time of old Russia. For about forty years after 1480 the Khanate remained amenable to Moscow, but in 1521 the Kazan Tartars revolted against this tutelage. The fortress of Vasil-Sursk was built at the confluence of the Sura and Volga as a base for operations against them, but it was not until 1552 that Kazan was successfully stormed, a new base having been built near by at Sviyazhsk in the previous year. Soon afterwards, in 1556, the Khanate of Astrakhan was annexed and Muscovite control of the Volga all the way to the Caspian Sea was established.

Anthony Jenkinson has left an account of Astrakhan at the time of its conquest:

> This Astracan is the farthest hold that this Emperor of Russia hath conquered of the Tartars towards the Caspian Sea, which he keepeth very strong, sending thither every year provision of men, and victuals, and timber to build the castle.
>
> There is a certain trade of merchandise there used, but as yet so small and beggarly, that it is not worth the making mention, and yet there come merchants thither from divers places.
>
> The chiefest commodities that the Russes bring thither are red hides, red sheep's skins, wooden vessels, bridles and saddles, knives and other trifles, with corn, bacon and other victuals. The Tartars bring thither divers kinds of wares made of cotton wool, with divers kinds of wrought silks, and they that come out of Persia . . . do bring sewing silk . . .

[1] *Fennell (1961), p. 67*

all such things in such small quantity, the merchants being so beggarly and poor that bring the same, that it is not worth the writing.[1]

The Crimean Tartars remained a serious threat, especially after they became the vassals of the Ottoman Turks in 1475. This meant that they were free to raid Russian territory as much as they dared, for neither the Lithuanian nor Muscovite princes would or could challenge the might of the Turks. It was probably beyond the capacity of a sixteenth-century Muscovite army, which normally moved along rivers, to cross the waterless steppe and invade the Crimea by way of the narrow Perekop isthmus. Kazan and Astrakhan had fallen because they could be approached by river, but a navy commanding the Black Sea would have been necessary to conquer the Crimea, as well as the ability to challenge the Ottoman armies in the steppe. Hence the Crimea was to elude Russian conquest for nearly two and a half centuries after the fall of the Tartar fortresses on the Volga.

Ivan III (1462-1505) had been successful in diverting the energies of the Crimean horde against both the Golden Horde and Lithuania. But the Lithuanian-held steppe borderland had become so devastated that it offered little return and the Crimean Khanate had now to look to Muscovy for slaves. Furthermore, in the sixteenth century, it came to recognize Moscow as its potentially most dangerous enemy and, despite the strengthening of the defences along the Oka by the building of new fortresses, there were repeated raids into Muscovite territory. Agricultural settlement, which had been venturing southwards into the wooded steppe belt south of Moscow, depopulated by the Tartar onslaught of the thirteenth century, again became impossible. It reverted to a frontier region in which armies had to be concentrated annually in case of attack. Despite these conditions, the Cossacks were able to establish themselves along the Don. Moscow itself usually escaped damage, but in 1571 the city suffered complete disaster, being sacked and burned. So, although the Mongol yoke had now been permanently thrown off, neither Moscow nor Poland-Lithuania could protect its Russian lands from continued depredations by steppe nomads.

In one direction, however, the Russians penetrated far into the Mongol Empire. Siberia, whose primitive tribes had long acknowledged Tartar authority, was invaded by Cossack bands in the employ of Russian commercial interests (1582) and Tartar rule was overthrown. As land beyond the Urals was annexed to the Muscovite tsar, so traders and colonists poured in.

Mongol suzerainty had been removed from Russia, but the results of its exercise remained. True, there was little voluntary admixture between Russian and Mongol nor did the Tartars establish themselves as settled inhabitants within the forest zone. *'Fortunately'*—to quote Karamzin—*'Russia's rigorous climate forced them to abandon any such idea'.*[2]

[1] *Hakluyt (1598), p. 326*
[2] *Karamzin (1820), vol. 5, p. 447*

Ignatius of Smolensk did not see *'his first Tartars'* until he had travelled well south of the river Don.[1] But they had established by terror the power to deal arbitrarily with the lives and property of the conquered. This authority they had transferred to the princes of Moscow who now used it and abused it to the full. The tribute was still collected, but it remained in the Tsar's treasury to be used at his own discretion. His expeditions within Russian territory, whether to punish or acquire, were as merciless as those of the Tartar. Karamzin gave full weight to the effect of the conquest upon the Russian people, attributing to it the *'ferocity of princes and people'* and the widespread use of corporal punishment. He admitted the possibility that the *'present-day character of the Russians retains some of the stains with which it was soiled by the barbarity of the Mongols'.*[2] Tartars and Tartaric frontiersmen served in the Russian armies and were present at the Tsar's court, the manners and customs of which resembled those of the former khans rather than of any European court. One of Ivan IV's many wives was a Circassian and Boris Godunov himself derived from a Mongol family.[3]

Besides acquiring independence from the Mongols in this period, Eastern Russia became ecclesiastically independent of the Greek Church at Constantinople. As the Ottoman Turks swarmed over the Eastern Empire of Byzantium, its leaders had looked west for help. Rome would not entertain this plea unless the Greek Church accepted union, which it did in 1439. The Russian Church refused to recognize this union, and in 1448 elected its own metropolitan without seeking confirmation from Constantinople. In 1453 Constantinople itself fell to the Turks and Moscow was left as the leading independent capital of the eastern Church. Although a separate Greek Orthodox Church was restored in Constantinople, it never recovered its authority over the Muscovites. Instead, in 1589, it consented to the elevation of the Russian metropolitan to the supreme dignity of patriarch.

This simultaneous acquisition of national and religious independence encouraged ideas among some Russians as to Russia's destiny. Although backward materially and isolated geographically, there were forces here which would develop a unique greatness and a distinct civilization. Such philosophy was opposed to any tendency to imitate the West or borrow blindly from its culture. Russia would evolve its own. One expression of these workings of the Russian mind or 'soul' was the doctrine of Moscow as the 'third Rome'. Rome had become the centre of a great civilization, and had then declined. Byzantium had taken its place and likewise known greatness and fall. Moscow would be the third great capital from which the light of truth would radiate, but this time there would be no decline: *'for two Romes have fallen, and the third stands, and a fourth will not be.*[4]

[1] *Khitrowo (1889), p. 132*
[2] *Karamzin (1820), vol. 5, p. 449*
[3] *Riasanovsky (1963), p. 172*
[4] *Filofei, quoted in Clarkson (1961), p. 96*

Although this idea was purely religious in its original conception, its wider implications appealed to secular Russians. Among all classes of Great Russians—as the eastern Russians or Muscovites had come to be called— there grew a remarkable self-confidence, sometimes assuming the form of an arrogant xenophobia. This pride buttressed their self-satisfaction with their material backwardness:

> *As touching their behaviour and quality otherwise, they are of reasonable capacities, if they had those means that some other nations have to train up their wits in good nurture and learning. Which they might borrow of the Polonians and other their neighbours, but that they refuse it of a very self pride, as accounting their own fashions to be far the best.*[1]

When the Holy Roman Emperor offered Ivan III a crown, the offer was disdainfully refused: the Russian prince derived his power direct from God and recognized no earthly authority. Instead, the title of Caesar or Tsar was assumed, the Byzantine imperial double eagle adopted as the state emblem, and ceremonial and ritual elaborated to befit the court of an emperor.

Several factors contributed to a widening of the gap between Muscovy and the West in this period. They included the pride and xenophobia just mentioned, the revulsion felt in the West at the barbarity of the Muscovite princes, the spiritual isolation of the Orthodox Church to which the Great Russians clung with fervour, and the physical difficulties of communication with Europe. Great Russia was divided from Europe by an immense semi-circle of hostile powers: Swedes, Livonians, Lithuanians, Poles, Tartars and Turks. Thus when Zoe travelled from Rome in 1490-1 to become the wife of Ivan III, she had to travel via Nürnberg lest she be seized by an enemy. Relations with Hungary had to be abandoned in the 1490s because communication between the two countries proved impossible. In 1547 a large party of foreigners, enlisted to serve in Great Russia, were prevented from going further than Lübeck by the Livonians. Ivan IV's plans for his Livonian wars, undertaken to free himself from economic isolation, were hampered by his inability to use his Baltic port of Narva and difficulties of communicating with England:

> *He made preparation accordingly, only doubting of some want of powder, saltpetre, lead and brimstone, and knew not how to be furnished thereof, the Narva shut up, but out of England. The difficulty was how he should convey and send his letters to the Queen, his countries environed and passages shut up.*[2]

This difficulty of access resulted in considerable ignorance of Russia in the West, and rumour and phantasy flourished. When, in 1553-4, English merchants established a free communication with Moscow, it was by way of the Arctic Ocean and the White Sea, a route closed by ice for much of the year and extremely perilous for the rest. But positive Russian

[1] *Fletcher (1591), p. 150*
[2] *Horsey, quoted in Bond (1856), p. 185*

action worsened the situation. Conquered Novgorod was forced to sever its longstanding relations with the West and in 1494 the Hanseatic League was expelled from the town.

Incentives for communication between East and West were not lacking. The Holy Roman Emperor and the Pope hoped to bring Moscow in against the Turk, and sent missions to Russia. The English and Dutch wanted trade for which they were prepared to brave the icy hazards of the northern sea route via Archangel. In 1561 an English merchant, Anthony Jenkinson, even penetrated the deserts of Turkestan, having crossed Russia from end to end. Muscovy for her part, wanted western doctors, engineers, teachers, craftsmen, etc., in order to overcome some of the more serious aspects of her backwardness. Despite the arrogant spiritual contempt felt by many Russians for the West, others were already fascinated by the material achievements of western culture.

In 1448 Ivan III asked the King of Hungary to send him men who could cast and fire cannon, as well as goldsmiths, silversmiths and masons.[1] He enlisted Italian architects to build churches in Moscow. His successor, Basil III, under the influence of his second wife who had been brought up in Lithuania, was induced to shave his beard, although the beard was becoming a symbol of anti-western conservatism.[2] German engineers were employed in the successful siege and capture of Kazan in 1551-2. The capable and cruel Boris Godunov strongly favoured westernization. He even sent a group of young Muscovites to study in England, France and Germany, but none of them chose to return.[3]

European states bordering on Russia saw in the backwardness of Muscovy their only defence against her overwhelming potential might. '*We seemed hitherto to vanquish him only in this, that he was rude of arts and ignorant of policies*', wrote the King of Poland to Queen Elizabeth in protest against English trade and friendship with Ivan the Terrible. He added: '*we that know best and border upon him, do admonish other Christian princes in time, that they do not betray their dignity, liberty and life of them and their subjects to a most barbarous and cruel enemy*'.[4]

The growing arrogance towards and isolation from the West in Great Russia was matched by the increasing westernization of Lithuania under Polish influence.[5] The split between West and East divided the Russian nation and resulted in many differences of character and outlook between the Great Russians of the forest zone, the White Russians of the western marshes, and the Ukrainians of the south-western steppes. These differences were political, economic, social, linguistic and even religious.

The Greek Church having, under Turkish duress, accepted union with Rome, Moscow had elected its own metropolitan (1448). For a while he

[1] *Fennell (1961), pp. 115-6*
[2] *Vernadsky (1959B), p. 163*
[3] *Pushkarev (1965), p. 141*
[4] *Quoted in Clarkson (1961), pp. 129-30*
[5] *Hrushevsky (1941), pp. 169-71*

was recognized also in Lithuanian Russia, but in 1558 Casimir of Poland and Lithuania accepted from Rome another metropolitan '*of Kiev and all Russia*' and he was later confirmed by the Greek Orthodox patriarch in Constantinople. Thus the Russian Church, which could have been a potent factor in holding the partitioned country together despite political schism, was itself divided, with rival metropolitans in Kiev and Moscow. Throughout the sixteenth century the Orthodox population of Lithuania, thus separated from its Great Russian brethren, had to withstand increasing pressure from the Roman Catholic Church, especially after large areas had been incorporated into Poland. Eventually, the Counter-Reformation and Jesuit activity succeeded in bringing into the fold of the Catholic Church a large section of the West Russian nobility, although making little impression upon the peasants. In 1595, supported by some of the Orthodox bishops, but opposed by most of the laity, the King of Poland proclaimed the union of the West Russian church with Rome. Thus by the year 1600 West Russia was itself divided in religion between those who accepted union (the Uniate Church) and those who refused it (the Orthodox Church).

CHAPTER SIX
THE ECONOMIC AND SOCIAL GEOGRAPHY OF RUSSIA IN 1600

Great Russia or Muscovy was now a single unified state and no longer a collection of principalities as it had been in 1400. It was much greater in extent, owing to expansion westwards, southwards and eastwards at the expense, respectively, of Lithuania, of the now extinct Golden Horde, and of the Siberian Tartars and native tribes. In Siberia the whole basin of the lower and middle Ob-Irtysh river system was now Russian. But access had only just (1598) been regained to the Gulf of Finland, the entrance to which, however, was controlled by Sweden on both sides; and not far distant from the Russian base of Ivangorod stood the Swedish fortress of Narva. In the south there was no access at all to the Black Sea, the shores of which were in the hands of the Ottoman Turks and their vassals the Crimean Tartars. The ferocious raids of the latter still carried terror into the heart of Muscovy.

To the west lay the united Polish-Lithuanian state which still possessed former Russian land, though less than in 1400. White Russia lay in Lithuania, while the former principalities of Galicia, Volynia and Kiev, now known as the Ukraine, formed part of Poland. Poland had also incorporated Livonia after the collapse of the German Livonian order in 1561. One of the chief contrasts between Muscovy and Poland-Lithuania was that, whereas the former lay under the unchecked tyranny of an absolute tsar—for the council of boyars (*duma*) had merely advisory capacity—the latter was a constitutional monarchy in which the nobles and landowners had ᴄat power. Russian remained an official language of Lithuania.

In the frontier zone between the Russians and the steppe nomads were the Cossack bands of horsemen. Of doubtful origin, they had recruited fugitives of all kinds from the neighbouring states, especially runaway peasants. They were Russian in language and religion, and lived adventurous lives independent of prince or khan. Each group was based on one of the main rivers which crossed the steppe; they existed by fighting, fishing, farming and robbing, according to the opportunities of the moment. The most formidable were those of the Dnieper, especially the Zaporozhye Cossacks whose headquarters were on islands in the river. They fought in the service of Poland against Turk and Tartar but resisted any Polish attempt to curb their independence. They lived mostly on booty, except for those married Cossacks who were sedentary farmers.

The Muscovite economy, having made a slow recovery during the fourteenth and fifteenth centuries, was roughly comparable to that of western Europe in the thirteenth. It had been dislocated in the sixteenth century by Ivan IV's terror, involving as it did the uprooting of populations as well as wholesale massacre by fire and sword. Agriculture had continued to progress: the three-field and fallow-grain systems had become general.

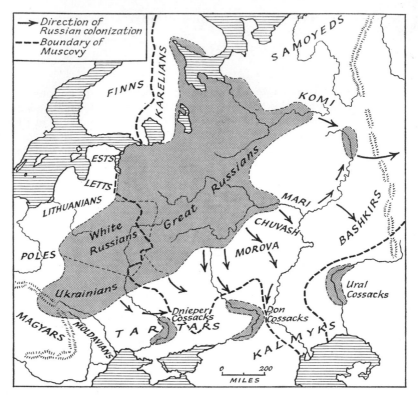

figure 23   Russia in 1600: peoples.

The horse-drawn *sokha* plough was universally used throughout the forest region and harrows, scythes and other implements had become more widespread; there had been an increased use of manure. Autumn-sown rye and spring-sown barley, millet and buckwheat were the principal grain crops, while flax and hemp now occupied a large acreage in the north-west.[1] The holding by households of intermingled strips of land in various fields made a communal form of farming essential. In the north and in many parts of the central area, climatic and soil conditions did not allow the peasants to support themselves wholly by agriculture. Hunting, fishing, the gathering of wax and honey, and the practice of domestic industry were also resorted to. The cultivated area now extended to the North Dvina and Kama basins and beyond the Urals. Farming on the steppe was on the increase again as the new Russian fortress towns gave some security from the Tartars.

The exploitation of forests for furs, and of seas and rivers for fish products, was now at its height. Hitherto the main source of furs had been

[1] *Lyashchenko (1956), vol. 1, pp. 230-1*

the former Novgorodian Empire, in the basins of the North Dvina and
Mezen rivers. These remained important and their towns continued to
flourish. But, as the demand from Europe grew, their declining yield failed
to suffice, and the hunt moved into the Pechora basin, the Urals and beyond.
By 1600, following the conquest of the Khanate of Siberia in the 1580s,
western Siberia had swiftly become the main source of furs, with the
Ob-Irtysh basin the most prominent area. New forts or ostrogs had been
founded as follows (see back endpaper map):[1]

Tyumen	*1586*	*Obdorsk*	*1596*
Tobolsk	*1587*	*Narym*	*1596*
Surgut	*1593*	*Ketsk*	*1597*
Pelym	*1593*	*Verkhoturye*	*1598*
Berezov	*1593*	*Turinsk*	*1600*
Tara	*1594*		

Siberia proved irresistible because of its wealth in sables, the most coveted
of all furs. Tribute or *yasak* was levied on the natives in sables; only if
they could not produce enough were they allowed to pay in other pelts.
As early as 1594 the Russians took from a single native chief 426 sables,
300 fox skins, 61 beavers and 1,000 squirrel. The number of pelts taken as
yasak alone in 1605 has been estimated at over 60,000.[2] The pelts moved
from the local ostrogs by way of river and portage to collecting centres in
northern Russia. These were towns that had grown up when their own
regions had been the most important sources of fur: Kholmogory, Ustyug,
Vologda, Solvychegodsk. Thence the furs moved to Archangel for export
or to Moscow which had long displaced Novgorod as the great central fur
mart.

Fletcher describes the extraction of seal oil:

> *Another very great and principal commodity is their train oil, drawn
> out of the seal fish. . . . When they first find the haunt . . . they come
> altogether and compass the seals round about in a ring, that lie sunning
> themselves together upon the ice, commonly four or five thousand in a
> shoal, and so they invade them every man with his club in his hand. . . .
> After the slaughter, when they have killed what they can . . . they flay
> them, taking from the body the skin, and the lard or fat withal that
> cleaveth to the skin. This they take with them, leaving the bodies behind,
> and so go to shore where they dig pits in the ground of a fathom and a
> half deep or thereabout, and so taking the fat or lard off from the skin,
> they throw it into the pit, and cast in among it hot burning stones to
> melt it withal. The uppermost and purest is sold and used to oil wool for
> cloth; the grosser they sell to make soap.[3]*

The newly-won control of the Volga and the foothold at Astrakhan on the

[1] *Kerner* (*1946*), *pp. 185-6*
[2] *Fisher* (*1943*), *pp. 97, 110*
[3] *Fletcher* (*1591*), *pp. 11-12*

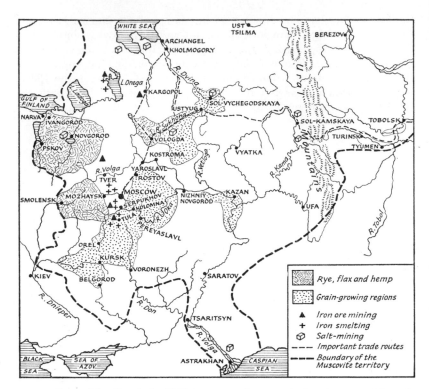

figure 24   Russia in 1600: towns and economic development. Note the development between Moscow and the White Sea, the main outlet of isolated Muscovy to the West.

Caspian had added valuable fisheries, yielding caviar, to the productive wealth of Russia.

The growth of mining and industry was restricted in the older settled parts by lack of labour, but salt extraction and evaporation continued to expand to meet the demand for salting more and more meat and fish. A large share of salt production had been monopolized by the Stroganov family whose works were to be found along the Kama, on the Ustyug and in the Urals, and whose headquarters were at Solvychegodsk. The Archangel district and the Volga delta were also salt-producing regions. As the Stroganovs dominated salt production, so the boyar Morozov controlled potash preparation from which he had made a vast fortune. Much potash came from areas of new colonization where forest clearing and burning were still actively prosecuted. The potash was used in the soap-making industry. (Fig. 24.)

Mica was mined in the north and its use is described by Fletcher:

> *In the province of Carelia, and about the river Dvyna towards the North Sea, there groweth a soft rock which they call slude. This they*

cut into pieces, and so tear it into thin flakes, which naturally it is apt for, and so use it for glass lanthorns and such like. It giveth both inwards and outwards a clearer light than glass, and for this respect is better than either glass or horn: for that it neither breaketh like glass, nor yet will burn like the lanthorn.[1]

Iron mining and smelting had grown enormously in the Tula area to satisfy an expanding armaments industry.

The handicraft industries, hitherto mainly rural, had traditionally provided occupations for peasants during the long winters. They were now developing more in the towns, often with the help of western immigrants. The Moscow region, with state encouragement, had become the most highly industrialized, with the manufacture of weapons of war, leather, soap and linen cloth. Metal-working also took place at Novgorod and Tula. Woollen cloth was made at Mozhaysk, linen at Tver and Yaroslavl. Leather was important at Novgorod, Pskov, Kostroma, Yaroslavl, Nizhniy Novgorod, Kazan, Serphukhov and Murom. English workshops making rope from local hemp had been set up at Vologda. Soap-boiling works were busy at Kazan, Nizhniy Novgorod, Kostroma, Yaroslavl and Vologda. Most of the towns had some woodworking crafts as well as weaving and tanning. Compared with western Europe, however, the quantity and quality of goods produced were low. There were almost no factories or even large workshops. Such industry as there was remained of the cottage type, whether rural or urban. The few larger enterprises that did exist were run either by state officials or by foreigners: private native entrepreneurs like the Stroganovs were exceptional. The tsars and some landowners tried to encourage industry by drafting peasants into new villages or suburbs built specially for the purpose and supervised by foreigners. The following table gives some idea of the relative importance of certain manufacturing towns:

Numbers of artisans in certain towns, 1638[2]

Moscow	2,367	Kazan	318
Novgorod	2,000	Mozhaysk	224
Nizhniy Novgorod	500	Kolomna	159
Serpukhov	331		

The unification of Great Russia into one state facilitated internal trade by removing the barriers constituted by the boundaries of numerous principalities and appanages. In the main there was an exchange of products between the newly-colonized wooded north-east and the cleared and old-settled centre. Tools, textiles, weapons, grain and miscellaneous manufactured goods went out to the colonists in return for furs, pitch, timber, salt, metallic ores and potash. Hemp and flax were grown in the new clearings and these too found their way to the towns.

[1] *Fletcher (1591), pp. 13-14*
[2] *Kochan (1962), p. 76*

Moscow was now the unrivalled commercial centre of the country and the focus of its major trade routes:

> *Hither flowed agricultural produce from the south, the products of hunting, fishing and trapping from the Siberian colonies and from the north, iron articles from Tula and the Urals, and all kinds of luxury and household goods from abroad.*[1]

The main road to Europe ran westwards from the town along the morainic ridge via Smolensk; the new and busy water route to Archangel went northwards via Vologda. The Moskva and Oka rivers led east to the Volga waterway with its terminus at Astrakhan, and to the Kama which led up into the Urals and to Siberia beyond. It was on these trade routes that Muscovy's fastest-growing towns stood: Ustyug, Vologda, Kolomna, Yaroslavl, Nizhniy Novgorod and Kazan, and the terminal ports of Archangel and Astrakhan. The relative importance of the commercial towns can be gauged from the amount of tax raised from trade, given as follows:[2]

Moscow	*450,000 R.*
Kazan	*140,000*
Nizhniy Novgorod	*50,000*
Yaroslavl	*35,000*

The last-named place impressed Fletcher:

> *But for situation, Jaruslav far exceedeth the rest. For besides the commodities that the soil yieldeth of pasture and corn, it lyeth upon the famous river Volga, and looketh over it from a high bank very fair and stately to behold.*[3]

Noteworthy was the large number of markets and annual fairs that had sprung up all over the country. The greatest was held at the confluence of the Volga and Vetluga: here goods from the East and West met in an impressive array. Commerce in Russia was now subject to a great deal of state interference and control. Even the merchants or *gosti* were state officials and often employed as tax collectors.

The second half of the sixteenth century had witnessed an increase in Russia's overseas trade with Europe, now that commercial relations had been established with the two rising maritime powers of England and Holland. The shipbuilders and mariners of these countries stood in great need of a range of commodities that were of less interest to other lands: hempen rope, sailcloth, pitch, whale grease, masts, etc. The scope of Russian commerce was thus widened. There was bitter rivalry between the English and Dutch for this trade, and Ivan IV, who saw that Muscovy stood to benefit from such competition, strongly resented an English attempt to exclude the Dutch:

[1] *Lyashchenko (1956), vol. 1, p. 269*
[2] *Lyashchenko (1956), vol 1, p. 291*
[3] *Fletcher (1591), p. 19*

This was taken in very heinous part by the Emperor and his Council, because of their practice by all means they can to enlarge that trade by the Bay of St Nicholas, as thinking it a far better and surer way to vent their own commodities and to bring in foreign than the other through the Sound by the Narva and Riga, which lie under check and are many times stopped up by reason of their wars with the Polonian and Sweden.[1]

Also to western countries went furs, hogs, bristles, walrus tusks, caviar, hides, tallow, seal oil, honey and wax. Among the goods coming in return were guns, munitions, tools and implements, chemicals, wollen cloth and luxury articles. Archangel was the port for this sea-borne commerce, and every summer merchants from all over the country made the long trek there to deal with the foreigners. It was a season of feverish activity soon terminated by ice. The English also had trading establishments in Moscow, Yaroslavl, Kazan and Astrakhan.

In 1600, apart from the White Sea trade, commercial exchanges with Europe had to be made overland. The Baltic outlet had been lost through the yielding up of the port of Narva to Sweden. But frequent wars with Poland interrupted the overland traffic. As the author of *De Russorum* (1582) had written: '*When there is peace, merchants bring the furs of wild animals from Moscow to Poland and Livonia. They then sell honey, wax and leather in great quantities to the foreigners.*'[2] But there seldom was peace, and Muscovy's isolation had produced grave economic consequences, especially for those parts of the country which were not well placed to use the new and distant outlet at northerly Archangel. Such regions had relied largely upon exportable staples which they were now unable to ship. Production of flax, hemp, etc., had therefore sharply fallen off in some regions:

> *The reason of this abating and decrease . . . is the shutting of the port of Narva towards the Finland Sea, which now is in the hands and possession of the Sweden. Likewise the stopping of the passage overland by the way of Smolensko and Plotsko [Polotsk], by reason of their wars with the Polonian, which causeth the people to be less provident in maintaining and gathering these and like commodities, for that they lack sales.*[3]

The hazards of communication with the West and the suspicious attitude of the tsars to Russian links with Europe restrained western trade. The conquest by the Turks of the eastern Empire and their control of the Black Sea had all but destroyed the once fabulous commerce via Constantinople. Trade with the Orient, despite the newly-gained Russian control of the Volga and the extension of the Tsar's power beyond the Urals, suffered from the depredations of the warlike Nogay Tartars and the Kalmyks. Imports from the East included silks, cotton cloth,

[1] *Bond (1856), p. 373*
[2] *Oderbornius (1582), B.5*
[3] *Fletcher (1591), p. 12*

precious stones, metals, spices, horses and sheep. Some of these were re-exported to the West via Archangel. Russian exports to the East included furs, weapons, textiles, leather goods and other manufactured articles.

Russia's chief eastern trading partner was Persia, with whom direct commercial relations began soon after the Muscovite conquest of Astrakhan. Silk, raw and manufactured, was the most valuable import from Persia. Russian exports thither are exemplified by the goods taken away in 1594 by a single Persian merchant: furs, suits of armour, tin, lead, birch bark, hides, glass, walrus tusks and paper.[1]

The population of Muscovite Russia at the end of the sixteenth century was possibly about 12 million, compared with an estimated 10 million for 1400, since when there had been a large migration from the central areas to the newly acquired lands to the east, south-east and south. The terror of Ivan IV, with its slaughter and uprooting of population, had fallen mainly on the older-settled areas. The burden of labour, taxes and army service fell so heavily on those who remained, that they too made every effort to get out:

> *Besides the taxes, customs, seizures, and other public exactions done upon them by the emperor, they are so racked and pulled by the nobles, officers and messengers sent abroad by the emperor in his public affairs . . . that you shall have many villages and towns of half a mile and a mile long, stand all unhabited: the people being fled all into other places, by reason of the extreme usage and exactions done upon them.*[2]

The new landowners with whom Ivan replaced the executed or expelled boyars were desperate for peasant labour. Ivan IV was compelled to end the wars with Poland-Lithuania and Sweden because he could not lay his hands upon enough recruits. The worst hit areas were those around Moscow, Novgorod and Pskov, that is the centre and the north-west. This was mainly the result of the Tsar's wicked harrying of the north-west (1570), the Lithuanian campaigns in that area, and the Crimean Tartar raid on Moscow (1571): '*What with the Crimme on the one side and with his cruelty on the other, he hath but few people left*'.[3]

The flight of the peasants took two main directions. Many went north-east and east beyond the Volga where, although the climate was harsh and the soil poor, there were no Tartars and the land was free. Work of all kinds was available in forest and mine to supplement the poor returns of farming. Monasteries did much to organize economic life and promote settlement in this region, where the two chief areas were the Sukhoma and Kama valleys (fig. 24). By 1600 there had even begun the colonization of trans-Ural land in the basin of the Tobol. Although most of the Russian population in Siberia at this early date consisted of Cossack fur-traders

[1] *Fisher (1943), pp. 215-17*
[2] *Fletcher (1591), p. 61*
[3] *Uscombe (1571), p. 170*

and soldiers, the government was already encouraging the settlement of peasant farmers:[1]

> In Siberia (where he goeth on in pursuing his conquest) he hath divers castles and garrisons, to the number of six thousand soldiers of Russes and Polonians, and sendeth many new supplies thither, to plant and inhabit as he winneth ground.[2]

There was also a large migration south of the Oka into the wooded steppe: cultivated land in the Tula district had doubled in the five years, 1585-9.[3] Where a neighbouring fortress guaranteed some measure of safety, settlers ventured into the steppe itself. Where such security was lacking the peasants joined the Cossacks. The steppe soil and climate were excellent for a variety of crops, but the Crimean Tartars were a real menace to life and property. Nor were farmers so free here as in the north-east, for landlords and state granaries, to which compulsory deliveries of grain had to be made, were soon established. From these granaries carts took supplies to Moscow or to the garrison towns. The second half of the sixteenth century had also witnessed a movement of Russian peasants from the Polish provinces across the Dnieper into the Kiev and Chernigov districts, which had lain waste since the Mongol conquest. But here too landlords soon appeared and the colonists were reduced to serfdom.[4]

The conquest of the Khanate of Kazan had brought under Muscovite control a group of non-Slavic peoples hitherto subject to the Tartars. These were the Chuvash, the Mordva, the Votyaks and the Mari. These middle Volga peoples had lived partly by farming and partly by hunting: they now either became the serfs of Russian landlords or were driven into the forest by Russian immigrants.[5]

The urban population amounted to perhaps 2 or 3 per cent of the total and much of it, possibly a quarter, was concentrated in one large town, Moscow. The inhabitants of the capital certainly numbered over 100,000, and its population was now so large that, as in Paris, the town mob was able to exert some influence on events. According to Fletcher there had been more than 41,000 houses before the Tartar raid of 1571, as a result of which it was 'now not much bigger than London'.[6] Apart from its excellent geographical position with regard to the waterway routes and the trans-continental morainic ridge, it enjoyed two further advantages: it was the administrative and ecclesiastical centre of a large and populous unified state, and the tsars, by compelling dvorians, merchants, artisans and others to live in it, artificially promoted its growth.

The ancient inner core of Moscow consisted of two parts, both strongly walled with brick, the Kremlin and the Kitaygorod. Within the former

---

[1] Lyashchenko (1956), vol. 1, pp. 322-3
[2] Fletcher (1591), pp. 83-4
[3] Kulischer (1925), vol. 1, pp. 108-9
[4] Lyashchenko (1956), vol. 1, pp. 340-1
[5] Mirsky (1952), p. 156
[6] Fletcher (1591), p. 17

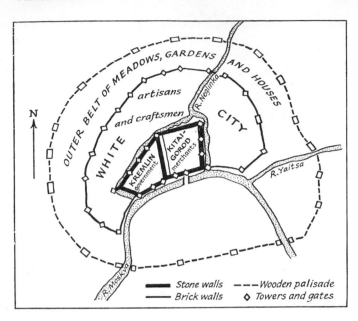

figure 25   Moscow in 1600.

were palaces and churches, while the latter had nobles' houses and the great market. This central area had now been adorned with a multitude of buildings in stone and brick, with a strange confusion of Byzantine, Italian and native Russian styles. In the Kitaygorod a great square was occupied by shops and stalls arranged in rows according to commodity or trade. Nowhere else in Russia was such a wide range of goods, both foreign and domestic, displayed. Both the Kremlin and the Kitaygorod were protected by water as well as by walls, being entirely surrounded by the river Moskva or its tributary streams. (Fig. 25.)

Round the city centre was the *Belygorod* or White Town which was enclosed by a white stone wall. Here there were nobles' and merchants' houses, many churches and more shops. The outer ring was formed by the *Zemlyanoygorod* or Earth Town, so called because it was surrounded '*with mud walls supported with planks*'.[1] The outer zone contained more houses, shops and churches, as well as barracks for the soldiery.

By 1600 there were several new towns or towns which had developed a new significance. *Archangel*, on the White Sea coast, had been founded in 1584 to handle trade coming in English and Dutch ships by the new sea route. *Vologda* had become an important trading town on the waterway route to Archangel as well as a centre of mining and manufacturing activity. *Ustyug* was another flourishing trading town on the North Dvina river route to Archangel and a centre of recent colonization. *Solvychegodsk*

[1] *Brace (1782), p. 81*

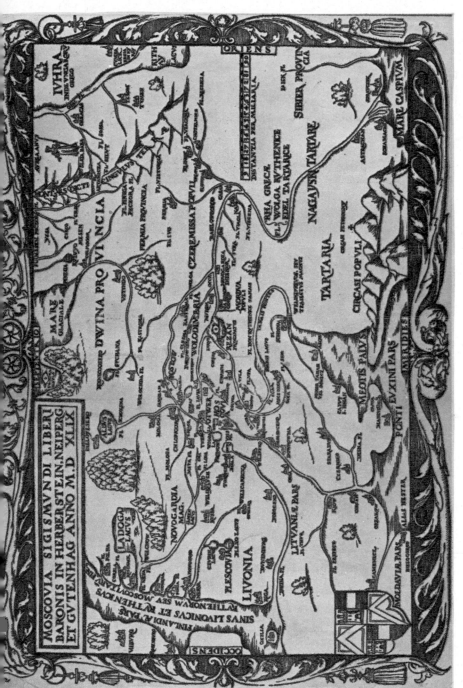

Plate 1   Herberstein's map (1549) was the first reasonably accurate map of Russia. It showed the Ural mountains for the first time, although these did not appear regularly on maps until the eighteenth century.

Plate 2   Part of Ortelius's first map of Europe (1570). The whole eastern area of the Russian lowland, including the Volga river and the Ural mountains, is called 'Tartaria' and designated 'Part of Asia'.

nearby was capital of the large private commercial empire set up in the north-east by the Stroganov family for the exploitation of forest and mine. Fortresses built to hold down the newly acquired steppe and Volga lands were fast growing into towns. Such were Orel, founded in 1564, Tsaritsyn (1589), Saratov (1590), Voronezh (1586), Kursk (1586) and Belgorod. Ufa (1586) was an outpost near the Urals and built in the territory of the Bashkirs to enforce payment of tribute. Infant towns, at present little more than trading posts, had been founded in newly-acquired West Siberia. Among them were Tyumen (1586), Tobolsk (1587), Berezov (1593) and Turinsk (1600). (Fig. 24.)

The forest left its stamp upon the towns of Muscovy, not only in the predominance of wooden buildings, but in the way the streets were paved: '*The streets of their cities and towns, instead of paving, are planked with fir trees, planed and laid even close the one to the other*'.[1] The influence of the forest was even more evident in the log houses which formed the dwellings of the peasants throughout Muscovy except where its new frontiers had extended southwards on to the steppe. Fletcher saw advantages as well as drawbacks in this type of housing:

> *Their houses are of wood, without any lime or stone, built very close and warm, with fir trees planed and piled one upon another. . . .*
> *Betwixt the trees or timber they thrust in moss to keep out the air. . . .*
> *This building seemeth far better for their country, than that of stone and brick: as being colder and more dampish than their wooden houses, specially of fir, that is a dry and warm wood. . . .*
> *The greatest inconvenience of their wooden building is the aptness for firing, which happeneth very oft and in fearful sort, by reason of the dryness and fatness of the fir, that being once fired, burneth like a torch, and is hardly quenched till all be burnt up.*[2]

In contrast to the wooden dwellings of the peasants were the large monasteries surrounded with stone walls. They were most numerous in the environs of the larger towns, but were also established in the northernmost parts of the country. They were often important agricultural and commercial centres.

The composition of the population of a Russian town at this time was very different from that of a western city. Boyars had houses in them and their servants were very numerous. In many towns the military garrison was a dominant feature. In others there would be *streltsy*, a new class, militarily trained who, while working at some profession or trade, could be called on to perform police duties in return for which they were exempt from tax. There were others of semi-official status—*dvorians* and *gosti*—as well as the usual artisans and labourers. There was nothing that could be called a middle class in the sense of a large body of independent professional and business men; almost everyone was an official or servant, whether of high or low degree.

[1] *Fletcher (1591), pp. 18-19*
[2] *Fletcher (1591), p. 19*

The social structure of Russia had undergone some change. The land-owning boyar class had been much weakened by the wholesale evictions, confiscations and executions during Ivan IV's terror. Over a large part of the country, known as the *oprichnina*, their land had been divided among the dvorians or lesser gentry, who owed service, usually military service, to the crown in return. In furthering the interests of these men, the Tsar was rewarding a class which tended to support the autocracy against the boyar resistance to centralization.

Most of the older-settled parts of the country had now been thus granted, so that fewer peasants were free in the sense that they had no lord, other than the Tsar, to whom they must pay dues and for whom they must work. Where dvorians replaced boyars, their exactions were much harsher than before. The peasants were left with less time and less land for their own use. Men determined to be free had to seek out the newly-opened lands, though here too the process of land-granting soon overtook them. Because of the shortage of labour, restrictions on the free movement of peasants were increasing and the transformation of the free peasant into the serf was well under way. In Poland-Lithuania the peasants' position worsened also: land reforms suppressed their rights and customs in the interests of the landlords. The organization of peasants in village communes, with elected elders who apportioned land and taxes and acted as intermediaries between landlord and peasant, was now general.

The cultural gap between the Russians and the West was at its widest. Foreign travellers were amused at the quaint behaviour of the Muscovites and disgusted at their bestial habits. It was between the upper classes of the two societies that the gulf was greatest. At a time when European courts and aristocracies were fast adopting many civilized refinements, the manners of the Muscovite noble were

> *those of savages; their behaviour, especially towards women, on their rare appearances outside Russia, led to diplomatic remonstrances. Filthily dirty, clad in long, cumbersome garments which prevented all free movement, unkempt hair down to their shoulders, and matted beards, they behaved hoggishly at table, dipping their black and greasy fingers indiscriminately into plates and dishes, always eating too much and drinking noisily and greedily out of unwashed vessels.*[1]

---

[1] *Marsden (1942), p. 27*

CHAPTER SEVEN
RUSSIA, 1600-1725: MUSCOVY AND THE WEST

(MICHAEL 1613-45, ALEXIS 1645-76, THEODORE II 1676-82, SOPHIA REGENT 1682-9, PETER I 1689-1725)

Throughout the seventeenth century, Russia was almost completely isolated from Europe by a zone of hostility extending from the Arctic Ocean to the Black Sea. She was also culturally isolated from the West by the immense gap which caused her to be looked upon by sophisticated Europeans as utterly barbarous. To cross the Russian boundary into Europe was, '*after a tedious association with a people barbarous and rude, to fall amongst those who were civil and urbane*'.[1] Although the clergy and the masses, ignorant or careless of this gap, regarded the Westerners as despicable heretics, there was a growing desire among the ruling classes to bridge it. But this necessitated breaking through the zone of enemy states so as to make effective contact with less inimical countries, to wit the Netherlands, Prussia, Austria and England.

Russia's principal foes were Sweden, Poland and Turkey. There was scarcely a year during this whole period when she was not at war with one or other of them. The main aims of Russian external policy made conflict with all three inevitable. Sweden barred her from the Baltic just as the Ottoman Turks and their Crimean Tartar vassals prevented access to the Black Sea. Poland-Lithuania still held on to a large area of Russian land and controlled the main land routes to the West.

The first years of the seventeenth century were known in Russia as the Troublous Times because the country was distraught by the struggles of rival tsars and their supporters. The ravaged countryside was stricken with famine between 1601 and 1609 and the population was reduced to cannibalism.[2] The enormous number of discontented, dispossessed and desperate people guaranteed initial support for any plausible pretender, and the threatened nobility were ready to consider calling in foreign aid. The Poles used this situation to invade Russia, capture Smolensk and enter Moscow. At the same time the Swedes seized a large part of north-western Russia including Novgorod. In 1613 the Troublous Times came to an end with the election by a *zemsky zobor* of a new tsar, Michael (1613-45). The *zemsky zobor* was a kind of estates general to which the absence of a recognized autocrat gave temporary power. Its decision was recognized because the dominant forces in the country, the dvorians or service gentry and the cossacks, whose military prowess had enabled them to join in the civil wars with great effect, accepted the new tsar.

Disadvantageous arrangements had to be made with both Sweden and

[1] *Anderson (1954), p. 153*
[2] *Bussow (1617), vol. 2, p. 68*

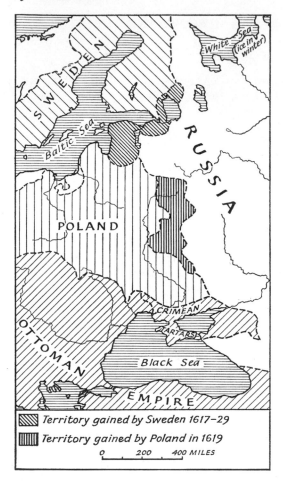

figure 26   Russia and her neighbours in the early seventeenth century. Russia was isolated from western Europe by a continuous zone of hostile states: Sweden, Poland, the Ottoman Empire. She had free access to neither the Baltic nor the Black and Azov Seas.

Poland to obtain peace for the new regime and a respite for the strife-torn country. The Peace of Stolbovo in 1617 gave Sweden complete possession of the Gulf of Finland coast although Russia recovered Novgorod. Russia was now completely cut off from the Baltic Sea (fig. 26). The 1618 truce with Poland allowed that country to keep Smolensk. The Poles were weakened, however, by the defection of the Dnieper or Zaporozhian Cossacks, who centred round their Sech on the lower Dnieper. During the seventeenth century, the Sech was the focus of resistance to Polonization amongst the Ukrainian peasantry and those landowners who had remained Orthodox in religion. In 1654 the Zaporozhian Cossacks transferred their allegiance

figure 27 Territorial gains from Poland and Sweden, 1640-1725.

from Poland to Moscow, after which the Ukraine became a battlefield and was devastated: the peasants in large numbers fled into Muscovite territory, helping to populate the southward-advancing frontier. In 1667 the Poles had to accept, at the Truce of Andrusovo, a settlement which brought Russia up to the Dnieper river and gave her Kiev on the other side: Smolensk was once more Russian (fig. 27). The truce was confirmed by the Peace of 1686. Under Tsar Peter I (1696-1725) it became clear that Russia was now the stronger of these two traditional enemies. He exploited Polish weakness and division, and Russian armies marched through Poland to Germany at will. Peter made a treaty with Prussia about Poland (1720)—the first of a series that was to end in the partition of the latter country.

Thus the Polish question was dealt with first. But some of those who, in the mid-seventeenth century, advised the Tsar, considered that Russia should have put access to the seas before territorial aggrandizement at Polish expense. They argued that the country needed to expand her restricted trade if she were to grow in wealth and power. Ordin-Nash-chokin would have preferred to have seen Riga and other Baltic outlets wrested from Sweden, rather than Kiev from Poland. Yet a successful war with Sweden (1656-61) ended with Alexis abandoning his Baltic conquests. A breathing space was badly needed after the Polish wars and Russia was dependent on Sweden for supplies of copper. The writer Kotoshikhin strongly urged a policy which would set Russian trade free from the hindrances it met in every direction—except for the long, arduous, distant and seasonally interrupted Archangel outlet.[1]

Wars with Turkey consisted in the main of Russian attempts to descend the Don and take the stronghold of Azov, giving access to the sea of that name. In 1637 the Don Cossacks had seized Azov but the Tsar relinquished it to the Turks in 1642. Campaigns across the steppe against the Crimean Tartars in 1687 and 1689 failed because the Russians could not adapt themselves to warfare where large uninhabited waterless distances had to be covered. They were accustomed to living on the country in which they fought. In 1696 Peter I took Azov but had to abandon it in 1711. No permanent progress was made therefore against this formidable enemy and the Black Sea remained out of reach.

In the north it was a different story. Although a massive Russian attack against the Swedish fortress of Narva ended in disaster in 1701, the Swedish king, Charles XII, made the mistake of underestimating his enemy and moved off to attack Poland. Whereupon Peter overran Estonia and Livonia and founded St Petersburg near the mouth of the Neva in what was now, by treaty, Swedish territory (1703). In 1704 the naval base of Kronstadt was built to protect St Petersburg from the seaward approach.

By the time Charles XII of Sweden was ready to turn again to Russia, Peter I had thoroughly reorganized his army which was now of enormous size. Charles did not follow the obvious invasion route via Smolensk to Moscow along the great glacial terminal morainic ridge, as the Poles had done a century before and as Napoleon was to do in 1812. The earth had been too well scorched. Instead he turned south into the food-rich Ukraine, hoping for support from disaffected Cossacks and possibly for help from Tartar and Turk. But his exhausted and numerically inferior army, cut off by distance and hostile guerillas from reinforcements and supplies, was crushed at Poltava in 1709.

---

[1] *Klyuchevskiy (1957), vol. 3, pp. 120, 343; Sumner (1950), p. 51; Kotoshikhin (1906), pp. 8-9*

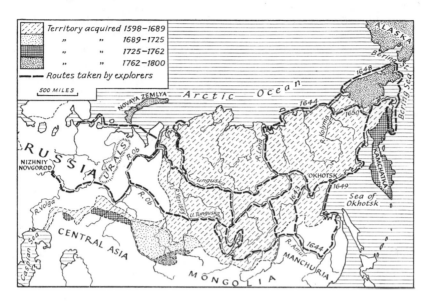

figure 28   Russian expansion into Siberia, 1598-1800.

Peter I was now able to extend and consolidate his Estonian and Livonian gains. The fortress and towns of Vyborg, Riga and Revel fell into his hands. Finland was overrun. A new Baltic navy strengthened his position and won the victory of Hango over the Swedes in 1714. But Britain, apprehensive at the prospect of Russian power in the Baltic, encouraged Swedish resistance. Not until 1721, following a devastating Russian raid on their coast, did the Swedes finally relinquish their dream of a Baltic empire. At the Peace of Nystadt in that year they ceded Estonia, Livonia and part of Karelia. The Russians had broken through the barrier of hostility and now had free access to the Baltic Sea (fig. 27).

The gains in the west were hard fought for against the most formidable military powers of the age. Eastwards, there was little to stand in the way of a rapid Russian advance across northern Asia to the Pacific Ocean. The Sea of Okhotsk was reached in 1639. By 1650 the Amur basin had been entered and hostilities with China ensued. These ended in 1689 when, by the Treaty of Nerchinsk, the Russians agreed to leave the Amur basin in return for commercial privileges. (Fig. 28.)

The speed with which the vast Siberian domain was acquired is remarkable: a mere 50 years had seen the addition of a territory 3,000 miles long and 1,000 miles wide. Not even the progress of the Europeans westward across North America beyond the Appalachians could compare in speed and distance with the Russian advance eastwards from the Urals. In both cases, fur traders took the initiative. The Russian achievement was aided by the arrangement of the river systems. Although the great natural waterways of northern Asia flow from south to north, a closer examination of the map shows that the river systems include long east-west tributaries which facilitated movement from one system to the next. The opening up of Siberia was the work of armed bands of Cossacks and fur traders. Where good soil was available, especially along the fertile black-earth belt that forms the southern margin of western Siberia, settlers soon came to farm in the vicinity of the fur-trading posts, where they could obtain supplies in return for their produce.

The far north-eastern limits of the continent were established when the Cossack Dezhnev sailed from the Kolyma estuary on the Arctic coast westwards to the Bering Strait between Asia and North America, and then southwards into the Bering Sea (1648). Bering, who gave his name to the strait and sea aforementioned, was commissioned to explore the northern-most Pacific in 1724. Peter I's reign also witnessed the conquest of Kam-chatka.

A premature attempt to subdue the trans-Caspian khanates ended with the ambush of a Russian expedition (1717); but in a successful war with Persia, aimed at controlling the lucrative silk trade, Peter I obtained a coastal strip along the Caspian (1722-4).

During the seventeenth century the southward advance of the Muscovite frontier and of Russian colonization continued, though progress was not so spectacular as in the east. About 1650 a fortified defensive line was made through Belgorod and Voronezh to Tambov. Not only peasants from the overcrowded north but Ukrainians from the Polish-held lands of the Dnieper pushed settlement and cultivation down the Donets beyond Kharkov, and the whole of the wooded steppe zone was thus occupied. Even farther south, on the open steppe, the Don Cossacks continued to flourish.

The continuous warfare of this period bore very heavily upon the peasant class who produced almost all the country's wealth. Disaffection developed principally in the south where Cossacks and runaway peasants were still ready to resist oppression, and in the south-east where non-Russian Tartaric tribes found their new masters' rule hard to bear. The revolts led by Bolotnikov in 1606 and Stenka Razin in 1669-70 were widely supported and initially successful, but the undisciplined mobs they led, intoxicated with blood and loot, were no match for the Tsar's armies. Exactions and extortions reached their height in Peter's reign. The enormous army and growing navy drained away the country's wealth. Apart from the wars themselves, the expense of westernization, involving costly importations and the salaries (which were not always paid) of hordes of foreign immigrants, further increased the need for taxation. By the end of his reign the Tsar had contrived to squeeze over five times as much from the country as at its beginning. A new poll tax which fell exclusively on the peasants was the chief means employed and a census (the first 'revision') was held in 1718-22 to make its collection more efficient.

From 1705 to 1711, the south and south-east were in a state of violent unrest, but after the battle of Poltava, Peter's great army was divided up into local detachments and quartered upon the country which it terrorized at will. The Cossacks were more strictly supervised henceforth, but allowed to retain their distinct administrative, military and cultural organization. This product of the wild open steppe was to prove of great value to the autocracy for, although Cossack rebellions would still occur, loyal Cossacks were to form a unique and terrible ingredient of the imperial army and police.

The period from 1600 to 1725 was one of increasing western influence. Ardent westernizers included the Tsar Alexis (1645-76) and three of his counsellors: Orduin Nashchokin, Matveyev and Golitsyn. Nashchokin gave his son a western education. Matveyev's house

> *was a source of never-failing delight to the receptive and inquisitive Tsar. It was like a bit of western civilization transferred bodily into another age and another continent. Within its walls could be seen all the wondrous half-forbidden novelties of the West: painted ceilings, rich pile carpets, ingenious clocks, pictures by French and German artists.*[1]

Golitsyn spoke Latin and could read Greek and German. Peter I (1689-1725) was but the most powerful, most thorough and most ruthless of the westernizers. He was by no means the first and '*the foundations of modern Russia were laid while he was still in his nursery*'.[2] European architecture (baroque), literature, drama, painting and music were all imitated by members of the wealthy class. Western—particularly German—modes of dressing, eating, drinking, smoking and shaving were imported, along with such objects as clocks, toys, carriages and glass. Despite ecclesiastical opposition, education made headway and Latin and Greek appeared on the syllabus. German rather than Russian became the language of the Court. But, whereas the westernization of the seventeenth century was the voluntary choice of certain courtiers, under Peter I it was enforced upon the whole boyar and gentry class by threats and punishments. Beards had to be shaved, western dress had to be worn, and the sons of the service gentry had to study according to a curriculum laid down by the Tsar. Many young Russians were sent abroad to further their education. The western method of counting the years replaced the old Russian custom. There was, however, an interlude of Muscovite reaction when Peter's mother and the church patriarchs were the dominant influence (1693-4): even military training in the European style was for a time proscribed.

The dispersal over the country, after the Battle of Poltava, of a large number of Swedish officers also did much to spread European civilization. These prisoners of war mixed freely with the Russians and, '*to support their tedious captivity*', taught music, painting, dancing, languages and '*several useful arts, which were almost unknown before their arrival*'.[3]

Apart from the cultural westernization of the upper classes of Russian society, foreign aid was enlisted to help reorganize the army, the navy and

---

[1] *Bain (1908), p. 275*
[2] *Bain (1908), p. 280*
[3] *Bell (1763), vol. 1, p. 187*

D*

the economy on Western lines. Patrick Gordon and James Bruce (Scots), Francis Lefort (a Swiss) and Münnich (a German) all did much for the Russian army. Peter enlisted a thousand Dutch officers and seamen for his new navy. Dutchmen also helped in the development of the textile industry and in the establishment of a post office. In 1652 Alexis allocated a special suburb, the German suburb as it was called, to foreigners in Moscow. Peter I himself learned all he could from the foreigners resident in this suburb and from those he met on his tours of Europe in 1697-8 and 1717. In 1694 he built a dockyard at Archangel and himself built a ship there following an English model. When Peter founded his future capital on the Neva in territory seized from Sweden (1703), it was no second Moscow, but an imitation of the great western capitals he had seen on his tour abroad. Even the name was Dutch (*Pieterburkh*) or German—*Peterburg* (Peter's Fortress).

Naturally there was intense resentment, widespread consternation and even active opposition to Peter's programme with its implied condemnation of the old Muscovite ways. The clergy, some of the older aristocratic boyars and the Russian masses looked upon the innovations and the innovator with a mixture of horror and dismay, bewilderment and awe. In the Tsar's absence on his first European tour, the *streltsy* of Moscow revolted. Peter's own son, Alexis, became a centre of reactionary hostility, and the Tsar, fearful of a reversal of his achievements, had him sentenced to death (1718). As well as sheer blind opposition to change, the philosophy later described as Slavophil now began to develop. The writer Krizhanich set forth such a viewpoint. He recognized that geographical factors, such as the country's isolation, its immense forested, marshy and desert tracts, and its vast size had handicapped its cultural development, and he conceded that a certain amount of judicious borrowing from the West might be desirable. But he did not think that the Russians should try to compete in matters of industry or material culture:

> *We should not compete with them in handicraft, nor display any silver vessels or other objects, with floral pattern, decorated or gilded, and for which the value is derived from the workmanship. For they are incomparably better than us in all craftmanship.*[1]

Instead, they should concentrate on the exercise of moral virtue in which they were so superior to the heretical and decadent West:

> *Let us compete in the temperate use of bedclothes, being content with one woollen mattress, or at the most, one feather bed and that not too thick, with a little straw underneath. And let us not use two or three feather beds underneath and a third or fourth above, as the Germans do, and sweat amongst the feathers as in the baths, almost suffocating.*[2]
> *Let us not imitate too much the curious and painstaking cleanliness of the Germans, who so often wash the floors of their houses, and where a guest may not spit or spew on to the floor. And if by chance he does so,*

[1] *Krizhanich (1860), vol. 2, p. 163*
[2] *Krizhanich (1860), vol. 2, p. 164*

straightway a servant wipes it up. Such men, in their voluptuousness and carnal cleanliness, attempt to make a heaven out of a mere earthly home.

And yet, with all this Epicureanism, cleanliness, splendour and delicacy, the Germans turn into the same dirt and dust as do other people. And therefore it should not be asked who has the cleanest floor or bedding, but who has the clearest conscience. . . . Such cleanliness is foul before God. Cleanse your heart and not your floor.[1]

Krizhanich expresses very strongly the antipathy between Teuton and Slav which grew rapidly with the increased contact between the races. He sees in the Germans all that is most evil amongst the corrupt heretics of western Europe. He deplored trade with the West as, through it, the Russians lost valuable and hard-won produce of soil and forest in return for *'pestiferous novelties'*. He likewise deplored imitating the West in military matters: *'They even persuade us to learn the art of fighting from them and to have them as generals, and to buy from them useless and ridiculous arms, such as swords, pistols and ill-made carbines'.*[2]

Russia, according to Krizhanich, was not only superior to the West in moral virtue, but in the absolutism of her government:

Absolute monarchy makes for perfect liberty on earth. For, in it, all just and honourable things are allowed to all men. But wicked men are not allowed to commit crimes with impunity nor to harm the good, as they are in your unbridled and disorderly licence. For what, O Germans, is there in your freedom that is conducive to right, honesty and the good of the State? What may we not do that is allowed to you? What we may not do is to commit crimes with impunity. Ours is the true and greatest liberty.[3]

Second only to his hatred of the Germans came his dislike of those ultra-conservative churchmen who would acknowledge nothing without Byzantine or Greek authority. He rejected their doctrine of Moscow's destiny to be the 'third Rome', which he did not fully understand.[4] It was bad enough that the Germans should claim supremacy over Russia for their Holy Roman Emperor. It was just as reprehensible to imply that Russia's power derived ultimately from Rome. She was inherently and independently great:

Russia never belonged to the empire of Rome nor was subject to the Romans. Neither their empire, name or insignia belong in any way to Russia. But the Russian realm is as high and glorious, and as powerful, as the Roman was: indeed, it is more solidly founded and more monarchical. The Roman emperors had no dignity or power that the most serene tsars of Russia do not have.[5]

---

[1] *Krizhanich (1860), vol. 2, p. 167*
[2] *Krizhanich (1860), vol. 2, p. 160*
[3] *Krizhanich (1860), vol. 2, pp. 169-70*
[4] *See* supra, *pp. 83-4.*
[5] *Krizhanich (1860), vol. 2, pp. 181, 184-5*

108

THE ECONOMIC GEOGRAPHY OF RUSSIA IN 1725, AT THE END OF THE REIGN OF PETER THE GREAT

The Russian Empire in 1725 extended from the Gulf of Riga on the Baltic shore to the Sea of Okhotsk and the Pacific; and, by the acquisition of central and eastern Siberia, it had more than doubled its area since the year 1600. Cossack adventurers were already in the peninsula of Kamchatka and looking towards America. The Baltic littoral, from Riga to Vyborg, had been won from Sweden in the war of 1701-21, though its value was limited by the presence of winter ice. The Russian hold on the lower Volga region had been strengthened and widened and, since the peace with Persia (1724), possession of the southern and western shores of the Caspian Sea had been added. But the Black Sea remained beyond the Tsar's reach, and although the lower Don valley was now firmly in Russian hands and Cossacks were active in the Kuban, the Tartars, vassals to the Turk, still held the Crimea and the shores of the Sea of Azov. (Fig. 27.)

The country's rulers were no longer content that the Empire should be known as Muscovy, a term associated with the old and the unreformed; instead the name 'Russia' came into general use abroad. Western influence was also evident in the use of the title of *Imperator* taken by the Tsar in 1721 and in the name 'Senate', given to the new council in 1711; and, whereas in 1600 the Russian noble families were mostly without European connections, in 1725 the Russian royal family was closely knit through marriage with several German princely houses.[1]

Agriculture

A brief contemporary account of Russian agriculture was given by Strahlenberg, a Baltic German who, as a Swedish army officer, spent twelve years in captivity in Russia. He was, however, given considerable liberty to pursue his geographical interests, including freedom to travel. He perceived that Russia's climate and vegetation, and likewise her soils and agriculture, could be divided into latitudinal zones.[2] The first and northernmost of these lay between 70° and 60°N, i.e. north of the latitude of St Petersburg. Here winters were long and cold and there were no trees; but there were berry-bearing bushes, as well as game, wild fowl and fish.

The second belt, from 60° to 57°N, i.e. from the latitude of St Petersburg to that of Kalinin (Tver), had a less severe winter and was admirably suited to livestock of all kinds—cattle, sheep, goats and horses, and was also capable of producing grain and vegetables in favoured places. The Novgorod district was, despite its many marshes, still famous for its flax

[1] *Sumner (1950), p. 203; Mirsky (1952), p. 184*
[2] *Strahlenberg (1730), pp. 173-5*

and hemp, its honey and its beeswax.[1] Beekeeping was still an important source of livelihood where soils were poor and where, therefore, forest remained. The bees were not kept in hives, but nested wild at the tops of fir trees in the woods. The newly-won Baltic lands lay in this zone. A sharp contrast could be drawn between Ingria, the sterile glaciated country immediately to the west of St Petersburg, and Estonia, to which the ice sheet had been kinder, bequeathing it a zone of fertile boulder clay. This had enabled it to become an exporter of grain, 'which foreign merchants preferred to that of Poland and other countries'.[2]

Thirdly, from 57° to 54° or from the latitude of Kalinin to that of Tula, was a zone where, because the climate was less extreme and because there were relatively few hills, marshes and forests, corn, fruit and vegetables were all abundant, together with much cattle and honey, '*so that the inhabitants lacked nothing but wine*'. This belt included the Moscow district. The land round Vladimir, distinguished by better soils than elsewhere in the region, attracted special notice: '*Wolodimir is situated in the most fertile country in all Muscovy*'.[3] It was in this zone also that arable farming had expanded significantly eastwards beyond the middle Volga and up the Kama valley. Since their conquest by Russia the inhabitants of this area, the Kazan Tartars and some of the Bashkirs, had settled as wheat farmers. In this they differed markedly from the nomadic and untamed Tartars farther south.

The fourth and richest division was from 54°, the latitude of Tula, to 48°N, the parallel that passes through the great bends of the Dnieper, Don and Volga. Here summers were warm and winters short, so that a wide variety of fruits and abundant grain could be grown. This belt corresponded broadly with the wooded steppe, where wheat-growing on the fertile black-earth soils was creeping southwards. It was already helping to feed the growing population of the central region round Moscow, where this newly-tapped supply of grain enabled the population to turn more to manufacturing.

Still farther south lay a fifth zone, potentially even richer, but, because it was in Tartar hands or lay exposed to Tartar depredations, it went uncultivated and almost uninhabited, except near garrison towns such as Astrakhan on the lower Volga and Terek in the Caucasian piedmont. Here fine large sweet grapes were grown, as well as '*the most excellent fruits, yielding neither for beauty nor flavour to any . . . apples, quinces, nuts, peaches and melons, . . . especially the water melon*'.[4] The grapes of the Astrakhan district were not good for wine because of the salty soil, but those from about Terki made a wine '*superior to that of Saxony*'. Perry thought these southernmost parts of the Tsar's empire had '*the best climate in the world*':

[1] *Bruce (1782), p. 110*
[2] *Weber (1721), p. 68*
[3] *Bruce (1782), p. 228*
[4] *Bruce (1782), p. 250*

> *In the spring of the year, as soon as ever the snow is off the ground,*
> *which usually does not lie above two or three months in these parts,*
> *the warm weather immediately after takes place; and the tulips, roses*
> *. . . and several other flowers and herbs spring up like a garden . . .*
> *the common grass in the meadows is up to the horse's belly.*

It was, he continued,

> *a thousand times to be lamented, that so rich and noble a country,*
> *situated on the side of the great river Wolga, which is perhaps the best*
> *stored with fish of any river in the whole world . . . should now lie in a*
> *manner waste without inhabitants, whilst many of the northern Russes*
> *I have seen, for want of sun enough to ripen their harvest, mingle roots*
> *of grass and straw with their corn to make bread.*[1]

Agriculture had made limited progress in Siberia because the main objective of the Russians beyond the Urals was still furs. But the growing number of fortified trading posts, some of which were growing into towns, created a demand for food. This demand, together with some state encouragement, had led peasant farmers to settle nearby. At Yakutsk, according to Ides, '*the land is very fruitful and corn grows in a very great abundance . . . great numbers of Russians have settled here and taken up hundreds of villages*'; but Strahlenberg, while noting that corn was grown at Yakutsk despite its northerly latitude, states that the inhabitants '*neglect cultivation, being more interested in hunting sables, foxes and other animals*'. At Ilinsk, Ides, travelling as the Tsar's ambassador to China, found that the Russians there '*go sable hunting, not tilling any more ground than necessity requires*'[2] Yakutsk was also known as a horse-breeding centre.

Fishing

It was now a commonplace with writers on Russia that its rivers abounded with fish of all kinds. The Volga had '*great plenty of sturgeon, sterlet, citera, salmon—both red and white, saudack, perch, crawfish, carp, pike, tench*'. Settlements on the shores of the White Sea still lived mainly by fishing, but Russia now had another great source of fish at the opposite end of the country. Of the Caspian Sea, Perry wrote that it was '*much the largest lake and perhaps the best stored with fish of any water in the world*'. From its waters the sturgeon was already contributing to Astrakhan's caviar industry. Fishing and curing prospered '*on account of their numerous fast days.*'[3]

Fur trading

The significance of furs in the national income had declined, partly as the

[1] *Perry (1716), pp. 90, 93*
[2] *Ides (1706), pp. 36, 39; Strahlenberg (1730), p. 378*
[3] *Bruce (1782), pp. 236-7*

state had acquired fresh sources of revenue and partly owing to depletion of the hunting and trapping grounds. The yield of furs had grown rapidly until towards the end of the seventeenth century, after which it fell off steeply. Depletion was especially severe around the older trading posts which had grown into towns. These had attracted a large population of farmers who were busy clearing the forest and frightening the animals away.[1]

Fur trapping had moved eastward as areas closer to Russia were exhausted and it was, in fact, the frantic search for new sources that caused the Russian dominions to spread so fast across northern Asia (fig. 28). As the Arctic and North Pacific coasts were reached, some compensation was found for the loss of forest fur in the new-found wealth of seal and other cold-water life:

> *The fishing of seals or sea dogs, about ten thousand a year, yields five thousand measures of oil; the skins and oil are sent to England. Morses or sea-horses, from Nova Zembla, used to load thirty boats a year with blubber; the teeth are esteemed next to ivory.*[2]

Had the getting of furs been left solely to the natives of Siberia, who hunted with bow and arrow, there would have been less serious depletion. But the Russians used traps, nets and dogs, systematically clearing district after district of its animal wealth. The natives themselves, eager to acquire clothing, equipment, utensils, ornaments and knick-knacks from the Russians, were stimulated to greater efforts in tracking down furs. But supplying them with arms and alcohol was forbidden. Although the actual fur trapping was normally a winter occupation, furs and fur traders travelled to and from Russia as much as possible in summer and by water.

The old route by which furs had left eastern Siberia (the upper Lena, the Vilyuy, portage to the lower Tunguska, the Yenisey at Turukhansk, portage to Mangazeya and the Ob estuary, thence by sea to Archangel) had been abandoned. Fur resources along this route had been depleted, the northern sea route was highly dangerous and only briefly open, and Archangel had been replaced by St Petersburg as the main port for Europe. Yakutsk rather than Mangazeya was now the chief fur-collecting centre, and the main route back to Russia went: up the Lena, by portage to the upper Tunguska via Ilinsk, thence to the Yenisey at Yeniseysk, by portage to the Ob at Narym, up the Irtysh to Tobolsk, up the Tobol and Tura rivers, by portage across the Urals, and finally down the Kama and up the Vychegda to Solvychegodsk. There were many other routes, most of which ended at Solvychegodsk. Other important fur-collecting depots were the Volga towns of Nizhniy Novgorod and Astrakhan.[3]

[1] *Fisher (1943), pp. 99-101*
[2] *Whitworth (1761), p. 201*
[3] *Fisher (1943), pp. 158-65*

Mining (fig. 29)

Peter I had ordered all landed proprietors to search for minerals on their lands. Mining was the one great occupation in which compulsory serf labour could be used effectively and this was a factor in Peter's success. In the development of the central Urals, where copper and iron had been known to exist long before, lands were granted to private individuals or placed under state management, while the inhabitants, whether Russian peasants or native Bashkirs, were forced to work in the mines. Because of the Tsar's military needs, the mining of iron ore had increased since 1600 more than any other mineral, and this increase came almost wholly from the Urals. Here there was not only a higher grade ore than in central Russia, but vast reserves of forest for charcoal making—a weighty consideration in view of the growing scarcity of wood fuel near the older centres.

Copper mining also greatly increased, again mainly in the Urals, but also at Olonets near lake Ladoga. This satisfied, besides military and domestic needs, the demand arising from the introduction of copper coinage. Silver-lead mining had, by 1719, begun at far-away Nerchinsk in the Amur basin.[1]

Salt remained the most essential mineral for the population generally. The main producing area was still the upper Kama district, where between fifty and eighty pits were sunk for brine; this was evaporated in large pans to produce three million *puds* of salt a year. The pits were chiefly at Nova Usolye and at several other places in the neighbourhood of Solikamsk, the headquarters of the Stroganov family business. Other producing areas were in the Vychegda valley at Solvychegodsk and Yarensk; in the upper Volga region at Rostov and near Kostroma; and in the Novgorod area at Staraya Russa. Rock salt was relatively unimportant, although the local needs of the Bashkirs and Tartars were met from mines east of Ufa.[2] The boiling of sea-water took place along the White Sea coast, and a mile below Astrakhan were

> *collected great quantities of common salt. The people dig pits, into which they introduce the water; which being exhaled by the heat of the sun, the salt is left upon the bottom: after gathering, they transport it along the river in large barques of about five or six hundred ton.*[3]

The Astrakhan area supplied the local fish-curing industry with immense quantities of salt as well as meeting the growing needs of southern Russia.

Sulphur, used for medical purposes and now more than ever for the manufacture of gunpowder, came from the Kazan region.[4] There were

[1] *Strahlenberg (1730), p. 331*
[2] *Lyashchenko (1956), vol. 1, p. 309; Strahlenberg (1730), pp. 417-18; Ides (1706), p. 5*
[3] *Bell (1763), vol. 1, p. 37*
[4] *Strahlenberg (1730), p. 241; Whitworth (1761), p. 204*

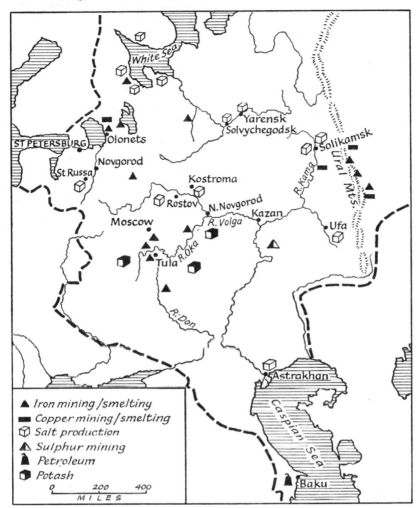

figure 29   Russia in 1725: minerals

several sources of potash south-east of Nizhniy Novgorod.[1] Near Solikamsk, besides salt, was '*found the fossil called asbestos of which is made a kind of cloth like linen, that may be put into the fire and taken out again unconsumed*'.[2] The petroleum deposits of the Caucasus, observed by Marco Polo, were now beginning to be appreciated. Strahlenberg speaks of '*excellent white naphtha*' and the '*black kind of bitumen*' found near Baku: '*all the land round this town is full of mineral oil*'.[3]

[1] *Lyashchenko (1956), vol. 1, p. 215*
[2] *Bell (1763), vol. 1, p. 170*
[3] *Strahlenberg (1730), p. 408*

Manufacturing Industry

During the seventeenth century, foreigners, at the invitation of the tsars, had established factories in Russia. These were mainly works producing ironware, armaments and glass.[1] Peter I's main economic achievement was the establishment of an industrial base for a large and well-equipped army and a powerful fleet. The central Urals were developed into the leading mining and metallurgical region in the world in a remarkably short time, in order to guarantee a supply of arms. The production of rope, sailcloth and uniforms was so expanded as greatly to reduce dependence on imports. St Petersburg was founded, not only as a new port, but as an industrial centre; and to the existing industries of the Moscow region, factory enterprises unprecedented in size were added.

An economic policy based on compulsion and oppression tended to make capital scarce by encouraging the hoarding and hiding of valuables. Yet it was all found at home, partly by extortion from the Russian peasant and partly by exploitation of other peoples of the expanded empire. The labour supply problem was aggravated by the establishment of industrial areas in regions where manpower was scarce, as in St Petersburg and the Urals. In the Urals, local peasants were ascribed to the works, while thousands of serfs were drafted to build the new capital city. The skilled labour came from Europe.

During Peter's reign the number of factories rose from a mere dozen to some two hundred, among which there were some really large establishments, consisting in the main of ironworks, armament works and textile mills. One or two factories employed over a thousand workers, and several had over five hundred. A large proportion of the labour force was drawn from the countryside and landowners could no longer reclaim runaway serfs once they had found factory work. In old-established industries the more skilled work was done by hired workers, only labouring tasks being performed by unpaid serfs. For the new industries, not only serfs, but orphans, beggars, whores and criminals were recruited and driven into the factories.[2]

Most of the newer and larger works had been established as state enterprises and protected by high tariffs or prohibitions on imports. But Peter soon realized that able private entrepreneurs, motivated by profit and with defenceless and unpaid labour available for exploitation, could outmatch his government officials in initiative, efficiency and productivity. Many state enterprises were accordingly transferred to private ownership.

The earlier works established by Peter were exclusively directed towards war needs: metals, armaments, uniforms, rope, sailcloth, ships. But as military needs declined and the Europeanization of the upper classes became the Tsar's chief preoccupation, the nature of the new factories

[1] *Lyashchenko* (1956), *vol. 1, p. 306*
[2] *Florinsky* (1953), *vol. 1, p. 389*

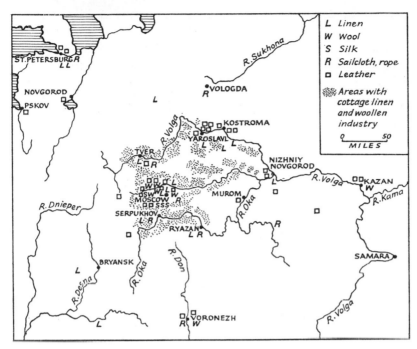

figure 30   Russia in 1725: factories making textiles, leather, etc., in Central Russia.

changed: they were to produce such wares as silks, velvet, china, glass, mirrors, wallpaper, etc.

This remarkable development of factory industry did not prevent cottage industry, particularly the weaving of wool and flax, metal-working and distilling, from rapidly expanding, especially in the Moscow region.

THE TEXTILE INDUSTRY (fig. 30)

The woollen textile industry was handicapped by the poor coarse wool given by the Russian and Siberian sheep. Even with an admixture of imported wool, the cloth made was *'only fit for soldiers'*.[1] Woollen cloth was still mainly a product of cottage industry in the basin of the upper Volga, although Peter had established large new factories at Moscow, Kazan and Voronezh.

The linen industry was favoured by Russia's production of excellent flax in abundance, but skill in its treatment was sadly lacking. Relatively little was made in factories: most came from the looms of peasants living in the flax-growing areas. The cloth so produced was too narrow to be of much general value, but the width was limited by the size of the cottage looms traditionally in use and could not easily be changed. The factory-made

[1] *Perry (1716), p. 268; Strahlenberg (1730), p. 419*

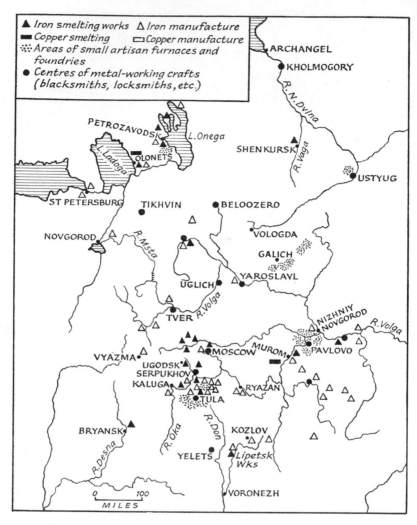

figure 31   Russia in 1725: the metal-working industries of the North and Centre.

product came from Moscow, Yaroslavl and other central towns. The manufacture of sailcloth and rope for the navy, goods hitherto imported from abroad, was concentrated at Moscow and St Petersburg in the largest factories yet established in Russia. Again the raw material, hemp, was a home product of good quality.

Novgorod and Pskov had been replaced by Yaroslavl and Kostroma as the chief centres of leather production, and there were now several leather-working establishments peripheral to the central Moscow area. To meet the increased needs of Peter's reign, the industry was expanded at Moscow, whither master tanners were brought from Revel to train the local workers.[1]

IRON AND STEEL MANUFACTURE (figs. 31, 32)
In 1725 Russia probably led the world in the production of iron, the annual amount being then about 150,000 tons, a total not matched in Britain until the end of the century.[2] Most of this production came from the many large works established by Peter I. The share of the Urals region, in which the industry had existed only in the form of very small artisan enterprises before Peter, was now 40 per cent, the rest coming from the central region (Moscow-Tula) and from the north-west. In the centre and north-west, several small works had been established during the seventeenth century, to which many large plants were added by Peter.

The skilled nucleus of the labour force for the new plant came either from Europe (mainly Saxony), or from old-established works in the Tula region, but the mass of the workers were peasants compelled to toil, not only in the works themselves, but in the ancillary iron-mining, wood-cutting and charcoal-burning activities. In parts of the Ural region there were local artisans with experience of small-scale iron-smelting and iron-working; and Hennin, Peter's director of state works there, found about 250 such in the Kungur district. But large numbers of local peasants as well as serfs from outside had to be conscribed into the labour force.[3]

Some of the principal works in the central or Moscow-Tula region are tabulated below:

Date of establishment	Position	Production, etc.
1632	Ten miles from Tula	Mortars, cannon, grenades
17th cent.	Near Kashira on the Oka	Mortars, cannon, grenades
17th cent.	Ugodsk on the Nara	Bar and roofing iron, anchors
17th cent.	Pavlovsk works, west of Moscow	Firearms, locks, miscellaneous
1696	Near Tula	'Twenty thousand muskets, ten thousand pairs of pistols annually, besides other iron goods.'[4]
1707 Peter's reign	Pushech, at Moscow Lipetsk, between Kozlov and Voronezh	Cannon (an older works modernized)[5] 'all sorts of arms for the supply of the Czar's army'[6]

[1] *Bain (1908), p. 303*
[2] *Watson (1960), p. 505*
[3] *Portal (1950), p. 69*
[4] *Strahlenberg (1730), p. 351*
[5] *Portal (1950), p. 28*
[6] *Perry (1716), p. 246*

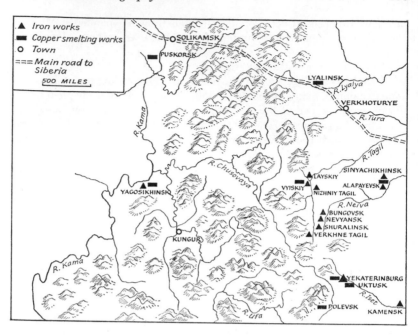

figure 32   Russia in 1725: the metal-working industries of the Central Urals.

Besides these and other large works, there were about fifty small artisan workshops in the Tula district in 1725.[1] This great activity in the central region was due to the presence of local iron mines, but by 1725 depletion of both ore and of wood for charcoal were causing difficulty.

The presence of ore and great forests in Karelia, together with the foundation of St Petersburg and the establishment of a naval base on the Baltic, led to the further development of iron-smelting and working in the north-west. Small-scale industry went back a long time here, but a larger works had been built in the seventeenth century at Shenkursk on the Vaga, a tributary of the North Dvina. Peter had founded three great centres. The first was at Olonets, near the east shore of lake Ladoga. The second was at Petrozavodsk, on the west shore of lake Onega. Its main purpose was to supply the new navy, and its output included a cannon a day, 12,000 muskets and 6,000 pair of pistols a year, anchors and other naval requirements.[2] This great works had four large blast furnaces, employed nearly 1,000 men, and became the centre of a new town. The third plant, at Sestroretsk, close to St Petersburg, was almost as large, employed nearly 700 men, and produced mainly armaments.

A combination of assets favoured the Urals area:

[1] *Portal (1950), p. 29*
[2] *Strahlenberg (1730), p. 351*

The ore is very good, and rises in many places to the very surface of the earth, and may be dug at small expense. As for wood to smelt it, no place in the world can have greater advantage. Besides, all the machines may be driven by water; and there is an easy communication by the rivers to St Petersburg for exportation, and to many other parts of Russia, for inland communication.[1] (Plate 3.)

Disadvantages were distance from the consuming areas and the insecurity of a region whose native population was non-Russian. Some of the main works of this region are tabulated below:

Date of establishment	Name or position	Production, etc.
1699	Nevyansk, on the river Neiva	Began to produce iron in 1701 at the rate of 2 tons of pig a day[2]
1700	Kamensk, on the river Kamenka	300 cannon in 1702; second blast furnace added in 1704[3]
1723	Nizhniy Alapayevsk	Finished 1727
1724	Yagoshikhinsk	The settlement here developed into the town of Perm
1725	Nizhniy Tagil, on the river Tagil	

But the most active Urals centre in 1725 was the newly founded (1723) metallurgical town of Yckatcrinburg (now Sverdlovsk). It already had 5 blast furnaces working, 2 steel furnaces and many other installations.[4]

NON-FERROUS METALLURGY

The only other metal besides iron to be smelted and worked in any quantity in 1725 was copper, and almost all came from works established in the central Urals during Peter's reign. There was also some copper smelting near lake Onega, at Murom in central Russia, and at Kazan.

OTHER INDUSTRIES

Shipbuilding was an entirely new industry which had been introduced by Peter I with the help of foreigners. Construction was mostly naval. For use on the Baltic, shipyards were at first established at Lodeynoye Pole on the banks of the Svir river between lakes Onega and Ladoga, but these were soon superseded by the new Admiralty yards at St Petersburg. At first the vessels were built of fir, which abounded in the neighbourhood, but ships so made scarcely lasted seven years. For plentiful supplies of good

[1] *Bell (1763), vol. 1, p. 169*
[2] *Klyuchevskiy (1958), vol. 4, p. 121; Portal (1950), p. 32*
[3] *Portal (1950), p. 33*
[4] *Portal (1950), p. 74; Strahlenberg (1730), p. 341*

oak, recourse had to be made to the forests of central Russia beyond the Volga in the former khanate of Kazan. Here, '*ten or twelve thousand Tartar inhabitants with three or four thousand horses*' were employed each winter '*in drawing the timber out of the woods to the bank of the Volga*'.[1] Even so, the Tsar's oaken ships did not last much longer than those of fir, partly because the felled timber was piled up in the snow and rain for months on end to await shipment and was therefore half rotten when it arrived at St Petersburg, and partly because, in felling, no regard was had '*to the season of the year and the age of the trees*'.[2] Having to bring the oak 1,000 miles to the yards meant that,

> *though men's labour is abundantly cheaper, and that he has the iron work and cordage out of his own country, yet the building of his ships with oak are as dear as to have them built in England.*[3]

For White Sea navigation, Archangel and Onega became shipbuilding centres. Yards had also been equipped at Voronezh-on-Don to supply river fleets for action against the Turks and, later, at Nizhniy Novgorod for the expedition via the Volga and the Caspian Sea against Persia.[4] River boats for the Dnieper were built at Bryansk on the Desna. All three places —Bryansk, Voronezh and Nizhniy Novgorod—lay back in the deciduous or mixed forest zone, although the ships were needed for service further south. On the far Pacific shore, Okhotsk became Russia's first Far Eastern shipyard.[5]

One result of the spread of western culture in Russia was a great demand for both window glass and looking glass. In 1725 Russia was no longer entirely dependent on imports and there were large glass-works at both Moscow and St Petersburg.[6] Peter I's war needs had led to the creation of a large gunpowder industry with mills built on several small rivers near Moscow, '*where a sufficient supply is . . . made, not only to supply the Czar's occasions, but may be spared to other nations*'.[7] His bureaucratic needs meant a vastly increased consumption of paper, for the manufacture of which large state mills had been erected at St Petersburg and soon transferred to private ownership. Peter had decreed that only paper of Russian make was to be used by government officials. Sugar refining was another new industry: the first mills refining imported sugar cane had been built at St Petersburg in 1718 and Moscow in 1723.[8] The Russian Ukraine was almost wholly without industry apart from distilling.

[1] *Bridge (1899), p. 110*
[2] *Bridge (1899), p. 110*
[3] *Perry (1716), p. 40*
[4] *Bruce (1782), p. 153*
[5] *Strahlenberg (1730), p. 298*
[6] *Lyashchenko (1956), vol. 1, pp. 306, 383; Bruce (1782), p. 153*
[7] *Perry (1716), p. 246*
[8] *Lyashchenko (1956), vol. 1, p. 521*

Trade and Transport

Since 1600 there had been a great increase in the internal circulation of goods, as a degree of specialized production developed. Industrial and commercial towns grew up in the north, but grain growing was beginning to move to the newly-settled wooded steppe lands to the south. Hence there was a growing movement of manufactured goods southward and of grain northward. Large estates began sending a variety of foodstuffs and industrial crops to the urban market to pay for the widening range of goods necessitated by the westernization of the upper class: thus wheat, rye, vegetables, flax, hemp, livestock and animal products moved off the farms, and potash also, where there were expanses of forest for burning. Back to the manor house came luxury goods, French and Italian wines, playing cards, window and looking glass, wallpaper, clocks, etc.

Despite the pull of St Petersburg and Riga and their importance in foreign commerce, Moscow remained an important centre of internal trade. The roads and waterways leading to it were still busy with laden carts and barges. The rapid growth of Peter's new town on the Finnish Gulf revived for a time the former prosperity of Moscow's old rival, Tver:

> The river Volga, which flows into the Caspian Sea, runs through the town, and as the kingdom of Kazan sends to Tver many thousand loads of corn a year by that river, it has become the real staple of the corn trade, and all that is required for the army and for St Petersburg is despatched from the town in sledges.[1]

But the construction of the Vyshniy Volochok canal (1720) had already begun to threaten this prosperity by taking traffic off the Volga below Tver in the navigable summer season.

The extracts that follow give some idea of how climate and other natural causes affected the movement of men and goods early in the eighteenth century. John Bell is the narrator and the date is 1718:

> Sept. 7th, leaving Astrakhan, we sailed up the Volga. Our progress, contrary to the course of the river, was very slow and tedious. In calms the boats were drawn up by men who went upon the banks; but in hard gales we were obliged to haul them near the side and lay still.
>
> Oct. 12th, after a voyage of five weeks, we arrived at the town of Saratoff. . . . The winter drawing on prevented our farther progress by water. We therefore unloaded, and discharged the boats, being resolved to remain here till the snow fell, when we might proceed by land in sledges.
>
> Nov. 1st, there had now been a little fall of snow, sufficient to smooth the roads, and this day we set out from Saratoff in sledges. . . . The 8th, we came to large town called Penze. . . . As we advanced to the north the frost and snow daily increased, which made the roads very smooth and easy. Before we left this place a sudden rain obliged us to halt a few days. . . .

[1] Weber (1721), p. 128

The 14th, the frost and snow returning, we set out from Penze. . . .[1]

WATERWAYS

The movement of goods on the waterways and connecting portages during the navigable season was by far the most important form of transport. Peter had seen the necessity for replacing portages by canals, thus avoiding the delays of repeated transhipment, but in most instances the physical and engineering difficulties proved insuperable. This was notably so with his attempted Volga-Don (Kamyshenskiy) canal which, *'after being greatly advanced, was at last found impracticable by the vast quantity of hard rock lying in the way'*.[2] Despite its obvious advantages, a Volga-Don waterway link was not successfully accomplished until 1952. Peter had been more fortunate in joining a tributary of the upper Volga, the Tvertsa, with a tributary of the Volkhov, the Msta, thus providing a continuous water route between Moscow and St Petersburg for shallow-draft craft—the Vyshniy Volochok canal. This was already being intensively used for bringing grain and oak to St Petersburg. But storms on lake Ladoga made the new communication very hazardous.[3]

The Moscow-Archangel waterway route, so busy in 1600, was now much less important because of the transfer of most of the northern port's functions to St Petersburg and Riga. But there was now much more traffic on the Volga. Flat-bottomed barges, carrying 800 or 900 tons, brought salt, fish, caviar, as well as goods from the Far East up to Moscow from Astrakhan, and returned with corn, timber and manufactured articles. Not only did the great river itself connect the growing industry of the centre with the agricultural and commercial progress of the south, but the tributary Kama system reached up into the Urals where it penetrated the new metallurgical region.

ROADS

Transport by roads was commonest in the winter season when they were frozen hard and when snow and ice provided a surface over which sledges could swiftly glide. At other seasons swamps made many roads impassable; the great distances involved made road surfacing impracticable and the best roads were very bad, especially after the spring thaw and the autumn rains. Consequently, *'excepting where there is opportunity of water carriage'*, goods were stored until winter came; at that season *'the price of land carriage . . . upon sleds is not above one fourth or fifth part so much as it is in the summer upon wheels'*.[4] Bruce found winter travel in Russia *'extremely commodious'*:

> *their sledges glide away on the surface of the ice or snow, in a flat country, with incredible despatch, and so very little labour to the*

[1] *Bell (1763), vol. 1, pp. 150-1*
[2] *Bruce (1782), p. 243*
[3] *Bruce (1782), p. 111; Klyuchevskiy (1958), vol. 4, pp. 120, 122-3*
[4] *Perry (1716), pp. 244-5*

horses, that they can easily perform fifty or sixty miles a day.[1]
There was not even a good all-season road between Moscow and the
new capital at St Petersburg. Up to 5 weeks had to be allowed for the 500-
mile journey at seasons other than winter. Peter had planned a straight
road, Roman fashion, from one city to the other, but was unable to master
the marshes and forests of the Novgorod area.[2] The Urals were almost
impossible to cross by road once the thaw had set in:

> *the multitude of the morasses and the deepness of the roads rendering
> that way utterly impassable in summer, for which reason all travelling
> officers as well as merchants are necessitated to lie still the whole summer
> in Solikamskoi till they meet with hard lasting winter roads.*[3]

Only in the dry south-east, where the caravan routes from Asia terminated,
did all-season land traffic flourish. Even here, because winds concealed
the roads with sand, the camel caravans had to be navigated by the stars.[4]

FOREIGN TRADE

Russia's foreign trade was much greater in 1725 than in 1600. A larger
population, increased foreign contacts, and the higher degree of westernization, which created new appetites for foreign goods, were the causes of this
increase. But the dependence on foreign sources was less for iron and
copper, previously imported from Sweden and now produced wholly in
Russia, and even exported therefrom; it was less also for woollen cloth,
glass and paper, now manufactured in large new works established in
Peter's reign.

The Netherlands were Russia's chief supplier, England her best
customer. She still had no merchant navy of her own. The Dutch carried
her trade with France, the Mediterranean world and overseas. Otherwise,
she dealt principally with Poland and Germany to the west, and with
Persia, China and the peoples of Siberia and Central Asia in the East.

Furs, though less preponderant than before, were still the chief export,
especially to Asiatic countries. Competition from North America was
affecting exports to the West, as was the great difficulty of bringing furs
to Europe now that western and central Siberia had been depleted of
pelts. Vegetable and animal products—hemp, flax, hides, tallow, honey,
wax, bristles, caviar, sealskins, sperm oil, timber, resin, pitch, tar and ash
—were, after furs, the main exports. These goods went, in the main, to
England, Holland and Germany. The main novelty among the exports in
1725 was iron, which had begun to find a market in England.

Exports eastward to China, Persia and India on the other hand, were
chiefly of European and Russian manufactured goods: soap, paper,
woollen and linen textiles, glassware, toys, etc., but here also furs were
by far the largest single item. To the Siberian tribes who supplied the

[1] *Bruce (1782), p. 104*
[2] *Perry (1716), p. 280; Klyuchevskiy (1958), vol. 4, p. 122*
[3] *Ides (1706), pp. 4-5*
[4] *Strahlenberg (1730), p. 320*

furs, Russian traders sold beads, needles, knick-knacks and, often, the prohibited but eagerly coveted firearms, swords, knives, etc.[1]

Imports from Europe continued to be of manufactured goods and metals other than copper and iron; textiles, especially English and Saxon woollen cloth; manufactured iron and steel goods and hardware, paint, paper, playing cards, glass; gold, silver, lead, tin, pewter and articles made therefrom; also fish and fruit. From China and Persia came raw silk and silk cloth, pearls, chinaware, gold, silver, ivory, teak and tobacco; and from the peoples of Central Asia, cotton goods and dates. Peter had hoped to bring all Europe's trade with the East through Russia and one motive in his Persian campaign had been to control the silk trade. For the same reason he was interested in the possibility of a north-east passage *'to receive goods this way from China and Japan, without crossing the torrid zone'.* Yet the Tsar personally doubted the existence of such a passage:

> *But he is notwithstanding of opinion that there is none; and says that he believes his country joins here to America, and that that part of the world was first peopled this way, when there was not such vast quantities of ice, and the cold had not so strongly possessed the parts near the Pole.*[2]

Russian maps of Peter's reign show that active exploration of the Bering Sea was being carried on from Anadyr *ostrog*, and that there was probably some knowledge of the opposite American coast, but whether America was joined to Asia or not was still an open question. Yet Semyon Dezhnev had sailed through the Bering Strait in 1648, and this strait had been shown on Hondius's 1659 map of Asia. This, however, was not known to Peter when, in 1725, the Danish sea captain Bering set out to discover if there was a passage between the two continents, on the Tsar's behalf.[3]

SEAPORTS

In 1725 Russia was no longer dependent upon the ice-hampered White Sea port of Archangel, but had acquired six hundred miles of Baltic sea coast with the ports of Riga, Pernau, Revel, Narva and Vyborg, to which Peter had added his own creations, Kronstadt and St Petersburg. He built the naval and commercial port of Kronstadt on Kotlin Island which guards the approach to St Petersburg, twenty miles to the east. Larger vessels are compelled to sail close to this island by shallow water to the north and by sandbanks off the southern shore of the Gulf of Finland. He had previously (1703) fortified the island with the Kronschlot fortress: *'thus the entrance to Petersburg is sufficiently guarded against every attempt of an enemy by sea'.*[4]

According to Strahlenberg, Kronstadt harbour had three serious disadvantages: the entrance was narrow and dangerous, the ice did not clear

---

[1] *Fisher (1943), p. 76*
[2] *Perry (1716), pp. 61, 70*
[3] *Efimov (1950), pp. 90-117*
[4] *Bruce (1782), p. 124*

until late in May, and the freshness of the water hastened the rotting of the ships. For these reasons, Peter had experimented with the creation of a new artificial naval port between Revel and Pernau—Rogerwyck.[1] Larger ships could not proceed to St Petersburg but unloaded at Kronstadt, whence their cargoes were taken on to the capital by smaller craft.

St Petersburg-Kronstadt had become, in remarkably short time, Russia's chief seaport and was fast growing in importance. It was used by 116 foreign ships in 1722 and 240 in 1724.[2] Although affected by ice in winter, it was not closed as long as Archangel. It has often been described as a purely artificial and even unnecessary result of Peter's caprice, yet the development of a port in this area was natural and inevitable if Russia was to have closer commercial and political relations with Europe. By canalizing portages as Peter planned, it was possible to bring Russia's waterway network to the sea at this point, which was, furthermore, closer to the heart of the country than any other place on a sea coast. Given the limitations of the Baltic Sea—ice-fringed in winter and land-locked at all seasons—the position of St Petersburg was ideal as a focus for sea routes from the West and river routes from the East. A further advantage lay in the fact that most of Russia's export staples—flax, hemp, tallow, timber—originated in this north-western part of the country.[3]

Riga, an established port, but largely isolated from its hinterland when Swedish, benefited from Russian annexation as did the other Baltic ports. It had a better natural harbour and a longer ice free period than St Petersburg-Kronstadt and, of course, a longer commercial tradition. Its hinterland was a main source of flax and hemp which moved towards it for export.

Archangel's trade was now limited to the needs of the northern provinces in order to encourage St Petersburg's development. It retained a considerable export trade in furs and timber to which Ural iron had been recently added.

In the south, the Tsar's firmer hold on the lower Volga and the shores of the Caspian was contributing to the rapid increase of trade at Astrakhan. But Azov and Taganrog, which Peter had hoped to develop as outlets to the Black Sea, were no longer in Russian hands.

[1] *Strahlenberg (1730), pp. 298-9*
[2] *Klyuchevskiy (1958), vol. 4, p. 124*
[3] *Pokshishevskiy (1956), pp. 106-12*

CHAPTER NINE
THE SOCIAL GEOGRAPHY OF RUSSIA IN 1725, AT THE END OF THE REIGN OF PETER THE GREAT

The inhabitants of the Russian Empire in 1725 numbered about 15½ million. This figure included over ½ million in the newly acquired Baltic territories and some 2 million in the western provinces won from Poland during the seventeenth century.[1]

The first 'revision' of 1719-24 reveals, when its data are mapped (fig. 33), a central axis of denser population, away from which population falls off in each direction. Yet the actual movement of population at this time was outwards from this axis in three directions: south-eastwards to the wooded steppe, eastwards beyond the Volga, and—in a more restricted sense—north-westwards to the Finnish Gulf and Peter's new town at the Neva mouth. (Fig. 34.)

Along the south-eastern borders a frontier zone, corresponding broadly to the wooded steppe vegetation belt, was being actively settled by new colonists. The region round Kursk was now as densely populated as any part of old Muscovy apart from the Moscow district itself. Many of the colonists were from this old-settled part of the country where famine, oppression and hardship were once more—as in 1600—causing flight from the centre. Many more were refugees from the Polish Ukraine. Others had come from the Baltic provinces, and *'finding their new slavery easier than their old, the earth more fruitful, and the climate more gentle, would I believe, never return back'*.[2]

The progress of settlement down the Volga was still delayed by the presence of the Kuban Tartars who:

> make frequent incursions into the outparts of Russia, plunder and fire villages, and often carry off cattle and horses and people, by reason of which there is a great tract of land on the west side of the Volga all the way between the town of Saratoff and the Caspian Sea lies wholly uninhabited, save only the islands about Atracan and the people that live within the towns of Camishinka, Czaritza and Terki where garrisons are kept.[3]

Fugitive serfs from old Muscovy had made their way eastwards across the upper Volga to the valleys of the Vyatka, the Kama, the Chusovaya and other Ural valleys, settling here among the Bashkirs. Thus Ides, when he went through these lands in 1706, found them *'perfectly well inhabited everywhere by the Russians'*.[4] These peasants had, by settling in the Ural valleys, unwittingly made easier Peter I's introduction of the iron and copper industries by providing a potential labour force.

[1] *Kabuzan (1963), pp. 159-63; Lorimer (1946), pp. 10, 204-8*
[2] *Whitworth (1758), p. 183*
[3] *Perry (1716), pp. 87-8*
[4] *Ides (1706), p. 10*

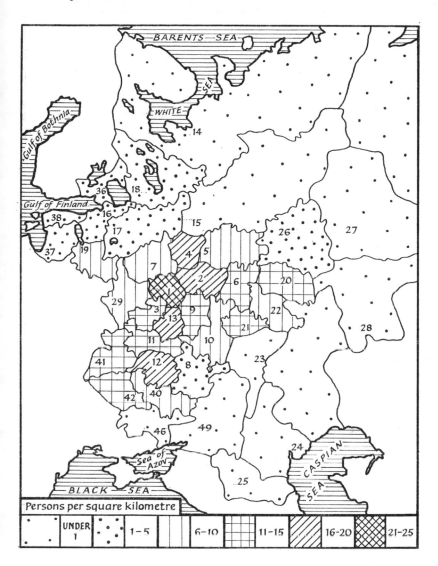

figure 33   Russia in 1725: density of population according to the 1719 Revision. For key to numbered provinces, see p. 395

Many Russians had left the central area for religious reasons. These included the *raskolniks*, who refused to accept changes of ritual introduced in the seventeenth century, as well as members of various persecuted nonconformist sects. These dissenters, like the Quakers of the West, often flourished in business. Those who had migrated north to the White Sea

figure 34   Russia in 1725: peoples, settlement and towns in southern and south-eastern Russia.

area came to dominate the fisheries there and to play an important part in mining and metallurgical enterprises such as those of Povenets.[1]

The tide of Russian peasant colonization had spilled over the Urals, and Ides followed it all the way to Tobolsk. Thence it is found intermittently right across southern Siberia in the neighbourhood of the fortress towns. The Siberian towns began as fur-trading posts and military forts situated strategically on rivers and portages, as in Canada. The posts developed into administrative centres and, with the increase of agricultural population around them, into market and commercial towns. The movement into Siberia now included—besides fur traders, Cossack garrisons, administrative officials and peasants—a stream of political, religious or criminal exiles: '*Siberia is the place whither the Czar banishes capital criminals and offenders, never to return*'.[2] The population of Siberia was now about 400,000, of whom perhaps a quarter were Russians.

[1] *Bain (1908), pp. 298-9*
[2] *Perry (1716), p. 78*

Plate 3   The Ural forests provided charcoal for the great iron industry of the region. The numerous rivers which rise in the hills facilitated transport to the works. (Atkinson & Walker, 1812.)

Plate 4   Tobolsk, founded in 1587, grew up where the Trans-Siberian road crossed the river Irtysh at its junction with the Tobol. It was Siberia's leading town throughout the seventeenth and eighteenth centuries. (Ides, 1706.)

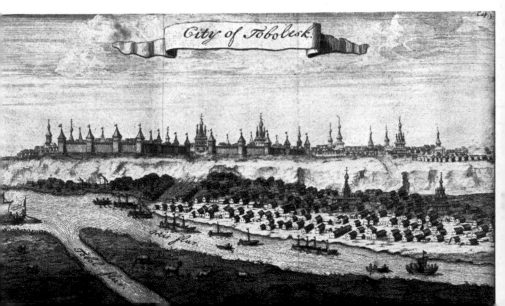

City of Tobolesk.

Plate 5   The *telega* was used for the transport of goods in summer, after the spring mud had dried up and roads were again passable. It could carry about half a ton. (Atkinson & Walker, 1812.)

Plate 6   Transport by sledge in winter was the easiest, fastest and cheapest form of transport in old Russia. It cost one third of the summer rate, and therefore, where possible, goods were stored until the winter season. (Atkinson & Walker, 1812.)

The Towns

The urban population of Russia in 1725 was only about ½ million or under 4 per cent of the total.[1] A large proportion lived in Moscow, and most of the rest in the old-established towns of the north and centre, such as Novgorod, Smolensk, Vladimir and Vologda. Most towns in the southern frontier zone were little more than garrisoned forts although some of them were growing fast as the surrounding countryside became settled.

The most remarkable feature of the urban scene was, however, Peter's new town at the head of the Gulf of Finland, still in the throes of building, but already a considerable place. Built in what until 1721 was Swedish territory, and with at first a Dutch (Pieterburkh) or German (Peterburg) name, this new capital was a planned attempt to give Russia a city comparable in style and magnificence to Paris, Vienna or London. In 1703 Peter had selected as the site of his new port and city a score of deltaic mud-flats where the Neva river enters the Finnish Gulf. He was aware that the Dutch had created Amsterdam in natural conditions hardly more propitious, and they had not possessed hordes of slaves. To build St Petersburg, serfs were fetched in thousands for pile-driving and other labour, and they died in thousands from frost, flood, hunger, disease and exhaustion. They came from all parts of the Empire and worked under the supervision of foreign architects and Russian artisans in the erection of buildings of wood, brick and stone. Work went on so fast that John Bell, after three years' absence (1715-18) found that *'the appearance of things was so changed that I could scarce imagine myself in the same place'.*[2] By 1725 there was a large and imposing town on the site, the residence of the royal family since 1710 and the seat of government since 1712. Most of the dwelling houses were as yet of rough-hewn timber, but the royal and wealthier noble families—and the Church—built in stone. Several local brick kilns and tile works had been set up, but their products did *'not last very well, and as the mortar also is poor, the newly built houses and palaces have to be repaired every two or three years'.*[3]

On the south shore of the central or Peterburg Isle was Peter's original log house, built by himself. On a small off-lying island, the hexagonal Peter-Paul Fortress raised its gloomy mass. Here the Tsar had had his son Alexis murdered, and it was now used as a prison. Rising from within it, and almost completed, was the Peter-Paul Basilica. This was to be the mausoleum of the Romanov family and Peter I was buried there. At the north-western corner of Peterburg Isle was a gunpowder factory. (Fig. 35.)

South-west of Peterburg Isle lay Vasilyevskiy Isle, distinguished by Prince Menshikov's grand palace and a *number of fine brick houses for*

[1] *Lyashchenko (1956), vol. 1, p. 396*
[2] *Bell (1763), vol. 1, p. 154*
[3] *Weber (1721), p. 223*

E

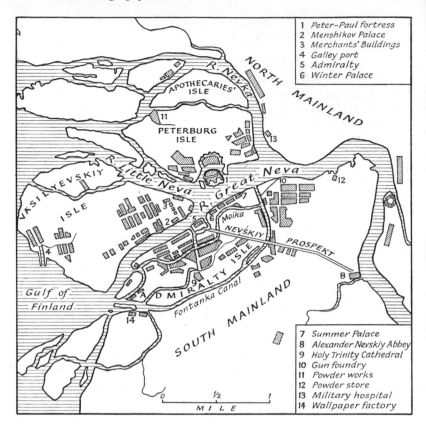

1	Peter–Paul fortress
2	Menshikov Palace
3	Merchants' Buildings
4	Galley port
5	Admiralty
6	Winter Palace
7	Summer Palace
8	Alexander Nevskiy Abbey
9	Holy Trinity Cathedral
10	Gun foundry
11	Powder works
12	Powder store
13	Military hospital
14	Wallpaper factory

figure 35   St Petersburg in 1725.

the accommodation of those belonging to his court'. Here too was

> *a large square brick building with a spacious court within, for merchants and tradesmen, where they have their shops below and store rooms above . . . the merchants all reside in this part of the town.*[1]

This was for European and Russian merchants. The '*habitations of Asiatic merchants, viz Armenians, Turks, Tartars, Chinese and Indians*', were relegated to Apothecaries' Isle (*Aptekarskiy ostrov*), north of Peterburg Isle. Foreign ambassadors' houses were also on Vasilyevskiy Isle while on its far western side was a small artificial harbour for use by the galleys of Peter's navy. A suburb of wooden houses and a wooden church stood nearby.

Opposite Vasilyevskiy and Peterburg Isles, across the Neva to the south, was Admiralty Isle, along the waterfront of which were Peter's great naval arsenal, dockyard and wharves. '*The people employed in shipbuilding are all quartered here, as also the officers and sailors belonging to the fleet*'. On the

[1] *Bruce (1782), pp. 116-18*

Neva waterfront immediately above (north-east of) the Admiralty, was the Tsar's winter palace, also the influential Admiral Apraxin's mansion. Peter's summer palace was at the eastern extremity of the island and set in gardens *'full of waterworks, Italian statues, covered walks and arbours'*. About the Admiralty was the foreign settlement, *'where all European foreigners live and have several Protestant and Roman Catholic meeting houses'*.[1]

The naval area was protected by a moat, the Moyka Canal. Other canals threaded the island, reminding foreigners of Amsterdam. As these were as yet without bridges, numerous ferries connected the various parts of Admiralty Isle with each other as well as with the other islands and the mainland. Admiralty Isle was separated by the Fontanka canal from the south mainland bank of the Neva, where a gun foundry and powder store were sited. On the opposite or Vyborg bank of the river, a large military hospital had been built.

St Petersburg was, unlike most contemporary towns, endowed with a plan, the main features of which were the two wide avenues, Nevskiy Prospekt and Voznesenskiy Prospekt, which radiated out from the Admiralty, crossing streets which ran parallel to the canals. At the end of each avenue, beyond the Fontanka Canal, two noteworthy buildings were rising: Nevskiy Prospekt led to Alexander Nevskiy Abbey, Voznesenskiy (now Mayorova) Prospekt to the Cathedral of Holy Trinity (*Troitskiy Sobor*).

By 1725 the courtiers and noble families who had been required to live in the new town had doubtless to some extent reconciled themselves to its many disadvantages, the chief of which seems to have been the very high cost of provisions. Little food could be grown in the area and it had therefore to be brought from afar. Perry summed up the reasons for the nobility's dislike of St Petersburg:

> *all manner of provisions are usually three or four times as dear, and forage for their horses, etc. at least six or eight times as dear as it is at Moscow; which happens from the small quantity which the country thereabouts produces, being more than two thirds woods and bogs . . . Peterburgh, which lies in the latitude of sixty degrees and fifteen minutes north, is too cold to produce these things. Besides, Moscow is the native place which the Russes are fond of, and where they have their friends and acquaintance about them; their villages are near, and their provisions come easy and cheap to them, which is brought by their slaves . . .*
>
> *. . . and though they seemingly compliment the Czar whenever he talks to them of the beauties and delights of Petersburgh; yet when they get together by themselves, they complain and say that there are tears and water enough at Petersburgh, but they pray to God to send them to live again at Moscow.*[2]

[1] *Bruce (1782), pp. 118-19*
[2] *Perry (1716), pp. 262-3*

The general plan of Moscow in 1725 was as described for 1600. There were in the inner Kremlin and Kitaygorod, surrounded by the White City (*Belygorod*) and the Earthen Town. Changes had taken place within these divisions, however. Many churches, bell towers and palace apartments had been built, extended or restored in the Kremlin, and the elegant Tsar's Tower had been added (1680) to the Kremlin Wall. There were a few wooden buildings left in the Kitaygorod, which now contained, besides new and improved mercantile buildings, a printing house (1694), the Mint, a library and an academy. This was Russia's first college, where Slavic, Greek and Latin studies were pursued and where Lomonosov, Russia's distinguished eighteenth-century scholar, was later to work. It was opposite the thirteenth-century Bogozhavlensky monastery and near the Printing house. The simply designed Church of Our Lady of Vladimir (1694) was another addition to the buildings of the Kitaygorod.

The Belygorod had not yet recovered from the great fire of 1712 which left whole districts derelict. But some of Peter's new industries had been set up here and the most notable building was the palace of Peter's favourite, Menshikov. The recurrent fires created a great demand for new houses which were prefabricated in the Earthen Town (*Zemlyanoygorod*): '*Here one may buy a wooden house of any dimensions, have it carried to the place where it is to stand, set up and ready to dwell in, the third day after the purchase*'.[1]

Outside the old town, the German suburb had grown up into a large and populous community inhabited chiefly by Dutch, Germans, English and Scottish. It was '*pleasantly situated on the river Neglinka on the banks of which are a number of pleasure houses with fine gardens*'.[2] It was served by four Protestant churches and one Roman Catholic. Many large nobles' residences were also found outside the town as well as new industrial establishments.

Most visitors were impressed when seeing the city from a distance, but disgusted by the squalor and stench of the unsanitary streets revealed by a closer view. As Perry put it:

> *When any traveller comes within a fair view of the city, the numerous churches, the monasteries, and noblemen's and gentlemen's houses, the steeples, cupolas and crosses at the tops of the churches, which are gilded and painted over, makes the city look to be one of the most rich and beautiful in the world . . . but upon a nearer view, you find yourself deceived and disappointed.*[3]

It is doubtful whether Moscow was very much larger or more populous in 1725 than in 1600, owing to the creation of St Petersburg and the enforced removal thither of many noble families with their vast retinues: '*this metropolis, once the pleasantest and most agreeable city in all Russia, became*

[1] *Bruce (1782), pp. 80-1*
[2] *Bruce (1782), p. 81*
[3] *Perry (1716), p. 263*

quite deserted, none remaining in it but the vulgar'.[1] The population was about 150,000.[2]

The northern towns of the Dvina route were losing their prosperity owing to the rise of St Petersburg, the restrictions on Archangel's commerce, and the decline of the fur trade. Those most affected, besides Archangel, were Kholmorgory, Solvychegodsk, Ustyug and Vologda. But the metallurgical activity of the Urals had brought new life to the old salt-working town of Solikamsk (*'a very fine large and rich city, where several very rich and considerable merchants reside'*[3]) and had resulted in the creation of the new town of Yekaterinburg. Although not founded until 1723, Yekaterinburg (now Sverdlovsk) was already a fortress to dominate the Bashkirs, the administrative centre of the Ural mining, smelting and manufacturing region, and an important iron-working town. It occupied a strategic position on the then southernmost trans-Ural route at the eastern end of the portage between the Chusovaya, coming up from the Kama and Volga, and the Iset, descending to the Tobol. (Fig. 32.)

The ancient city of Novgorod had now shrunk to a collection of wooden hovels within the old walls, beyond which it had formerly extended for many miles. A disastrous fire about the year 1695 had destroyed the town, but traces of its former extent were still visible along with some stone buildings which had survived the flames.[4]

Nizhniy Novgorod and Kazan, two great cities on the middle Volga, had benefited enormously from the progress of Siberian and Uralian enterprises, and from the growth of Volga traffic. The river had now been made more secure with garrison towns all the way to Astrakhan and the Caspian Sea, and had been linked by a continuous navigable waterway with St Petersburg and the Baltic. Both towns were the meeting places of European and Russian manufactures from the West and Asiatic produce from the East. Near Nizhniy Novgorod, at Makaryev, was held the famous annual fair, the greatest in the Russian Empire. These two towns were probably next after Moscow and St Petersburg in wealth.

The size, activity and commerce of Astrakhan made an even stronger impression on travellers. The town stood on a deltaic island in the Volga mouth at the opposite end to St Petersburg of that great waterway axis that now ran across Russia from the Baltic to the Caspian. It was the great centre for trade between Russia and Central Asia, Persia, India and China. It was *'of a considerable bigness'* and *'the site of an immense trade'*, and its suburbs spread out from the original fortified island to the surrounding country.[5] It abounded with merchants of many nationalities and, according to Strahlenberg, thirty languages were spoken there.[6]

[1] *Bruce (1782), p. 100*
[2] *Marsden (1942), p. 142*
[3] *Ides (1706), p. 5*
[4] *Weber (1721), p. 127*
[5] *Bruce (1782), p. 246*
[6] *Strahlenberg (1730), p. 320*

The most numerous group were the Armenians who had '*one of the suburbs of this city allotted for their residence, and carry on a great trade from hence into Persia*'.[1] The Tartars also had a suburb apart. '*built with earth only, and clay hardened by the sun, where they reside during the winter season; but when it is summer time, they live in the open country*'. As a reminder to them of Russian power there were, in their part of the town, '*an abundance of gibbets erected . . . on each of which hung no less than six Cossacks, perfectly naked.*' The Indians were '*obliged to transact their affairs in their caravanserai*', which was '*modern, large and surrounded by a square stone wall*'.[2]

The town was noted for its markets, one for each commodity. The fish market was '*full twice every day . . . and the Volga yields such a profusion of them, that what they have not for sale is given to the hogs,*' Besides the commodity markets there was the Tartar bazaar, '*where the Armenians as well as the Russians have the privilege of exposing their respective merchandise to open sale*'.[3] Also some forty or fifty Armenian families kept large shops.

The military function was still an essential one at this Caspian outpost of the Russian Empire. The town was fortified with a strong wall which had ten gates. There was a garrison of 3,500 men, and the largest of all the suburbs, lying to the east, was inhabited by soldiers. Except for one church, the buildings were all of wood, even the governor's palace. The surrounding countryside was enriched by gardens, orchards and vineyards which depended on irrigation:

> they frequently sink pits in their gardens, and furnish them with water by subterraneous pipes. And from these pits they draw up what water is from time to time wanted with a large wheel, whereto proper buckets are fastened, which throw it into wooden gutters, or spouts, from whence it is distributed.[4]

With the spread of settlement southwards there had also been marked urban development in the wooded steppe. The soils were not yet producing much grain, but livestock farming—horses, cattle and swine—was bringing prosperity to the countryside, and some of the frontier towns began to lose their exclusively military look, notably Kharkov, Belgorod and Voronezh. The last-named town had scarcely a hundred wooden huts before Peter I brought in the boat-building industry; now:

> Within the city there is a remarkably long ropewalk; and without the wall there are several magazines or storehouses for their powder . . . the inhabitants are principally employed as ship's carpenters or in other professions of a similar nature.[5]

Kharkhov had become a livestock market centre and its fairs were achieving wide fame.[6] But three quarters of the population of Kiev—still a

[1] *Bruce (1782), p. 252*
[2] *Le Brun (1759), pp. 130-3*
[3] *Le Brun (1759), p. 130*
[4] *Le Brun (1759), p. 133*
[5] *Le Brun (1759), p. 92*
[6] *Mirsky (1931), p. 192*

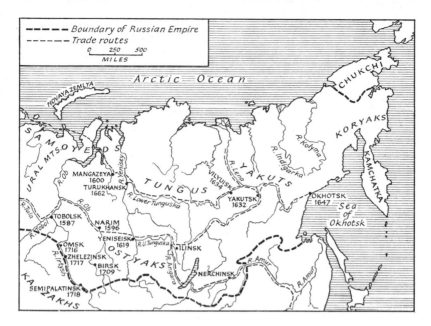

figure 36   Siberia in 1725.

frontier town—were military.[1] On the other hand, Bryansk, farther north, at a crossing point on the Desna, which had ceased to be a frontier town with the territorial gains of the 1667 treaty of Andrusov, had also developed a prominent livestock market and fair and benefited from expanding trade with Poland and Germany. Like Voronezh, it too had gained a boat-building industry during Peter's reign.

Several Siberian fur-trading and military posts had grown into towns since 1600. Tobolsk, administrative and ecclesiastical capital of Siberia, was the largest. It had developed at the intersection of one of the main east-west trans-Siberian routes with the north-south Irtysh-Ob waterway, at the junction of the Tobol and Irtysh rivers. In the seventeenth century it had been the principal fur-trading centre east of the Urals. That function had now been yielded to towns farther east. In 1725 it was a general trade centre, attracting merchants from Central Asia in particular. It was also a market town for the extensive agricultural area that had grown up around it. Its Russian inhabitants—soldiers, officials, traders—lived mostly upon the hill beneath which, by the river, dwelt the remains of the ancient inhabitants of these parts'.[2] (Plate 4.)

Farther east, where the same trans-Siberian route crosses the Yenisey, was the town of Yeniseisk, an outfitting centre for fur-trading expeditions and for intending settlers from Russia. Still farther east, and on the same

[1] *Clarkson (1962), p. 244*
[2] *Bell (1763), vol. 1, p. 185*

route, was Ilinsk, on the portage between the Angara and the upper Lena. According to Ides it was a large town, most of whose inhabitants were Russians who went sable-hunting in winter and did a little farming in summer. Five hundred miles south-east of Ilinsk was Nerchinsk in the Amur basin. Nerchinsk had become the point of departure for caravans to China, following upon the 1689 treaty with that country. Russian Cossack farmers had settled the surrounding district. Yakutsk was now the chief fur-collecting centre of Siberia and its eastward position on the Lena showed how rapidly depletion had swept through western and central Siberia. Ides found it provided with strong fortifications, outside of which were suburbs with Russian farming villages around.[1]

Peoples of the Russian Empire

THE RUSSIANS

The Great Russians were by far the most numerous of the Tsar's subjects, and although the ruling class was drawn from them, this distinction meant little to the mass of the people, who remained poor, ignorant and oppressed. The enormous cost in lives, money and goods, not to mention labour, of Peter's military operations, of his mines and factories, of his new capital city, and of his ports, canals and roads, came from the toil of the peasants. Not only had a poll tax been instituted from which other classes were exempt, but new taxes were imposed on necessities of all kinds as well as luxuries. Monopolies on the sale of such goods as coffins, pitch, potash, salt, tar, tobacco, vodka, were farmed out to greedy exploiters.[2] For $4\frac{1}{2}$ million peasants serfdom was degenerating into slavery. In practice, if not in law, they had lost their remaining rights and were at the mercy of their masters. On top of all this, they had to suffer the unrestrained depredations of Peter's army which lived upon the defenceless countryside:

> *The military detachments whose job it was to collect the taxes were more ruinous than the taxes themselves. The collection was made three times a year and each expedition lasted two months: for six months of the year, the villages and hamlets lived in panic-stricken terror of the armed collectors who maintained themselves at the expense of the inhabitants in the midst of tortures and executions. One could not say that the Tartars, in the time of Batu, behaved worse to conquered Russia.*[3]

The 'serving class', those upstarts who already in 1600 had benefited largely from Ivan IV's confiscation of the boyars' lands, had seen their importance greatly increased under Peter; they formed the basis of the new nobility who held their rank in return for service to the state. Their lower and middle orders, apart from the occasional military service which

[1] *Ides (1706), p. 35*
[2] *Klyuchevskiy (1958), vol. 4, p. 131*
[3] *Klyuchevskiy (1958), vol. 4, p. 98*

they performed, also engaged in trade and industry; they were the principal class from which the merchants and industrialists were drawn. In Siberia they were able to combine military or administrative duties with fur trading. Their existence prevented the growth of a real middle class as an independent economic and political force in Russia.

WESTERN PEOPLES

The inhabitants are chiefly those called Muscovites; the rest swell the bulk, but add little to the strength of the country; the Laplanders and Samoyedes being too heavy and dispirited; the several nations of Tartars too wild, and the Cossacks too full of freedom and privilege to be of any great advantage.[1]

The above statement (1710), while pertinent to Russia's eastern dominions, takes no account of those European peoples—usually more advanced than the Great Russians—who had recently become the Tsar's subjects. These included the Ukrainians or Little Russians, who had become sharply differentiated from the Great Russians or Muscovites as a result of centuries of Polish rule and of living in a distinct geographical environment. They had not been isolated from the West, nor had they been subjected to Mongol influence, and their higher culture was exemplified in their Church, in their national poetry and puppetry, and in their music. Ukrainian clergy were increasingly recruited into the Russian Church where they exerted great influence, modifying the stagnant Muscovite orthodoxy with western ideas and after western models.[2]

The White Russians were worse off than the Ukrainians in almost every way. They occupied poorer lands under cloudier skies; most of their territory was still under Polish rule and they were being subjected to an intensive Polonization at a time when many Ukrainians were escaping from it. With all land held by the Polish and Lithuanian gentry, and commerce monopolized by the Jews, they were a people of serfs living in poverty.

The newly acquired Baltic provinces were left in the hands of the German squires and merchants who had dominated the country since the Middle Ages. They were not incorporated into Russia nor, according to some authorities, were lands in them granted to Russians.[3] But a contemporary German who had travelled through the area wrote that Peter *had brought from Russia into Ingria a large number of prosperous peasants, with their families, and given them productive lands in this country, which had been laid waste by war and disease.*[4]

The native Estonians and Letts, working as peasant serfs on large estates, had borne the brunt of the military campaigns that had devastated the Baltic territories during the Swedish war.

[1] *Whitworth (1758), pp. 174-5*
[2] *Mirsky (1931), pp. 177, 232*
[3] *Sumner (1950), p. 119*
[4] *Weber (1721), p. 31*

E*

TARTARS

Immediately east and south-east of the Great Russians, along and beyond the middle and lower Volga, were various peoples all of whom were loosely known as Tartars. The Kazan Tartars, eastwards from the middle Volga, were the *'most civilized of all the Tartars'*, having been by now entirely Russianized.[1] The Ural Tartars, most of whom were Bashkirs in the south, inhabited *'quadrangular wooden rooms, like those of the Russians'* and lived by hunting. To the west of the lower Volga were the Kuban Tartars, *'who are a very strong-bodied well-proportioned people'*. They made the country between the Black and Caspian Seas uninhabitable because of their plundering raids.[2]

Eastwards from the lower Volga were the Kalmyks, *'generally of a swarthy complexion, black hair, low noses and broad cheeks, with little or no beard'*. They moved *'northward and southward, according to the seasons of the year, with their flocks, their herds and their wives and families'*.[3] Their portable tents were *'composed of laths, which are three or four inches in breadth, and are covered over with nothing but a felt or hair cloth . . . When they change their situation, they throw their tents into waggons'*.[4] Their women folk were engaged in weaving cotton cloth which they sold in Astrakhan.

Beyond the Bashkirs were the Central Asian Tartars. To their north, along the southern margins of Siberia, were the Siberian Tartars, prominent among whom were the Ostyaks. Within reach of the Russian posts they had *'learned to dwell in houses, to till the ground, and pay the Czar an annual tribute of furs'*, but *'the other Tartars, who continue to range about with their tents, do not acknowledge the Czar's sovereignty'*.[5]

COSSACKS

The Cossacks, still an independent force in 1600, had, by 1725, after the failure of various revolts, notably that of Stenka Razin, lost their autonomy and had been forced to enter the service of the Tsar. Those of the Dnieper were resettled in the Terek region, north of the Caucasus, and others went to the Ural river. The Cossacks retained many valuable privileges, including exemption from taxation and remained distinct from the rest of the population. The tsars used them in frontier wars and for garrisons. Of the Ukrainian or Dnieper Cossacks, Whitworth wrote: *'they drive a great trade in hemp, potash, wax, corn and cattle; they live in much ease and plenty'*.[6] The Don Cossacks *'sow little corn . . . nor do they eat much bread, roots or herbs; their chief diet being fish, flesh and fruits; their riches consist in*

[1] *Bruce (1782), p. 234*
[2] *Perry (1716), p. 87*
[3] *Perry (1716), p. 83*
[4] *Le Brun (1759), p. 135*
[5] *Whitworth (1758), pp. 175-6*
[6] *Whitworth (1758), p. 180*

cattle, horses, dromedaries and camels'.[1] Those settled father east, along the Ural river, lived by fishing *'when not at war'*, and sent *'annually large amounts of caviar and sturgeon to Moscow and other towns for sale'.*[2]

SIBERIAN PEOPLES

The two principal Siberian tribes with whom the Russians were now in contact were the Samoyeds in the north-west and the Yakuts in the east. The Samoyeds lived in the tundra by the White Sea, on both sides of the Ob estuary and on Novaya Zemlya. They were *'a people of a strong swarthy countenance, full cheek bones and short noses;' 'their stature is low, their figure very disagreeable, their apprehension and understanding scarce above that of brutes'.*[3] They lived by hunting and fishing and paid tribute to the Russians in furs. As these were now becoming hard to get, they had increasingly to substitute sealskins; the seal hunt took place in March and April. Their use of dogs and their dependence on reindeer were now familiar facts. Perry remarked how well adapted these animals were to their habitat along the zone of transition between the tayga and the tundra: they *'feed upon a kind of moss that is upon the ground and on the trees in the woods';* they have a *'broad thin flat hoof, which spreads so much that they run over the frozen snow without sinking in to it'.*[4] The natives depended on the reindeer for food and transport, and also for clothing:

> *Their skins are a very thick warm fur with which they clothe and defend themselves from the severity of the winter. Their shirts are made of the skins of young deer. . . . Their coat and cap (fur within and without) is made all of a piece so that the snow cannot blow in at their necks; and a flap is made to button down upon their face upon occasion, with holes only for their eyes and their nose . . . when the weather is severe.*[5]

And *'the thread which they generally use is made of the sinews'.* The way of life of those living within reach of Archangel had been more affected by contact with the Russians:

> *we found them all in general very busy making of oars and bowls for throwing water out of boats, as also little chains and other trifles . . . which they sell in the streets of the city and amongst the sailors.*[6]

Although they could not practise agriculture in their climate, *'some few of them that live near the borders of Archangel, purchase some small matter of corn of the Russes, of whom they have learned to eat bread'.*[7]

The Yakuts inhabited the tayga forest of the Lena basin and it was in their territories that the Russian fur traders were now most active. They

[1] *Whitworth (1758), p. 178*
[2] *Strahlenberg (1730), p. 345*
[3] *Whitworth (1758), p. 175*
[4] *Perry (1716), pp. 64-5*
[5] *Perry (1716), pp. 65-6*
[6] *Le Brun (1759), pp. 8-9*
[7] *Perry (1716), p. 64*

likewise did not farm, but hunted and fished; they procured a kind of meal from the inner bark of young pine trees. They were nomadic in summer, when they lived in tents made of birch bark, but their winter abode was in log huts. They were very fond of tobacco, which the Russians brought from China and traded for furs.[1]

The Tsar and his People: the Human Resource

Peter, by the end of his reign, had brought unbridled despotism to a high pitch. He not only harnessed the nobility and subordinated the Church, but he destroyed the arrogant power of the *streltsy*. The great changes he had brought about in the economic and social geography of the country were made possible by his possession of this unchecked absolute power.

Whatever opportunities the seas, rivers, forests, soils, mines and factories may offer, the human resource—the character and skills of the inhabitants—remains the determining factor in a country's prosperity. In using this resource Peter relied upon foreigners for the skill, and on compulsion for all else. *'Was it not all accomplished by force?'* Peter himself exclaimed in 1723.[2]

He did attempt to lessen the dependence on foreigners by enforcing a limited education upon the upper and 'serving' classes, and by sending some Russians to Europe, but the reliance on force was complete. The English engineer Perry failed to persuade the Russian leaders that wages and incentives would produce better work and bring forth unsuspected talent:

> *If it be known in a country town or place where a man lives that he is ingenious, he gets no rest but is constantly sent for and employed either by the governor or petty officers under him, or by the gentlemen of the country, whose slaves they are, without being able to call their time their own, or having any suitable encouragement to themselves; but in the place thereof, if they do not please, or murmur . . . they often get stripes for their labour . . .*
>
> *And therefore, this being the custom of Russia, when I have made my utmost application for the encouragement of some few persons who have been really ingenious, that they might have but a copeck a day reward allowed them to animate the rest. I have received for answer, particularly from my lord Apraxin . . . that there was no such precedent for the giving of money out of the Czar's treasure for men to do their duty for which they were sent; but in the place of it they had battoags that grew in Russia, and if they did not do their work when required, they must be beaten to it.*[3]

[1] *Strahlenberg (1730), pp. 375-8*
[2] *Klyuchevskiy, vol 4, p. 110*
[3] *Perry (1716), pp. 257-60*

Military Geography

By no means all the territory shown on fig. 34 as belonging to the Russian Empire in 1725 was securely held, and frontier peoples, both within and without its boundaries, were not yet pacified. Consequently a frontier zone of garrison towns from Kiev in the west and curving round to the Volga at Simbirsk and Samara was still mainly military in character. So were the lower Volga towns. At Penza, *'a very large place in which the fortress is surrounded by a wooden wall'*, the inhabitants were *'soldiers . . . kept there to defend the country against the [Kuban] Tartars'.*[1] Samara had a *'garrison of regular troops and cossacks'* while Saratov was *'garrisoned by a great number of Russian soldiers and cossacks who are put here as a guard against the incursions of the Kalmuck Tartars'.* Kamyshin was *'a well fortified town . . . and has a numerous garrison of soldiers and Cossacks'.*[2]

These towns formed part of defensive lines constructed during the seventeenth century. The latest and southernmost line was built by Peter and ran eastwards from Pavlovsk on the Don to Tsaritsyn on the Volga. The projected but abandoned Volga-Don canal was to have been part of this line, *'a defensive moat against the Tartars'.*[3]

The territory in southern Siberia, newly acquired in the teeth of Ostyak Tartar opposition was held down by forts along the upper Irtysh, upper Ob and upper Yenisey rivers: Minusinsk (1707), Biysk (1709), Omsk (1716), Zhelezinsk (1717), Semipalatinsk (1718). And in the Far East and North East, the Chukhotsk peninsula and Kamchatka were not wholly tamed, although some forts had been established on them. (Fig. 36.)

[1] *Strahlenberg (1730), p. 186*
[2] *Bruce (1782), pp. 238-43*
[3] *Perry (1716), p. 89*

CHAPTER TEN
RUSSIA FROM 1725 TO 1815

After Peter I, the traditional hostility between Russia and her neighbours—Sweden, Poland and Turkey—continued. But there was now an additional aspect to Russian foreign policy. The Empire now played its part in the European system of alliances and counter-alliances. This change was reflected in the marriages made by Russian royal princes: previously they had married Russians; during the eighteenth and nineteenth centuries they all married foreigners—almost always Germans. Further, whereas on Peter's accession Russia had no ambassadors abroad (except in Poland), at the end of his reign Russian representatives were found in almost all the courts of Europe.[1]

As France had long been the ally of all three of Russia's chief enemies, Russia normally found herself in alliance with Austria against France. The emergence of Prussia, challenging at once the pretensions of France on the Rhine and of Austria in Germany, forced these two inveterate enemies together for a time, and Russia temporarily joined this anti-Prussian grouping. But, although Prussian aspirations in the Baltic area conflicted with Russian interest there, ties between the Russian court and the German princely families, many of whom were coming under Prussian influence, militated against any sustained Russian opposition to Prussia. Britain was usually on the same side as Russia, partly because of the close commercial relations between the two states and partly because Britain also sought to contain French ambitions; but as time went on, a division of interest between Britain and Russia developed, particularly in the Near East.

Although Peter I had succeeded in seizing Sweden's territories on the south shores of the Baltic, warfare between the two countries continued, mainly because Sweden was prepared to accept French or Turkish subsidies in return for intervention in Russia. Also, Russia wished to put a greater distance between her new capital, St Petersburg, and the frontier, and this could only be done at the expense of Swedish Finland. At the Peace of Abo in 1743, after war with Sweden, Russia added to her territory north of the Finnish Gulf, pushing the Swedish border back seventy miles. But this did not prevent a serious Swedish threat to St Petersburg during another war in 1790. Eventually, at Tilsit in 1807, Napoleon gave Russia a free hand against Sweden, and Finland was conquered in 1809. Russian possession of Finland as an autonomous Grand Duchy was confirmed by the Congress of Vienna in 1815, Sweden being recompensed with Norway which was taken from Denmark. (Fig. 37.)

Russia's position on the Baltic had been secured in Peter I's reign, but she was still on the defensive in the south, where the Turkish and Tartar-held steppes separated her from the Black Sea. Peter I planned

[1] *Sumner (1950), p. 188*

figure 37   Russian territorial gains, 1762-1825.

defensive lines against the Turks between the Dnieper and the Donets rivers and the fortification of these lines continued until 1738. Hitherto, such was the strength of the Ottoman Empire that serious Russian operations against it had not been possible. By the second half of the eighteenth century, however, Russia's position had improved: she had less to fear from Sweden and Poland and could concentrate more on Turkey; her war industries and population had greatly increased; she was now able to cooperate closely with Austria; and her generals had learned to master the peculiar conditions of steppe warfare. Two wars, characterized by inhuman ferocity and immense slaughter (1768-74 and 1787-92) gave Russia the Black Sea steppes and the Crimea so that, at long last, Russian superiority was established from the shores of the Baltic Sea to those of the Black, that is over the whole of the Russian lowland. A north-south political unit had, by force of Russian muscle and metal, both forged in the forested regions, been stamped across the east-west geographical zones of forest and steppe. Napoleon at Tilsit (1807) sanctioned further Russian moves against Turkey also and in 1812 Bessarabia was annexed. (Fig. 37.)

Russia's triumph over the Turks brought more than territorial aggrandizement. It gave her naval command of the Black Sea and freedom to enter the Mediterranean through the Dardanelles. It taught the Christian subjects of the Turk to look to Russia for succour and protection. But it also attracted the suspicions of Britain, who now took France's place as chief western backer of the Turk; and it meant the eventual end of the Austrian alliance since the Austrian Empire regarded Turkish Europe as its own sphere for influence and expansion.

Russia's quarrel with Sweden and Turkey had arisen from their possession of the Baltic and Black Sea littorals, thus standing between Russia and her natural limits. The quarrel with Poland was different, originating in Polish and Lithuanian acquisition of Russian territory in the past and embittered by almost continual invasion and counter-invasion ever since.

Poland's history has been dominated by the fact that she possesses no natural geographical boundaries. The Polish heartland developed in the valley of the Vistula; from this centre, Poles spread in all directions, unimpeded by physical barriers; in periods of military strength, the expansion of Polish settlement had been particularly vigorous. But in the absence of clear bounds, Germans and Russians had also expanded towards the Polish heartland from either side. Thus Poland, when she had the strength to assert her claims, could establish a large state and justify it on the grounds that she was extending her frontiers to include the farthest Poles (or Lithuanians). But a weak Poland had to contend with the counterclaims of Prussia, Austria and Russia to extend their frontiers to include the farthest Germans or Russians. This would leave a very small Poland indeed.

Poland, ruled by a selfish and purblind gentry class and cursed with a system of elective monarchy which invited foreign intervention each time the throne became vacant, sank rapidly, during the eighteenth century, into helplessness. Surrounded by autocratic regimes with powerful armies, and without any natural defences, the country was doomed. In 1764, a Russian army, invited by one faction, entered the country. Russia, who now dominated Poland, was reluctant to partition the country, but Prussia, determined to seize West Prussia, forced the issue; in 1772, Austria, Prussia and Russia annexed the outer parts of Poland. Russia obtained about 40,000 square miles. The second partition (1793) gave Russia another 100,000 square miles of Polish territory. When, in 1795, Poland was totally dismembered, Russia obtained yet another 45,000 square miles. Although Russia finished with by far the larger part of the original

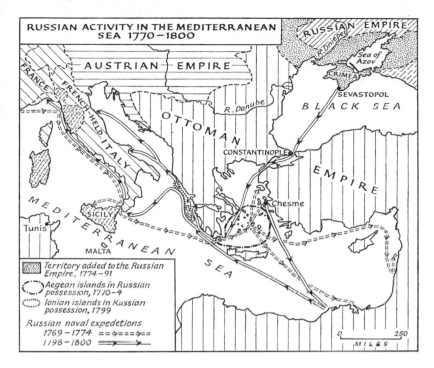

figure 38   Russian activity in the Mediterranean Sea, 1770-1800.

Polish state, most of this territory had been part of ancient Russia and many of the population spoke Russian and were Orthodox in religion. The whole Dnieper basin was once more Russian. But much of the land gained was ill-drained and infertile, particularly to the north, and brought little real wealth to the Russian state. (Fig. 37.)

Napoleon's Grand Duchy of Warsaw, constituted from those parts of Poland seized by Prussia and Austria at the three partitions, fell into Russian hands after Napoleon's retreat from Moscow (1812). The Congress of Vienna (1815) agreed to the Russian Emperor becoming king of a reconstituted Polish kingdom. Thus Polish weakness and the French collapse, together with Russia's immense strength, had brought the Russian frontier six hundred miles westward.

It is remarkable how well the Russians took to the sea as soon as they had secured access to it. At the same time that he founded St Petersburg (1703), Peter I began the construction of the naval base at Kronstadt at the head of the Gulf of Finland. In 1769 a Russian fleet left this Baltic base and made its way to the eastern Mediterranean where it scattered a larger Turkish fleet off Chesme (1770) and later destroyed it. For a time the Russians controlled these waters and captured several of the Aegean islands which were returned to Turkey at the peace of 1774. (Fig. 38.)

No sooner had the Crimea been won than a Black Sea fleet was built with a new base at Sevastopol. This fleet took command of the Black Sea after sinking the Turkish fleet at the mouth of the Dnieper in 1788. Eleven years later the Russian Black Sea fleet sailed through the Straits and seized the Ionian Islands from the French; Tsar Paul accepted the Grand Mastership from the Knights of Malta. These achievements in the Mediterranean aroused British hostility and later Alexander I yielded his position in the Mediterranean to Great Britain.

The tour made by Tsar Peter at the end of the seventeenth century in Europe had not only given rise to much curiosity, but also to a certain alarm lest such uncouth Russian visitors might, at a later date, return in larger numbers, armed, and with hostile intent. By the end of the eighteenth century, Russian soldiers had overwhelmed two European capitals— Warsaw and Berlin—leaving a lasting terror behind them, and in 1814 they were to enter Paris triumphantly. They had appeared in northern Italy, chasing out the French; they had won naval victories in the Mediterranean; and they had even planned an overland expedition to India. Alongside the admiration felt for their achievements, there was growing uneasiness lest this new force in European power politics should get out of control.

Another aspect of the Russian territorial gains of the eighteenth century was that they placed under Great Russian dominion large numbers of people of a different nationality. The Little Russians or Ukrainians and the White Russians had been too long under alien rule to assimilate easily to the customs and institutions of Moscow; the Lithuanians, Jews, Estonians, Latvians, Finns and Poles considered themselves as more advanced culturally than the Russians whom they regarded as semi-barbarous.

Compared with the preceding and succeeding centuries, the eighteenth century saw little territorial expansion of the Empire other than in the west. The hold on the Chukchi and Kamchatka peninsulas was con-solidated, and there was a slight southward movement of the Siberian boundary. Russian fur-traders having crossed the Bering Strait, Russia was now established in the North American continent, not only in Alaska, but with trading posts along the Pacific coast as far south as northern California where Fort Ross was built in 1812.

The main advance was in the Caucasus, at the very end of the century. Here the Russians were able to benefit from national and religious antagonisms in an area where Turkish and Persian influences had hitherto been the strongest. The Christian kingdom of Georgia had asked for the Tsar's help in 1586 against surrounding hostile Moslems, but this was a distant and difficult environment into which to extend the Russian arm. Now, two hundred years later, further pleas for aid were received, this time to be met with military expeditions which defeated the Persians in 1783 and 1795, and which were followed by the annexation of the country: eastern Georgia in 1801 and the western part in 1804 and 1810. In the ensuing Persian (1804-13) and Turkish (1806-12) wars, the Russians were again victorious and their possession of Georgia was confirmed. (Fig. 37.)

Not only did Russia continue throughout the eighteenth century to form part of the European system of military alliances and counter-alliances, but she continued to undergo rapid westernization. In almost every aspect of culture the Russian nobility became Europeanized and increasingly Gallicized, a process accelerated towards the end of the century by the French Revolution and the consequent availability of numerous French aristocratic exiles as tutors for their Russian imitators.

> *There was a veritable flood of savants, scholars, engineers, technicians of all kinds, architects, painters, musicians, singers, dancers, specialists in both the military and the culinary arts, tutors and governesses, adventurers, courtesans, and valets de chambre from whom lessons could be had in how to behave and even how to write. The Academies, the universities, the schools, the principal manufactures and all the departments of state were, at first, so many western colonies called in to act as nurseries for the new Russia.*[1]

This process went on despite constant changes in the attitude of government. Under Peter I contacts with Europe had reached unprecedented proportions, but for the few months during which his grandson, Peter II (1727-30), was in the hands of the reactionary Dolgorukis, the Court returned to Moscow and turned its back on the West. During the ten years of Anne's reign (1730-40), Germans ruled Russia, but their hated influence came to an end with the reign of Elizabeth, Peter's daughter (1741-62). She, unlike all other Russian autocrats after Peter, was the all-Russian daughter of Russian parents and she ruled through Russians. Yet she herself was permeated by the powerful influence of French culture. Her successor—after the brief interval of Peter III (1762)—was Catherine II (1762-96) who, though a German, continued to rule through Russians and to speed the Frenchifying of the upper classes. But her son Paul I (1796-1801) tried to halt it. Edicts were issued against wearing French fashions; foreign travel and residence abroad were forbidden. Clarke wrote (1800):

> *When we returned to Moscow we found the inhabitants murmuring in consequence of new prohibitions. An ukase had appeared, which forbade the importation of any kind of foreign literature; and under this head were included maps, music and whatever might be construed a medium of science.*[2]

Paul's son Alexander (1801-25) opened Russia once more to western influence, although according to his words to Sir Thomas Wilson, he was not too happy with the gallicization of his country under his predecessors:

> *I am to be pitied, for I have few about me who have any sound education or fixed principles: my grandmother's court vitiated the whole education of the Empire, confining it to the acquisition of the French language,*

[1] *Weidlé (1949), p. 78*
[2] *Clarke (1810), vol. 1, p. 99*

French frivolities and vices, particularly gaming. I have little, therefore, on which I can rely firmly.[1]

As westernization was confined to the gentry, and as the vast majority of the population continued to live according to their native customs, an unbridgeable gap was created between the aristocracy and the masses, a gulf widened still farther by accretions of privilege to the nobility and the peasants' loss of their remaining rights.

For a hundred years the nobility wielded great political power, mainly because, after Peter I's death, no rule of succession to the throne prevailed. It was left to each autocrat to indicate an heir. Tsars and tsarinas owed their acceptance to a clique of court nobles who demonstrated, by the murder of two tsars, that they could destroy as well as make an autocrat. The price of their favour was the grant of state lands on an unprecedented scale, converting millions of free peasants into serfs. Through the edicts of those to whom they had given the supreme power, they freed themselves of all obligations to the state while increasing their authority over their serfs to such a degree that these became their personal property, to do with as they chose. But they failed to formalize or institutionalize this power into any kind of constitutional limitation upon the autocracy, so that, when a direct line of hereditary succession to the throne was once more established, their power vanished. Only in local government were they allowed, as a class, to exercise administrative functions.

The desperation into which the peasants were driven by the burdens imposed upon them by their omnipotent landlords and by the taxation necessary to support a lavish court and continual wars, found vent in several revolts, the most serious of which was that led by the Ural Cossack Pugachev. For a few months in 1773 and 1774 he was able to lead a huge band of disaffected men through eastern Russia, doing a vast amount of material damage, but failing before the regular armies of the government. His supporters were, besides Cossacks and serfs, the inhumanly-treated workers of the Ural mines and foundries and the dispossessed non-Russian peoples of the lands beyond the Volga.

It was Catherine the Great, the disciple of French philosophers and the 'enlightened' monarch, who reduced the Russian peasant to unprecedented depths of misery and servitude, and who extended his unenviable status to the Ukraine and into the new territories won from Turkey. After 1785 the Ukraine became part and parcel of the Russian Empire; its Cossack bands were dispersed or enlisted into cavalry regiments in the regular Russian army.

Napoleon's Invasion of Russia, 1812

The men, the ideas and the results of the French Revolution were anathema to established Russian society, and Napoleon had been condemned by

---

[1] *Wilson (1860), p. 117*

the Orthodox Church as Antichrist. The normal hostility of the Russian Empire to French ambitions was therefore stronger at the beginning of the nineteenth century than it had ever been, and Russia naturally found herself a partner in the various coalitions against France. But allied reverses and French successes bred a distrust of and an impatience with her associates that led to an occasional rapprochement with the French. The chief of these was in 1807: Napoleon, master of all continental Europe from the Atlantic, came to an arrangement with Alexander, lord of the remainder of Eurasia to the Pacific. They met at Tilsit on the river Niemen which formed the boundary between their respective empires. Alexander was to support Napoleon by joining his anti-British blockade and was given, in return, freedom to attack France's one-time allies, Sweden and Turkey, and to win territory at their expense.

This was not an easy arrangement for Alexander to maintain. Napoleon, thought of as Antichrist by the mass of his subjects, was not a popular ally. Napoleonic reform and Russian feudalism were strange partners. Russian commerce depended much on Britain, and its interruption was inconvenient to most Russian landlords and merchants and ruinous to many. Nor, with the Poles and Lithuanians as Napoleon's most enthusastic supporters, would it be easy for the Corsican to resist becoming their champion by attempting to re-establish their ancient kingdom. On the other hand, Russia's ambiguous attitude after 1810, when she no longer even pretended to enforce the embargoes against British trade, was a standing cause of hope and incitement to the increasing number of Napoleon's discontented German and Austrian subjects.

The decision was made to invade Russia in 1812 with an overwhelming force. The French emperor thought that the vastness of his army, his reputation for invincibility, and the discontent of the wretched Russian masses would suffice to bring the Tsar to satisfactory terms with or without a decisive battle. It was not so much territory Napoleon wanted from Alexander—although, to satisfy his friends, he would probably have asked for the return of Russia's partition gains from Poland. His real aim was to compel the Tsar to a more positive cooperation and to leave the world in no doubt as to which of the two emperors was the greater and more powerful.

Napoleon saw himself as the champion of Europe: its civilization, its cultural, scientific, administrative and military superiority; he visualized Russia as Tartaric or Asiatic, semi-barbarous, with masses of slaves awaiting liberation. He knew that recent progress had enabled Russia to intervene in European affairs with increasing weight and usually to French disadvantage. He wished to put her back in her old place as a backward, isolated and innocuous giant.

The armies which crossed the Niemen frontier on 24 June 1812 were European rather than French, and included German, Dutch, Austrian, Polish, Lithuanian, Italian, Swiss, Spanish and Portuguese recruits, besides the French. The combined force amounted to over 617,000, although by no means all of these took part in the Moscow campaign. The

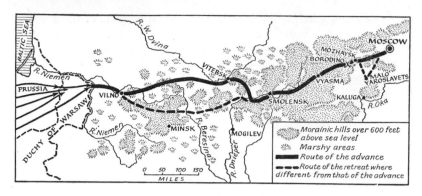

figure 39   The routes of Napoleon's advance and retreat in 1812, and their relationship to the terminal moraine deposited by the last ice sheet at the southernmost limit of its extent.

multi-national nature of the army led to linguistic difficulties and to many deserters who hung back and consumed much of the supply destined for the army ahead. The large Polish contingent often caused confusion because of the similarity between its language and Russian.

The route chosen for the main advance was the road across the morainic country which divides rivers flowing north from those flowing south to the Black Sea. After Smolensk the great terminal moraine itself was followed to Moscow. These morainic roads utilized ridges and low hills of sand to avoid the surrounding marshes. (Fig. 39.)

It took Napoleon 82 days to cover the 640 miles to Moscow—a month longer than the retreat, despite the shorter days and terrible conditions in which the latter took place. His slow progress was in part due to the immense trains of provisions and artillery waggons, ambulances, cannon and droves of cattle which had to accompany the expedition; but in the main it was caused by Napoleon's own procrastination: he wasted 15 irresolute days in Vitebsk. To a lesser degree, Russian tactics were responsible. The Russian commander refused to offer battle but fought delaying actions in the towns to cover his retreat. These were enough to ensure that each town the French army left behind was filled with wounded; supplies that otherwise might have followed Napoleon were consumed in these hospital towns which also attracted stragglers and deserters. The Russians' pride forced upon their army one pitched battle before Moscow was abandoned: that at Borodino on 7 September. Here, despite enormous losses on both sides, the battle was inconclusive and the Russian army continued its withdrawal in good order.

Russian policy hit Napoleon in other ways. By being denied a pitched battle he was drawn farther into the country than he had intended and compelled to adopt diplomatic moves towards the obdurate Alexander. Because of the Russian evacuation and burning of towns, the French failed to find in them the comforts they hoped for. Vitebsk, Smolensk,

Vyazma, Mozhaysk and Moscow itself were all found abandoned, burnt or burning.[1] Outside Moscow, Napoleon confidently expected to be met by a welcoming deputation from the submissive citizens. Instead it was Tsar Alexander who was to receive such a deputation outside the gates of Paris in March 1814.

Not only were the towns empty, but the countryside also was devoid of peasants and provisions. This again disconcerted the French who expected that the Russian serfs, more than any European peasant, would welcome a liberator. But the brutish moujik, in his ignorance, had never heard of the revolutionary ideals of liberty and equality; taught by his priests to regard the invaders as devils in the pay of Antichrist, he wished to avoid all contact with them. No doubt in the misery of the peasantry there lay ultimately possibilities which Napoleon could have made use of in time; but he hoped to win over, and not to alienate, the powerful class of landowners. Not only did the Church help Russia by filling the peasantry with hatred of the French, but it aroused religious fervour to a high pitch before battles, as at Borodino, enabling the soldiers to confront the French with fanatical feats of bravery.

For much of the campaign Napoleon toyed with the idea of marching on St Petersburg rather than Moscow. It was the political capital and the country's chief link with Britain and the outside world; but it was farther off and did not have the symbolic value in Russian eyes that Moscow had. Apart from delays on the road, Napoleon frittered away another 35 days in Moscow (14 September-19 October) despite the lateness of the season, vainly hoping to come to terms with Alexander. He was forced to leave eventually because the whole district around the city had become completely denuded of food and horses.[2]

He decided to return in a south-westerly direction via Kaluga, hoping to find more provisions along a fresh route. But the Russian army obstructed him at Malo Yaroslavets, and he returned to the terminal-moraine road by which he had come. After Smolensk he continued along this road instead of taking the rather more northerly route by which he had come. This was partly because the latter was blocked by a Russian army and also because he intended to travel via Minsk where he hoped to find plentiful provisions and accommodation; however, Minsk fell to the Russians. This more southerly route involved crossing the icy, swift and swollen Beresina where panic-induced stampedes caused extremely heavy loss of life. (Fig. 39.)

The retreating army suffered terrible hardships and catastrophic casualties from the severity of the oncoming winter, lack of supplies and fuel, and continual harassing by the Russian armies, by cossacks and guerrillas. Of the vast army which had crossed the Niemen in June, only between 30,000 and 50,000 returned in December. Baggage and munitions were abandoned, weapons cast away, horses eaten and waggons broken up

[1] *Ségur (1825), vol. 1, pp. 152, 214, 253, 310*
[2] *Ségur (1825), vol. 1, p. 231; vol. 2, pp. 70-1*

for firewood. Awful though the sufferings were before the Beresina was reached, they were even more calamitous during and after the crossing. Forty thousand perished between the river and Vilno, and 20,000 in the town itself, where the Russians came upon them just as they thought they had gained some respite.

The geographical factors of distance, relief, rivers and climate were all important in the 1812 campaign. The great distances involved were too much for Napoleon's administration to cope with—at Moscow he was over 700 miles from his Polish and Prussian bases. The dismal morainic countryside, with its sandy hillocks and marshy hollows, black woods and fields of rye, was unfamiliar and depressing. Only the lighter waggons could negotiate the stretches of loose sand; the Russian roads proved to be poor unsurfaced tracks. The woods which clothed the sandy hills sheltered the Russians who appeared and disappeared as it suited them. At Borodino the Russians were defending similar morainic wooded sandy hills separated by deep stream-cut ravines, and the French, for all their furious valour, could not dislodge them from these vantage points. On the retreat, as winter set in, a combination of icy slopes and soft muddy bottoms made the hummocky morainic country particularly difficult to negotiate with horses and waggons.

Each season contributed to the problems and discomforts of Napoleon's army. The tardy spring delayed the start of the expedition until late June, for there would not be fodder for the cattle and horses before then. The summer proved dry and hot, inducing thirsts that were often assuaged with vodka. This liquor of the rye land, unfamiliar to westerners habituated to the gentler grape, led to sickness and death.[1] The summer heat caused many to discard the heavy coats which they were to need so much on the wintry retreat. When rain did come it fell, after the fashion of this continental climate, in violent thunderstorm downpours which, by producing sudden quagmires, arrested the progress of the long columns. Autumn, bringing its customary rains, handicapped the first stages of the retreat with ubiquitous mud. But winter was not far off. On 6 November, 18 days after the army left Moscow, the first blizzard struck; the snow covered everything and the freezing winds bit into the ill-covered flesh of the afflicted marchers. Rivers, easily forded in the summer, had now become raging torrents, soon laden with swirling masses of ice which added yet another formidable hazard to the crossing.

Conditions worsened as temperatures dropped and snowfall increased. Each night took its toll of frozen men just as each day saw hundreds falter and fall at the roadside. After Napoleon had abandoned the army, leaving incognito in a carriage for Paris, order and discipline, long on the decline, broke down utterly.

The disaster which overtook the French army on its retreat has tended to overshadow the heavy losses which it suffered on its advance. For a variety of reasons already mentioned—many of them geographical in character—

[1] *Ségur* (1825), *vol. 1, p. 224*

the main French army had lost two-thirds of its strength by the time it reached Moscow, and in the opinion of Clausewitz, who was in Russia at the time, was no longer strong enough to enforce either a military or a political decision. The Russians knew this and therefore no longer thought in terms of talking peace or making concessions.[1]

[1] *Clausewitz* (*1843*), *pp. 67, 96-100.*

CHAPTER ELEVEN
RUSSIA AT THE BEGINNING
OF THE NINETEENTH CENTURY:
GENERAL GEOGRAPHY,
AGRICULTURE, MINING AND MANUFACTURING

Between 1725 and 1800, the territory of the Russian Empire had increased in size from 5·8 to 6·5 million square miles. The acquisitions resulting in this increase were to the west, to the south and in the Far East.

The three partitions of Poland had brought the Russian frontier over 250 miles closer to the states of western Europe, but most of the ex-Polish territory had formed part of old Kievan Rus seven hundred years before, and it contained many White Russians and Little Russians (Ukrainians).

In the south, Russia was at last, for the first time in a thousand years, firmly planted on the Black Sea as a result of her successes against Turkey (1774-92). The Sea of Azov was now a Russian lake and the Crimea a Russian peninsula. By 1825 most of the Caucasian and Trans-Caucasian territory had also been brought into the Empire, including Georgia and Azerbaydzhan. Control of the northern shores of the Black Sea proved, however, to be of little strategic value while Turkey controlled the Straits leading to the Mediterranean. In the Far East, Kamchatka was firmly in Russian hands and Russian power had overflowed into Alaska in the far north-west of North America.

Physical Geography

During the eighteenth century the Imperial Academy of Sciences had produced many savants who interested themselves in the geology, physiography, climatology and botany of their country. Several foreign visitors had similar interests, while others were merely observant. Thus there were, by 1800, many reasonably accurate accounts and scientific descriptions of the country's physical geography.

The uniformity of relief over the country as a whole was remarked upon. Chappe d'Auteroche, crossing Russia from St Petersburg eastwards beyond the Volga, *'had met with no mountains worthy of the name'*;[1] Forster, travelling from Astrakhan to Moscow, *'had not seen any land so much elevated as to merit the name of a hill'*.[2] But the geographer Pinkerton, after mentioning that Russia is *'rather a plain country'*, points to a more elevated part, *'by some called the mountains of Valday'* and *'which sends forth the three rivers of Duna, Volga and Nieper'*. But these hills were only:

> *about 1,200 feet above the sea: the height is inconsiderable, and gives a*

[1] *Chappe d'Auteroche (1768), vol. 1, p. 38*
[2] *Forster (1798), vol. 2, p. 283*

striking impression of the gentle and plain level, through which such
extensive rivers must pursue their course.[1]
The Empire had real mountains, however. There was the '*immense*
Uralian chain', but even its summits reached '*an inconsiderable height when*
compared with Mt Blanc'.[2]
The newly-gained territories in the south are described by many observers. There are the steppes, '*perfectly level*', their turf '*smooth and firm*'.[3]
The Crimea, where '*a hard grey lime-stone arranged in inclined strata forms,*
with beds of schist and clay, the framework of the Crimean Mountains'.[4] As
for Siberia, not only were the mountain ranges bounding much of it on
the south described, but also the ill-drained flats of the north:

> *the northern verge of Siberia towards the shores of the frozen ocean,*
> *for several hundred versts in width, is one prodigious watery morass,*
> *grown over with moss, and entirely destitute of wood, and which in*
> *summer is only thawed to the depth of about a span.*[5]

And the volcanoes of Kamchatka:

> *Many traces of volcanoes have been observed in the peninsula; and*
> *there are some mountains which are at present in a burning state.*
> *The most considerable of these volcanoes is situated near the lower*
> *Ostrog. In 1762 a great noise was heard issuing from the inside*
> *of that mountain, and flames of fire were seen to burst from different*
> *parts.*[6]

Serious research was now being undertaken into climate by members of
the Academy of Sciences and, for the first time, statistics covering lengthy
periods were available. It was now realized '*that the farther a district lies*
towards the east, so much is their weather proportionately colder'. The reason
that foreigners, '*according to the universal testimony of them all*', suffered
less from the cold than they did in the milder conditions at home, was
'*from the dryness of the atmosphere*'.[7]
In the Far North there was '*hardly any summer; for the three or four*
months in which it does not snow in some districts scarcely deserves that name'.
But in the extreme south, at Astrakhan, '*the heat is sometimes so intense that*
the mercury in Fahrenheit's thermometer is up at $103\frac{1}{2}°$, *and rain is then so*
rare, that without artificial irrigation, all the plants are withered'.[8]
The monthly precipitation at St Petersburg over a 10-year period was
as follows (more modern averages are given in brackets):[9]

[1] *Pinkerton (1802), vol. 1, pp. 323-4*
[2] *Pinkerton (1802), vol. 1, pp. 323-4*
[3] *Clarke (1810), vol. 1, p. 212*
[4] *Reuilly (1803), p. 11*
[5] *Tooke (1799), vol. 1, p. 84*
[6] *Coxe (1780), p. 6*
[7] *Tooke (1799), vol. 1, pp. 40, 53*
[8] *Tooke (1799), vol. 1, pp. 33, 40*
[9] *Tooke (1799), vol. 1, pp. 41-3; Cox (1784), vol. 1, p. 477;*
  Kendrew (1953), p. 295

Precipitation in inches			days with rain	days with snow
January	1·0	(0·9)	2	11
February	1·0	(0·8)	2	12
March	0·8	(0·9)	2	11
April	1·2	(0·9)	7	4
May	1·3	(1·7)	13	some snow
June	3·1	(1·8)	13	0
July	2·8	(2·7)	14	0
August	2·7	(2·7)	16	0
September	3·5	(2·0)	16	some snow
October	2·5	(1·7)	13	5
November	1·5	(1·4)	4	11
December	1·0	(1·2)	3	16

Between 1726 and 1789, the earliest recorded break-up of the ice on the Neva was 25 March, the latest, 27 April. The earliest date that the river froze over during the same period was 20 October, the latest, 1 December.[1] In 1778: *'on 15th November the Neva was entirely frozen, and soon after-wards the Gulf of Finland was covered with ice, and sledges began to pass from Petersburg to Cronstadt'*.[2]

The academician Gmelin had discovered that in some parts of Siberia, *'the climate is so cold that one may find several places where the ground does not thaw below a depth of three feet'*. At Yakutsk an attempt to dig a well in July had been frustrated by permafrost. But the worst feature of the Siberian climate was not the extreme cold, but *'a certain tremendous kind of winter hurricane, which they call* burane, *and which not infrequently buries both men and cattle in whirlpools of snow and sand'*.[3]

THE FORESTS

Despite the enormous forests still covering large areas of northern and central Russia, a shortage of wood was keenly and increasingly felt in many inhabited districts:

> *With all her wealth in forests, Russia, however, contains districts that are totally destitute of timber and fuel; and even in the governments where these necessaries of life were lately in abundance, the increasing population and industry have made the decline of them very sensibly felt.*
>
> *The immense consumption of wood in a territory where it is necessary for eight or ten months of the year to provide against the cold, and where almost all the habitations in town and country are constructed*

[1] *Tooke (1799), vol. 1, pp. 40, 51*

[2] *Coxe (1780), vol. 1, p. 478*

[3] *Chappe d'Auteroche (1768), vol. 1, pp. 90-2; Tooke (1799), vol. 1, p. 65*

of timber, rises in the same proportion in which the number of people increase.[1]

The chief causes of dearth were: clearing and burning for agriculture; felling for export; burning for potash; felling for house-building, ship-building and road-surfacing; bark-stripping for mat and shoe making; felling for domestic fuel and for charcoal burning; the wasteful use of the axe instead of the saw.[2] In the southern steppe regions, where there was almost no natural woodland, the lack of wood was, of course, greater. In the north the peasant still preferred to burn away forest for the high yield which came in the first year or two, rather than cultivate old land in areas where the poor light podzol gave rapidly diminishing returns.

Potash was prepared from oak or pine, the peasants bringing their ashes to the works where they were washed out in long vats. The saturated lye was then boiled in large coppers and the potash calcined white in a furnace. The largest Crown potash works in the country was at Arsamas, fifty miles south of Nizhniy Novgorod. Other Crown works were at Murom, Alatyr and Sviyazhsk, all in the middle Volga region.

Shipbuilding in Russia was almost entirely naval: the country's over-seas trade was mostly carried by foreign ships. The chief yards therefore, were the Crown naval ones at St Petersburg, Kronstadt, Astrakhan, Kherson and Nikolayev. The fine oak forests in Kazan province were reserved for the royal navy and immense quantities of timber took the waterway to St Petersburg. It is surprising that ships continued to be built there, since they had to be *'got over the bar by means of camels, or floating hulks constructed for that purpose'*.[3] However, with the erection of new dockyards at Kronstadt, the building of large men-of-war at the capital was about to be abandoned. At Kherson there was a similar snag, namely of *'being obliged to carry down every new ship to the sea on camels, for want of depth in the water'*.[4] The great disadvantage of Nikolayev was its

being placed in the Scythian desert, where no wood ever grew. . . . As the best oak comes down the Dnieper it must afterwards make the tour by sea, and mount the Bog. . . . The same remark applies to all the other naval materials and stores.[5]

Archangel alone was wholly concerned with the building of merchant ships. Vessels for the fur-hunting voyages to Alaska and for seal-hunting on the Kurile Islands were built at Okhotsk, with a few on Kamchatka. They were *'commonly built without iron, and in general so badly constructed, that it is wonderful how they can weather so stormy a sea'*.[6]

Not all the economic uses of the forest involved its destruction. Turpen-tine and pitch were prepared from the oily resins exuded from the

[1] *Tooke (1799), vol. 3, p. 365*
[2] *See French (1963), vol. 3, p. 365*
[3] *Oddy (1805), p. 116*
[4] *Guthrie (1802), p. 6*
[5] *Guthrie (1802), p. 7*
[6] *Coxe (1780), p. 8*

coniferous trees of the northern forest, while both bees and swine were kept in the mixed woodlands. The age-old method of apiculture had changed little in a thousand years. All over the country, wherever there were lime or linden trees, honey was taken from wild bees. In White Russia, Martha Wilmot '*saw a man climb a tree to a wild beehive with the help of his rope*', and in Livonia, Mary Holderness reported that '*the peasants hang their beehives in the woods, that the bees may have the first flowers of the lime, whence they make fine honey*'.[1]

The fur trade was, in part, another use of the forest. It was now most active in the newly-conquered far eastern extremities of the Empire. Many skins came from the Kurile Islands and Alaska. The natives of Kamchatka paid a '*fixed annual tribute of 279 sables, 464 red foxes, 50 sea otters with a dam, and 38 cub sea-otters*'.[2] In addition there were the furs obtained in trade by the Russian and native traders and trappers.

Since most timber was used at a distance from its source, an enormous amount had to be transported, almost all by water:

> *The various kinds of timber are floated down the small streams and collected in the large navigable rivers in rafts of a prodigious length; I have seen some in the Ladoga canal of more than twelve hundred feet long; they are dragged by horses in the canals and floated down by the current in the rivers.*
>
> *They frequently have the appearance of villages, as the proprietors send ready-made houses, stacks of hay and even sometimes animals for sale, which, added to the smoke that arises from their cooking, completes the deception.*[3]

Agriculture

'*There is certainly no country in Europe where agriculture is practised so negligently*'.[4] Some few landowners, especially in the west and south, were zealous for agricultural reform and were introducing artificial fertilizers and agricultural machinery, the latter having been permitted to enter the country free of duty in 1806.[5] But most landowner agriculture and all peasant farming continued in the old way. Yet the amount of land in cultivation had increased greatly during the eighteenth century, partly as a result of Peter I's poll tax, which forced the peasants to increase their production in order to pay the tax.

Rye in the northern and central provinces, wheat in the south, with barley and oats widespread, continued to be the chief cereals grown in Russia. Hemp and flax maintained their position as the leading industrial

[1] *Wilmot (1803-8), p. 125; Holderness (1823), p. 22*
[2] *Coxe (1780), p. 68*
[3] *Atkinson & Walker (1812), vol. 2*
[4] *Storch (1801B). vol. 2, p. 222*
[5] *Lyashchenko (1956), vol. 1, pp. 500-1*

crops. But the acquisition of the southern territories had made possible the introduction of new crops, notably sugar-beet, tobacco, cotton and maize, although production of each of these was as yet small. Few potatoes were grown in Russia, other than those found on the farms of foreign colonists.

Livestock, although numerous, were of poor quality almost everywhere. Cattle were now numerous on the steppes where there were even more sheep. Horses were so common all over old Russia that it was 'rare to find a peasant, even among the poorest, who does not own one or more horses; they are employed everywhere in cultivating the land except in the Ukraine'.[1] Pigs likewise were extremely common and provided the chief source of meat for people in the forested parts of the country; by European standards they were undersized.

In the following pages attention is confined to regions in which noteworthy changes had taken place in agriculture, or which had been recently acquired.

THE BALTIC PROVINCES

The German squires of Livonia were quietly carrying out an agricultural revolution. Having obtained the abolition of serfdom, they were consolidating their estates under efficient and progressive management, the Letts Estonians becoming their landless labourers. These landlords showed more intelligence and took more care than their Russian counterparts. They made profitable use of their rye surpluses by converting them into vodka. They imported cattle from the Ukraine and fattened them up again, after their long journey, for the St Petersburg market. They reared a good class of sheep on the coastal salt marshes and derived from them an exportable surplus of semi-fine wool.[2]

THE NORTH

In the cold-winter/cool-summer lands of northern Russia, the people of Finnish origin still relied on the primitive clearing and burning of new lands, taking as many crops as the temporary fertility so produced would permit, and moving on. Rye and barley were sown as far north as Mezen (65°N), but the rye did not always ripen and the barley was grown as green fodder rather than for grain[2]. In contrast to this wretched primitive and sporadic agriculture was the new livestock farming introduced into the Archangel province by Catherine II. She had imported good breeds of European cattle so as to make use of the region's excellent summer pastures, and now Kholmogory calves were highly esteemed at St Petersburg for their fine-quality meat.[3]

[1] *Storch (1801B), vol. 2, p. 181*
[2] *Storch (1801B), vol. 2, pp. 159, 168-9, 235; Mirsky (1931), p. 238*
[3] *Tooke (1799), vol. 1, p. 29; Storch (1801B), vol. 2, pp. 157-8, 229*

THE WOODED STEPPE AND STEPPE

A vast area in the south, comprising the wooded steppe and the steppe, was now free from the military troubles which had prevented settlement and cultivation from prospering before the end of the eighteenth century. For the first time for a thousand years men were able to make fuller use of its rich soils and long hot summers, hindered only by the threat of drought. The new agriculture set up here was differently organized than that of old Russia to the north. Whether the landholdings were those moderate in size granted to foreign colonists or the large estates given to Russian nobles, a new capitalist technique predominated. Production was mainly for the market rather than for local use, and new methods, especially the use of machinery, found a warmer welcome. The Ukrainians had a heavier plough drawn by oxen instead of the lighter horse-drawn implement used in Great Russia.

The newly-colonized wooded steppe and steppe regions of southern Russia and the Ukraine had a mixed agriculture producing livestock and grain, with the latter more prominent in northern areas close to the older-established towns like Tula, Kaluga and Orel, or along waterways such as the Don. Clarke, crossing the wooded steppe, found that '*you travel for miles and miles and see nothing but corn*'.[1] Also grown were barley, oats, millet, peas, lentils, flax, hemp, sugar-beet and poppies, with buckwheat on lighter sandier soils.[2] Orchards were frequent in the south (New Russia). At Chernigov '*dried fruits begin to be abundant*' and good raisins. The Don Cossacks made '*delicious wine*'; water melons grew in the gardens and poultry filled the yards. But vegetables were few and dear.

Throughout these regions cattle were numerous and still more important than grain on the open steppe. The Don Cossacks prided themselves on the quality of their herds. Many cattle were killed in the autumn for their tallow. Others, brought from the Tartar peoples of the south-east, were fattened in the Ukraine and then exported on the hoof to the Baltic region. Vast flocks of sheep also roamed across the southern steppes: they were mostly the long-tailed Circassian sheep and gave better wool than the native Russian breeds. Between 1800 and 1809 the merino breed was introduced into the provinces of Poltava, Kharkov, Kursk, Simbirsk and Voronezh, as well as into New Russia.[3]

The Ukraine west of the Dnieper, which became Russian in 1772-91 did not yet share the progress and prosperity of that to the east. It was still suffering from the devastation that had resulted from war and repeated rebellions against the Polish gentry.

THE CRIMEA

The northern part of the peninsula was covered with arid steppe, and what

[1] *Clarke (1810), vol. 1, p. 189*

[2] *Storch (1801B), vol. 2, p. 232*

[3] Khozyaistvenno-statisticheskiy atlas *(1857), pp. 76-8; Storch (1801B), vol. 2, p. 156*

water was to be had from wells was often brackish. It was inhabited by Tartar shepherds. Their sheep were so numerous that '*an ordinary Tartar has a thousand, a wealthy one up to five thousand*'. These animals were '*famous for their valuable furs and the sweetness of their flesh*'. The Russian conquest, followed by expropriation and the introduction of serfdom, had deprived them of the right to roam at will, and those who remained were increasingly compelled to settle in villages and cultivate the dry ground. Their attempts at agriculture met with but limited success.[1]

Southwards, relief becomes more undulating, precipitation increases, and soil deepens and darkens until the mountains are reached. This belt had a '*surprising fertility in corn and other vegetables*' but it too was predominantly given over to sheep.[2] Besides the native Tartars, many French emigrés were established here and had introduced merino sheep from Spain. Towards the east, in this richer belt, Bulgarians were settled and were good farmers and careful shepherds: they kept goats too, which '*are turned to more profit than those of the Tartar flocks, for they milk them regularly, and make a rich good cheese of the milk*'. They also grew grain and flax. But at the eastern extremity of this belt, near the coast at Kaffa, the soil was thin and gravelly, giving meagre yields of corn yet grazing thousands of sheep.[3]

Along the eastern coast and on the Kerch peninsula, Greek settlers kept cattle and grew tobacco. The south coast valleys, sunny, well-watered and protected by the mountains from northerly winds, were luxuriant with fruit trees, nut trees and vineyards.[4]

THE SOUTH-EAST (KUBAN AND CAUCASUS)

The Kuban was still '*covered by fine pasture herbage*' and with cattle and sheep, but Russian and Cossack colonists were introducing corn: Clarke (1800) noticed '*some corn mills worked by undershot wheels*'. But the eastern foothills of the Caucasus and the Caspian coastal region to Baku were richly blessed and bore '*the best wheat, the choicest orchard fruits, wild and cultivated vinestocks, mulberry trees, wild olives, figs, chestnuts, almond and peach trees, saffron, etc.*' as well as pomegranates, sweet melons, water melons, cotton and '*a special kind of long red onion*'.[5] The Caucasus valleys not only yielded varied fruits and nuts, but carried verdant pastures with sheep and goats. The hot dry Astrakhan region, besides its orchards and gardens, was now growing a little cotton. But it was still productive of '*no grain and but little pasturage*'.[6]

[1] *Reuilly (1806), p. 185; Storch (1801B), vol. 2, p. 169; Guthrie (1802), p. 225*

[2] *Guthrie (1802), p. 207*

[3] *Holderness (1823), pp. 135, 166*

[4] *Guthrie (1802), pp. 128, 130; Reuilly (1806), p. 58*

[5] *Tooke (1799), vol. 1, p. 33; Reinegg (1796), vol. 1, pp. 145-6*

[6] *Storch (1801B), vol. 2, p. 250; Forster (1798), vol. 2, p. 272*

F

Fishing

Peasants all over northern and central Russia still fished with hoop nets through holes in the ice of rivers and lakes in winter. But the increased growth of flax in response to sustained foreign demand meant increased contamination of the rivers through retting, to the detriment of the fishermen.[1] The principal fisheries were still those of the White and Caspian Seas. The fishermen of Archangel, Kholmogory and Olonets not only fished off the White Sea shores for cod, plaice, sole and herring, but visited Spitzbergen for whales and walruses, sometimes wintering on these frigid islands.[2]

Sturgeon was still the main catch of the lower-Volga Caspian fishery. Kalmyks here proved to be the best fishermen, but the salting and preparation of caviar on shore was done by Ural Cossacks. Among the newly acquired fisheries was that of the Crimean Greeks who also sought sturgeon in the Sea of Azov, where the quantity of fish taken was '*truly astonishing*'.[3] The newly-tamed peoples of north-eastern Siberia—Chukchis, Kamchadales and Kuriles—lived mainly by fishing. The Chukchis and Kamchadales made great use of the whale; they also caught salmon and sea trout, and the Kuriles went after sea otters.

Mining

The Urals remained the most important single mining region, and were already known to contain granite, porphyry, jasper, quartz, whetstone, topazes, amethysts, porcelain and pipe clay, serpentine, asbestos, marble, gypsum, coal, mineral oil, naphtha, sulphur, salt, saltpetre, natron, iron, copper, gold, silver and lead.[4] But new mining regions had now been developed, especially along the southern mountain fringe of the Asiatic part of the Empire.

The permanent mining of coal on the Donets coalfield began in 1790 in the Lugan valley.[5] Some of this coal went by river to Nikolayev and as a result, Mrs Guthrie could write from that town in 1796: '*I am now sitting at a cheerful fire made . . . with coals*'.[6]

Production of petroleum from the Baku region, which became Russian in 1806, was only 200,000 puds or 3,000 tons in 1818. A detailed description of the oil wells was given by Dr Jacob Reinegg in 1796:

The Baku region must hold an incredible store of petroleum, for in

[1] *Storch (1801B), vol. 2, p. 247*
[2] *Tooke (1799), vol. 3, pp. 101-7*
[3] *Clarke (1810), pp. 330, 341*
[4] *Tooke (1799), vol. 1, p. 44*
[5] *Semenov (1862-85), vol. 2, p. 106*
[6] *Guthrie (1802), p. 9*

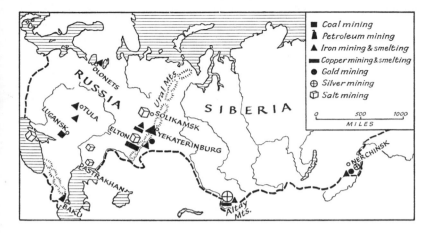

figure 40   The Russian Empire in 1815: mining.

Balaghan, a district twelve versts from Baku, there are 25 open oil wells. These often dry up, so that it is necessary to dig new wells; the old ones are not filled in, however, but kept open for a long time, as the oil often reappears after some months.[1]

Mrs Guthrie noted '*springs of naphtha and petroleum*' around Kerch in the Crimea, a district important today for natural gas.[2]

The Urals were far and away the richest source of iron ore, which was now mined over a wide area from Perm and Ufa on the west to Verkhoturye, Yekaterinburg and Chelyabinsk in the east. But mining was still active in the old Olonets and Tula districts as well as in the basin of the upper Don. Many mines were now working in Siberia, notably in the Altay and the Nerchinsk Mountains. The Russian ores in general were said to have a metal content above 50 per cent.[3]

Copper came almost entirely from the western Urals and the basins of the Kama river and its tributaries: Kargalinsk was the district of most intensive mining. There was a growing quantity from the Kolyvan silver mines in the Altay Mountains.

Gold mining was now of some importance, almost all the ore coming from the Beresov mine near Yekaterinburg. In 1799 another Ural mine was opened at Miask. Some gold was also obtained from the Nerchinsk silver mines.[4]

There were now two great centres of silver mining. The Nerchinsk mines, noted before in 1725, had increased their output of ore to about 2

[1] *Reinegg (1796), vol. 1, pp. 149-50*
[2] *Guthrie (1802), p. 174*
[3] *Tooke (1799), vol. 3, p. 419*
[4] *Tooke (1799), vol. 3, p. 414; Storch (1801B), vol. 2, p. 377;*
Hermann (1810), table 6a

million puds by 1779, after when there had been a steep decline to about half that amount. The metal content was poor. Rather more important were the Kolyvan mines in the Altay Mountains, first worked by the Demidovs in 1728 and by the Crown since 1745; they now yielded over 2 million puds of ore of decreasing quality.[1] The ores referred to above, although poor in silver, were very rich in lead. However, it was easier to import lead into Russia than transport this heavy metal from Siberia. Consequently it was only used locally.

It is possible to give a statistical estimate of the leading sources of common salt at the end of the eighteenth century:[2]

District	Source	Average annual output (thousands of puds)
Solikamsk (Perm Province)	brine pits	5,681
Elton (Saratov province)	salt lake crust	5,592
Crimea	,,	3,000
Astrakhan	,,	677
Kolyvan (Siberia)	,,	486
Ilekskaya (near Ufa)	rock salt	444
Archangel	sea water	150/200
Staraya Russa	salt marsh water	150

Manufacturing (fig. 41)

During the eighteenth century and especially during the reign of Catherine II, there was a sharp rise in the number of Russian manufactories. One estimate gives the number of industrial establishments at different dates as follows:

1725	233
1762	984
1796	3,161
1814	3,573

However, less than a tenth of the figure for 1814 employed over a hundred workers, and many were small artisan workshops.[3]

Catherine had done all she could to promote industry: by encouraging foreigners, who were privileged to buy serfs for employment in factories; by giving subsidies and freedom from tax to promoters of new industries; and by prohibiting imports. In some instances the government itself set up and ran factories, but there was now much more *laissez faire* than in Peter's time when state supervision was ubiquitous. A surprising aspect of this greater freedom is the number of serfs who had become successful

[1] *Storch (1801B), vol. 2, pp. 378-80*
[2] *Storch (1801B), pp. 408-12*
[3] *Kulischer (1922), p. 152; Lyashchenko (1956), vol. 1, p. 442*

figure 41   Russia in 1800: manufactures.

industrialists. Many pioneers of the new cotton industry were serfs of Count Sheremetyev.

Although the eighteenth-century industrial *essor* was impressive quantitatively, it left much to be desired in quality. Official reports deplored the low standard of woollen cloth and other goods, and foreign visitors were contemptuous of the Russian product:

> The manufactories of Russia are all far behind ours in the attainment of excellence . . . scarcely anything bought of Russian manufacture is worth having. . . . All kinds of cutlery are very bad.[1]

The Abbé Chappe d'Auteroche visited the copper works at Solikamsk (1761) and found its products all of '*the coarsest work*'. Almost all Russian industrial processes remained either entirely primitive or were crude imitations of western techniques. Yet individual Russians were already

[1] *Holderness (1823), pp. 69-70*

giving unmistakable evidence of remarkable skill and inventiveness. In 1763 the self-educated Polzunov built a steam engine; and Lomonosov (1712-65) had made contributions to physics and chemistry which were ahead of contemporary European science. But the suppression of all initiative by autocracy and serfdom meant that such scientific progress had no practical application in Russian economic life.

Wage labour was gradually displacing compulsory serf labour in the factories. This was possible, even under serfdom, since landowners whose estates were within reach of industrial towns were ready to commute their peasants' obligations for a money rent or *obrok*. This was paid, either from the serf pursuing some trade in his cottage and selling the product to a merchant or on the market, or from his migrating seasonally to a town to find factory or building work. According to Tugan-Baranovski, about a third of the adult male population of Yaroslavl province left home each year. Whereas only 39 per cent of the labour force was hired in 1767, the percentage was 48 in 1804 and 54 in 1825. But it was, in the main, the new industries depending largely on imported raw materials, which accounted for this increase: 80 per cent of the cotton factory workers were hired in 1804, 91 per cent in 1825.

In those industries still under the control of nobles, the proportion of serf labour actually increased. These were usually industries, like woollen cloth, linen and glass, in which the raw material was produced on the estate. In this form of manorial industry, the noble had no outgoings whatever for raw materials and labour, and was thus able to compete as an industrialist, despite the inefficiency and low productivity of serf labour. Far from being obsolete, manorial industry using serfs was being introduced by the Russians into newly-acquired territory, e.g. the Crimea, where, at Simferopol, '*the Governor, Mr Beresdina, has established some manufactories on his property . . . one of them a fabric for blue cloth*'.[1] As only foreigners could now buy serfs for factory work, the nobles were left with a near monopoly of this form of cheap labour. Thus it is not so surprising that in the woollen industry, in which three-quarters of the establishments were owned by nobles, the percentage of serf labour increased from 38 per cent in 1804 to 61 per cent in 1825. There was a similar increase for the glass industry.[2]

Estimates that the total number of industrial workers was a mere 100,000, as suggested by Gille and others, are too low. According to Hermann's lists, which are incomplete, there were 81,000 workers in the metallurgical industry alone, besides 167,000 'ascribed serfs'. There were about 20,000 in the linen workshops and about the same number in the woollen mills. These figures do not include artisans, members of artels, and those working at home.[3]

[1] *Holderness (1823), pp. 91*
[2] *Florinsky (1953), p. 714*
[3] *Gille (1949), p. 124; Florinsky (1953), pp. 561-62; Hermann (1810), tables 6 and 7; Hermann (1790), pp. 378-9*

Except in metallurgy and one or two new industries such as cotton, urban artisan and rural cottage manufactures accounted together for far more production than factory industry. Some artisans, craftsmen or tradesmen were to be found in all towns, but they were most numerous in St Petersburg where they were to be numbered in thousands. As a fast-growing city it employed thousands of bricklayers and carpenters. Most of these building workers were attached to country villages: '*Besides the bricklayers and masons that lived constantly in Petersburg, above 6,000 of them came annually from the provinces to work during the short summer*'. The wealth and luxury of the capital and its devotion to foreign modes demanded a host of carriage builders, bookbinders, watchmakers, dressmakers, milliners, embroiderers, cabinet makers, landscape gardeners, jewellers, silversmiths, goldsmiths, etc. Many of these craftsmen were German or Dutch. Even in metallurgy there were still many thousands of artisan smiths making tools and equipment for the peasants. These were to be found especially in the Oka basin, round Tula, along the upper Don and the middle Volga, in the Olonets district and in some of the Siberian towns.[1]

Even more numerous and important than the urban artisans were the rural craftsmen or *kustari*. Many of these worked independently and sold their wares in markets and fairs, but a rapidly growing number worked up material supplied by merchants who bought the finished goods at a low price and marketed them themselves. The merchants had recourse to this method of laying out their capital and increasing their business because of the nobles' monopoly of serf labour and the great shortage of wage labour. The villages in several districts acquired fame in one or other branch of industry or handicraft, as for example:

> *Villages near Moscow:* woollen, silken, linen and cotton cloth
> *Gzhel, near Moscow:* pottery
> *Khouy, near Vladimir:* ikon painting
> *Ivanovo-Voznesensk:* linen, cotton printing
> *Gomel:* glassware, linen
> *Pavlov, near Nizhniy Novgorod:* hardware, padlocks, guns
> *Upper Volga region:* woodworking (wheels, yokes, sleighs); tanning, leather working
> *Kimry district, upper Volga:* boot making
> *Sidorovsk, Kostroma district:* silversmiths, goldsmiths
> *Tula district:* hardware, cutlery, curiosities
> *Penza:* woollen carpets
> *North Dvina valley:* artistic handicrafts, e.g. walrus bone carving

Almost all the nails used in Russia were made by *kustari* in the Volga provinces, and the boats and barges used on the navigable rivers were

[1] *Kulischer (1922), pp. 154-6; Storch (1801B), vol. 2, pp. 279-80, 382*

built by the rural villagers who lived nearby.[1] Already craftsmen and tradesmen were meeting the problem of finding capital by combining into cooperative artels. In the last quarter of the nineteenth century, factory industry was to take advantage of the presence of these regional concentrations of specialist skills.

Moscow remained the most important centre of manufacturing industry, but St Petersburg was of growing importance. There was a fundamental difference between the two cities as industrial centres. Moscow worked up mainly Russian resources; St Petersburg depended on imported raw materials. Moscow flourished as a natural geographical centre and focus of routes; St Petersburg because, as capital, it was a centre of wealth, society, and such educational and scientific institutions as there were. St Petersburg was well ahead in the use of modern methods and machinery.

TEXTILES AND LEATHER (fig. 42)
Tugan-Baranovsky gave the following figures for 1804:[2]

	Number of factories	Number of workers
Woollen cloth	155	28,689
Linen	285	23,711
Cotton	199	6,566
Silk	328	8,953
Leather	850	6,304

The Russian factory linen industry was at its zenith at the end of the eighteenth century. Its decline in the first quarter of the nineteenth was rapid, the number of factories and workshops dropping from 285 to 196 between 1804 and 1825.[3] According to Hermann the main centres of the factory industry were Moscow (3,479 workers) and Yaroslavl (2,637 workers). The cottage industry was widespread in the central provinces of Moscow, Kostroma, Vladimir, Yaroslavl and Tver. Russian linen was excepted from the strictures passed by foreigners upon the quality of Russian goods and it loomed large in Russian exports. English spinning machines were introduced in 1809, but the industry was already beginning to feel the effects of competition from cotton. Sailcloth and cordage were manufactured principally at St Petersburg (12 works) and Archangel (10 works); also at Novgorod, Kolomna, Tambov, Bryansk, Nizhniy Novgorod and Saratov.[4] Although still handicapped by the poor quality of the native wool and

[1] *Tugan-Baranovsky (1900), pp. 59-60; Mirsky (1952), pp. 196-7, p. 222; Lyashchenko (1956), vol. 1, pp. 440-1; Tooke (1799), vol. 3, pp. 512-13*
[2] *Tugan-Baranovsky (1900), p. 98*
[3] *Tugan-Baranovsky (1900), p. 78*
[4] *Tooke (1799), vol. 3, pp. 357-8*

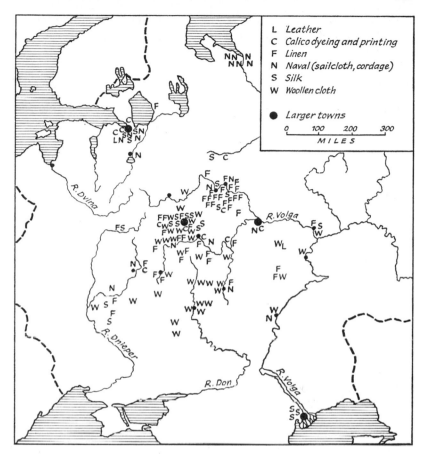

figure 42   Russia in 1800: textile factories (data from Hermann and Lyashchenko).

heavily dependent upon imports of better quality fibre, there had been some improvement in the woollen industry because of the finer wool now available from the newly acquired territories in the south and from the Baltic provinces. But Russian woollen cloth was still far from having the high reputation of the country's linen. There were about 60 large factories, most of them near Moscow and in the Voronezh-Tambov region. Near Kaluga was the Polotnyany factory: *'a great cloth manufactory. There is not in England a more extensive establishment or a mercantile residence more magnificent'.*[1] The mills at Kazan made, *'along with other materials, a fine camel's hair cloth which is left in its natural colour'.*[2] At St Petersburg there was a tapestry manufactory that *'produces such excellent work that better is*

[1] *Wilson (1861), vol. 1, p. 206*
[2] *Hermann (1790), pp. 378-9*

F*

not to be seen from the Gobelines at Paris'. Hats were made at Moscow, St Petersburg and Smolensk, the largest factory being at the latter place.[1]

There were at least 40 larger silk factories in various parts of the Empire, half of them in and about Moscow, with others at St Petersburg, Yaroslavl and Astrakhan. This industry was now at its peak.[2] Lace manufacture was concentrated at St Petersburg (5 establishments).

Cotton was the newest of Russia's textile industries, stimulated in part by the interruption of British supplies during the Napoleonic Wars and by the growing demand for cottons, which were displacing linen. The industry had begun in Russia in the mid-eighteenth century at Ivanovo near Vladimir, with the printing of imported cloth; next came the weaving of imported yarn, followed by the introduction of cotton spinning. In 1793 the first spinning machines had been introduced at the state cotton works at Schlüsselburg. In 1799, a state spinning and weaving factory was established at Alexandrovsk, and by 1812 Moscow had 11 cotton spinning mills with 780 machines between them. Most yarn was still imported, however. The industry had also spread rapidly amongst the peasants, especially in the area between Moscow and Vladimir. The new techniques of the industrial revolution were already coming into use: in 1805 the first steam engine in the cotton industry began work at St Petersburg.[3]

One of Russia's oldest industries, the preparation of leather, was still widespread, and *'the white-tanned leather made at Moscow from elkskins, buckskins, goatskins, etc.'* was *'very much esteemed'*.[4]

Metallurgy (fig. 43)

During the eighteenth century, the iron industry had greatly increased its capacity and, under the stimulus of almost continuous warfare, was now producing more than ever before. The total annual production of factory-made pig and cast iron had doubled from 5 million to nearly 10 million puds between 1767 and 1807, and these figures do not take into account *'the little smithies and forges scattered here and there'*.[5] In many parts of the country there were *'a great number of boor smiths who smelt the ore at home, and of the iron make various kinds of utensils'*. Clarke found (1800) that Yelets, near the upper Don, was a centre of the artisan industry:

> *We observed a number of forges at work, and found that the number of smiths and other artificers in iron alone, amounted to two hundred. Eletz is renowned for the celebrity of its forges.*[6]

[1] *Storch (1801A), p. 274; Tooke (1799), vol. 3, p. 513*

[2] *Took (1799), vol. 3, pp. 509-10; Lyashchenko (1956), map 7*

[3] *Lyashchenko (1966), Vol. 1, pp. 512, 518–20*

[4] *Tooke (1799), vol. 3, pp. 541-2*

[5] *Oddy (1805), p. 72; Portal (1950), p. 358; Hermann (1810), tables 6 and 7*

[6] *Clarke (1810), vol. 1, p. 193*

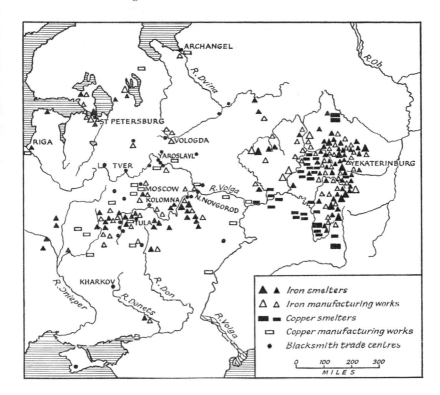

figure 43   Russia in 1800: metallurgical works (data from Hermann and Lyashchenko).

The works production of pig and cast iron in Russia at the beginning of the nineteenth century was nearly 160,000 tons compared with about 15,000 tons in Peter the Great's reign. But British production was now rising at an even faster rate as a result of the new techniques: it had moved, under the stimulus of war, from only 68,000 tons in 1788, a figure well below the contemporary Russian level, to 258,000 tons in 1806.[1] The Russian industry, still dependent on charcoal, on serf labour and water-powered hammers, could not rival such revolutionary progress and, despite its own development, was falling further and further behind.

Since 1725 the proportion of pig iron produced in the Urals had risen from 40 per cent to 75 per cent in 1802-6. All the largest works were there, and almost all of them had been founded before 1762. Works of recent date were few because older works were added to rather than new ones started. The largest producer of pig iron outside the Urals was the Alexandrovsk works at Petrozavodsk.

The Urals were no longer, as in Petrine times, merely a producer of

[1] *Watson (1960), p. 505*

iron for working up in other areas, but now dominated the production of wrought iron also. Their share of production—over 90 per cent of an annual total of 100,000 tons—was greater even than that for pig iron. All the leading works were in or near the Urals region except for Velet-minsk (Nizhniy Novgorod province) and Klimsk-Kholunitsk.

Steel production remained small and mainly in the hands of a few skilled artisans in the older metallurgical regions. But some four or five of the Ural works were making steel, chiefly Izhevsk, with a yearly average of 3,412 puds and Votkinsk (847 puds); production at the others was negligible. A little refined steel was made at Yekaterinburg. This, the only modern steelworks in Russia, had been built in 1785.[1]

Most of the ironworks had only one or two blast furnaces, although the largest, Nizhniy Tagil, had four. The more modern furnaces had an annual capacity of about 100,000 puds (125,000 at Nizhniy Tagil). The number of hands employed was about 65,000, to which number must be added some 150,000 'ascribed peasants'.[2] Production often ceased in summer, so that workers could labour in the fields.[3] Working conditions were appalling and discontent was rife; revolts were numerous and Ural metallurgical labourers had joined Pugachev's Cossack revolt in thousands.

Cannon and firearms were still the main product of the Russian iron industry and some large works of recent foundation, such as Petrozavodsk (1772), St Petersburg (1801), Kronstadt (1789) and Lugansk (1798), were wholly devoted to them. Kamensk, an older works of Petrine date, also cast cannon. The Lugansk works is of special interest because it was founded on the Donets coalfield, in a district where coal and iron occurred together, with a view to their joint use on the British model:

> *Higher up the Donets, where it receives the Lugan, are the Lugan ironworks and cannon foundry, belonging to the Crown. From thence the Emperor's artillery passes by water to the Black Sea . . . very excellent coal at Lugan; in consequence of which discovery, as well as its convenient situation for water carriage, the foundry was there established.*[4]

It was under the management of a Mr Gascoigne, who had had experience of coke smelting at the Carron works in Scotland (founded in 1760 as the first Scottish works to use coke). But by 1807 it had not yet been found possible to use coal in the works. Nevertheless it was then producing 400 tons of cannon, bombs, etc., a year and employing 1,500 men.[5]

The old Tula works was now in a decrepit state, but it still made firearms and turned out hardware, cutlery, trinkets and curiosities of all kinds. According to Clarke:

> *The machinery is ill-constructed and worse preserved. Everything*

[1] *Tooke (1799), vol. 3, p. 552; Hermann (1810), table 6*
[2] *Hermann (1810), tables 6 and 7*
[3] *Vigel (1891), vol. 2, p. 149*
[4] *Clarke (1810), p. 256*
[5] *Hermann (1810), table 7a*

seemed out of order. Workmen with long beards, stood staring at each other wondering what was to be done next, while their intendants and directors were drunk or asleep.[1]

The district around Tula abounded in artisans and cooperative artels; these also made hardware and cutlery for the peasants, and curiosities for tourists:

> *As soon as you arrive at the inn, a number of persons crowd the room, each bearing a sack filled with trinkets, knives, inkstands, incense pots, silk reels, scissors and corkscrews.*[2]

Martha Wilmot writes (1804) of '*steel candlesticks of Tula manufacture*' and explains that a curiosity from Tula is '*a machine for perfuming the room*'.[3]

Cutlery was made in St Petersburg, Moscow and the Pavlovo district as well as at Tula. But there were '*as yet no manufactory of scythes in Russia*', few needles or shears, and '*no fine files, nor a hundred other steel wares*', all of which were imported in large quantities.[4]

A small start had been made with engineering (machine building). Gascoigne had established at Olonets in 1786 what was perhaps Russia's first machine works and in 1790 it produced a steam engine. In 1805 a large factory making textile machinery was set up in St Petersburg. Another works making steam engines and metal-working machinery appeared in St Petersburg in 1790, followed by one manufacturing agricultural machinery in 1802 and another turning out textile machinery in 1805. The capital had become an important engineering centre in a very short time.[5] The growing demand for machinery in the newly-opened wheatlands of the south led to the setting up, by an Englishman, of a factory in Moscow, in 1802, which made simple threshing machines.[6]

During the five years 1802-6, Russia smelted an average annual amount of 200,000 puds of copper. 90 per cent of this came from the Urals, 8 per cent from the Kolyvan mines in the Altay Mountains of southern Siberia, and the remaining 2 per cent mainly from Georgia. Petrozavodsk had stopped copper smelting in 1781.

The Urals copper came from 34 works with 218 furnaces. Besides the operational works there were some 16 where copper was no longer smelted. All but one of these were in the central Urals and had closed down because the ore had given out. Voznesensk (built in 1756) ceased working in 1774 when it was destroyed in Pugachev's rising.[7]

The copper, brass and bronze works, which converted the copper metal into articles of use, were mostly in central and north-western Russia, although the imperial mint was at Yekaterinburg, and there was

---

[1] *Clarke (1810), p. 183*
[2] *Wilmot (1803-8), p. 180*
[3] *Wilmot (1803-8), p. 273*
[4] *Tooke (1799), vol. 3, pp. 553-5*
[5] *Gille (1949), p. 150*
[6] *Lyashchenko (1956), vol. 1, p. 513*
[7] *Hermann (1810), table 6c*

still the ancient copperworks at Solikamsk, which made mainly household utensils. The Kolyvan mint turned out about 100,000 roubles' worth of copper coinage a year (1803-9 average) as well as silver and gold money.[1]

Gold and silver were refined from the copper ores of Kolyvan in the Altay Mountains and the lead ores of Nerchinsk in Transbaykalia. The Kolyvan ores were not smelted at the mines since wood fuel was scarce there. Instead they were transported north-eastwards to smelters at Barnaul, Novopavlovsk and Susunsk *'in a country abounding with trees'*.[2] With the decline in the mineral content of the ore, production of silver had declined from about 13,200 puds to 600, and of gold over 40 puds to under 20. Over 5,000 workers were employed at the Kolyvan mines and smelters, besides the labour of more than 50,000 ascribed peasants, *'who, in lieu of paying the poll tax in money, cut wood, make charcoal, and transport the ore to the foundries'*.[3]

At Nerchinsk the metallic yield of the ore was declining, and the annual yield of silver had decreased from about 450 puds in 1772 to 200; that of gold from 5 puds to little more than 1. The number of men employed was about

> *1,900 free colonists, between 1,000 and 1,800 convicts, and 11,000 Russian peasants of the district of Nershinsk: 6,000 of these latter are employed in cutting and carrying wood, making and transporting charcoal, while the rest, who live at some distance from the mines, cultivate a certain portion of ground, and bring in winter the produce to the magazines of the foundries.*[4]

The gold and silver were not separated at the Siberian smelters but in St Petersburg.

The main centre of gold production in the Empire was now Yekaterinburg. The gold was obtained by washing and there were 9 lavatories, 5 of which had been erected in 1803 and 1804. This was an indication of a rapid increase in production from 3 or 4 puds in the first years after its inception in 1753 to over 20 puds in 1809. According to Hermann, the 41,250 ascribed peasants were replaced in 1807 by a regular labour force of 1,237 men.[5]

To sum up, annual gold and silver production at the beginning of the nineteenth century seems to have been:

	Gold	Silver
Yekaterinburg	*20 puds*	*600 puds*
*Barnaul-Novopavlovsk-Susunsk**	*19*	
Nerchinsk	*1*	*200*
	40	*800*
* *from Kolyvan ore*	*—*	

[1] *Coxe (1784), vol. 2, p. 285; Hermann (1810), tables 10hh, 6, 7a*
[2] *Coxe (1784), vol. 2, p. 284*
[3] *Coxe (1784), vol. 2, p. 285; Storch (1801B), vol. 2, p. 378*
[4] *Coxe (1784), vol. 2, p. 287*
[5] *Hermann (1810), table 6a*

Apart from the demands of the imperial mints at Yekaterinburg and Kolyvan, the gold and silver went chiefly to the smiths of Petersburg, Moscow and Ustyug *'where much silver has been wrought from time immemorial . . . a great number of silver boxes for snuff, etc.'*[1]

INDUSTRIES WORKING UP THE PRODUCE OF AGRICULTURE AND FISHERIES

Animal fat was an important raw material. The preparation of tallow was widespread and it was an important article of export. Kolomna, Moscow, Voronezh, Rostov and Tula were the principal centres. At Voronezh, part of the town was

> *covered by storehouses, cauldrons and tubs, for the preparation of grease, which is a great article of trade here, and which they send to England and to America in vast quantities. The stench from the bones and horns of animals, slaughtered for the purpose of obtaining grease, made the spot absolutely intolerable.*[2]

Chandleries of especial repute were found at Vologda, Kostroma and among the Moravian colonists at Tsaritsyn. Soap-boiling, a related industry, flourished in the same places, as well as Moscow, Kazan and Murom. The pressing of vegetable and fish oils, also widely used in the soap industry, took place in many parts of the Empire. Many raw materials contributed: hazel nuts (Kazan province), cedar nuts (Siberia), poppy seeds, juniper (Yaroslavl), turpentine (Tver and Vologda), hemp and linseed (rural peasants in many parts), train oil (*'from the blubber of the morshes, which is boiled in great quantities on the coasts of Archangel and Olonets. It is commonly melted at home in copper kettles over the fire.'*) Oil was made on the Caspian shores from the fat of the beluga or great sturgeon.[3] Isinglass, a product *'almost peculiar to Russia'* was made from sturgeon air bladders, mainly along the Caspian shores but also on the lower Ural, Volga, Don and Dnieper rivers. Caviar production was found in similar places.[4]

The distilling of vodka from rye and other grain was widespread in Livonia, Lithuania and White Russia, and in the Ukraine. It was a convenient and profitable way of using a grain surplus. By 1780 there were 976 distilleries in the Kharkov area.[5] Brewing beer was more of an urban industry and is mentioned at St Petersburg, Moscow, Nizhniy Novgorod and Riga. *'That of Riga is said to approach very near to the English'* while on the Oka river in Nizhniy Novgorod province:

> *are several large brewhouses in which, with the water of that river (for the Volga water is unfit for that purpose) an excellent light brown beer is brewed, little inferior to Burton ale.*[6]

[1] *Tooke (1799), vol. 3, p. 556*
[2] *Clarke (1810), pp. 204-5*
[3] *Tooke (1799), vol. 3, pp. 463-5, 469, 470*
[4] *Tooke (1799), vol. 3, pp. 463-70*
[5] *Wilmot (1803-8), p. 127; Lyashchenko (1956), vol. 1, pp. 533-4*
[6] *Tooke (1799), vol. 3, p. 471*

The old sugar refineries at St Petersburg and Moscow, mentioned in Chapter 8, worked on imported cane sugar. By the early nineteenth century a beginning had been made with the cultivation of beet sugar in the wooded steppe and in 1802 the first refinery to treat it opened at Tula.

INDUSTRIES WORKING UP MINERALS OTHER THAN METALS

Pottery was the chief of these. There were earthenware potteries at Moscow, St Petersburg, Revel, Kiev and several other places, but their products *'do not last like the English plates, as the glaze wears off in a short time'*.[1] There were 3 porcelain factories including the imperial works at St Petersburg. It served the Court and had 400 workpeople. The clay, formerly brought from the Urals, now came from the Ukraine. An Englishman had set up the porcelain works at Dmitrov, north-west of Moscow, in 1766.[2]

Glass was now manufactured in several of the older towns of central Russia, as well as at St Petersburg, Archangel and in the Baltic provinces. Russian plate glass was excepted by Mary Holderness from her general condemnation of Russian manufactures.[3]

Vitriol was produced in Tambov and Voronezh provinces where the ground was impregnated with sulphides and sulphates of iron, and also at Konchozersk in Olonets province, where similar conditions prevailed.[4] Clarke saw *'a building for the preparation of vitriol'* at Voronezh.[5] Saltpetre works were numerous, especially in southern Russia. Alum was prepared with sulphuric acid at the large vitriol works in Tambov province where 1,700 workers were employed.[6]

Moscow was the chief centre for the manufacture of paper, wall-paper, playing cards, etc. (12 factories). The other towns making paper were in central Russia round Moscow. There were now several printing works in both Moscow and St Petersburg, with others at Reval and Riga in the north-west, Kiev and Kremenchug in the south-west, and at Astrakhan in the south-east.[7]

[1] *Holderness (1823), p. 69*
[2] *Storch (1801A), pp. 275, 280; Tooke (1799), vol. 3, pp. 545-6*
[3] *Holderness (1823), p. 69*
[4] *Hermann (1810), tables 6 and 7*
[5] *Clarke (1810), p. 205*
[6] *Hermann (1810), table 7b*
[7] *Tooke (1799), vol. 3, pp. 504-6*

CHAPTER TWELVE
RUSSIA AT THE BEGINNING
OF THE NINETEENTH CENTURY:
COMMERCIAL GEOGRAPHY

THE TRADE OF RUSSIA

Russia's foreign trade increased by leaps and bounds during the eighteenth century. According to customs returns, admittedly unreliable, the total value of trade in 1802 was 120 million roubles, whereas sixty years before it had been but 8 million. Although the bulk of this commerce was seaborne, overland traffic was quite considerable, as Table 1 shows:[1]

Table 1: Value of Trade, 1802 (millions of roubles)

	Imports	Exports	Total
Overseas	36·3	54·8	91·1
by the Baltic Sea	33·0	46·9	79·9
by the White Sea	0·5	4.8	5·3
by the Black Sea	2·1	3·0	5·1
by the Caspian Sea	0·7	0·1	0·8
Overland	20·3	8·5	28·8
across the Swedish frontier	0·1	0·1	0·2
across the Prussian and Austrian frontiers	10·6	4·5	15·1
across the Turkish frontier in Europe	2·5	0·8	3·3
across the Turkish frontier in Asia	0·2	0·0	0·2
with Central Asia	2·4	1·1	3·5
with China	4·5	2·0	6·5
Total	56·5	63·3	119·9

Whether Russia really had such a favourable balance is doubtful. According to Oddy, '*it is generally reckoned that the imports should be 10 per cent more, and the exports 10 per cent less, in which case Russia has a losing trade*'. It is clear, however, that with European countries the balance was more favourable than with those of Asia. The customs returns for 1802 give a favourable balance of nearly 12 million roubles with Europe and an adverse gap of nearly 4 million roubles with Asia. European countries badly needed Russian raw materials. But, whereas the Russian demand for Asian livestock, silk, spices, tea and pearls was great, China preferred European to Russian manufactured goods. Compared with Russia's own exports to

[1] *Oddy (1805), p. 205*

Asia, valued at 3 million roubles, European goods valued at 5·6 million roubles went to Asia by way of Russia.[1]

The general nature of the trade, according to commodities, is summarized in Table 2;

Table 2: Russian Trade by Commodity Groups, 1802
(in thousands of roubles)

	Imports	Exports
RAW MATERIALS	10,223	36,390
	(textile fibres, dyes, raw sugar, etc.)	(hemp, tallow, flax, leather, timber, etc.)
METALS	11,465	4,680
	(silver, gold, tin, lead, etc.)	(almost wholly iron)
FOOD AND DRINK	15,636	12,453
	(wine, sugar, salt, fruit, coffee, etc.)	(rye, wheat, barley, etc.)
MANUFACTURES	17,536	7,882
	(woollen and cotton goods, etc.)	(flaxen, hempen and leather goods, etc.)
OTHERS	1,707	1,880
	(horses, cattle, pearls, etc.)	(horses, cattle, etc.)
TOTAL	56,567	63,285

The trade in the leading individual commodities is not so easily computed, and the list below (Table 3) does not include the full value of some goods. It is based on the amounts recorded at the Baltic and Black Sea ports only, with additions where ascertainable. When the figures are supposedly complete, they have been marked with an asterisk; where they are certainly too low, with a plus sign.

Table 3: Russian Trade by Commodities, 1802[2] (in thousands of roubles)

	Imports		Exports	
1	Woollens	5,832+	Tallow	9,664*
2	Refined sugar	4,832	Raw hemp	9,346*
3	Silver	3,363+	Raw flax	5,773*
4	Cottons	3,289	Rye	5,604*
5	Dyestuffs	2,494	Iron	4,618*
6	Wine	2,361+	Wheat	4,056*
7	Salt	1,323	Leather, leather goods	3,057*
8	Coffee	997	Linseed & hempseed	2,519*
9	Fruit (fresh & dried)	995	Sailcloth & canvas	2,253

[1] Oddy (1805), p. 205
[2] Compiled from data in Oddy (1805)

	Imports			Exports	
10	Gold in foreign coin	798+	Hempseed & linseed oil	1,560*
11	Live animals	710*	Live animals	1,445*
12	Fish	589	Timber	1,442*
13	Raw silk	526	Linen & linen goods	1,285*
14	Silk manufactures	523	Barley	1,004*
15	Pearls	433*	Potash	804
16	Turpentine	413	Ropes and cordage	635
17	Raw sugar	326	Vodka	531*
18	Raw cotton	325	Caviar	290+
19	Iron manufactures	294	Furs	270+
20	Sandalwood	276	Butter	247
21	Salad oil	275	Candles	227
22	Incense	269	Wax	220

Britain was easily Russia's chief customer and bought much more from her than she sold. After Britain came Russia's western neighbours by land: Sweden, Prussia, Austria and Turkey. Prussia and Austria sent manufactured goods and metals, and imported—besides Russia's staple exports—large numbers of live cattle. Turkey sent fruit—fresh, dried and preserved.

The bulk of Russia's foreign trade was still carried in foreign vessels. As will be seen below, English ships predominated and the Dutch no longer had the lion's share:[1]

Ships Arriving at Russian Ports by Nationality, 1803

English	1,312	Austrian	294
Swedish	450	Lübeck	154
Turkish	339	Mecklenburg	92
Danish	336	American	85
Prussian	304	Hamburg	51

Only 30 Dutch ships are recorded.

Although tallow heads the list of individual commodity exports, if all hempen and flaxen products are put together, they far and away exceed any other export in value; they formed in 1802 over 35 per cent of the total.

Russian exports of iron, which had soared from 2,000 tons in 1740 to over 50,000 in the 1780s, while still important, had begun to decline as the new techniques in England and elsewhere began to have effect.[2]

Some commodities, such as tobacco, vegetable oil and salt, were both imported and exported. Russia's great sources of salt supply were in the eastern part of the country, and the demand in the Baltic provinces and the north-west was partly met by imports. These were only partly offset by exports from Black Sea ports. Despite her large exports of linseed and

[1] *Oddy (1805), p. 204*
[2] *Oddy (1805), p. 73; Portal (1950), p. 156*

hempseed oil, Russia had to import considerable quantities of fine edible oils, especially olive oil. Raw cotton was a new import. American ships brought 97,000 roubles worth to St Petersburg in 1803 for Russia's nascent spinning industry, but imports of yarn were still much larger.

The Baltic Sea: Trade and Seaports (fig. 44)

The Baltic carried two-thirds of Russia's total trade in 1802, and nearly 90 per cent of her seaborne trade, a remarkable fact when it is remembered that she had had access to these waters for less than a hundred years. There was a considerable excess of exports (47 million roubles) over imports (33 million roubles). As the former were much bulkier than the latter, the excess was much greater by volume than by value. The leading commodities of the Baltic trade in 1802 were as follows:[1]

Imports		*Exports*	
		(thousands of roubles)	
Woollens	*5,811*	*Raw hemp*	*9,059*
Sugar	*4,831*	*Tallow*	*8,712*
Silver	*3,281*	*Raw flax*	*5,583*
Cottons	*3,169*	*Rye*	*4,041*
Dyestuffs	*2,494*	*Iron*	*3,742*
Wine	*2,002*	*Leather and leather goods*	*2,945*
Salt	*1,319*	*Sailcloth and canvas*	*2,253*
Coffee	*992*	*Hempseed oil*	*1,492*
Gold	*720*	*Wheat*	*1,319*

The trade was divided among the ports by value as follows:

St Petersburg-Kronstadt	*70%*
Riga	*18*
Libau	*4*
Revel	*3*
Pernau	*2*
others	*3*

ST PETERSBURG-KRONSTADT

Kronstadt was the port of St Petersburg because the bar at the Neva mouth prevented access to vessels drawing more than seven or eight feet. But, as Kronstadt was on an island, goods coming to or from the capital had still to be transported by lighters or 'galliots':

> *flat-bottomed and with a round bar and stern. They carry from fifty to a hundred tons of hemp. Sailing boats of about thirty to fifty tons burthen are likewise employed in this trade for the sake of quicker dispatch.*[2]

[1] *Oddy (1805), pp. 109-12*
[2] *Atkinson and Walker (1812), vol. 1*

figure 44   Russia in 1800: relative trade of the principal ports (data from Oddy).

Exports from the port were greater than imports in the ratio of three to two. As with Russian trade as a whole, Britain was by far the best customer:

Principal Exports from St Petersburg-Kronstadt by Volume, 1802
(in thousands of puds, arsheens or pieces)

Iron	2,055	puds, of which	70%	to Great Britain			
Raw hemp	1,986	,, ,, ,,	48%	,,	,,	,,	
Tallow	1,773	,, ,, ,,	85%	,,	,,	,,	
Hempseed oil	392	,,	*(figure not available)*				
Flax	303	,,	of which 67%	to Great Britain			
Potash	285	,, ,, ,,	24%	,,	,,	,,	
Linen goods	4,001 arsheens	,,	76%	,,	,,	,,	
Deals	1,113 pieces	,,	95%	,,	,,	,,	

St Petersburg's trade was distinguished by an extremely wide range of commodities, for many of which it was the sole Russian inlet or outlet.[1] This was especially true of imports, of which there were some 240 different categories listed, the chief of which were: cotton and woollen goods, refined sugar and molasses, wines, gold and silver coin. Among the items imported were also listed: arsenic, beaver skins, chocolate, corks, crucibles, elixir, sealing wax, statues of alabaster and walking sticks.

RIGA

Riga had established itself as the second port in the Russian Empire, though far behind St Petersburg. Good inland water communication gave it a hinterland extending as far south as the western Ukraine and Austrian Galicia, but it suffered from a bar at the Dvina mouth which compelled larger vessels to load out in the road, exposed to north-west winds. Hence vessels frequenting it were, on an average, much smaller than those using Kronstadt. At Riga, exports predominated even more than at St Petersburg. There was nothing like the range of goods, but five main staples: raw hemp, raw flax, linseed, rye and timber.

For certain goods, notably rye, linseed, masts, yards, spars and bowsprits, Riga was the leading exporter. This position she owed to the quality of the goods exported, the result of inflexible insistence on high standards and thorough Germanic inspections of which the Russians were incapable. Thus we learn that Riga flax was 'of a finer harl, cleaner and better quality than from any other port in the Baltic'; that the linseed was '*a particular and superior sort*', as a result of which the Dutch bought large amounts for sowing; that '*the grain . . . from its being dried, bears longer voyages, on which account it is generally shipped to Spain or Portugal, or other southern markets*'. As for the masts and other ships' timber, it was '*the great attention and excellent regulations paid to the bracking system which has hitherto preserved this branch to Riga exclusively*'.

Linen is remarkably absent from Riga's exports, but little of it was manufactured in the hinterland. Among the port's inconsiderable imports, the chief were salt, refined sugar, coffee, cheese, fruit, hardware, scythes and lead. Britain did not loom so large among the port's customers as at St Petersburg, but Spain, the Netherlands, Denmark, Sweden, Prussia and the city of Lübeck were all considerable buyers.[2]

OTHER BALTIC PORTS

Libau, third after St Petersburg and Riga, but with only 4 per cent of the Baltic trade, was the port of the former Polish province of Kurland. It was handicapped by lack of inland waterway communication. Its trade was chiefly with the Dutch who bought linseed for sowing and rye for distilling, both products of the agricultural province of Kurland. The remarkable fact about Revel and Pernau was that their imports exceeded their exports:

[1] *Oddy (1805), pp. 113-16*
[2] *Oddy (1805), 138-52*

at Revel they were four or five times as great. Revel had natural advantages:
*Its harbour ranks among the first in the gulf. . . . There is a sufficient
depth of water near the town for the largest ships, which may work
into the roads with almost any wind.*
Further, Revel was superior to other Baltic ports in that:
*When they are choking up with floating ice, or fast altogether by it, its
harbour is not so soon frozen, on account of having no fresh water river
falling into it, and having a sufficient depth of water. From these
advantages, at the close of the year, vessels with cargoes intended for
Petersburg, put into Revel.*
But there was no inland waterway. Its trade was mostly with Lübeck to
which it sent rye and from which it imported manufactured goods.[1]
Pernau, like Revel, exported the rye and other grains of its immediate
hinterland. Narva and Vyborg, on opposite sides of the Gulf of Finland,
both exported timber.

The White Sea: Archangel

Almost wholly carried on at Archangel, the White Sea trade had increased
rapidly in value during the eighteenth century, the rise of St Petersburg
notwithstanding:

> *Trade of Archangel (in thousands of roubles)*
> 1726   279
> 1750   489
> 1776   1,764
> 1802   5,040*
> *this figure is artificially exaggerated because Baltic trade was
> interrupted by war. In 1803 it was 2,592,000 roubles.*

The rise in the value of exports had been faster than that of imports, and
the latter were normally about a quarter of the former. The chief commodities exported were tallow, iron, deals and rye. Archangel's oldest
customer, Britain, still dominated her trade, taking, in 1802, 94 per cent
of the deals, 88 per cent of the tallow and 75 per cent of the iron; but she
took only 3 per cent of the rye, most of which went to Dutch distilleries.[2]

The Black Sea and Sea of Azov: Trade and Ports

Russian trade in the Black Sea began in 1758, but was interrupted by
successive Turkish wars until 1793, after which date it had grown un-
interruptedly. As the table below shows, there were important differences

[1] *Oddy (1805), pp. 155-7*
[2] *Oddy (1805), pp. 93-102*

between the main commodities in the trade of the ports of northern and southern Russia:[1]

Trade of the Black Sea Ports, 1802 (*in thousands of roubles*)

Imports		Exports	
Fruit and fruit jelly	398	Wheat	1,755
Wine	360	Iron	334
Edible oils	275	Caviar	225
Incense	229	Butter	169
Gold and silver coin	160	Linen goods	141
Cotton goods	120	Furs	52
Raw silk	75	Rope and cordage	52
Raw cotton	71	Salt	49
Nuts	65	Felts	39

The Black Sea ports have obviously taken advantage of the opportunity to import Mediterranean products in large amounts in exchange for the wheat of the newly-cultivated steppes. This trade was, in 1797, distributed amongst the ports as follows (thousands of roubles):

Port	Imports	Exports	Total
Taganrog	379	693	1,072
Yevpatoriya (*Kozlov*)	85	244	329
Odessa	129	79	208
Feodosiya (*Kaffa*)	51	69	120
Ochakov	39	33	72
Sevastopol	63	5	68
Nikolayev	0	37	37
Kherson	0	35	35
Kerch	14	13	27

TAGANROG

The Russians had first secured a foothold where the Don enters the Sea of Azov. Temporarily in Peter I's reign, and again in 1739, the Don mouth became Russian, but while the Turks held the Azov shores and Crimea, any trade was completely at their mercy. Once these also had become Russian, the Don outlet became of value and Taganrog, where a colony of Armenian traders established itself, soon became an important port. Although linked by established waterways and portages with central Russia, the Urals and western Siberia, it suffered from severe drawbacks. The Sea of Azov freezes from November to March, and there was never enough water through the Taman Strait. Nevertheless 200 ships, mostly Greek, entered the port in 1803.[2] Clarke summed up the trade of the place:
They receive fruit from Turkey, such as figs, raisins and oranges;

[1] *Oddy (1805), pp. 175–6*
[2] *Reuilly (1806), p. 280*

also Greek wines from the Archipelago, with incense, coffee, silks, shawls, tobacco and precious stones. Copper comes to them from Trebisond, but of a very inferior quality and is all sent to Moscow. Among their principal exports are caviare, butter, leather, tallow, corn, furs, canvas, rigging, linen, wool, hemp and iron, of which last article above a million poods were exported during the year in which we visited the place. The greatest advantage which the town enjoys is being the deposit of Siberian productions. From Orenburg they receive tallow, furs and iron, which, with the caviare of Astrakhan has only the short passage by land which intervenes between Zaritzin on the Volga and the Don, a distance of 40 English miles, where Peter the Great projected a canal, and which it was Paul's intention to have completed.[1]

Iron, carried to Constantinople and Smyrna, was the main commodity to pass through Taganrog.

YEVPATORIYA (KOZLOV)

The old Tartar town of Kozlov, renamed Yevpatoriya, with its dangerously exposed harbour, became, for want of a better, the main outlet for the growing surplus of wheat from the steppes until Odessa took its place. It imported some rice, coffee, sugar, dates, dried figs and cotton cloth.[2]

ODESSA

The difficulties and dangers of Taganrog, Yevpatoriya and alternative harbours, led Catherine II to decide upon the building of an entirely new port on the north shore of the Black Sea, between the mouths of the Dniester and the Bug, as soon as this territory had been acquired (1791). Founded in 1794 and open to traffic in 1795, the new port made fast progress, encouraged by immense government subsidies and special privileges. By 1797 it had risen to third place amongst the southern ports by value of trade, and by the early years of the nineteenth century it had undoubtedly outstripped all its rivals. Oddy (1805) thought it *'likely to become a second Petersburg'*. The following figures, though incomplete, give some idea of the growth of this infant port:

	Ships arriving	Value of trade
1795	35	68,000
1796	87	172,000
1797		208,000
1803	502	

The site was an open bay and breakwaters were being built, under Dutch guidance, to provide sheltered water.[3] The water was deep—six fathoms—

[1] *Clarke (1810), pp. 330-1*
[2] *Reuilly (1806), p. 129; Holderness (1823), p. 139*
[3] *Guthrie (1802), p. 25*

and anchorage good on sand and gravel. Frost interrupted navigation only briefly and in some years not at all.

Cotton and dried fruit, olive oil and wines, were already coming to Odessa in large quantities; Ukrainian wheat was the main export. Of the 500 ships that arrived in 1803, 278 were Austrian, 96 Russian and 56 Turkish. Ochakov, Taganrog, Yevpatoriya and Kherson all suffered from the vigorous growth of this place, as it was more advantageously placed than were they for dealing with all the staples except Uralian iron and Siberian furs.[1]

FEODOSIYA

Kaffa, once the most flourishing of the Genoese ports on the Crimean coast, was now in decline under its new name. Despite a fine natural harbour protected by a promontory, it could not compete with Taganrog and Odessa for communication with the interior. However, its trade was not yet insignificant. It consisted:

> *chiefly in the export of wheat; besides which barley, salt and a few manufactures in iron and woollens. The imports are somewhat more numerous: Greek wines, dried fruits, Turkish stuffs, silks and other manufactures, raw cotton and a few copper utensils.*[2]

Ochakov, nearer to the Bug than Odessa, had been the chief Turkish port on the north shore of the Black Sea and enjoyed a short-lived prosperity under the Russians. The decline in its trade after the foundation of Odessa was rapid.[3]

1794	*546,451 roubles*	
1795	*140,747*	,,
1796	*126,835*	,,
1797	*72,304*	,,

SEVASTOPOL (fig. 45)

The fine natural harbour of Sevastopol, consisting of deep inlets sheltered by promontories, but backed by mountains, was more suited to become a great naval base than to be a commercial port. An imperial *ukaz* closed it to commerce in 1804. Henceforth it was the headquarters of the Russian Black Sea fleet where, in 1803, there were stationed 14 ships of the line and 4 or 5 frigates.[4]

NIKOLAYEV

This place was founded in 1789 to replace Kherson as the Black Sea naval headquarters. After the establishment of Sevastopol, a flotilla of 70 to 80 galleys was stationed here. It was also a fishing port.[5]

[1] *Oddy (1805), pp. 168-80; Reuilly (1806), p. 262*
[2] *Holderness (1823), p. 138.*
[3] *Oddy (1805), p. 175*
[4] *Reuilly (1806), pp. 207-8*
[5] *Reuilly (1806), pp. 207-8; Holderness (1823), p. 85*

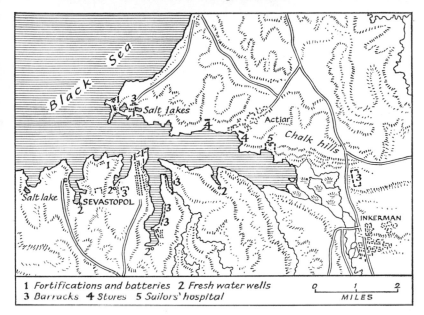

| 1 Fortifications and batteries | 2 Fresh water wells |
| 3 Barracks | 4 Stores | 5 Sailors' hospital |

figure 45   Sevastopol in 1803 (after Reuilly).

KHERSON

The rise of Odessa had left Kherson with very little trade. The great advantage of a situation on the Dnieper was more than offset because

> goods are obliged to be transported in lighters to the ships in the open roads, which is often attended with danger from the weather, and always great risk on account of pillage.

It had also been tried as a naval port, but found to be too unhealthy.[1]

KERCH

Kerch, strikingly placed at the foot of a steep hill, had an excellent harbour, but its trade had nearly vanished.[2]

The Caspian Sea: Astrakhan

Astrakhan, if the figures given above (p. 177) are to be credited, transacted in 1802 less than 1 per cent by value of the total trade of the Russian Empire. This would place it eighth as a port, after St Petersburg, Riga, Archangel, Libau, Revel, Pernau and Taganrog. It had perhaps been adversely affected by the rise of the Black Sea trade.

In 1806 Russia gained, in Baku, another Caspian port, described by Coxe as follows:

[1] *Oddy (1805), p. 177; Guthrie (1802), pp. 32-3*
[2] *Reuilly (1806), p. 140*

*Baku is esteemed the most commodious haven in this sea, as vessels may
there ride securely at anchor in seven fathom of water; but the number
of shoals, islands, and sandbanks, render the entrance in some places
extremely difficult and dangerous . . .
Baku is a fortress surrounded with high brick walls; its inhabitants . . .
are Persians, Tartars, and a few Armenian merchants. The principal
articles of exportation which support the trade of the place are naphtha,
and the finest rock salt, of both of which there are mines on the east
side of the bay.*[1]

The Pacific Ocean

Russia now had two Pacific seaports in Okhotsk and Petropavlovsk, but
there is little information available about them at this time.

WATERWAYS

The barges used on the rivers and canals were
> *perfectly flat-bottomed, and many of a great length: the largest fir
> planks are selected for the purpose of building them; the timbers and
> crooks are generally selected from such trees as have roots of a proper
> shape.
> The depth of one of these vessels is seldom more than four feet; some
> few more: the sides are perpendicular, and not much regard had to
> shape; they load them to draw from twenty to thirty inches of water,
> or more, according to the season of the year and to the water they expect
> to find in their respective navigations.*[2]

The Don

The newly-gained Russian hold on the Black Sea inevitably brought
increased traffic on the Don, and at Pavlovsk: '*barges, laden with corn,
were seen moving with its current towards the Sea of Azov*'. The ancient
practice whereby the barges made a single journey and were then broken
up for their timber was now found at the Don mouth, especially as these
lands lacked wood:
> *The vessels from Woronetz, unfit to encounter the sea, are broken up,
> and their cargoes, the product of Russia, shipped on board lighters and
> small vessels and sent to Taganrog, to load the vessels lying in the
> roads of that place.*[3]

[1] *Coxe (1784), vol. 2, p. 260*
[2] *Oddy (1805), p. 69*
[3] *Clarke (1810), pp. 217, 313*

The Volga-Neva Waterway (fig. 46)

The waterway linking Moscow and the Volga with St Petersburg and the Gulf of Finland was now the busiest in Russia. There were two artificial canals: the Vyshniy Volochok, linking the upper Volga system with that of the Volkhov; and the Ladoga canal which skirted the southern shore of the lake.

The former, completed in Peter's reign, ran through the middle of the small town of Vyshniy Volochok, as did the main St Petersburg-Moscow road, so that the place was full of activity. The traffic was one-way, and throughout the navigable season a stream of barges laden with timber, tallow, hemp, grain, iron and copper made its way from lock to lock before beginning the perilous descent of the Mtsa and the Borovichi rapids where

> *the fall of the river is 122½ yards perpendicular in twenty miles; and the stream is so violent that the boats not infrequently shoot along this space within the hour: but they are sometimes dashed against the rocks, or overset by accident: in the year 1778, above thirty were lost.*[1]

Each barge was towed up the Tvertza to Vyshniy Volochok by 10 horses, making 10-12 miles a day. They were then rowed downstream. Vessels passing through the canal in 1797 were: 3,958 barges, 382 half-barges, 248 one-masted vessels and boats, and 1,676 rafts; they carried 82½ million puds of goods (1,334,000 tons), together with over 13 million chetverts of goods measured by capacity (75,800,000 bushels), and 123,000 barrels.[2] After descending the Mtsa to lake Ilmen, the barges went down the Volkhov. They were no longer, as in 1725, exposed to the storms of lake Ladoga, but entered the Ladoga canal, completed in 1732. This canal was 67½ miles long with a summer depth of 7 feet. The journey from Vishniy Volochok to St Petersburg took a fortnight in spring when the rivers were full and fast, three weeks in summer, and a month in autumn, when they were shallow and slow.[3]

Two other waterways linking the Volga and the Neva had canals newly completed or under construction. One route left the Volga at its northernmost bend to follow various streams, the last of which, the Syas, enters lake Ladoga; a canal, finished in 1801, extended the Ladoga canal to the mouth of this river. The other route ran northwards from the Volga to lake Onega: the Mariinsk canal on this waterway was also finished in 1801; a canal along the southern shore of lake Onega, and the Svir canal, joining the Svir to the already extended Ladoga canal, were under construction.

---

[1] *Coxe (1784), vol. 2, p. 293*
[2] *Oddy (1805), p. 68*
[3] *Coxe (1784), vol. 2, p. 294*

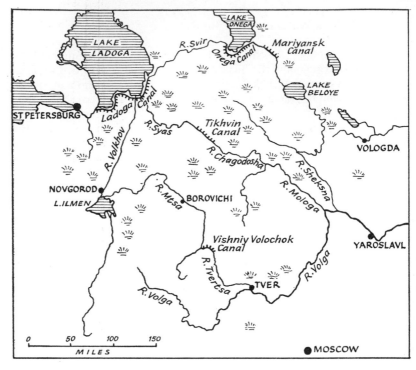

figure 46   Waterways linking the Volga with St Petersburg.

LAND ROUTES

There had been little improvement in the roads generally since 1725, although some had been 'corduroyed', i.e. surfaced with logs or planks. Even in winter they were well nigh impassable in places:

> *From the constant passage of merchandise on the roads they are ploughed up into rocks of frozen and refrozen snow over which you must drive. . . . In these dreadful holes one is sometimes rooted for twenty minutes at a time, the miserable horses falling with the exertion of pulling one out, and lashed up again and again by dozens of people and servants who aid in supporting either side of the carriage.*[1]

After spring thaw or autumn rains, roads could become so impossible as to prevent movement altogether. Bridges were still few and far between and Forster noted no fixed bridges on the route from Astrakhan to Moscow, but had to cross rivers by ferries or floating bridges. Normal winter trans-

[1] *Stewart & Hyde (1934), p. 220*

port was still by sledge. For goods, these were large, but for passengers the small swift light *kibitka* was used. This was not confined to roads, but

> *its being considerably less [wide] gives it an advantage for travelling through the extensive woods of Russia, where the track is so narrow in winter, as scarcely to admit two horses abreast; they are extremely light, and are drawn with the greatest ease by one horse, though for greater expedition they sometimes use two. Such is the simplicity of their construction that a peasant, with no other tool than his hatchet, will knock one together in a very few days.*[1]

In summer the *telega* or cart was used for transporting goods; these appeared lightly constructed, but were '*strong enough to carry a load of 20 to 25 puds for one horse, or 30 to 40 drawn by two horses*'. The sledges could carry nearly a third more than the carts, in a shorter time, and with less risk of damage or breakdown. Consequently, while it cost a rouble a pud to send goods in summer, the rate was only 35 kopeks in winter. Both winter and summer loads went in caravans of about fifty.[2] (Plates 5, 6.)

The Moscow–St Petersburg Road

The direct road between Moscow and St Petersburg attempted by Peter I was now finished and followed an almost straight line across the 400 miles separating the two cities. It was without doubt the best road in the country and enormous trouble was taken to improve the worst parts with timber. Coxe gives the details:

> *trunks of trees are laid transversely in rows parallel to each other, and are bound down in the centre, and at each extremity, by long poles or beams fastened into the ground with wooden pegs; these trunks are covered with layers of boughs and the whole is strewed over with sand or earth.*

Yet the road was considered as indescribably bad by travellers. The timber stretches soon deteriorated:

> *When the road is new, it is remarkably good; but the trunks decay or sink into the ground, and as the sand or earth is worn away or washed off by the rain, as is frequently the case for several miles together, it is broken into innumerable holes, and the jolting of the carriage over the bare timber road can better be conceived than described.*[3]

The Trans-Uralian Road

The old route via Solikamsk and Verkhoturye was being displaced by a more southerly one by way of Perm and Yekaterinburg. The pacification of Bashkiria had made this possible.

[1] *Atkinson & Walker (1812), vol. 2*
[2] *Atkinson & Walker (1812), vols. 1 and 2*
[3] *Coxe (1784), vol. 1, p. 434*

The Ukraine

Now that southern Russia had been secured from marauding Tartars, not only agriculture but land transport developed rapidly, and caravans of loaded waggons were met with everywhere. Up and down the Don, between central Russia and the Sea of Azov, Clarke was

> *continually met by caravans from the Don, the Crimea and other parts of the south of Russia. These caravans formed a line of waggons, thirty or forty in number, bearing brandy, wool, corn, etc.*

Lower down the river he: '*observed trains of from sixty to a hundred waggons, laden entirely with dried fish, to feed the inhabitants of the south of Russia.*'[1] One important route came out of Germany, crossed the Dnieper at Kiev and the Don at Voronezh, and continued across the Volga into Siberia and thence to China:

> *The carriers of Woronetz go every three years to Tobolsky in Siberia which is a rendezvous for all caravans bound to Kiatka, on the frontiers of China. From Tobolsky they form one immense caravan to Kiatka. From Siberia they bring furs; from Kiatka, Chinese merchandise of all sorts, as tea, raw and manufactured silk, porcelain and precious stones.*
>
> *The Chinese, upon their arrival at Kiatka, also furnish them with the productions of Kamschatka, brought from St Peter and St Paul [i.e. Petropavlovsk]. Thus laden, many of them set out for Francfort, and bring back muslin, cambric, silks, the porcelain of Saxony, and the manufactures of England.*[2]

These new nomads, many of whom were Ukrainians (*chyumaki*), also penetrated into the north-west, linking southern Russia with Riga and the Baltic:

> *We passed on our road several caravans of Tchumaks or Little Russians, with their four-wheeled carriages drawn by oxen. Each waggon holds from one or two, even two and a half tons weight of salt or corn. The Tchumaks travel in caravans of twenty or forty waggons or even more. . . .*
>
> *The extraordinary journeys which these Tchumaks undertake with their loaded waggons is very remarkable—setting out from Riga, or other port towns of the Baltic in the spring, when the snow is dissolved, and travelling to Moscow, Kaluga, Tula, etc., and then to the Black Sea, with corn, and returning laden with salt in the autumn.*[3]

[1] *Clarke (1810), pp. 195, 259*
[2] *Clarke (1810), p. 206*
[3] *Holderness (1823), pp. 90-1*

Plate 7 Moscow: Red Square. This open space, the scene of uprisings, executions and processions for many centuries, separates the Kremlin (right) from the Kitaygorod or merchants' town. St Basil's cathedral is in the centre. The circular enclosure on the left is the 'scaffold' where public executions took place. (Lyall, 1823.)

Plate 8 Moscow, from the south. The Kremlin hill, with its walls, towers and churches, is in the centre. The river Moskva flows in the foreground. (Porter, 1809.)

Plate 9   The river Neva at St Petersburg froze over in November, and was soon covered by sledges and skaters. The pontoon bridges were dismantled before the freeze. The north bank of the river, with the building of the Academy of Arts, is shown in the background. (Rechberg, 1812–13.)

Plate 10   'Montagne russe' at Tobolsk. Owing to the lack of steep natural slopes, artificial tobogganing structures were built for recreation. They were known throughout Europe as 'montagnes russes'. (Rechberg, 1812–13.)

CHAPTER THIRTEEN
RUSSIA AT THE BEGINNING
OF THE NINETEENTH CENTURY:
SOCIAL GEOGRAPHY

The population of the Russian Empire, based on the 1794-6 Revision, was $37\frac{1}{2}$ million, and according to the 1811-12 Revision, $42\frac{3}{4}$ million.[1] These figures show a substantial increase on the $15\frac{1}{4}$ million calculated for 1719-22, although $8\frac{1}{2}$ to 9 million had been added to the population by the acquisition of new territory.

The density of the population according to the 1795 Revision is shown on fig. 47. The percentage increases above the figures for 1719-22 are shown on fig. 48. It should be remembered, when studying this latter map, that large percentage increases in scantily populated areas very often represent much smaller absolute increments than small percentage increases in densely peopled areas. Fig. 49, by showing the percentage increases—and decreases—between the 1795 and 1811-12 Revisions, shows actual trends at the beginning of the nineteenth century.

The most striking feature of the population density map for 1795 (fig. 47) is the emergence of a continuous belt of denser population which follows the wooded-steppe vegetation zone north-eastwards, towards the heart of old Muscovy in the mixed-forest zone. This map, compared with that for 1719 (fig. 33) includes an added area to the west as a result of the annexation of Polish territory, and here the effect of the Pripyat marshes is visible in the lower density of Minsk 'government' (no. 32).

When the changes between 1719 and 1795 are examined, it is clear that the largest proportional increases in population have taken place on the steppes and the trans-Volga lands to the east. The pacification of the south and the development of the Uralian metallurgical industry have obviously been the decisive factors here.

The northernmost wooded-steppe provinces and the bordering steppe, blessed with rich black-earth soils and hot summers, had now ceased to be a militarized frontier populated mainly by a military caste. They were now becoming a richly cultivated land colonized by Ukrainians, Russians and immigrant Serbs and Germans. The westernmost of these provinces were termed Little Russia, and Sir Robert Wilson was
> greatly surprised in 'la petite Russie' to see as great a population and as richly cultivated land as almost any province in England can produce. I do not think we saw a barren acre for five hundred miles.[2]

Away from the densely populated middle Don and Dnieper valleys, the density in the newly-won steppes (fig. 47, nos. 46 to 50 inclusive) was still very low. Nevertheless, in 1811, 2 million people inhabited a region where, in 1725, there was little settlement at all away from the Don, and where

[1] *Kabazan (1963), p. 164*
[2] *Wilson (1861), vol. 1, p. 145*

G

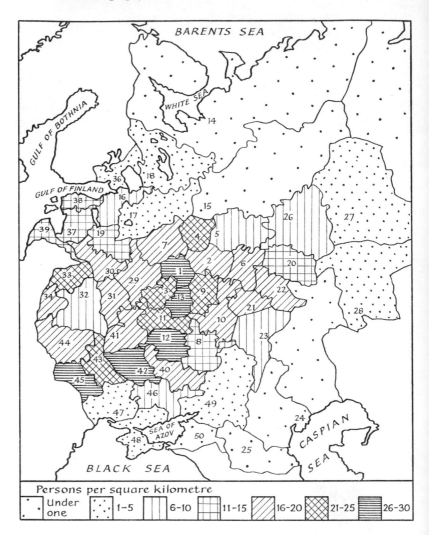

figure 47   Density of population according to the 1795 Revision (data from Kabuzan). For key to the numbered provinces, see p. 395

Cossacks and roaming Tartars and Kalmyks had been almost the only inhabitants.

The coming of Russian power to the southern steppes and Crimea resulted in drastic population changes. The introduction of serfdom in the Crimea caused thousands of Tartars to flee to Turkey, while the established Greek and Armenian settlers were moved to the steppes of the lower Don. In their place Russian troops were introduced as garrisons in the towns, and the new province of Tavrida was now being resettled by

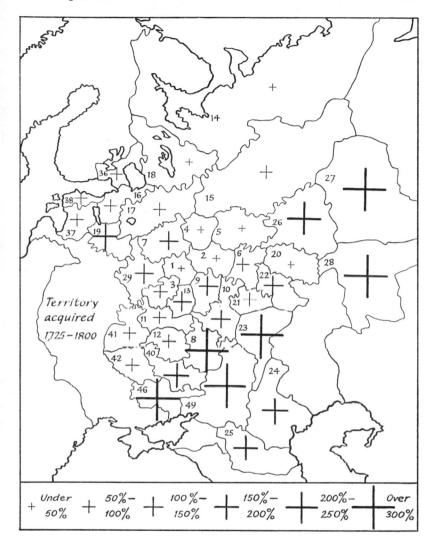

figure 48 Percentage increase of population, 1719-95 (data from Kabuzan). For key to the numbered provinces, see p. 395

Great Russians, Ukrainians, Greeks, Germans, Armenians and Bulgarians.

In the steppe, Serbs had colonized the land between the Bug and the Dnieper. They were now joined by Moldavians, Germans and exiles from revolutionary France, who settled along the Dnieper. Ukrainians and Germans were peopling the north shores of the Sea of Azov, and new Russian settlers were invading the territory of the Don Cossacks. Dnieper Cossacks had been recently established in the Kuban. Greeks and

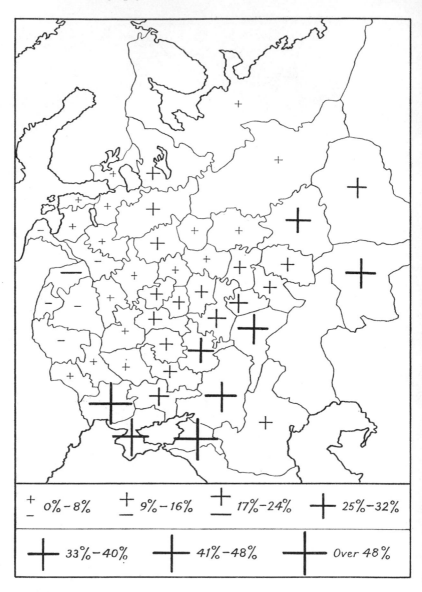

figure 49 Percentage increase and decrease of population, 1795-1811.
For key to the numbered provinces, see p. 395

Armenians from the Crimea were moving into the towns to dominate trade and commerce there.

In the northern forested part of the region east of the Volga, the population consisted mainly of the Ural iron and copper workers and the Kama salt workers but, farther south, the wooded-steppe zone between Samara and Ufa had attracted numerous colonists including some Montenegrins, and Germans had settled along both banks of the Volga.

In the south-east, the semi-desert lands bordering the Caspian Sea, including the province of Astrakhan, were virtually unpopulated, apart from the town of Astrakhan itself. These lands had a density even less than that of the bleak north.

The smallest increases since 1719-22 were in the already densely-peopled central 'governments' of Moscow, Vladimir, Yaroslavl and Kostroma, where land shortage was becoming acute, and in the far north which had lost the vitalizing stimulus of Archangel's primacy as a seaport. Instead, the lands between the ancient centre and the Baltic reflect, with moderately large increases, the transfer of commercial activity from the White Sea to the Baltic.

As for the map of actual trends about the year 1800 (fig. 49), the high rate of population growth in the steppe 'governments' is prominent; the Trans-Volga and Uralian provinces are still receiving many settlers, but their growth has slowed somewhat. The Baltic states are not maintaining the rate of increase which followed Peter's annexation, and most of the territory recently taken from Poland is losing population. This may be due in part to the flight of Jews and Poles from Russian rule, and in part also to the exodus of White Russian peasants to more easterly parts of the Empire in which they now found themselves. Within these ex-Polish lands, the southern wooded-steppe province of Podolia (no. 45 on fig. 47) was much more densely populated than the rest.

By and large, the north and west were losing people or growing but slowly in population, while the south and east were increasing fast. An exception to this generalization was the moderately large increase taking place in Tver and Novgorod 'governments' (nos 7 and 17). This was a result of the vigorous commercial activity along the waterways and road connecting Moscow and St Petersburg, routes which ran through these provinces. But Novgorod 'government', with its poor soils and many swamps, remained nevertheless but thinly inhabited.

The population of Siberia, according to the Revision figures, had increased from ½ million in 1719-22 to 1,200,000 in 1795 and to nearly 1,400,000 in 1811. The eastward march of settlement is clear. In 1719 the westernmost 'government', Tobolsk, had more population than the other two combined, but by 1795 its share had fallen to 37 per cent. In 1811, when Tobolsk's share was only 30 per cent, the easternmost province of Irkutsk had the largest population.

90 per cent of the population of Siberia was Russian. Whereas in 1725 fur traders and soldiers still predominated, mine workers and peasants were now more important, the latter settling in the steppe lands of southern Siberia. Some of them were free migrants from the non-Russian Volga peoples—the Mordva, Chuvashi, Mari and Votyaks. Others were Great Russians seeking freedom or sanctuary. A great number were now political exiles and transported felons.

Urban Settlement

The urban population of the Russian Empire had grown considerably during the eighteenth century, but at a rate not much faster than the population as a whole. At about 1½ million it was still only 4 per cent of the total. The lists tabulated below gives estimates of the populations of the larger towns in 1788 and 1811.[1] They should be taken as approximate only, because the urban population was subject to very large seasonal fluctuations.

Well over a third of the people living in towns were to be found in St Petersburg and Moscow. Most estimates from the turn of the century give Moscow rather more and St Petersburg less than 300,000 inhabitants, but it is likely that the Baltic city was growing faster and may have overtaken Moscow early in the nineteenth century. According to Semenov its population rose from 220,000 in 1800 to 308,000 by 1812.[2] The 1811 figure given below for St Petersburg probably includes Kronstadt and may be thereby inflated by 35,000 or so. The estimate for Moscow in the same year is a conservative one. Semenov put Moscow's population at the time of Napoleon's invasion (1812) at 400,000 in winter and 250,000 in summer: during the latter season the gentry left it for their estates or for the cooler Baltic capital, while peasants returned to their villages to work on the land.[3]

Table 4:
Estimated Populations of Russian towns in 1788 and 1811

1788 (*Hermann*)		1811 (*Rashin*)	
Moscow	300,000	St Petersburg	336,000
St Petersburg	200,000	Moscow	270,000
Kronstadt	30,000	Vilno	56,000
Riga	30,000	Kazan	54,000
Astrakhan	30,000	Tula	52,000
Yaroslavl	25,000	Astrakhan	38,000
Tula	20,000	Riga	32,000
Kazan	20,000	Saratov	27,000
Archangel	15,000	Orel	25,000
Tver	15,000	Yaroslavl	24,000
Kaluga	15,000	Kursk	24,000
Novgorod	12,000	Kiev	23,000
Orel	12,000	Kaluga	23,000
Kursk	12,000	Voronezh	22,000

Polish and Siberian towns are not included in the above. Thirty-seven towns were listed in 1788 as having populations between 30,000 and 10,000 (fig. 50).

[1] *Hermann (1790), p. 20; Rashin (1956), pp. 90-3*
[2] *Semenov (1862-85), vol. 5, p. 450*
[3] *Semenov (1862-85), vol. 3, p. 323*

MOSCOW (fig. 51, plates 7, 8)
In 1784 Coxe called Moscow *'certainly the largest town in Europe'* and Martha Wilmot found it in 1803 *'a town of such magnitude as is astonishing'*.[1] Whereas the rampart enclosing the city (except for the German suburb) in 1725 was 12 miles long, the earthwork which now surrounded the suburbs was 26 miles in circumference. Largest city in area it may well have been, because of the great extent of gardens attached to nobles' mansions, and the extraordinary number of ecclesiastical buildings, but the population—estimated variously between 200,000 and 360,000—was only a third of London's. The size of the town, coupled with the appalling condition of the streets—some ill-paved, some logged or planked, others unmitigated dust or slush, frozen ruts or mud, according to season, and all filthy—made travel from one part to another slow and unpleasant.

The odd mixture of palatial mansions, tumbledown hovels and gaudy churches puzzled and intrigued visitors (including Napoleon's troops), as did the motley appearance of the inhabitants:[2]

> *you behold nothing but a wide and scattered suburb, huts, gardens, pigsties, brick walls, churches, dunghills, palaces, timber yards, warehouses.*[3]
> *It is not a city of houses in mere rank and file of streets, but rather a collection of mansions, each embosomed amidst its own lawns, gardens, pleasure grounds, and the dwelling of its necessary slaves.*[4]

Inside the city there had been much building since 1725. Within the Kremlin, the new barracks and arsenal had been built, and the Saviour's Tower (*Spaskaya Bashnya*) rebuilt in the Kremlin wall. In the Belygorod many new nobles' houses, mostly built in neo-classical style, were to be seen, especially west and north-west of the Kremlin. One of these was Prince Dolgoruki's house (1803) described in Tolstoy's *War and Peace*. The University building (1786) was here as well. Much building, including new barracks, had taken place in the suburb contained in the south-western loop of the Moskva river, and handsome country houses were springing up in the Lenin Hills. Large residences, including the Petrovskiy Palace, used by the tsars and by Napoleon in 1812, had also been built along the main St Petersburg road, to the north-west of the town. In the east, the old German suburb of Lefortov had been transformed by the building of splendid palatial residences and new churches to serve them.

Another part of the town to have undergone extensive redevelopment was Zamoskvorechye, the district across the Moskva river from the Kremlin and Kitaygorod. Here the land had been drained and wealthy merchants had built not only their homes but new churches as well.

Coxe noted that some of the great houses of the wealthy, though of brick and stone on the ground floor, were of wood above. This was

[1] *Coxe (1784), vol. 1, p. 264; Stewart & Hyde (1934), p. 63*
[2] *Roos (1911), p. 92*
[3] *Clarke (1810), p. 47*
[4] *Porter (1809), vol. 1, p. 206*

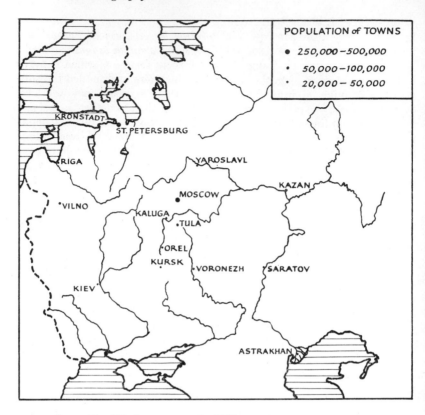

figure 50   The larger towns in 1811.

because '*wooden houses are by many persons in this country supposed to be warmer and more wholesome than those of brick and stone*'. Custine also remarked that 'true Muscovites' were of this opinion.[1]

An 1803 list classified the buildings in Moscow as follows:[2]

10 cathedrals	79 horse-hiring establishments
275 parish churches	199 eating houses
15 monasteries	162 public houses
9 nunneries	64 public baths
56 public buildings	216 manufactories
9 market places	194 breweries and distilleries
6,450 shops	115 smithies
8,360 dwelling houses	285 inns

A similar list, giving the composition of the population in 1805, shows that

[1] *Coxe (1784), vol. i, p. 281; Custine (1843), vol. 3, p. 334*
[2] *Lyall (1823), p. 530*

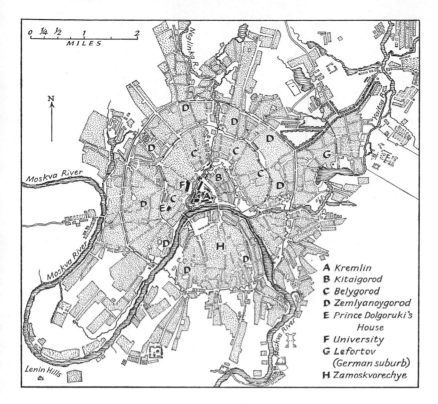

A Kremlin
B Kitaigorod
C Belygorod
D Zemlyanoygorod
E Prince Dolgoruki's
   House
F University
G Lefortov
   (German suburb)
H Zamoskvorechye

figure 51   Moscow at the end of the eighteenth century.

there were twice as many males in the city as females. This arose mainly from the large number of troops and from the many merchants and tradesmen who were living temporarily in Moscow while their families resided elsewhere. The more important categories of the male population are listed below:[1]

	per cent		per cent
Nobles	8	Merchants	5
their serfs and servants	29	Burghers	5
Permanently resident serfs	6	Tradesmen	9
Temporarily resident serfs	25	Industrialists	1
Troops	8	Foreigners	2

Germans were by far the most numerous of the foreigners, followed in order by French, Italians, Greeks, Georgians, Tartars, British and Austrians.

Moscow had continued to grow, despite the rise of St Petersburg. As the

[1] *Lyall (1823), p. 530*

G*

fortunes of various groups and cliques rose or fell at the capital, so the discarded, discredited or disgraced courtiers returned to Moscow with their retinues.[1] Perhaps they found some consolation there, as *'the superiority of this metropolis over that of St Petersburg in the general beauty of the females'* was *'beyond comparison'*.[2] Foreigners often termed Moscow 'Asiatic' in contrast to the European character of the Baltic capital.[3]

ST PETERSBURG (fig. 52, plate 9.)
During the eighteenth century, St Petersburg was transformed from a group of muddy streets lined with ill-built wooden houses around a few unfinished stone erections, into a city that excited the wonder of foreign visitors.[4] It was *'difficult to imagine a more beautiful town'; 'no city I have seen can equal it in external magnificence'*; it was *'this marvellous city'; 'such grandeur and symmetry in building, I never before beheld in any of the different capitals to which my fondness for travel has conducted me'*.[5] The predominance of classical architecture and of Finnish granite produced a somewhat ponderous effect, lightened by the bright colours in which the buildings were painted.

The Neva, now banked with imposing quays of granite blocks, was not crossed by fixed bridges. Its great depth would have made their construction difficult; they were unnecessary in winter when the ice could be crossed at will, and in spring floating ice would have threatened them with destruction. The main bridge over the Great Neva was a pontoon bridge, but the narrow canals of Admiralty Isle and the South Bank had drawbridges.[6]

Building and rebuilding were still going on actively in all parts of the city and the streets were being paved. Large numbers of labourers drawn from many parts of the country still invaded the town in spring to work on the buildings through the summer, returning home with the onset of winter.

The inner section of Admiralty Isle, between the Neva and the Moyka Canal, had established itself as indubitably the heart of the city. Here Rastrelli's baroque-classical Winter Palace (1754-62), Velten's baroque Hermitage (1771-5) and Quarenghi's classical Riding School (1804) were among the imposing buildings erected since 1725. Between the Moyka and Catherine Canals many new palaces had been built for wealthy nobles, e.g. the baroque Stroganov palace by Rastrelli (1752-4), and Emperor Paul's new summer palace (1796-1800) in which he was murdered. Between the Catherine and Fontanka Canals were the City Hall (1802), the Merchants'

[1] *Wilmot (1803-8), p. 213*
[2] *Porter (1809), vol. 1, p. 207*
[3] *Wilmot (1803-8), p. 222*
[4] *For the story of this transformation, see Marsden (1942)*
[5] *Wilmot (1803-8), p. 176; Cochrane (1824), vol. 1, p. 52; Carr (1805), p. 218; Porter (1809), vol. 1, p. 19*
[6] *Storch (1801A), p. 17; Swinton (1792), p. 395*

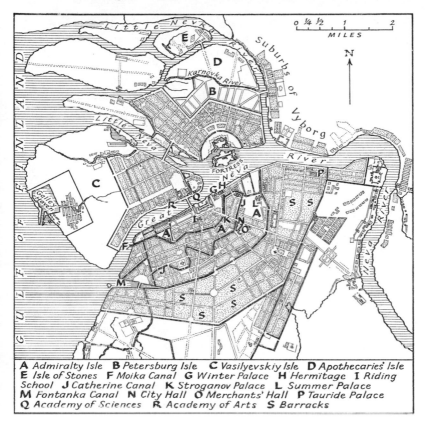

A *Admiralty Isle*   B *Petersburg Isle*   C *Vasilyevskiy Isle*   D *Apothecaries' Isle*
E *Isle of Stones*   F *Moika Canal*   G *Winter Palace*   H *Hermitage*   I *Riding
School*   J *Catherine Canal*   K *Stroganov Palace*   L *Summer Palace*
M *Fontanka Canal*   N *City Hall*   O *Merchants' Hall*   P *Tauride Palace*
Q *Academy of Sciences*   R *Academy of Arts*   S *Barracks*

figure 52   St Petersburg at the end of the eighteenth century.

Hall (*Gostiny Dvor*, 1785), and many nobles' palaces, including the Tauride
Palace (1782), built for Potemkin, and which was to house Russia's short-
lived Parliament, the *Duma*, from 1906 to 1917. Most of these splendid
buildings were ranged along Nevskiy Prospekt, '*the finest in the capital, as
well for its breadth as for the splendour and magnificence of its buildings*'.[1]

Of the two large islands opposite the Admiralty quarter, Vasilyevskiy
was '*the seat of commerce and learning*'. Commerce had been there in 1725,
but the building of Quarenghi's classical Academy of Sciences (1784-7)
opposite the Admiralty, and of La Mothe's neo-classical Academy of Art
('*one of the most elegant structures in all Petersburg*'), had added the
'learning'. In 1819 the University was to be founded in this same district.
However,

> except this line of buildings upon the banks of the Neva, the whole
> of this quarter of the city consists of wooden houses: these are built
> very regularly in streets, cutting each other at right-angles: canals run

[1] *Svinine (1814), p. 64*

through the middle of the streets, but owing to the level surface of the ground, the water in them, in the heat of summer, stagnates and is offensive. They serve no good purpose and it would be proper to fill them up with earth.

The lines of houses nearest the Academies were '*inhabited by merchants and literary men*'. The western half of the island was still wilderness except for the galley-port district.[1]

Petersburg Isle remained without large stone buildings; it was now '*mostly built upon, though only with timber, and its streets are not all paved*'. Apothecaries' Isle was graced with the Botanical Gardens and '*several small country houses, serving the inhabitants of the town for their summer residence*'. To its north, on the Isle of Stones, a large palace with ornamental grounds had been built in 1785, but the Vyborg mainland beyond had '*the most rural appearance of all; as besides the street along the Neva, it is only occupied by the cottages of the peasantry*'.[2] The southern part of the city, forming an outer zone enclosing Admiralty Isle, had several large barracks.

Food was brought from abroad and from all parts of Russia to satisfy the appetites of the wealthy court and aristocracy. Coxe wrote:

I have frequently seen at the same table, sterlet from the Volga, veal from Archangel, mutton from Astrakhan, beef from the Ukraine, and pheasants from Hungary and Bohemia. The common wines are claret, Burgundy and Champagne; and I never tasted English beer and porter in greater perfection and abundance.

He had previously seen '*numberless herds of oxen, moving towards Petersburg for the supply of that capital*'.[3]

A three-day market was held annually on the Neva ice at the end of the long fast on 24 December. Here the inhabitants bought whole carcasses of oxen, sheep, swine, geese, etc., for the remainder of the winter, during which season they remained naturally refrigerated. Thousands of carts brought the dead animals to this market, where they were piled up in great heaps.[4]

Admiralty Isle, within the Fontanka, now had few houses of wood. Instead they were '*mostly of brick, and plastered, painted every variety of colours! No wooden house is suffered to be rebuilt within the canal.*'[5] The number of brick houses, most of which were four storeys high—and therefore replaced several wooden ones—had increased from 460 in 1762 to 1,291 in 1787, and the number of wooden ones had decreased from 4,094 to 3,431.[6]

The population of the capital was variously put at about 193,000 in 1784, 218,000 in 1789, and 220,000 or 230,000 in 1800. These figures show

[1] *Storch (1801A), p. 53; Swinton (1792), p. 391*
[2] *Storch (1801A), pp. 54-7*
[3] *Coxe (1784), vol. 1, pp. 433, 504*
[4] *Georgel (1818), pp. 250-1*
[5] *Swinton (1792), p. 395*
[6] *Storch (1810A), pp. 23-4*

how fast the town was growing. The 230,000 inhabitants were roughly divided according to origin as follows:

200,000 Russians
18,000 Germans and Dutch
4,000 Finns
2,000 Swedes
1,000 English

But Swinton in 1791 also met Danes, French, Italians, Portuguese, Venetians, Poles, Persians and Turks, the latter having arrived as prisoners of war. The Germans were cabinet makers, painters, mechanics, tailors, shoemakers; the Dutch were landscape gardeners; the Italians were architects and singers; the English were merchants, and the French, tutors.[1]

Kronstadt, with about 35,000 inhabitants, most of whom were connected with the navy, was still a town of wooden houses to which St Andrew's Cathedral and a sea cadets' academy had been added. Twenty miles south of St Petersburg, on a morainic hill, and elevated above the swamps, was Tsarskoye Selo, the Russian Versailles. Here a magnificent collection of palaces, churches, monuments and gardens formed the summer resort of the Imperial Court.

Tula, on the southern borders of old Muscovy, was one of the largest provincial towns, with 30,000 inhabitants (52,000 in 1811). With '*its numerous white buildings, domes, towers and rising spires*' it was imposing at a distance; at closer view '*its shops and public places present a greater appearance of activity and industry than is usual in Russia*'. Its streets were paved, and although most houses were wooden, the number of stone ones was '*considerable and increasing daily*'. The population included 6,000 iron workers and 4,000 merchants and shopkeepers.[2]

Tver, about half the size of Tula, was also prosperous, partly because it lay on the main water and land routes between Moscow and St Petersburg, and partly because Catherine II had spent large sums on its improvement. She had built a new town on the opposite side of the Volga to the old. Not only did she erect a governor's house, bishop's palace, law courts, a prison and schools, but offered a loan '*to every person who would build a brick house*'.[3]

Voronezh (10,000 in 1788, 22,000 in 1811), on the northern margin of the steppe, was '*now a very handsome town*' and an important centre of commerce, being situated where a main east-west trade artery crossed the north-south line of the Don:

> By means of the Don, it possesses an easy intercourse with the Black Sea. Every year, vessels go laden to Tscherkaskoy with corn; and they

[1] *Storch (1801A), pp. 85-8; Swinton (1792), p. 229*
[2] *Clarke (1810), vol. 1, pp. 184-6*
[3] *Coxe (1784), vol. 1, p. 421*

accomplish their voyage in about two months. In winter they receive merchandise by sledges from the Crimea and Turkey. Its merchants travel into Siberia for furs and then carry them even to the fairs of Francfort.[1]

And it benefited from *'its remarkable situation'*, being *'placed so as to enjoy the advantages both of warm and cold climates'*. Its prosperity was enhanced by the rapid settlement and development of southern Russia. It was also an industrial town.

The lower reaches and the mouth of the Don had several busy commercial towns. Chief among these was the island capital of the Don Cossacks, *Cherkassk* (15,000):

Although not so grand as Venice it somewhat resembles that city. The entrance is by broad canals, which intersect it in all parts. On either side wooden houses built on piles, appear to float upon the water . . . not an inch of dry land is to be seen.

There were 3,000 houses, 7 churches, 6 prisons, 2 public baths, and numerous shops *'kept chiefly by Greeks. They contain the produce of Turkey and Greece, as pearls, cloth, shawls, tobacco, fruit, etc.*[2]

A few miles lower down were the adjoining towns of *Nakhichevan* (2,000) and *Rostov* (4,000 in 1811). The former was a new Armenian colony which *'had about 400 shops'* and which possessed *'neat and comfortable houses, many of which are limestone and covered with tiles'*.[3] Rostov was a new garrison town, but older Azov, at the mouth of the river, once an important fortress town, had decayed to a village of less than 50 houses.

Kiev, after centuries as an exposed frontier military post, had at last begun to flourish again. Its population was estimated at 15,000 in 1788 and at 23,000 in 1811. Sir Robert Wilson found it in 1812 *'a very large city'*, and shortly afterwards Mary Holderness dubbed it *'much the best town which we have seen, and of far greater extent than any except Riga. The shops are very superior.*[4]

In the Dnieper bend stood *Yekaterinoslav*, new centre of steppe colonization. The town, founded in 1786, was meant to be a great memorial to Catherine and enormous sums were spent on it. Yet,

in 1795, the only inhabitants . . . were a few officials, a few soldiers and a few peasants. All that remained of the original dream were the imposing palace and the expensive orangeries of Potemkin on which millions had been wasted.[5]

Near the Dnieper mouth was the new fortress town and port of *Kherson*, founded in 1774.

Close to the Bug mouth stood *Nikolayev* (4,000 in 1811), founded in 1789, and now a handsome town with wide streets, stone houses and public

[1] *Clarke (1810), p. 199*
[2] *Clarke (1810), pp. 275-99*
[3] *Clarke (1810), pp. 304-12*
[4] *Wilson (1861), vol. 1, p. 144; Holderness (1823), pp. 59-70*
[5] *Bain (1908), p. 415*

buildings: the admiralty, the naval academy and a hospital. These were built of '*a fine white calcareous stone full of shells*'. The population consisted mainly of soldiers, sailors and shipwrights, as it was a new base and ship-yard for the Black Sea fleet. Its main lack was of fresh water and timber.[1]

Of all the new towns in the region, one was to outdistance the rest. *Odessa*, 30 miles east of the Dniester mouth, with little winter ice, and with the moister western section of the steppes and Russia's Polish acquisitions behind it, experienced an immediate boom. Founded in 1795, it had 506 stone houses and nearly 5,000 people by 1799; 2,900 houses and 15,000 people by 1804; 40,000 people by 1820. Although the streets were not yet paved and could therefore be unpleasantly muddy or dusty, the houses were of the same white limestone as those of Nikolayev, giving a bright clean appearance. Two-thirds of the population consisted of Italians, Jews and Greeks.

The largest town of the Crimea was *Karazubazar* (8,000), central to the richest agricultural region of the peninsula. It was an important centre for articles of sheepskin and goatskin leather. A garrison of 1,500 troops was stationed here. At *Simferopol* (Akmechet, 3,000), in a valley among the northern foothills, a new administrative centre for the Crimea was being built, close to the old Tartar town. *Bakhchisaray* (5,000) was the old Tartar capital. The new naval town of *Sevastopol* (3,000) was built on a natural amphitheatre above the harbour. Its population was said to be sometimes swollen to 14,000 or 15,000 by sailors, soldiers and shipwrights.[2] Many Crimean towns of ancient splendour were now reduced to ruins, among which lived a few Tartar shepherds or Greek fishermen. Such were Balaclava, Yalta, Sudak, Feodosiya and Kerch.

Across the Sea of Azov, in the Kuban, the new town of *Yekaterinodar* (now Krasnodar), founded in 1792 as the capital of the Kuban Cossacks, was as yet '*a number of straggling cottages*'.[3]

Astrakhan (35,000) was still one of the largest towns in Russia, and its population was sometimes put as high as 70,000 or 80,000, probably because of the large numbers temporarily resident: '*there is perhaps a more diversified assemblage of nations than in any other spot on the globe*'. It was still mainly a town of wooden houses.[4] Higher up the Volga, Tsaritsyn (5,000) and Saratov (10,000) were expanding from small fortress towns into the growing centres of newly colonized districts. The latter was growing particularly fast and reached an estimated population of 27,000 in 1811.[5]

The *Ural towns*, non-existent as such in 1725, were now of fair size. In 1788 Yekaterinburg, Perm and Ufa were said each to have 8,000

[1] *Guthrie (1802), pp. 5-8; Reuilly (1806), p. 271*

[2] *Reuilly (1806), p. 200; Holderness (1823), p. 214*

[3] *Clarke (1810), pp. 356-7*

[4] *Hermann (1790), p. 20; Pinkerton (1802), vol. 1, p. 313; Forster (1798), vol. 2, pp. 267-72*

[5] *Rashin (1956), p. 90*

inhabitants, and Orenburg, 6,000. The latter had been founded in 1735 as a military post to hold down the Bashkir territory.

Hermann's list (1788) gives population figures for the following *Siberian towns:*

Tobolsk	*20,000*	*Krasnoyarsk*	*5,000*
Irkutsk	*15,000*	*Yakutsk*	*5,000*
Barnaul	*10,000*	*Nerchinsk*	*3,000*
Tomsk	*6,000*	*Okhotsk*	*3,000*

In addition there were many Cossack garrisons like Chita which were developing into small trading towns and even centres of agricultural settlement.

From Lesseps there is early mention of two Kamchatka towns. A Pacific naval base was planned for *Petropavlovsk*, formerly the native village of Kamchadale, because of its natural harbour; but at present (1788) there was only a fort, a small garrison of some 40 Cossacks, and 30 or 40 native huts. *Bolcheretsk*, on the opposite side of the peninsula, was the chief Russian centre. Here there was a disreputable collection of Cossacks, Russian merchants and sailors who, between them, fleeced the natives and reduced them to misery by plying them with vodka.[1]

Rural Settlement

The normal Russian village in the central mixed forest zone consisted of '*one street only, pretty wide, presenting to the eye a row of gable ends*'. The cottages were usually of one storey only and: '*square of shape; formed of whole trees, piled upon one another, and secured at the four corners with mortices and tenons*'. The interstices between the logs were filled with moss. The tree trunks were left with the bark on the outside, but smoothed with the axe within. Often no other tool was used, most Russian peasants having no saws.[2] (Plate 11.)

The steeply-pitched penthouse roofs were of bark or wooden shingles, on which turf was sometimes laid. The roof projected

> to defend its inmates from the sun during the summer, and the weather in the severer season. I understand that no habitations are cooler than these during the hot months, nor any warmer through the whole of the cold.

While some dwellings were rough hovels, in most villages the peasants had taken pride in ornamenting the exteriors of their cottages with carvings. The windows were '*apertures of a few inches square, closed with sliding frames*', often surmounted by carvings, and on the shutters '*a variety of flowers, stars and strange devices*' were crudely painted. The courtyards were *filled with sheds, old kabitkas, and other carriages of the country;*

[1] *Lesseps (1790), vol. 1, pp. 79-81*
[2] *Porter (1809), p. 178; Coxe (1784), vol. 1, p. 254*

besides an accumulation of dirt, rotten straw, jaded horses, pigs and nuisances; completing a musuem of nastiness scarcely to be found in any other civilized spot on the globe.[1]

The habitable interior of the *izba* consisted usually of one room in which the stove was the most prominent feature, taking up about a quarter of the space. It was used as a bed at night; by day, in winter, those not otherwise occupied *'loll over its baking warmth for hours'*. Often there was no bed as such, and those who did not find a place on the stove slept on benches: *'they spread out their mats and sheepskin coats in any place that best suits them'*.[2] For lighting they used, not lamps or candles, but burning laths. These made the cottages *'very black, and the glowing parts dropping off, occasion frequent fires'*.[3] (Plate 11.)

The steppes appeared to the traveller to be much emptier than they were because settlement concentrated in the sunken river valleys and was therefore *'concealed by the depth of the banks of the river below the level of the plain'*.[4] In the western steppes most settlers were Ukrainian and had a distinctive type of village; it was composed of cottages built thus:

> *Their method of building cottages is both cheap and expeditious, and very warm and comfortable when well finished. The corner posts are of wood, proportioned to the size of the house to be built, with light rafters and beams, and spars at regular distances from the walls, over which is laid, both within and without, a covering of reeds; the roof is of reeds also.*
>
> *When the plastering is dry they are whitewashed, and the window frames and doors painted, which renders them the neatest cottages I have seen.*[5]

More so than the forest-conditioned Russians they had adapted their village architecture to the absence of timber. For firing they used reeds or *'straw or kisseck, which is the manure of the cowyard, cut in the spring, and properly dried for the purpose'*. For lighting the common people here used *'tallow and linseed oil, which they burn in pans, or they make tapers of herbs and rushes'*.[6]

The Great Russian settlers in the steppe zone were often newly arrived and too busy grappling with their new environment to embellish their dwellings:

> *Usmani is entirely inhabited by Russians, and whenever that is the case, towards the south of the empire, a village resembles nothing more than a number of stacks of straw or dried weeds. . . . They were said to be settlers from Tver.*[7]

[1] *Porter (1809), p. 178*
[2] *Pinkerton (1833), p. 24*
[3] *Oddy (1805), p. 89*
[4] *Clarke (1810), pp. 246-7*
[5] *Holderness (1823), p. 96*
[6] *Holderness (1823), pp. 98-9; Tooke (1799), vol. 3, p. 377*
[7] *Clarke (1810), pp. 213-14*

Peoples of the Russian Empire (plates 11-16)

THE GREAT RUSSIANS

> *Is it fair to make a comparison between the Russians and European nations which have been civilized and polished for many centuries?*[1] *I must own I was astonished at the barbarism in which the bulk of the people still continue. . . . I am ready to allow that the principal nobles are perfectly civilized, and as refined in their entertainments, mode of living, and social intercourse, as those of other European countries. But there is a wide difference between polishing a nation and polishing a few individuals.*[2]

The greatest change in the culture of the upper classes since 1725 was the substitution of French influence for that of the Germans and Dutch. Catherine II had brought with her to Russia the German princeling's admiration for the French court and had determined to surpass it in magnificence. She would most likely have succeeded, even had the French monarchy not fallen, for she and her courtiers had more wealth at their command and more defenceless peasants to extort from. The affectation of French manners went hand in hand with hostility to French policy in Europe, and Catherine Wilmot thought there was

> *something childishly silly in their reprobating Buonaparte when they can't eat their dinner without a French cook to dress it, when they can't educate their children without unprincipled adventurers from Paris to act as tutors and governesses, when every house of consequence, that I have seen at least, has an outcast Frenchman to instruct the heir apparent; in a word, when every association of fashion, luxury, elegance and fascination is drawn from France.*[3]

Outdoor amusement, however, remained peculiarly Russian, a result of climate. 'La montagne russe', in which an artificial slope was built for tobogganing, was found, both in St Petersburg and in the most distant parts of the Empire. Captain Dundas Cochrane, R.N., who crossed Siberia on foot in 1820-1, was at Nizhne Kolymsk in January. Here

> *The ice mountain was of course one of our amusements, and our time was far from hanging heavy. I descended it daily during the fêtes with one and sometimes two young girls on my knees, who expressed no fear in trusting themselves with a novice.*[4] (Plate 10.)

In summer '*all kinds of machines . . . set up in the public squares*', were patronized by all classes of society.[5] A public spectacle, if not an amusement, was the administration of corporal punishment to serfs, at the behest of their masters or mistresses. This consisted of the 'battocks', the knout

[1] *Lyall (1823), p. iv*
[2] *Coxe (1784), vol. 2, p. 95*
[3] *Wilmot (1803-8), p. 194*
[4] *Cochrane (1824), I, 284-5*
[5] *Storch (1801A), pp. 416-17*

(light) and the knout (heavy). Those sentenced to the latter seldom recovered. (Plates 15, 16.)

Another native custom which survived was the bathing ritual, observed by all classes. The bather first visited the steaming hot bath, the temperature of which few Europeans could stand, and in which hot water was *'poured over the victims till every pore is wide open'*. He then plunged into the cold bath or a stream, or in winter, into the snow, and underwent flagellation. Porter (1806) saw

> *naked persons of both sexes, who waded or swam out from the bath in great numbers, without any consideration of delicacy or decency . . . a wooden pail in one hand and a huge bunch of umbrageous birch twigs in the other.*

They then entered the river, where

> *as soon as any of these nymphs lost sight of her lower extremities in the stream, she instantly applied herself with no small degree of vigour, to pour cold water on the top of her head, by the help of a wooden utensil.*[1] (Plate 14.)

After a century of intensive westernization, there was now a gulf between the *'higher and travelled nobility'* who were *'easy, elegant and imposing'*, and the lower nobility, who, having less contact with St Petersburg, were *'affected, consequential, overbearing and sometimes rude'*. The style of living of the upper nobility was boundlessly extravagant and, apart from the numerous retinues who attended them, even greater numbers slaved that they might indulge themselves in a superabundance of food and drink of all kinds. Martha Wilmot, referring to the social round at Moscow, writes (1804):

> *Many a bad dinner have I made from the fatigue of being offered fifty or sixty different dishes by servants who come one after the other and flourish ready carved fish, flesh, fowl, vegetables, fruits, soups of fish, etc., etc., in their turn before your eyes; wines, liqueurs, etc., etc., in their turn.*[2]

Some observers thought such living, combined with the high degree of unhumidified heat endured in unventilated rooms in winter, very unhealthy and saw its effects in the appearance of members of the upper class:

> *the higher orders, from indulgence, luxurious living, little exercise and hot stoves, are very susceptible of colds; indigestions, unwieldiness and shortened lives are the natural consequences.*

As for the ladies:

> *Like exotics in a hot house, the artificial heat brings them to untimely maturity, and they fade away, even at the moment when we expect to find them at their highest bloom.*

The lower orders, by contrast, were generally considered to be very healthy, except where drunkenness left its mark:

---

[1] *Porter (1809), p. 231*
[2] *Wilmot (1803-8), pp. 75, 81*

> *I never saw a race more healthy than the common people are in Russia;*
> *and were it not for their excessive use of brandy, I believe the rigour*
> *of the climate and their constant exercise would prolong their days to*
> *an almost patriarchal date.*[1]

Some thought the hot and cold baths contributed to this robust health, but most put it down to early habituation to the severity of winter:

> *They bring up their children with great hardiness, suffering them always*
> *to be in the air and exposed to the severest weather, with no other*
> *clothing perhaps than a little linen shirt.*[2]

All observers agreed about their drunkenness: '*every third person you meet is drunk.*'[3] The relative prosperity of members of some dissenting sects was doubtless due, in part, to their eschewing this indulgence.

Peasant dress continued unchanged in the old national style. In summer, over a coarse linen shirt and wide linen trousers were worn a linen or woollen double-breasted coat or kaftan, long enough to reach below the knees, with a sash round the waist '*in which he tucks his gloves, his whip or his axe*'. Boys usually dispensed with the trousers and went bare-legged and bare-footed. A flattish-topped felt hat with upturned brims might also be worn. Winter dress consisted of a fur or sheepskin hat and a greasy sheepskin coat, while

> *thick swathes of rags are rolled about their legs to keep out the cold,*
> *over which they pull a pair of large and ill-constructed boots. Those*
> *who do not arrive at the luxury of these leathern defences, increase the*
> *swathing to such a bulk by wrappings and cross-bandages, that their*
> *lower extremities appear more like flour sacks than the legs of men.*
> *When thus bulwarked, they stuff them into a pair of enormous shoes,*
> *made ingeniously from the bark of the linden tree.*[4]

The merchants were reputedly sharp-witted, frugal and simply attired, even when immensely wealthy; but they spared no expense to deck their wives out in all the finery imaginable, including 'diadems of gold set with coloured stones and pearls'.[5]

Whereas the merchants were now beginning to intermarry with the nobles, owing to the impoverishing extravagance of many of the latter, the clergy remained a socially isolated caste: '*parishes were handed over from father to son or son-in-law; for priests' daughters were invariably married to prospective priests*'.[6] They made no special claim to righteousness and it was by no means uncommon for the local priest to be drunk and incapable, even on a holy day.[7]

---

[1] *Porter (1809), pp. 191, 251*

[2] *Atkinson & Walker (1812), vol. 2*

[3] *Swinton (1792), p. 128*

[4] *Porter (1809), p. 112; Storch (1801A), pp. 473-4*

[5] *Porter (1809), pp. 228-9; Atkinson & Walker (1812), vol. 2; Carr (1805), p. 238*

[6] *Mirsky (1952), pp. 210-11*

[7] *Wilmot (1803-8), p. 305*

OTHER PEOPLES OF THE RUSSIAN EMPIRE

The expansion of the Empire, together with immigration, had greatly increased the number of non-Great Russian peoples within its bounds.

Clarke thought the Ukranians vastly superior to the Russians, but they had lost what remained of their independence and autonomy. The Russified gentry became landowners on a large scale; the peasants became serfs with the tiniest of holdings.

Several thousand German immigrants came to Russia in the reign of Catherine II. Some were settled along the Volga in Saratov 'government', some on the steppes of New Russia, and others in the Crimea. At first there was much hardship and little success: many of the settlers were unfamiliar with farm work and all found the climatic conditions harsh. The Volga settlers had suffered from Tartar and Bashkir depredations and the destruction wrought by Pugachev. But there were now some well-established and flourishing settlements, notably Katharinenstadt near Saratov and the Moravian colony of Sarepta near Tsaritsyn.[1]

The most successful German colonies on the steppes were those established in Yekaterinoslav 'government', around the Dnieper bend, by Anabaptist Mennonites.[2] They

> came over with plenty of money, knowledge of business, and are at present a wealthy race, having built large farm-houses and offices, planted extensive orchards, and laid out great gardens, possessing the finest breed of cows in the country, and growing a great abundance of corn. They are a most industrious and religious class of people, deservedly held in high estimation.[3]

But other Germans, settled in the Crimea, owed it 'to their own idleness and drunkenness that they are not in the most flourishing circumstances.'[4]

At the other end of the country the Baltic Germans were beginning to exert a strong influence on Russian life. Having qualities of self-discipline, application, frugality and rectitude, besides a good education, they became valued recruits in all government services. They made their impress upon the army and on the growing bureaucracy, and throught it upon the Russian people. Their presence contributed to a national dislike of the Germans which spread rapidly during the nineteenth century. It is seen in Pushkin's *The Queen of Spades* and in many other literary allusions. It contributed to the conflict with Germany in 1914.[5]

Their incorporation into the Empire enabled thousands of Greeks and Armenians to secure a position in Russian commercial life which the Jews would already have occupied had they been free to do so. The Black Sea trade was wholly in their hands.[6] The Bulgarians settled on the Black Sea

---

[1] *Bonwetsch (1919), pp. 29, 47*
[2] *Klaus (1887), pp. 180 et seq*
[3] *Holderness (1823), p. 160*
[4] *Holderness (1823), p. 215*
[5] *Laqueur (1965), pp. 17-18; Haxthausen (1852), pp. 14-21*
[6] *Oddy (1805), pp. 179-80*

steppes and in the Crimea were '*a sober, industrious and meritorious class*' and their houses were '*remarkable for cleanliness and order*'. Jews, who had not been allowed to reside in old Muscovy, now composed perhaps 2 or 3 per cent of the population. The Polish provinces had some in almost every town and village. They had also succeeded in infiltrating New Russia where they were '*very numerous indeed in all the colonies, composing from one-fifth to one-tenth of the whole population*'. They were all said to be shopkeepers.[1]

The Cossacks, though nominally Russian, speaking the language and practising the Orthodox religion, had intermarried with the various Tartar and Turkish breeds to such an extent that racially as well as by culture, they constituted a distinct people. There were considerable differences between the Cossacks of different geographical locations. Those of the Don were the most numerous, there being 230,000 of them in 1800, 35,000 of whom were in arms. They lived '*in large villages in content and abundance*'. Unlike the Russians, they intermarried freely with their Kalmyk neighbours. Nothing distinguished them more from the Russian peasant than the wealth and comfort which their free life in a rich land, oppressed and mulcted by neither landlord nor tax gatherer, brought them.

To the south of the Don Cossacks and eastwards from the Sea of Azov were the Kuban or 'Black Sea' Cossacks, moved hither by Catherine II from their homes on the Dnieper in 1783. Their original function was to guard the frontier from the Circassians of the Caucasus, but they had already begun to plough the Kuban steppe.[2] Not only were their dress and customs different from those of the Don, but having been recently uprooted, they did not yet possess the same wealth and comfort. (Plate 17.)

At the opposite end of the Caucasus were the Terek Cossacks, still actively engaged as military frontiersmen. The Bug Cossacks, settled along and about the river of that name, were originally Moldavian and Wallachian Christians who had revolted against the Turks, organized themselves as Cossacks, and joined the Russians in the mid-eighteenth century. They too had become cultivators. But the Ural Cossacks, located in semi-arid lands where cultivation was out of the question, still lived by fishing and livestock rearing.

Finally there were the Siberian Cossacks, manning forts all the way across the continent to Kamchatka. Where conditions permitted, they settled down as farmers around the forts or became traders.

The Crimean Tartars, despite emigration after the Russian conquest, were still the most numerous of the inhabitants of the Crimea. They were considered sober and chaste, and inordinately fond of horses and horseriding. A Tartar would '*never walk two hundred yards from his own door if he has a horse to ride on*' and horse racing was their chief amusement. They dressed in felt cloaks made from the wool of their own sheep and, in winter, wore sheepskin coats and lambswool caps.[3]

[1] *Holderness (1823), pp. 163, 171, 178*
[2] *Rechberg & Depping (1812-13)*
[3] *Holderness (1823), pp. 243-93*

The Kalmyks still wandered over the lands between the Don, the lower Volga and the Caspian. Like the Don Cossacks with whom they intermingled—there were 30,000 of them in the Don Cossack territory—they furnished units to the Russian army. They ate raw horseflesh and drank kumiss. Their tents, still covered with mats or felts, could be transported on a single camel. Their amusements were chiefly hunting, wrestling, archery and horse racing. Near the Caspian they were employed in the sturgeon fishery.[1] (Plate 18.)

The Bashkirs, *'the most negligent and slovenly of the Tartars'*, still occupied land in the southern Urals and westwards to the Volga. Since 1725 they had suffered from the growth of the Ural metallurgical industry, from increased Russian colonization, and from the pacification which followed Pugachev's revolt. They now had to furnish special cavalry units, whose appearance with the Russian armies on the European scene in 1813-14 attracted much attention, usually unfavourable. Martha Wilmot had a preview of them in 1806 at St Petersburg:

> *We have been today to look at a regiment of Bashkirs marching into the town. This savage looking race live on the borders of Siberia and to a European eye, accustomed to regularity and good order in a regiment, the one we have seen today appears no better than a rabble assembled Lord knows how . . .*[2] (Plate 19.)

Finally mention should be made of the Kamchadales of Kamchatka whose country was now dotted with Russian fortified trading posts (*ostrogi*). In summer they lived in light bark wigwams and spent much of their time fishing, but in winter they moved into log houses and were chiefly occupied in hunting. They were easy prey for the Russian merchants, Cossacks and sailors who fleeced them of valuable furs:

> *No sooner have the traders made them drunk, than they contrive to take in exchange . . . all the pelts they can get, often the result of a whole season's hunting . . . the brief pleasure of emptying a few glasses of vodka reduces them to the most abject misery.*[3]

Russian Society

To an even greater extent than in pre-Revolutionary France, all possible wealth produced by the labour and skill of miners, craftsmen and peasants, was extracted from them and concentrated in the hands of an aristocracy who formed the Court at St Petersburg. This concentration made possible an unparalleled splendour. Sir James Harris wrote: *'prepared as I was for the magnificence and parade of this court, yet it exceeds in everything my*

---

[1] *Clarke (1810), pp. 236-44; Forster (1798), vol. 2, p. 258; Craven (1789), p. 176*

[2] *Wilmot (1803-8), p. 287; Scenes (1814), pp. 86-7*

[3] *Lesseps (1790), vol. 1, pp. 79-81*

ideas', while John Carr remarked (1804): '*the princely magnificence in which some of the Russian nobility live is prodigious*'.[1]

To some English observers, who were not mere tourists but had lived for years in Russia, the peasant was not an object of pity. Coxe thought the peasants '*well clothed, comfortably lodged*' and enjoying '*plenty of wholesome food*'. Martha Wilmot wrote that '*those who imagine the Russian peasantry sunk in sloth and misery imagine a strange falsehood*', and thought them better off than the Irish. In South Russia, Mary Holderness '*had several opportunities of remarking the plenty and comfort of the Russian boor*'; '*certain it is*', she concluded, '*that the Russian peasant is happier, and has fewer wants unsatisfied than the peasantry of that country whose liberty is her boast*'.[2] Catherine Wilmot was more discerning than her sister:

> *When she [Princess Dashkov] appears, they fall down before her and kiss the ground with that senseless obeisance that stupefaction feels at the approach of superior power.*
>
> *Her lenity makes their lot better perhaps than that of others, but that is saying very little for the system. Each noble is omnipotent! He may be either an angel or a devil! The chance is on the latter side and it must be almost an angel indeed who is not ruined by the possession of uncontrolled authority. I look upon every noble as an iron link in the massy chain that manacles this realm.*

Later she describes the fate of some serfs who had dared to make some mild remonstrance. They

> *were conveyed to the public place of punishment and 'tis a literal fact that both were lashed in a manner that humanity shudders at, and the man's life was despaired of the night after. This is a master's or mistress's power over their miserable slaves.*[3]

The extent of serfdom varied considerably. As a general rule it was most widespread in Central Russia, and least in the periphery, but it was soon established on the good lands of the south (fig. 53). The peasants of the Far North had most freedom: powerful nobles did not want land there, and therefore the Crown had not granted it. The region had, for that reason, been chosen as a place of voluntary exile by many whose religious beliefs, rebellious nature or love of freedom made life intolerable further south. Others had been sent there by the state. It is probably no coincidence that here alone initiative and creative spirit are found in handicrafts, arts and science, and that the people of the North Dvina valley and of Archangel were considered superior in intellect to other Russians. The merchants of that place were termed '*the most honest and intelligent*'; they were mostly able to read, write and cast accounts. These attributes—which may also have derived from their contact with the English—helped Archangel to

[1] *Putnam (1952), p. 197; Carr (1805), p. 291*

[2] *Coxe (1784), vol. 1, p. 437; Wilmot (1803-8), pp. 146-7; Holderness (1823), pp. 76, 125*

[3] *Wilmot (1803-8), pp. 223-4, 282*

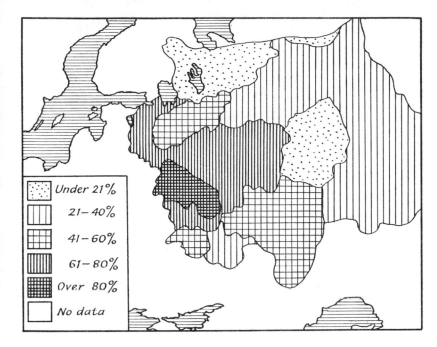

figure 53   Percentage of serfs, 1782 (after Lyashchenko).

remain a busy and prosperous port throughout the eighteenth century, in spite of Peter I's attempt to strangle it.

The ancient communal *mir* of parts of central Russia had spread rapidly during the eighteenth century, and the commune was now the prevailing form of peasant landholding. This was because it suited three strong forces in society: collective responsibility made it simpler for the state to collect taxes and for the gentry to enforce feudal dues; an egalitarian system of tax-paying and due-rendering suited the stronger and wealthier peasants. This policy of favouring the commune was to boomerang eventually, since it: *'was the commune that educated in them that capacity for mass action which made the Russian peasant movements so formidably single-minded'.*[1] (Plate 13.)

Two types of peasant serfdom can now be clearly differentiated: that where dues had been commuted for money (*obrok*) prevailed in the centre and north; that where labour on the land (*barshchina*) predominated, survived in the south (fig. 54). The reasons were economic: population was dense and labour abundant in the old-settled lands of the north and centre; the labour needs of the landlord were limited by the relatively low agricultural potential of the land; and the peasants had several opportunities of earning money—by going to the towns

[1] *Mirsky (1952), pp. 219-20*

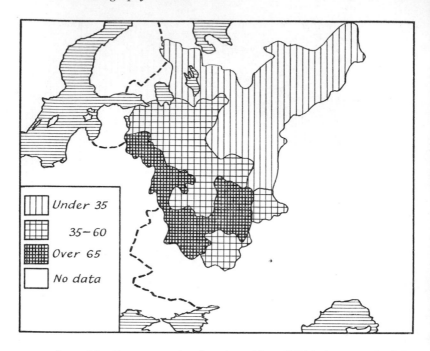

figure 54   Percentage of serfs on barschina, *1782 (after Lyaschenko).*

as labourers, by working at home at crafts, by joining in cooperatives or artels. But in the south the supply of labour could not keep up with the demands of the rapid spread of cultivation, largely because serfdom restricted the flow of settlers into the area. Here the landlords needed all the field labour they could possibly get out of those serfs they did possess.

Nevertheless, where industrial and commercial opportunities made it possible and the master permitted, a few serfs could become wealthy. John Carr saw a man (1804) *'who had paid £15,000 for his freedom, and had amassed by indefatigable industry a fortune of £100,000'.* Serfs elsewhere had *'become so considerable that they have made large purchases of land'.* This, however, had to be done in their master's name.[1]

Such peasants as were not the serfs of a noble did not go scot free. The growth of government bureaucracy afflicted them with a new kind of persecutor:

> *The boors are subject to many vexations, from the abuse of power by the officers of the government. . . . Armed with the most absolute authority, they are chiefly men of low rank and humble estate . . . they have*

[1] *Carr (1805), p. 241; Wilmot (1803-8), p. 103*

recourse to all the abundant means within their power of establishing that income. . .

These men are seen at all times and in all places, putting into requisition the boors and their horses, and galloping over the district, to the annoyance of the peasant who is frequently called from the harvest field, or other important occupation, to furnish the required duty. They eat and drink wherever they go . . .[1]

[1] *Holderness* (*1823*), *p. 115*

RUSSIA FROM 1815 TO 1861

During this brief period, the fundamental antithesis between Russia and Europe, which had been papered over by the eighteenth-century westernization and by Russia's active and successful participation in European affairs, reasserted itself. The period ended in war between Europe and Russia. The most noteworthy features of the struggle from a geographical point of view were the inaccessibility of Russia's heartland to western countries, especially maritime powers, and the difficulties of movement within the Russian Empire, particularly the transport of supplies from the industrial centre across the steppe to the Black Sea shores.

For forty years after the Congress of Vienna, Russia was indisputably the strongest military power in Europe, and this strength was used to maintain the order established in 1815, that is by supporting the 'legitimate' monarchies against subversion. In this aim she was associated with Austria and Prussia, both of whom looked to her for comfort in times of revolutionary danger. Tsar Nicholas I (1825-55), who had crushed a Polish revolution in 1831, used a Russian army to suppress the Hungarian republic in 1848, returning the subdued kingdom to its Austrian masters. Britain and France, however, removed by distance from the Russian colossus, drifted away from the principles which had inspired the Congress of Vienna. British public opinion became increasingly 'liberal' and therefore antagonistic to the absolutism and repression which characterized the Russian system; and it was from France that the revolutionary impulses that threatened established monarchies everywhere, emanated. Britain was traditionally opposed to any power exercising an unbalanced military hegemony in Europe, and therefore hostile to any Russian expansionist moves in general and to aggrandizement at the expense of Turkey in particular. In this she was supported by France, regarded coolly by the three eastern monarchies after 1830 for her revolutionary ardour.

The Eastern Question

Russian foreign policy was at this time chiefly concerned with the fate of the Turkish Empire, now showing unmistakable signs of decay. At all other points on the long Russian frontiers, satisfaction had been achieved or progress was continuing; but the south-western area abounded in uncertainties and problems. Russian interests in the nineteenth century focused on the Turkish-held Balkans and the Straits leading from the Black Sea to the Mediterranean. The Turkish subjects of the Balkans were mostly Slavs and Orthodox, that is of the same race and religion as the Russians, who therefore saw themselves as their natural protectors. To Russian public opinion, increasing in depth and range with the growth of literacy and political awareness, their welfare seemed a prime object of

Russian concern and a legitimate reason for Russian intervention. As early as 1695 the Sultan's Christian subjects had appealed to Peter the Great, and that tsar had enlisted the help of the more venturesome of the Balkan leaders for his catastrophic war against the Turks (1710-11). But Russian strength had not then been equal to the task.

Since Turkey lay athwart the link between the Black Sea, with its largely Russian coastline, and the Mediterranean, dominated by foreign fleets, it appeared to St Petersburg as essential for Russian security that such a buffer state should be amenable to Russian influence only. There was an economic interest as well as the obviously strategic one. The steppes of the Ukraine and South Russia were fast developing as wheat-lands with large surpluses which were exported from Black Sea ports via the Straits. Control of the Straits was therefore necessary for the protection of this trade.

Unfortunately for the achievement of these aims, the other great European powers had interests of their own in the Balkans and the Near East, interests which conflicted with those of Russia. And, after the brief period of Anglo-French-Russian cooperation which won the Battle of Navarino against an Ottoman (Egyptian) fleet in 1827 and led to the formation of an independent Greek state, these powers proved ready to combine to prevent the implementation of Russian policy.

The long history of Austro-Russian cooperation ended in this area. The first Austro-Russian alliance (1697) had been against the Turks, who at that time were a formidable threat to both, not a decaying force. Austria, having borne the brunt of resisting the Turkish onslaught upon Europe in the past, felt entitled to be the chief beneficiary of any dissolution of the Ottoman Empire; and since she had many Slav subjects of her own she could not but view with alarm the spread of plan-Slav ideas. Nor could Austria allow the Danube river or its delta to pass under foreign control: that river was the chief artery of her own trade.

Prussia had no interest in south-east Europe during this period. But, as she became responsible for the great industrial and commercial development of Germany in the latter part of the nineteenth century, so she began to view south-east Europe as a most important region for economic expansion. To achieve this economic domination of the region, she required that it lie within the jurisdiction of one—or at the most two— states whose governments would facilitate her economic aims: preferably Austria, possibly Turkey, but not Russia. Nor would it suit her dreams of commercial hegemony in this area to have it split up into many small fragmentary states. The Germans planned the railway from Vienna to Baghdad as the spearhead of their penetration in this direction. They consistently backed Austrian policy in the region and in 1889 Kaiser William II visited the Sultan at Constantinople.

France also developed imperial ambitions in the eastern Mediterranean and, although these conflicted with British interests, both powers were ready to unite against any Russian initiative. Britain was opposed to any further Russian aggrandizement anywhere and regarded the maintenance

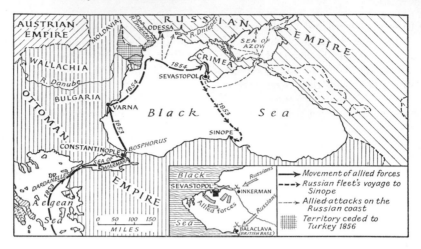

figure 55 The Crimean War, 1853-6, with, inset, the siege of Sevastopol.

of an 'independent' Turkey—that is a Turkey independent of Russia—as essential. With the cutting of the Suez canal and its importance in the route to India, the growth of foreign influence in the area became even more undesirable.

Britain took the lead in each successive combination to restrain Russia in this part of the world. At the Treaties of Adrianople (1829) and Unkiar-Skelessi (1833), Russia had established a protectorate over Turkey's Christian subjects and had made Turkey herself dependent on Russian support against rebellious Egypt. Foreign warships other than Russian were to be refused passage of the Dardanelles. But in 1839 Britain brought in Austria and Prussia to substitute four-power aid to Turkey for purely Russian help; and in 1841 an international Straits Convention closed the Bosporus to all warships when Turkey was at peace, thereby denying Russia egress to the Mediterranean.

The Crimean War, 1854-6 (fig. 55)

By 1851 it seemed to Tsar Nicholas I that the time was ripe to settle the Near East question in Russia's favour. He had stood aside from the Austro-Prussian alliance so that it would be nicely balanced by Britain and France, leaving him a free hand in Turkey. Austrian gratitude had been deserved by Russian intervention in Hungary (1848), and the Tsar had stood between the King of Prussia and the revolutionary aspirations of his subjects. 'The four of you could dictate to me; but that will never happen. I can count on Vienna and Berlin.'[1]

[1] *Taylor (1954), p. 54*

Despite every effort to propitiate Britain, his demands for a protectorate over the Orthodox subjects of the Turkish Empire was answered by an Anglo-French alliance. Notwithstanding, he sent Russian troops to occupy Moldavia and Wallachia (Rumania), whereupon Britain and France sent their fleets to the Dardanelles. Sure of support, Turkey now declared war on Russia but the Turkish fleet was destroyed at Sinope on the south shore of the Black Sea (1853). British opinion, already antagonistic to Nicholas because of his suppression of Hungarian liberties, became remarkably inflamed by this naval victory which portended Russian control of the Straits and of Constantinople.

In 1854 Britain and France declared war and Austria prepared to do so unless Russian troops were immediately withdrawn from the Danubian principalities (Moldavia and Wallachia). Russia complied, and Austrian troops occupied these provinces in her place. But Russia would not surrender her naval position in the Black Sea as Britain and France demanded. Their troops, originally landed on the Bulgarian coast, as if to invade the Danubian provinces, were now moved to the Crimea and given the task of taking Russia's Black Sea naval base at Sevastopol. The original intention of a campaign in the Danubian basin was abandoned, because of serious outbreaks of disease among the troops under summer heat on the swampy Bulgarian shore.

Although the Russians were fighting on their own soil, they were handicapped by two factors, apart from muddle and inefficiency. One was that the Crimea was not yet connected to central Russia by railways, nor were there any good roads: troops and supplies took weeks to move. The other was that Austrian pressure kept the main Russian army watching the Galician frontier. For, although Austria had already secured her war aims on the Danube, Britain and France had a hold upon her because of their ability to raise revolt in Austria's Italian provinces.

The death of Nicholas in March 1855 took some of the resolution out of Russian conduct of the war: the new Tsar wanted peace in which to introduce reforms. In June, Austria demobilized, but this was too late in the year for Russia to transfer her army to the Crimea before winter, and Sevastopol fell in September. Allied success had been delayed for months by ineptitude. The Crimea had no surfaced roads and, there being no skilled roadmakers in the army, the winter of 1854-5 was wasted as guns could not be moved. Eventually tramlines were laid down.[1]

The belligerent allies—Britain, France, Turkey—could not think what to do next. Invasion of Russia from the Crimea was impossible, the peninsula being connected to the mainland by a narrow isthmus. The Caucasus frontier area, where some fighting between Russians and Turks took place, with the Russians taking Kars, was too inaccessible. It was thought of intensifying the war in the Baltic where naval expeditions had so far accomplished nothing to Russia's detriment except the seizure of the

[1] *Woodward (1938), p. 274*

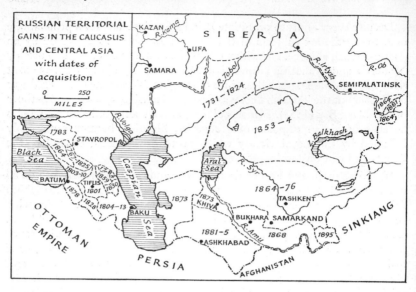

figure 56   Russian territorial gains in the Caucasus and Central Asia, with dates of acquisition.

Aland Islands. Sweden was drawn in to facilitate these Baltic plans (November 1855). But Russsia had now suffered enough. Unable to dislodge the allies from the Crimea, she accepted the humiliating terms of the Peace of Paris (March 1856). She gave up her protectorate over the Danubian provinces and ceded the Danube mouths to Turkey. Worst condition of all, she undertook to maintain no fortifications or bases on the Black Sea coast and to keep no navy on the Black Sea, thus surrendering control of these 'home' waters to Turkey and her allies.

Russia in Asia (fig. 56)

The nineteenth century saw Russia effectively take possession of the whole of northern Asia as far as—and sometimes into—the great mountain chains which divide it from Turkey, Persia, Afghanistan, India and China. Wars with Persia in 1804-13 and 1826-8, and mountain campaigns between 1857 and 1864, completed Russian control of the parallel ranges of the Caucasus Mountains and the intervening valleys. The mountaineers were too diverse ethnically as a result of the broken and isolated nature of their upland fastnesses to combine against the Russians, yet their bravery made them hard to conquer. Once conquered, they were resettled on the plains, although large numbers of them preferred to migrate to Turkey.

The Kazakh territory, ranging from grass steppes in the north to desert in the south, was penetrated by Russian traders and Cossacks early in the century. Military domination over the nomads followed with the

Plate 11   The one-roomed log house or *izba* was the traditional home of the Russian peasant. Benches, tables, and even the top of the stove, often served as beds. (Chappe d'Auteroche, 1770.)

Plate 12   Russian peasant games were of a simple and primitive kind, and included a kind of skittles played with bones. (Rechberg, 1812–13.)

Plate 13   A village council. Peasant agriculture and village affairs were run on a communal basis, and the landlord dealt with the elders when he wanted work done or taxes collected. (Atkinson & Walker, 1812.)

building of forts, beginning with that of Akmolinsk in the north in 1830 and ending with the foundation of Verny beyond lake Balkhash in 1854. Verny, as Alma Ata, is now the capital of the Kazakh Republic. The end of this period saw great activity in the Russian Far East. In 1853, Nikolayevsk was founded at the mouth of the Amur, and Sakhalin, north of the fiftieth parallel, annexed. Nikolayevsk would have been useless with this part of the island in hostile hands. In 1858 and 1860 a large area north of the Amur, and following the Pacific coast south to the Vladivostok district, was annexed and Vladivostok itself was founded (1860).

Russia and the West

During the eighteenth century and for the early part of the nineteenth, Russia behaved on the political and military plane as a European power and was accepted as such. By the mid-nineteenth century a new tendency, that of the other powers to sink their differences and unite against her, had appeared. An ambiguous relationship with Europe was found also in the internal affairs of the country.

The eighteenth century had been a period when the West was slavishly imitated. This process did not continue throughout the nineteenth century. Instead, ideas, arts, techniques, manners and institutions, borrowed from the West, developed in Russia in peculiarly Russian ways. This was particularly noticeable in literature, and later, in the other arts. To quote Sumner:

> westernization . . . involved the absorption of new attitudes of mind, new habits of thought, and new values. Out of these there emerged with astonishing rapidity in the nineteenth century the great flowering of Russian literature, thought, music and art.[1]

Or, in the words of Trotsky:

> The indubitable and irrefutable belatedness of Russia's development under influence and pressure of the higher culture from the West, results not in a simple repetition of the West European historic process, but in the creation of profound peculiarities demanding independent study.[2]

The Russian government found such nineteenth-century fruit of the eighteenth-century westernization unpalatable. Both Alexander I and his brother Nicholas were anxious to remain active participants in European affairs and to support the European order as it had been in the eighteenth century, but they were determined to shut out the new movements and ideas that grew with the new century in the West. This in itself meant placing obstacles in the way of further Europeanization and led to further differentiation of Russia from the West: police invigilation and control were elaborated to a degree unparalleled elsewhere. There was little

[1] *Sumner (1951), p. 13*
[2] *Roberts (1964), p. 7*

H

philosophical basis for such a policy, although Uvarov, a minister of Nicholas I, tried to give it one in his doctrine of Official Nationality, whereby it was held necessary to maintain Autocracy in government, Orthodoxy in religion, and the peculiar virtue of the people, so that a national identity could be preserved.[1] But government actions were really little more than the clumsy and heavy-handed attempts of an inefficient dictatorship, alarmed by democratic ideas and revolutionary acts in the West, to preserve itself from subversion at home.

The effect upon Russian minds of contact with Europe in 1813-14 was described by Turgenev:

> *With the return of the Russian armies to their country, liberal ideas, as they were called, began to spread in Russia. Independently of the regular troops, great masses of reservists had also seen foreign lands: these recruits of every rank, when they recrossed the frontier, returned to their homes, where they related what they had seen in Europe.*[2]

Measures were taken after 1848 to prevent the assimilation of foreign ideas: '*almost insurmountable obstacles are placed in the way of Russians either leaving Russia, or having their children educated abroad*'.

> *As a general rule, to which very few exceptions are allowed, no Russian can be absent from his country between the age of twelve years old and twenty-five, or the whole time during which the character is supposed to be forming; and after the age of twenty-five a medical certificate is necessary in order to obtain permission to travel, and a tax of one hundred silver roubles . . . is levied during each year of absence.*

> *No Russian can be absent more than five years from his country without ceasing to be a Russian subject, and forfeiting all his property.*[3]

It was now too late merely to close the door to western ideas. The seeds brought from the West during the eighteenth century were now bearing fruit in the effervescence of critical thought within Russia herself. A century of travelling in Europe, reading European books, listening to European savants and following European curricula in universities and schools, was now producing independent Russian thinkers and Russian writers with both Russian and European experiences to draw on. Some of these were for, and others against, Russia taking her place as a European power with a European culture, but neither party could find much satisfaction in things as they were.

Those who accepted European standards were distressed at Russia's backwardness and her seeming inability to move in step with the West. Spurts of energetic westernization were followed by long eras of stagnation. To some, Russia seemed, because of her peculiar past, to be an inert mass beyond the power of enlightened men to drag forwards. Of such thinkers, Chaadayev was the most pessimistic. In his *Letter* (1836) he condemned Russia's past history as purely negative: '*While the whole world was building,*

---

[1] *Riasanovsky (1963), p. 359*
[2] *Quoted in Carr (1956), p. 363*
[3] *Seymour (1855), pp. 260-1*

we created nothing; we remained squatting in our hovels of log and thatch. In a word, we had no part in the destinies of mankind.' And the responsibility for this futility he ascribed to Russia's exclusion from western Christianity:
While the edifice of modern civilization was rising out of the struggle between the energetic barbarism of the peoples of the North and the lofty philosophy of religion, what were we doing? Driven by a fatal destiny, we were seeking in wretched Byzantium, the object of the profound contempt of these people, the moral code in which we were to be reared.[1]
To Byzantium's malign legacy the Westerner Belinsky added the results of Mongol rule. To this, rather than to any inherent defects, were to be attributed the national vices of ignorance, superstition low cunning and servility.[2] I. S. Turgenev became one of the most emphatic of the Westerners: *'If I were asked in which direction the Russian people is destined to travel, I would answer that the question is in fact already resolved: it must move towards European civilization.'*[3] As Gershenkron has pointed out in an illuminating essay, Turgenev's desire for westernization was an intellectual one only. He, like many other leading Westerners, jibbed at the thought of the practical application of their philosophy. For Russia to follow the West in industrialization would be *'at the expense of the true interests of the nation'.*[4]

If the Westerners lamented Russia's long exclusion from Europe and were disappointed with her relative backwardness, the Slavophils regretted Peter the Great's forcible interruption of her natural evolution. They were steeped in idealism and romanticism, believing that in the autochthonous customs and institutions of the Russian people were to be found the seeds of a contribution to mankind greater than that yet made by any other people, and that, left to themselves, under the guidance of pure Autocracy and true Orthodoxy, unsullied by western individualism, Russian communal life would flower into universal brotherhood. They were encouraged by the national pride that followed the military and diplomatic successes of the years 1812-15. Their ideas had developed from those of Herder and other German philosophers down to Hegel; thus the Slavophil movement was another nineteenth-century fruit of the eighteenth-century transplantation of western ideas on to Russian soil. German romanticism had arisen as a reaction to French classicism and it had fortified German nationalism in its struggle against outside influences. It was therefore particularly suitable for development by those Russians who wished to free their own country from an alien culture.

The Romanov dynasty could find little comfort in either camp. Westerners were ashamed of its naked absolutism and hoped to dress it in constitutional garb, while the Slavophils could not close their eyes to its

[1] *Quoted in Carr (1805), p. 366*
[2] *Mazour (1958), p. 88*
[3] *Turgenev (1847), vol. 3, p. 4*
[4] *Gershenkron (1962), p. 161*

Germanic blood, its French manners, its Baltic officials, its corrupt and ineffective rule. Both Haxthausen and de Custine observed that the Slav temperament was antipathetic to the German element in the Russian government.[1] The autocracy was caught in a dilemma, a dilemma which led to defeat in the Crimean War. To preserve itself it must shut out western influences, yet by so doing it deprived its subjects of the skills and means needed to defend themselves against the West.

Yet it appears that, until the Crimean War, such public opinion as there was, backed the Tsar, accepted the doctrine of Official Nationality, and had little sympathy for the liberals and intellectuals who questioned his rule:

> *Giving generally the fruit of my observations among many classes of Russians for several years, I believe they think their government a wise and good one on the whole, although they are not slow to criticise it in its details.*
>
> *They believe that an iron hand is necessary to keep the empire together, and that a great destiny is in store for it, and as long as progress is made, and I think my opinion has been borne out by recent events, that they would be willing to rally round their Government, and make every sacrifice required by it.*

As for the restrictions on travel and residence abroad, these were accepted as attempts '*to rouse a national feeling in the country*'. They

> *seemed generally approved of, on the grounds that young Russians came back with such very absurd notions after having been to foreign countries, and that, without understanding what was good in them, they aped everything that was bad.*[2]

The Crimean defeat made it impossible for the government to answer the Westerners' devastating criticism as voiced, for instance, by Granovsky:

> *With all our vast territory and countless population, we are incapable of coping. . . . When we talk of the glorious campaigns against Napoleon, we forget that since that time Europe has been steadily advancing on the road of progress while we have been standing still. We march not to victory, but to defeat, and the only grain of consolation which we have is that Russia will learn by experience a lesson that will be of use to her in future.*[3]

Hurt national pride found vent in more direct but anonymous attacks upon the autocracy:

> *Awake, O Russia! Devoured by foreign enemies, crushed by slavery, shamefully oppressed by stupid authorities and spies, awaken from your long sleep of ignorance and apathy! You have been long enough held in bondage by the successors of the Tartar Khan. Stand forward calmly before the throne of the despot, and demand from him an account of the national disaster.*[4]

[1] *Custine (1843), vol. 3, p. 328; Haxthausen (1852), pp. 14-21*
[2] *Seymour (1855), pp. 260-1*
[3] *Wallace (1905), vol. 2, p. 91*
[4] *Wallace (1905), vol. 2, p. 97*

There were others besides the Slavophils who held strongly that Russia should free herself from Europe and go her own way, if need be in opposition to Europe. Danilevsky was a realist who saw that, however the Westerners might yearn for a place in the European family, the facts of geography, history and culture made this undesirable for Russia. He argued that Europe, as a separate continent divided from Asia by the Urals, did not make geographical sense: India, backed by her mighty mountain barrier, had a much better claim to such status. Europe could only be a cultural term and, by common consent among the western peoples, Europe was coterminous with western Christianity and the Latin-Teutonic world. Russia had no place in this civilization and had not shared in the experiences which had produced it. In this he was at one with Ranke.[1] Nor could western culture be successfully grafted on to the native Russian plant as the Westerners hoped.[2]

Danilevsky pointed out that, although Westerners claimed that Russia could serve Europe by acting as a missionary for western civilization in the East, the European powers would not allow this in practice. When Russia attempted to fulfil this mission in Turkey, the Caucasus or Persia, the Europeans at once cried '*Hands Off!*' Nor must she come near India nor touch China. '*We are trusted only with a few nomads*'.[3] His conclusion is that Russia and Europe are two irreconcilable civilizations and that Russia should ready herself for inevitable conflict with the West.[4]

From the European side, Custine had come to the same conclusion thirty years earlier:

> *I left Paris under the impression that only the intimate alliance of France and Russia could settle the affairs of Europe. But after I had seen the Russian people at closer range and had come to realize the true nature of its government, I felt that she was separated from the rest of the civilized world by a powerful political interest backed up by religious fanaticism, and I am now of the opinion that France should seek her allies elsewhere.*[5]

The word 'Europe' still meant a distinct and distant land to most Russians, even to those most westernized. Thus in Dostoyevsky's *Idiot*, one goes 'abroad' to Europe and there are countless other examples.[6] Westerners themselves were fully aware of a spiritual difference between Russia and Europe. In a letter to Chaadayev (1836), Pushkin wrote that in Russia '*only the government was European*'.[7] Many Europeans also continued to refuse to accept Russia in any but the narrowest geographical or political sense. The suppression of the Polish rebellion in 1830-1 and

[1] *Ranke (1824), p. 31*
[2] *Danilevsky (1920), pp. 17-22, 191 et. seq.*
[3] *Danilevsky (1920), pp. 23-5*
[4] *Danilevsky (1920), pp. 235-6*
[5] *Custine (1843), vol. 4, pp. 365-6*
[6] *Dostoyevskiy (1911), vol. 11, pp. 451, 448*
[7] *Schelting (1948), p. 14*

of the Hungarian Revolt of 1848 provided them with ammunition, and Crimean War propaganda against Russia was of a different nature than was then customary between two warring European powers. The struggle was represented as one between civilized Christian countries and barbarism, between freedom and slavery, and between Europe and 'Anti-Europe'.[1] However much European nations feuded among themselves, they felt a sort of community when confronted with Russia. Rousseau had expressed this feeling when he wrote that

> *there are no longer Frenchmen, Germans, Spaniards, nor even Englishmen, although these names are still used. They all have the same interests, the same feelings, the same manners. . . . They all, in similar circumstances, will behave in the same way.*

but as for the Russians, only contempt could be felt for their behaviour.[2] Governments took fundamentally the same view:

> *the allies would not have presented such terms to any Power whom they regarded as truly European. At bottom, the British and to a lesser extent the French regarded Russia as a semi-Asiatic state, not much above the level of Turkey and not at all above the level of China.*[3]

Visitors from the West often returned with a similar opinion:

> *The mere fact that a certain number of wealthy nobles have picked up European manners, can speak Western languages with facility, and live surrounded by every luxury of France or England, does not suffice to make Russia a civilized country.*

This writer also made an anthropological distinction:

> *Nor are the faces of these men like European faces; their foreheads are broad and low, their cheek-bones stick out, their eyes are sunken, their noses flattened, with wide open nostrils, their mouths large, and their complexion of a yellow hue not common in the West.*[4]

The debate in Russia over her relationship to Europe showed that the westernization of the country had not been absorbed by the national consciousness and had failed wholly to satisfy and convince the educated classes who themselves were a product of it. Only in the literary field was a successful symbiosis of the two cultures achieved, and this must be attributed to the genius of Pushkin and a few others in reconciling the irreconcilable. Both Westerners and Slavophils were uneasily aware of the gulf which isolated them from the mass of the people, although the former hoped to bridge this by transforming the people, the latter by bringing the ruling class back to a truly Russian culture. But the dichotomy existed and undermined the self-confidence of the aristocracy and the intelligentsia. Those who sought to become better Europeans could do so only by alienating themselves further from their own people. Having paid this price, they often found only disillusion and frustration in return:

[1] *Schelting (1948), pp. 194-7*
[2] *Rousseau (1826), pp. 289-91*
[3] *Taylor (1954), p. 85*
[4] *Dicey (1867), pp. 21, 232*

'*alienated from both their own past and their people, they could not identify with a Europe that did not conform to their idealized image and failed to fulfil their hopes and aspirations*'.[1] Those who sought constitutional reform could not base their movements on a broad popular support. The mass of the people remained innocent of western ideas. When the soldiers who wished the liberal Constantine to follow Alexander on the throne, instead of reactionary Nicholas, shouted '*Constantine and Constitution*' in the Decembrist revolt of 1825, those within earshot thought that *Constitutsiya* was Constantine's wife.

Suspected by the government, which now relied mainly upon its bureaucrats and its policemen, and cut off from the people, many liberals and intellectuals of the gentry class felt themselves both useless and rootless. In contrast stood the peasant mass, still unaffected by westernization except in that they had ultimately to pay for it:

> *The faith and toil of the humble folk, their strong belief in God, their veneration of the holy man, the monk and the pilgrim, the annual cycle of work and prayer, their legends, costumes, and folksongs, these had not altered much since the dawn of Russian history.*[2]

Thus psychosomatic disorders of the Russian body politic arose in the nineteenth century from the doses of westernization swallowed in the eighteenth.

In the arts and sciences and in geographical discovery and exploration, the eighteenth-century investment in westernization bore more wholesome fruit. New universities were founded and old ones expanded. Not only did literature enjoy a 'golden age' but a genuine Russian historiography was introduced with the work of Karamzin, and oriental studies made notable progress. European Russia was surveyed and mapped, and a Geographical Society was founded in St Petersburg in 1845. The exploration of Siberia continued and the necessity of sailing southwards of Africa, to link the Baltic and Pacific coasts of the Empire, led to important discoveries in the south Pacific, including that of Antarctica (1821), which was named Alexander I Land.[3]

[1] *Raeff (1964), p. 16*
[2] *Obolensky (1950), p. 43*
[3] *Wawilow (1952), vol. 2, p. 1,419*

CHAPTER FIFTEEN
RUSSIA IN 1861,
AT THE TIME OF THE EMANCIPATION OF THE SERFS

Although this chapter will concentrate on changes in the economic and social geography which had occurred since the beginning of the nineteenth century, the importance of these changes should not obscure the most remarkable aspect of Russia's economic geography in 1861. This was the persistence so far into the nineteenth century of its traditional characteristics. The technological revolutions that had transformed agriculture, industry and transport in Europe, though not altogether absent, were but little advanced. Grain, tallow, flax and hemp were still the main farm products. The Urals still dominated mining and metallurgy. Industry was still confined almost exclusively to the working up of the produce of farm and forest. Raft and barge, cart and sledge remained the main means of transport. The same commodities as in the sixteenth century continued to make up the bulk of Russia's overseas trade.

The principal cause of this economic lethargy was the rigidity of the social system, and particularly the institutions of serfdom and the commune. These restrained the mobility of labour, and thus inhibited the rapid growth of factory industry and of a large urban working class. They militated against innovations in agriculture, mining, industry and transport, and they ensured the continuance of human inefficiency and technical backwardness. In each and every aspect of economic geography, the paralysing effect of the social structure is seen as a decisive factor. In the Crimean War military weakness had exposed this economic stagnation, and led therefore to a questioning of the social structure which underlay it. The Emancipation of 1861 was the result. But many Russians still clung to the fallacy that unpaid labour motivated by fear of corporal punishment was adequate. They refused to admit that the incentive of earning money to buy goods would result in more co-operation, more efficiency and more skill. An English engineer employed by the Russians to fortify Sevastopol in the 1840s, had exactly the same problems to face as Perry in Peter I's reign (see p. 140):

> *The serfs were said to do so little work, that Colonel Upton, as well as all other Englishmen that I have known employed by the Russian government, were of the opinion that it would be far more economical to pay free labourers than to feed and keep the serfs for their gratuitous services.*[1]

Under the system of serfdom, the labourer employed all his cunning to avoid as much work and responsibility as he could.

Russian agriculture was typified by a combination of subsistence farming with the growing of cash crops for export. This reflected the division of land between small peasant holdings and landlord estates worked by serfs.

[1] *Seymour (1855), p. 69*

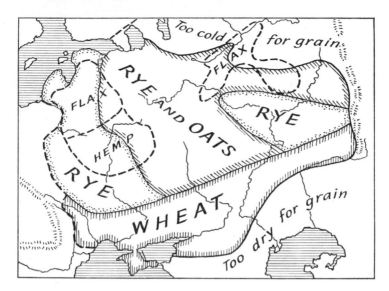

figure 57   Russia in 1861: crop zones.

The poorer serfs in the podzol-soil areas of the west and centre grew rye, buckwheat and oats to feed themselves and their horses, while their land-lords made vodka from rye or grew flax and hemp for sale (fig. 57).

In the black-earth soil provinces of the south, the growing market for grain at home and abroad led to extensive wheat growing on landlords' estates, while peasant holdings, cultivated perforce on a subsistence basis, were so encroached upon by the landlords that poverty and hunger were extreme.[1] But besides these fuedal estates, which predominated in the densely populated wooded-steppe belt, there were now large commercial 'capitalist' farms on the steppe, using machinery and hired labour. In some districts such farms prevailed—they were often owned by foreign colonists, mostly German—and serf agriculture was relatively unimportant.[2] Despite the rapid extension of wheat and sugar-beet growing, sheep-rearing re-mained important on the steppe.

This geographical factor—the division of agricultural Russia into a northern forested zone with podzol soils, an intermediate zone with black-earth soils, and a grass steppe—was decisive in the distribution of serfdom, and in the relative importance of *obrok* (money payment to the landlord) and *barshchina* (labour on the landlord's fields). The proportion of serfs was highest in the more densely populated central provinces of the mixed-forest belt and the adjoining wooded steppe; it fell away in the colder drier lands to the north, east and south (fig. 58). In the north, land had not been widely granted to gentry on account of its poor quality; in the

[1] *Florinsky (1953), vol. 2, p. 783; Robinson (1932), p. 38*
[2] *Lyashchenko (1956), vol. 1, pp. 500-1, 562*

H*

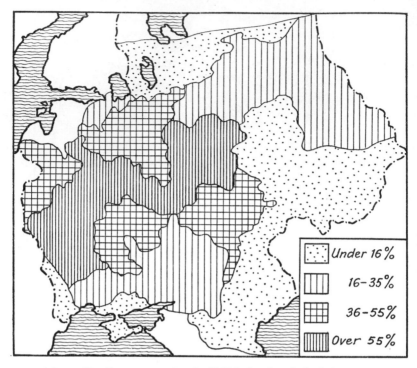

figure 58   Percentage of serfs, 1858 (after Lyashchenko).

east and south it had been more recently colonized and therefore without a
large settled population of peasants who could be reduced to serfdom.
Although serfdom was eventually introduced here, hired workers, free
peasants, Cossacks and foreign colonists were more numerous than serfs.

The proportion of serfs discharging their feudal dues by money payment
or *obrok* was highest in those central provinces whose soils were the poor
podzols and where population exceeded the possible labour needs of a
limited agriculture (fig. 59). It here suited the landlord to let his serfs earn
money through manufacturing, whether in their own cottages or in the
towns, and then to extract it from them in dues. But on the black-earth
soils of the wooded steppe and grass steppe, where population was sparser,
where the agricultural potential of the land was greater, and where industries and towns were fewer, the serfs were compelled to labour on the manorial estate for periods often in excess of the customary three days a week:

> *many landlords in Tula, Ryazan and other agricultural provinces,
> increased* barshchina *in summer, not only to four, but to five and even
> six days, leaving the peasant only Sunday for his own work. Some
> landlords in Tula province, according to Tuchkov, forced the serfs to
> come out on* barshchina *on Sunday as well.*[1]

[1] *Lyashchenko (1956), vol. 1, p. 495; Blum (1961), pp. 444-5*

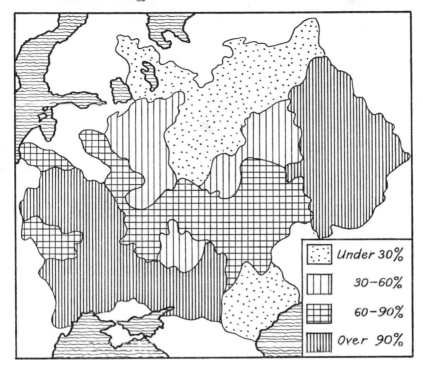

figure 59 Percentage of serfs on barshchina, *1860 (after Lyashchenko).*

The serfs had often to contribute, besides the labour of their hands, the use of their horses and implements.[1]

Low productivity and inefficiency were the inevitable results of serfdom and *barshchina*. Labour was cheap, but it was unwilling and unskilled, and its availability discouraged the introduction of machinery. Abundant unpaid labour, by favouring arable cultivation, worked against any increase in pasture and livestock, and so led to soil erosion. The feudal organization of agriculture perpetuated the primitive three-field system and, by widespread repartition of holdings, gave no incentive to improvements by the peasants themselves. As knowledge of progressive agricultural methods entered Russia from the West, not a few landlords and some peasants greeted the innovations with enthusiasm. Turgenev's Islayev, in *A Month in the Country*, represents such a landlord. But the social system occasioned many frustrations to such landlords: Tolstoy made Levin experience them in *Anna Karenina*. Only on the newly-opened steppe lands of the south could the modern agriculture be practised unhampered by feudalism. In these conditions, many landlords, rather than attempt to increase productivity through improved techniques, did so by the more ruthless exploitation of their serfs.

[1] *Robinson (1932), p. 58*

The declining fertility of the soil, caused by the three-field system, overcropping, and an insufficiency of livestock, added to the farmer's difficulties. On the black-earth land, which was considered to be '*so fertile as to have no need of manure and where cattle are not reared except for drawing the plough, for milking, or for sale*',[1] soil erosion was proceeding at an alarming rate:

> *Since so much of the land was ploughed, there was throughout the nineteenth century a chronic shortage of pasture in the chernozem belt, with the consequence that slopes too steep for ploughing or areas of light sandy soil were overgrazed. Overstocking led to weakening or total destruction of the grass cover in the very areas most liable to gully or wind erosion.*
>
> *The intensiveness of erosion was increased by cropping practises. Frequently the large estates were concerned only to produce as much grain as possible, especially for the export market and far too often land was sown to wheat year after year. If it were rested at all, it lay fallow and exposed to erosion.*[2]

Yet vast deposits of untouched phosphorite underlay the impoverished fields of central Russia, and the refuse from the fisheries of the lower Volga was allowed to putrefy and infect the air. Both could have been used to increase the production of grain by millions of bushels. Very little fertilizer was imported—only farmers in the Baltic area and some of the Ukrainian sugar-beet estate proprietors made use of it.[3]

Agricultural Regions

The North. North of a line approximating to the sixtieth parallel, such agriculture as there was remained of the primitive shifting type. Clearings were made in the forest, the trees burned, and a little barley and rye grown for as many seasons as the declining fertility of the soil allowed. A new clearing would then be made. Flax was grown to the east of lake Onega and round Vologda and Vyatka. Surplus grain and flax moved to Archangel for export. The number of cattle relative to population was high and those from the Kholmogory district of Archangel province moved to St Petersburg to help feed the capital.

The Baltic provinces, western Russia and White Russia. Rye, flax and hemp, with an increasing amount of potatoes, were the chief crops grown here. The rye was mainly converted into vodka, while the flax and hemp were either manufactured locally or moved to Riga, St Petersburg and other Baltic ports, for export. Cattle were relatively numerous and the amount of pasture was greater than that in central Russia. In the vodka-distilling areas they were fattened for the St Petersburg market with the

[1] *Tegoborsky (1852), vol. 1, p. 71*

[2] *French (1963), p. 52*

[3] *Matthaei (1885), vol. 1, p. 237*

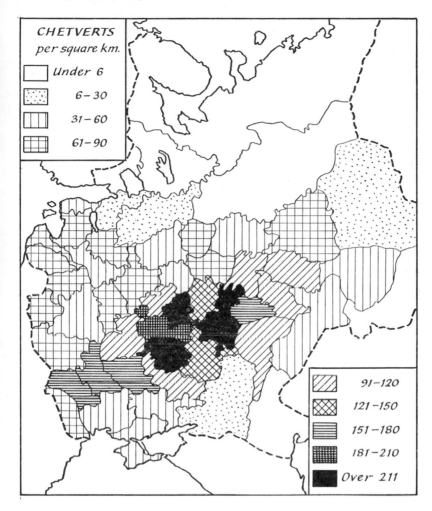

figure 60   Yield of cereals, 1870.

residue from the distilleries.[1] In the Lithuanian and White Russian provinces, where soils were poor and there was no alternative occupation to agriculture, the serfs were exploited to the limit and the peasantry was in a most wretched condition. They lived on buckwheat mash, rye bread and honey, and seldom tasted meat. Because poor communications prevented their landlords from sending their rye grain to market, they converted it into vodka, for the purchase of which the peasants mortgaged their meagre crops ahead of the harvest.[2]

---

[1] Khozyaystvenno-statisticheskiy atlas *(1857), p. 104*
[2] *Lyashchenko (1956), vol. 1, p. 527; Haxthausen (1847), vol. 1, p. 78*

The Baltic provinces stood apart. Serfdom had been abolished in them fifty years before, and crop rotations had replaced the three-field system. The cereal yield was double that of neighbouring Russian provinces.

North Central Russia: the podzol zone of the mixed forest. This region, corresponding to old Muscovy, was poor agriculturally. There was peasant subsistence farming of rye, oats and buckwheat, but this failed to feed the dense and largely industrial population, so that increasing amounts of grain were imported from the south. There was a flax-growing district in the north-east round Kostroma and Yaroslavl. The flax was grown as a textile fibre for local manufacture.

South Central Russia: the black-earth zone of the wooded steppe. This region, once fertile, productive and prosperous, was deteriorating as an ever-increasing emphasis on grain for the expanding population of the Moscow region to the north led to smaller peasant holdings, fewer live-stock and to soil exhaustion. Rye was the chief cereal grown. In this region the number of cattle per rural inhabitant was the lowest in the Empire.

The Ukraine west of the Dnieper. Here Polish landlords had begun successfully to exploit their vast estates with serf labour in the production of sugar-beet. Some *'converted their estates almost literally into slave plantations, by merging the village fields with those of the manor'.*[1] The prosperity and efficiency of their farms were in marked contrast to the conditions prevailing in the high-serf areas of Great Russia.

New Russia and the steppe. East of the Dnieper, the Ukrainian and south Russian steppes, earlier in the century the exclusive domain of the merino sheep, were being rapidly invaded by wheat growers—landlords, peasants, Cossacks and Germans. Hired labour and machinery were here the rule. Sugar-beet was grown in the north of this region and flax in the south. A British M.P., who knew Russia well, wrote in 1855:

> *This union of the black earth with a temperate climate in the Steppes between the Dniestr and the Don already enables the inhabitants of those countries to send, as from Mariopol, the finest wheat to the European markets, and justifies economists in looking forward to this region as one destined to a brilliant future.*[2]

The Crimea. Here also sheep farming was giving way to wheat growing, and nomadic Tartars were still being removed to make way for Russian colonists. These evictions were intensified during the Crimean War. Wine making had been revived along the south coast.[3]

Caucasia and Transcaucasia. The rich lands of the Kuban and Terek, made safe for settlement by the pacification of the mountains, were now settled by Cossacks, Russians and Volga Germans, and converted into rich wheat and sheep farms. The luxuriant valleys of the mountain area prospered. Their gardens and orchards produced grapes and other fruit, tobacco and sunflower seed, for which a growing market was found in the

[1] *Robinson (1932), p. 40*
[2] *Seymour (1855), p. 17*
[3] *Seymour (1855), pp. 227-32*

Russian Empire. The hills were covered with flocks of sheep. Evicted Circassian mountaineers made way for Russian colonists, and the Georgian nobles, their hands strengthened by support from the Russian government, were able to harness the lower orders in the ruthless exploitation of their lands.

Siberia. Agriculture continued to expand around Cossack fortresses and fur-trading posts. Some farming was found down the Irtysh-Ob valley as far as Demyansk (60°N), '*but beyond that village northwards throughout the whole extent of country, not a speck of tillage was seen*'.[1]

STATISTICAL SUMMARY

About one-third of Russia (west of the Urals) was used for agriculture, as the following estimates show:

	c. 1850[2]	*1875*[3]
	per cent	*per cent*
Arable	18	21·5
Pasture	12	11·9
Forest	36	30·2
otherwise unsuitable	34	36·0

Although too much reliance cannot be placed on such data, an increase in the amount of arable at the expense of both forest and pasture over a period of 25 years was not unlikely. The 98 million desyatins of arable land in 1875 were divided as follows:[4]

	Million desyatins
Fallow (about one-third of the whole owing to the prevalance of the three-field system)	32
Grain-growing	63·5
—of which, food grains	51
—of which, rye	24
oats	12
wheat	11
barley	3
buckwheat and millet	1
Potatoes	1·5
Flax	0·8
Hemp	0·5
Sugar-beet	0·2
Tobacco	0·04

[1] *Felinska (1852), vol. 1, p. 109*
[2] *Tegoborsky (1852), vol. 1 pp. 50-2*
[3] *Lyashchenko (1956), vol. 2, p. 63*
[4] *Lyashchenko (1956), vol. 2, pp. 63-4*

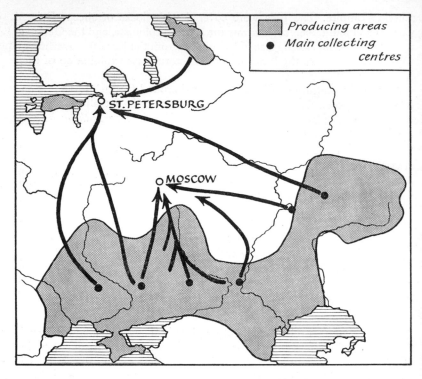

figure 61   The movement of cattle for slaughter (after Khozyaystven-no-Statisticheskiy Atlas, *1857).*

A large increase had taken place in the area sown to grain between 1800 and 1860: from 38 million desyatins to 58 million. The proportion on black-earth soils had risen from 53 to 60 per cent (fig. 60). But yields were not maintained and an estimated annual production of 266 million quarters for the 1860s was little more than the 250 million estimated thirty years before. 'In other words, during the first sixty years of the nineteenth century, serf agriculture produced an almost stationary harvest'.[1]

Livestock. Total numbers are given from different sources as follows (in millions):

	1853	*1862**	*1872*
Horses	*16·3*	*15*	*16·4*
Sheep		*41·5*	*49·5*
Cattle	*21·8*	*21·7*	*24·6*
Swine		*10·5*	

* *European Russia only.*

[1] *Lyashchenko (1956), vol. 1, pp. 506-8*

Plate 14   The public bath, in which the bather moved from steam heat into cold water or even snow, reproduced the extremes of Russia's continental climate. The practice was prominent in Slavic society at least as early as the ninth century, as is witnessed by Arab writers. It was considered to promote health and longevity. (Chappe d'Auteroche, 1770.)

Plate 15   The 'great knout'. Corporal punishment was widely used against peasants by the police at the behest of the landlords, and the practice was regarded as a result of Mongol influence. The 'great knout' was its most severe form, and often led to the death of the victim. (Chappe d'Auteroche, 1770.)

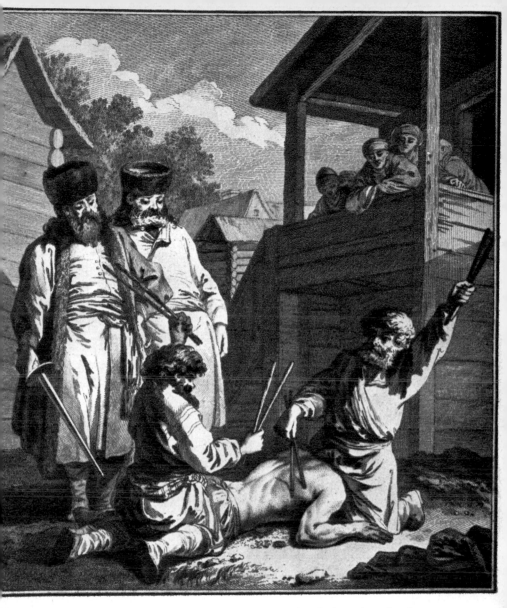

Plate 16   Punishment by 'battocks' was less severe than the 'great knout' and a more normal retribution for a serf's dereliction of duty. There was also the 'common knout' which consisted of the administration of lashes to the back.
(Chappe d'Auteroche, 1770.)

Plate 17   A Black Sea Cossack. The allegiance of the Cossacks was a powerful asset to the tsars in building the Russian Empire. They had long experience of living and fighting in the arid steppes, where the forest-dwelling Muscovites had difficulty in adapting themselves. (Rechberg, 1812–13.)

Plate 18   A Bashkir soldier. The Bashkirs, who inhabited the southern Ural and Middle Volga area, had been rebellious earlier in the eighteenth century and had taken part in Pugachev's rising. By the end of the century, they had been pacified, and now provided a regiment of horse for the Russian army. (Rechberg, 1812–13.)

Plate 19   A Tartar camp. The nomadic Mongol Tartars had been masters of the steppes until the sixteenth century. They were excellent horsemen, and kept large herds of sheep. Their tents or *yurts* could be readily dismantled and transported in their waggons. (Atkinson & Walker, 1812.)

These numbers were too small to maintain the fertility of the soil under the three-field system.[1] In addition, the northern province of Archangel possessed 140,000 reindeer and Astrakhan in the south-east had 26,000 camels.[2]

Central Russia had the largest density of horses because here they were necessary for the extensive land transport occasioned by the active internal trade of the region. As they were needed in any case for transport, they were also used instead of horned cattle for field labour. This was one reason why Central Russia had fewest cattle, another being the three-field system and the concentration on grain. Cattle were densest in relation to population on the steppe lands of the south where they were used for labour, and whence large numbers were sent northwards for slaughtering (fig. 61).

Of the sheep population, nearly 8 million were fine-woolled merinos, the vast majority of which were pastured on the steppes.

Mining and Metallurgy

Mineral production in 1860-1 can be summed up statistically as follows:

Coal	*300,000 tons*
Petroleum	*29,000 tons*
Pig iron	*284,000 tons*
Wrought iron	*200,000 tons*
Steel	*1,600 tons*
Copper	*6,000 tons*
Gold	*1,569 puds*
Silver	*1,000 puds*
Platinum	*227 puds*

Production of coal in the Donets coalfield, which began in 1790, had at last started to rise significantly, from under 1 million puds in 1840 to $3\frac{1}{2}$ million puds in 1850 and 6 million (100,000 tons) in 1860.[3] The growth of steam navigation on the rivers and on the Black and Caspian Seas was the chief factor in this increase. The coal mined was mostly anthracite. The 1850 production was consumed as follows:[4]

In steam navigation	*1,050,000 puds*
As domestic fuel	*932,000 puds*
For melting tallow, etc.	*612,000 puds*

[1] Khozyaystvenno-statisticheskiy atlas *(1857), pp. 86, 93; Pauly (1862), p. 11*

[2] *Pauly (1862), p. 11*

[3] *Lyashchenko (1956), vol. 2, p. 17; Semenov (1862-5), vol. 2, pp. 104-8*

[4] *Semenov (1862-85), vol. 2, p. 106*

In smithies and foundries   585,000 puds
In the Lugansk ironworks   300,000 puds
For burning lime, baking bricks, etc.   161,000 puds

It was said at the time that only lack of a market prevented a rise in coal production here to 20 million puds. Despite its small production, the Donets field was already the chief in Russia, although coal was also mined in Tula province, to the east of Yekaterinburg, and near Kuznetsk.

Production of oil in the neighbourhood of Baku was also small but increasing. It had risen from $1\frac{1}{4}$ million puds in 1850 to 1·7 million puds (28,000 tons) in 1860.

The Urals remained far and away the main source of iron ore. Here were smelted $14\frac{1}{2}$ million puds (234,000 tons) of pig in 1860 compared with 120,000 tons at the beginning of the century. This mountain region continued to dominate Russian production with 83 per cent of the total. The works at Nizhniy Tagil were still, as in 1800, the largest in Russia: *'the smelting furnaces, rolling mills, machine shops, and other works, with their machinery, are on a magnificent scale'*.[1] This works, which in 1861 produced 1 million puds (16,500 tons) of cast iron, was powered by 23 water wheels, 4 turbines and 3 steam engines.[2]

The moderate increase in Uralian production was not sufficient for Russia to maintain a leading place as a world producer, as the following table clearly shows:

Production of Pig Iron (tons), 1800-60

	Britain	Russia	Urals	Ural Percentage of Russian total
1800	160,000	160,000	120,000	75%
1860	3,900,000	284,000	234,000	83%

Russia, the leading producer of pig iron in the eighteenth century, ranked seventh in 1859. Exports declined from 58,000 tons in 1793-5 to an average of only 8,000 tons in the years 1851-60. There had been relative stagnation, with most of the Ural works still using eighteenth-century methods and equipment. Both Tsarist and Soviet economic historians attribute this to the system of forced serf labour.[3] The new techniques in England enabled that country to outprice the Russian product.

Besides the Urals works, with their manufactures of all kinds of iron objects, from guns and shells to *'wire, both strong and fine . . . which produces a very good price in the fair at Nizhniy Novgorod'*,[4] there were the various public armament works. These, as at St Petersburg, Petrozavodsk, Tula and Lugansk, had all been founded in the eighteenth century, but they

[1] *Atkinson (1858), p. 78*
[2] *Semenov (1862-85), vol. 5, p. 13*
[3] *Tugan-Baranovsky (1900), p. 92; Zlotnikov (1946), p. 41*
[4] *Atkinson (1858), p. 44*

had since been expanded and renovated. Petrozavodsk in 1865 produced 2,500 tons of arms and projectiles; the Tula works had been rebuilt in 1835-43.[1] Of Tula it was said that it might '*be justly called the Birmingham or Sheffield of Russia*'.[2] It remained famous for samovars, and employed 1,528 men in 47 works on this article alone. Locks, guns, cutlery and hardware were also made. Lugansk was unique in its use of Donets coal. Nizhniy Novgorod was the only other noteworthy iron-working town in Russia. Iron was smelted and steel made here, and two factories produced machinery: one of these was doubtless the 'steam-engine manufactory' seen by Moor in 1862. Here also was the Sormovsky steamship works, established in 1849, when the steam navigation of the Volga began.[3]

The Urals remained important for their production of copper and gold, to which platinum had now been added. Copper production had risen slowly from 200,000 puds in 1802-6 to 375,000 puds in 1850-4. Most gold now came from the Tunguska and Angara districts of Siberia where it had been discovered in 1838. Silver production at Nerchinsk, which averaged 285 puds a year in 1815-24, had shrunk to 26 puds in 1861, but the Altay mining district yielded 1,000 puds in 1860. Lyashchenko comments: '*these paltry figures show that here too the institution of serfdom paralysed the growth of production*'.[4]

Manufacturing

As for many centuries before, manufacturing industry in Russia was still concerned mainly with the working up of animal and vegetable raw materials. In town after town, and in the countryside, tallow melting, candle making, soap boiling, vodka distilling, leather working, tobacco manufacture were amongst the leading industries. They were found throughout the land. More concentrated geographically were the textile industries, flour milling and sugar refining. Brick and tile works and iron foundries were the only mineral-using industries of any general importance. Mining and metallurgy were, with few exceptions, confined to the Urals.

The first half of the nineteenth century was a period of stagnation compared to the speed of technological progress and expansion of industrial production in the West: the gap between Russian industry and that of the advanced countries of western Europe and North America was much wider in 1861 than it had been in 1800. Nevertheless some noteworthy changes had taken place.

There had been a significant growth in factory industry. There were nearly three times as many factories in 1861 as in 1804, and six times as

[1] *Semenov (1862-85), vol. 4, p. 96 and vol. 5, p. 242*
[2] *Beeton (1872)*
[3] *Moor (1863), p. 150; Baranskiy (1950), p. 175*
[4] *Lyashchenko (1956), vol. 1, p. 515*

many if small workshops are included. The number of factory workers, excluding the smallest establishments—but including mines and metal-lurgical works—rose from 225,000 to 860,000. The percentage of these who were paid wages rose from 27 per cent in 1804 to 56 per cent in 1860, but this still left a large proportion condemned to forced labour in the most appalling conditions.[1]

This continued increase in factory industry was hardly an approxima-tion to Western industrial culture, since so little of it represented capitalist enterprise. Many, if not most, factories were run by nobles using forced serf labour; several were winter factories, taking advantage of the climatic-ally enforced pause in agricultural activity. This explains the predominance of factories and works in the countryside instead of in the towns. By 1861 the production of woollen cloth, linen, beet sugar and vodka had all been remarkably developed on feudal estates. The Emancipation of 1861 came as a blow to landlord industrialists, although they were compensated by being paid a higher price than the market value for the land they had to give up to their peasants. According to Dicey:

> The old proprietors, who can no longer get their work done below the market price of labour, complain that the country is going to rack and ruin. The foreign employers, who pay wages, and have no longer to compete with unpaid labour, are well satisfied with the new state of things.

The Emancipation also hit the factory entrepreneur when peasants were no longer compelled to go to the town to earn the money to pay *obrok* to their landlords:

> a manufacturer who employs some twenty odd thousand workmen assured me that, since the abolition of serfdom, he finds it difficult to get labour during harvest time, because all the peasants have taken to cultivate small plots of ground of their own.[2]

In some areas serfs themselves were the entrepreneurs, though often working in their master's name. How this came about is described by Blum:

> The peasant who owned a factory usually started his manufacturing career as an artisan working in his home or shop. Possessed of more initiative and daring than his fellows, he began to put out materials to other peasants for them to work up. If things went well he opened a small factory, hiring his neighbours as his workers, and continuing to put out work . . . a few went on still further to become owners of great enterprises, with hundreds and even thousands of employees.[3]

Peasant-directed factory industry was particularly advanced in the cotton-cloth processing village of Ivanovo in Vladimir province and in the cutlery, tool and hardware manufacturing centres of Pavlovo and Vorsma in Nizhniy Novgorod province.

Kustar or peasant cottage manufacture shared in the general industrial

[1] *Blum (1961), pp. 295-6, 324; Lyashchenko (1956), vol. 1, p. 523*
[2] *Dicey (1867), pp. 124-5; Rashin (1958), p. 8*
[3] *Blum (1961), p. 299*

advance: 'one of the phenomena peculiar to nineteenth-century Russia is undoubtedly a partial return to domestic industry'.[1] This was especially true of the linen industry in which the factory form found it impossible to compete with kustar competition. In 1852 there were about three times as many domestic producers of linen as there were factory workers, and the number of factories declined from 285 in 1804 to 100 in 1861. Even in the cotton industry, although there had been an advance in factory spinning and printing, a decline took place in factory weaving. Imports of raw cotton and yarn were over three times as great in 1857 as in 1836, but the number of weavers working in factories declined from 95,000 to 76,000.[2] There must therefore have been a large increase in the number of domestic weavers.

A powerful cause of this recrudescence of cottage industry was the noble's monopoly of serf labour. Merchants and others responded to this by supplying peasants with raw materials for working up in their own homes. Either way the noble profited. If not himself an entrepreneur, he benefited from the *obrok* payments levied on industrialized peasants. This *kustar* type of manufacture flourished particularly in central and northern areas where agriculture could not support the growing population.[3]

Capitalist-style industry using steam-power and machinery did not begin seriously in Russia until the 1840s. The repeal in 1842 of British laws prohibiting the export of machinery gave it an impetus. The value of machinery entering Russia rose from 384,085 R. in 1839-43 to 3,103,510 R. in 1856-60. Mechanization had as yet, however, made little progress outside of the cotton-textile and flour-milling industries, and most machinery was still driven by man power or horse power. It was almost all imported, and two-thirds of the mechanized factories and works were in St Petersburg province, i.e. close to the port of entry. In St Petersburg province, 103 out of the 374 larger factories were using steam power in 1862. After St Petersburg, with steam engines giving 3,872 horsepower (1862), came Moscow province with 3,115 horsepower (in 1857).[4] The triumph of capitalist technology was still to come.

Perhaps the most remarkable feature of the industrial picture in 1860, as compared with 1800, was the improved position of the cotton industry which now held first place in the number of establishments and of workers:

Factories and Workers in the Textile Industry, 1860[5]

Cotton		Woollen		Linen	
Factories	*Workers*	*Factories*	*Workers*	*Factories*	*Workers*
1,200	152,236	706	120,025	117	17,284

[1] *Gille (1949), p. 148*
[2] *Tugan-Baranovsky (1900), pp. 78, 277*
[3] *Mirsky (1931), pp. 196-7; Wallace (1905), vol. 1, p. 135; Blum (1961), pp. 301-3*
[4] *Zlotnikov (1946), pp. 44-7*
[5] *Blum (1961), p. 295*

In cotton spinning Russia now held fifth place after Britain, France, U.S.A. and Austria. Weaving was less advanced and less mechanized.

The growth of the cotton industry was mainly at the expense of linen which, like the hemp-using industry, was suffering from the decline in the demand for sailcloth and rope. But although the manorial serf-using factory linen industry was in sharp decline, the cottage linen industry still flourished in parts of Yaroslavl, Kostroma, Vyatka and Vologda provinces.[1] Cotton spinning was concentrated in and about St Petersburg where most raw cotton was imported. Wallace mentions a factory at Narva, built in 1856, which was driven by water power and had nearly 500,000 spindles, while Heywood (1858) describes another on the Neva at Okhti three miles from the capital

> *worked by four engines of 250 and 260 horsepower, spinning yarn about 40 and 50 hanks, and employing 700 or 800 hands, chiefly serfs from the neighbouring villages, with managers, mostly English, occupying cottages surrounding the establishment.*[2]

In the capital itself there were, in 1866, 10 cotton spinning mills, employing over 6,000 workers, and it was the city's leading industry. A second cotton-spinning centre developed at Tver after the opening of railway communication with St Petersburg (1851). But this branch of Russia's industry—the most advanced—owed its success almost wholly to foreign enterprise. The weaving and printing branches were located in the Industrial Centre. Ivanovo's manufacturing had begun as *kustar* industry in the homes of the peasants. The factory industry had developed there through the enterprise of some of Count Sheremetyev's serfs who belonged to the non-conformist sect of *raskolniki* and had become wealthy entrepreneurs.[3] At Ivanovo in 1861 there were 26 print factories employing 1,790 workers, 2 cotton cloth mills employing 4,313 workers, 1 cotton-spinning mill with 511 workers and 1 textile machinery factory; and at neighbouring Voznesensk, cotton spinning and weaving employed a further 2,111 workers.[4] The cotton manufacturers of the Moscow area suffered competition within the Empire from the more highly mechanized and more efficient industry at Lodz in Poland.

Another industry that had made striking progress since 1800 was the refining of sugar-beet (fig. 62). Figures for the number of refineries vary, but there was undoubtedly a sharp increase to between 400 and 500 in 1860, employing some 65,000 workers, and producing over $1\frac{1}{2}$ million puds of sugar, or double the production for 1848. Unlike the cotton industry, the beet sugar industry was mainly manorial: most of the refineries were on landlord estates in the black-earth soil zone and employed serf labour, although some were in towns. Sugar was the most important

[1] Khozyaystvenno-statisticheskiy atlas *(1857), pp. 32-5, 41*

[2] *Wallace (1905), vol. 2, p. 361; Heywood (1918), pp. 36-7*

[3] *Lyashchenko (1956), vol. 1, p. 519*

[4] *Semenov (1862-85), vol. 2, p. 300*

figure 62   Sugar-beet refineries by province, 1851.

industry at Tula and St Petersburg, although at the latter place it was imported cane sugar which fed the refineries.

Of urban industries, leather manufacture and tallow preparation were the chief, and were found, along with candle and soap manufacture, in almost all Russian towns. Voronezh and Kolomna were no longer the chief tallow centres, the industry having moved eastwards and southwards to Samara, Yekaterinburg, Yekaterinoslav and Saratov.

The leading industrial towns in the 1860s are listed in Table 5 (fig. 63):[1]

Table 5:

Town	*Value of factory production (thousands of roubles)*	*Leading industries*
1 *St Petersburg*	48,703 (1863)	*Cotton spinning, sugar refining*
2 *Moscow*	29,200 (1864)	*Cottons, woollens, sugar refining*
3 *Tver*	6,169 (1872)	*Cotton spinning*

[1] *Data from Semenov (1862-85)*

Table 5—continued

Town	Value of factory production (thousands of roubles)	Leading industries
4 Odessa	4,887 (1866)	Flour-milling, tobacco
5 Riga	3,033 (1863)	Tobacco, woodworking
6 Ivanovo	3,030 (1861)	Calico printing, cotton spinning
7 Saratov	3,000 (1867)	Flour-milling, tallow
8 Kazan	2,896 (1861)	Leather, liquor, wax candles
9 Tula	2,726 (1870)	Samovars, sugar refining
10 Kiev	2,347 (1860)	Sugar refining, leather
11 Samara	2,168 (1869)	Tallow-melting
12 Yaroslavl	2,000 (1862)	Tobacco
13 Kharkov	2,000 (1879)	Woollen cloth, tobacco
14 Kostroma	1,900 (1863)	Linen
15 Yekaterinburg	1,544 (1860)	Tallow-melting
16 Stavropol	1,292 (1870)	Wine making
17 Taganrog	1,125 (1870)	Macaroni, meat packing
18 Yekaterinoslav	1,080 (1861)	Tallow-melting
19 Kronstadt	over 1,000 (1862)	Engineering, tallow
20 Orel	1,000 (1862)	Hemp
21 Yelizavetgrad	1,000 (1862)	Tallow-melting
22 Kaluga	939 (1861)	Leather, furs, bristles
23 Tyumen	904 (1870)	Leather
24 Vishniy Volochok	805 (1860)	Flour milling
25 Penza	766 (1861)	Woollen cloth

The leading industries of the two large cities are given below for 1864 (thousands of roubles):

St Petersburg		Moscow	
Cotton spinning	12,032	Cotton manufactures	6,706
Sugar refining	10,324	Woollen manufactures	6,390
Distilling, brewing	7,138	Sugar refining	2,589
Tobacco manufactures	3,716	Tallow preparation	1,904
Iron foundries	3,575	Leather manufactures	1,700
Textile weaving	2,076	Tobacco manufactures	1,552
Leather manufactures	1,976	Gold manufactures	1,347
Rope and cord	1,366	Silk manufactures	1,189
Shipbuilding	1,090	Distilling, brewing	1,110
Tallow, candles, soap	1,057	Chemicals	688
Oil mills	770	Iron manufactures	635
Printing works	744	Bleaching and dyeing	529

It was still true, but not as wholly as before, that St Petersburg manufactured mainly imported raw materials (cotton, cane sugar, tobacco), and

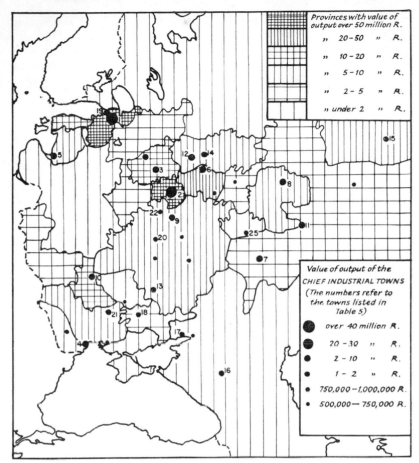

figure 63   Russia in 1861: factory production by province and town (data from Semenov).

Moscow, home-produced commodities (wool, sugar-beet, animal hides and fats). There were now similarities as well as points of contrast: cotton textiles, sugar refining, tobacco manufacture and vodka distilling were leading industries in both towns. Industrialization had made more rapid progress in the Baltic capital where the value of industrial production was now double that of Moscow. But whereas St Petersburg and its immediate environs stood in isolation, Moscow was the heart of a large industrial region.

Trade

Foreign trade also bore the strong imprint of the social system, for commodities produced by serf labour continued to dominate exports (tallow, hemp, flax, grain, timber) and goods consumed mainly by the landlord class (sugar, wine, fruit, coffee, silk) figured largely in imports. The chief change since 1800 was the enhanced place of grain in exports: its proportion by value had doubled from 18 per cent to 36 per cent of the total. Wheat amounted to about two-thirds of these grain exports which almost doubled in volume after the repeal of the British Corn Laws in 1846.[1] Other changes were a decline in the position of iron goods, as the obsolescent Urals industry could no longer compete in price with the European product, and a sharp decline in exports of sailcloth, consequent upon the growing use of steam. 60,000 pieces of hempen sailcloth a year had been exported in the 1830s; by the 1850s this number had declined to 12,000. On the import side, the main change was the increased proportion of industrial raw materials, especially cotton and dyestuffs.

Overseas trade was still carried mainly in foreign ships and England remained the chief customer, taking 50 per cent of the exports and sending 40 per cent of the imports. 90 per cent of total trade came by sea, and the share of the Black and Azov Seas had greatly increased since 1800. Trade was now distributed as follows:

	per cent		*per cent*
Baltic Sea	*58*	*Azov Sea*	*14*
Black Sea	*23*	*White Sea*	*3*
		Caspian Sea	*2*

THE BALTIC SEA: TRADE AND SEAPORTS (fig. 64)
Whereas at the beginning of the century, exports by way of the Baltic Sea greatly exceeded imports, by 1860 imports (annual average, 1850–60 = 58,546,413 roubles) had overtaken exports (52,455,947 roubles) by value. By bulk, exports were still far ahead. The leading commodities of Baltic trade were (annual average 1850-60):

Imports		*Exports*	
	(thousands of roubles)		
Cotton	*14,141*	*Flax and linen*	*11,397*
Manufactured goods	*9,435*	*Tallow*	*11,211*
Dyestuffs	*5,772*	*Grain*	*9,970*
Wines and spirits	*5,269*	*Hemp and hempen goods*	*5,678*
Vegetable oils	*2,315*	*Timber*	*2,627*
Wool	*2,173*	*Metals*	*2,352*

The nature of the export trade is very similar to that which obtained in 1802 (cf. p. 178 above), except that iron has lost its place. Raw cotton has displaced woollen textiles as the leading import, while sugar and silver, second and third respectively in 1802, are no longer near the top

[1] Khozyaystvenno-statisticheskiy atlas (*1857*), *p. 70; Florinsky* (*1953*), *vol. 2, p. 781*

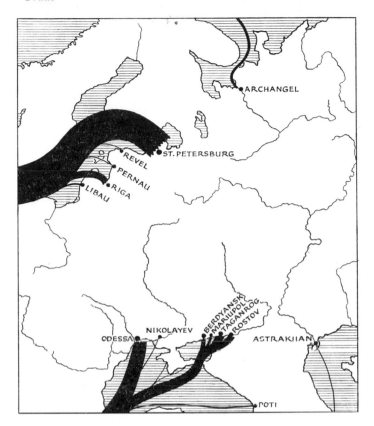

figure 64   Russia in 1861: relative trade of the principal ports (data from Semenov).

of the list. The production within the Empire of both commodities had greatly increased.

St Petersburg had now an even larger share of the total trade than in 1802; Riga has maintained its position, while the other ports have lost ground:

Percentage of Baltic trade, 1850-60

	per cent		per cent
St Petersburg	78	Revel	1·1
Riga	17	Pernau	1·0
Libau	1·6	Narva	1·0

At all the ports, exports exceeded imports in value, except at St Petersburg and Revel. At St Petersburg, as the main point of entry for raw cotton, manufactured goods, dyestuffs, wines and spirits, imports were half as much again in value as exports. St Petersburg continued to be the main outlet for hemp, Riga for flax. Riga's trade differed little in nature from the beginning of the century (*Exports:* flax and linseed 56 per cent, hemp 21 per cent, grain 13 per cent, timber 7 per cent; *Imports:* salt 22 per cent, fish 20 per cent, wines 15 per cent).

THE WHITE SEA: ARCHANGEL

The White Sea trade was almost entirely carried on at Archangel where exports (grain, flax and linen, linseed, timber, pitch and tallow) formed 90 per cent of the port's commerce.

THE BLACK SEA AND SEA OF AZOV: TRADE AND PORTS

It was here that the greatest increase in activity had taken place, the share of Russia's overseas trade having risen from 5 per cent in 1802 to 37 per cent. This ever-expanding traffic was divided amongst the ports as follows:

	per cent		*per cent*
Odessa	60	Nikolayev	4
Taganrog	12	Mariupol	3
Rostov	11	Poti	2
Berdyansk	6	others	2

Odessa had now become the second port of Russia with a total trade worth some 40 million roubles (*Exports*, 30·3 million R: grain 54 per cent, wool 16 per cent, linseed 6 per cent, tallow 3 per cent; *Imports*, 10·4 million R: manufactures 12 per cent, metals and metal goods 11 per cent, fruit 9 per cent, machinery 8 per cent, olive oil 8 per cent). It was the chief beneficiary of increased sales of wheat abroad, and Russia's acquisition of the Polish provinces had endowed it with a large and productive hinterland. The Dniester, Bug and Dnieper rivers brought the produce of this hinterland to the Black Sea whence it was carried to Odessa. Much of the freight leaving the Sea of Azov was also brought here by sea for export abroad. In 1861, 1,035 sailing vessels and 338 steamers took part in the coasting trade. Goods also converged upon the port by land.

The Azov trade consisted almost wholly of exports of Russian produce, notably grain, linseed, tallow, wool and iron. There was also some Donets coal. Imports were negligible at all ports except Taganrog where they included fruit, wine and olive oil. Rostov and Taganrog were now fourth and fifth in order of trade. Both ports benefited from increased Russian settlement and German colonization in the Don and Volga steppes, and their hinterland extended into the heart of old Russia by way of these rivers. The short railway linking the Volga and Don, built about this time, improved communications with the Volga and the Caspian. Berdyansk had grown to its present importance in a mere twenty years since its foundation about 1840. It had the best anchorage in the Sea of Azov, and was the port for neighbouring German colonies.[1]

[1] *Seymour (1855), pp. 308-11*

THE CASPIAN SEA: TRADE AND PORTS

The small trade on the Caspian amounted (1853-62) to only some $2\frac{1}{2}$ million roubles a year, distributed between ports as follows:

	per cent
Astrakhan	51
Baku	29
Astara	20

Astrakhan imported silk and silks, cotton and cotton goods, fruit and rice from Persia, Turkey and Caucasia, also fish and caviar from the Caspian shores. Most of these goods were shipped to the Volga delta from the Azerbaydzhanian ports of Baku and Astara, which imported metals, metal goods and manufactures from Astrakhan. But Astrakhan's seaborne trade represented only about 5 per cent of its total commerce, most of which travelled in overland caravans or on the Volga.

OVERLAND TRADE

There had been a marked increase in the overland trade with Central Asia, whose supplies of cotton saw Russia through the crises caused by the Crimean and American Civil Wars. Trade with Bokhara, Khiva and Kokand amounted to about 22 million roubles or about 5 per cent of the total: raw cotton made up a third of the imports from Central Asia, followed by lambskins, dried fruit, cashmere shawls and silk. Textile and leather manufactures constituted one third of the exports, followed by precious metals, iron and non-ferrous goods.[1]

Trade with China was, in comparison, small—about 11 million roubles a year in 1849-53. It consisted in the main of an exchange of Chinese tea for Russian manufactured goods.[2]

INTERNAL TRADE

Internal trade continued to grow during the first half of the nineteenth century, but was still small in amount compared with the country's potential.[3] Obsolete means of transport were a limiting factor. As railways began to spread in the 1850s, the increase in movement became more rapid, but in 1861 traditional methods still predominated. Carts, sledges and barges moved towards the villages, towns and ports, carrying serf-produced goods from the landlord estates: flax, linen, wool, tallow, vodka, grain. Back to the estates in return, smaller in bulk though higher in value, came goods for landlord consumption: tea, sugar, caviar, wine, whisky, coffee, furniture, carriages. The mass of the people, the peasants, had little money to spend. The vast majority were on a subsistence economy, and those who did earn money saw most of it go in *obrok* payments and

[1] *Vambéry (1864), p. 425; Lyashchenko (1956), vol. 1, p. 547*
[2] *Tegoborsky (1852-5), vol. 4, pp. 600-7*
[3] *Gille (1949), p. 154*

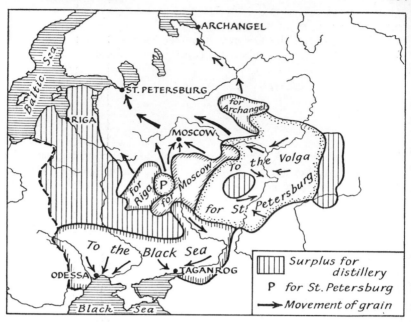

figure 65   Russia in 1861: the movement of grain (after Khozyaystvenno-Statisticheskiy Atlas, *1857*).

taxes. Nevertheless, purchased manufactured clothing was beginning to
replace the homespun product in some districts.

Grain and cattle moved the longest distances, because both were produced mainly in the southern part of the country and consumed in the
north. The main movement of grain was still northwards from the black-
earth soils to the Industrial Centre and St Petersburg, but an increasing
amount was descending the rivers for export from the Black Sea ports and
those of the Sea of Azov (fig. 65).

The busiest centres of internal trade were the river wharves where goods
were transhipped. Often this activity was concentrated within a few weeks
when the fair was held. The great fair at Nizhniy Novgorod was but the
greatest of many such marts. Here the Volga waterway was crossed by the
Kama-Oka route, and it was here that Moor saw

> *tea from China, and Russian wine and brandy; there were turquoises
> from Bokhara, and Russian train-oil and caviar; there was wool from
> Cashmere and Russian hempen textures; carpets and raw silk from
> Persia, and silks and cottons from China; refined sugar from Archangel,
> and soap from Kazan; there were horses' hides and dried fish, porcelain
> and washed rags, glass and mirrors, paper, horses' tails, furs, worked
> skins, and copper goods, coffee and cochineal, feathers and drugs, hogs'
> bristles, tobacco, ceintures and slippers . . .[1]*

[1] *Moor (1863), pp. 152-3*

Statistically, Nizhniy Novgorod's average annual waterborne trade was as follows (1859-62):

	puds	*value*
		(roubles)
Loaded:	*16,827,425*	*23,308,881*
Unloaded:	*23,863,499*	*27,498,589*
	40,690,924	*50,807,470*

In addition, 5,594,124 puds entered or left the town by the new railway, making a total of over 46 million puds or 760,000 tons. The leading waterborne commodities, by bulk and value, moving through Nizhniy Novgorod were (1859-62):

By bulk	*puds*
Grain	*9,780,579*
Salt	*8,358,424*
Metal and metal products	*7,347,240*
Fish and fish products	*1,870,277*

By value	*roubles*
Metal and metal goods	*9,319,704*
Tea	*5,964,913*
Grain	*5,534,557*
Cotton goods	*4,594,853*

The total annual value of the trade transacted at Nizhniy Novgorod was 100 million roubles (1859-62). Of this 74 per cent originated in Russia, 12 per cent in Europe and overseas, 3 per cent in Persia and Transcaucasia, and 1 per cent in Central Asia.

Transport

As overseas and internal trade grew in volume, so the inadequacy of Russia's natural communications—her rivers, her ice and snow, her unmade roads—was aggravated. Serfdom and lack of capital together hampered improvement whether in the form of new and deeper canals, steamships, surfaced roads, or railways. Steamers had been introduced on the Volga (1849), where the journey between Nizhniy Novgorod and Kazan took 38 to 40 hours,[1] and on the Dnieper, the Volkhov and the Neva. By 1861 there were two hundred steamboats on the Volga, but they were used more for the transport of passengers than for freight. The forced human labour of the *burlaki* (towing men) was too cheap to encourage the

[1] *Moor (1863), p. 165; Blum (1961), p. 284; Florinsky (1953), vol. 2, p. 789*

introduction of modern methods. Also, Russian rivers, vital though they had been in the early days of Russian commerce, when the draught of vessels was very small, were not only frozen in winter, but often too shallow during the summer or autumn for deeper draught vessels. And their nuisance as barriers to overland traffic came to offset much of their diminishing advantages as a means of transport.[1] Grain, the chief commodity on the Volga, could go up no higher than Rybinsk which therefore became an important transhipment point. Every year 2 million quarters of wheat, as well as large quantities of flour, were unloaded there.[2]

The Kama and the Oka in reality formed a single waterway running transverse to the north-west–south-east line of the Volga, and carrying Uralian and Siberian timber, metals, grain and livestock products to Moscow and central Russia. Craft for this traffic were constructed at Utkinsk on the Chusovaya, a tributary of the Kama:

> *This is the place where most of the barques are built to convey the produce of the Oural mines and ironworks, belonging to the crown, to Nizhniy Novgorod, Moscow and St Petersburg. It was now a scene of great activity, there being four thousand men in this small village, brought from various places, all diligently engaged in loading the vessels with guns of large dimensions.*

The barges

> *are flat-bottomed, with straight sides 125 feet long, have a breadth of 25 feet, and are from eight to nine feet deep . . . there is not a nail or an iron bolt in them, they being put together with wooden pins. . . . Each barque, whose cargo has a weight of 9,000 puds, requires 35 men to direct it; and one with a cargo of 10,000 puds, has a crew of forty men.*[3]

There was a fair traffic on the Ob, and great activity broke out at Tobolsk immediately after the thaw:

> *During the week a great bustle prevailed at Tobolsk. The mercantile portion of the citizens were busied in freighting boats and vessels destined for the Oby Sea, whence, after discharging their cargoes, they bring back loads of fish and fur.*[4]

The vessel referred to above carried bags of flour to the Arctic. Commerce on the Yenisey had shrunk to a mere shadow of what it had been in the heyday of the fur trade.[5]

In 1800 all the roads in Russia had been 'natural' and therefore full of ruts and completely at the mercy of the weather. Some, it is true, were 'corduroyed' with logs or surfaced with planks, but these devices were scarcely an improvement on nature. By 1861, however, over 5,000 miles of roads had been surfaced, i.e. those from Moscow to St Petersburg, Warsaw, Kursk, Nizhniy Novgorod and Yaroslavl. The main road across

[1] *Pauly (1862), p. 10*
[2] Khozyaystvenno-statisticheskiy atlas *(1857), p. 60*
[3] *Atkinson (1858), pp. 14-15*
[4] *Felinska (1852), p. 86*
[5] *Nansen (1914), p. 180*

the Urals was described as a *'macadamized chaussée'*.[1] But, as these highways were inadequately maintained, their condition was often deplorable. Even the main St Petersburg-Moscow road was *'very bad, the great traffic between the two capitals having cut it into such deep holes that the sledge went down every four minutes with a fearful shock'*.[2] Except when hardened by frost and covered by snow, vast areas of the country were still without passable roads. Caravans from China and Central Asia crossed the steppes to Astrakhan and Orenburg without benefit of made roads.

Railways were, to many foreigners, the obvious solution to Russia's transport problem:

> *The resources of the country are, no doubt, immense; but they are made unavailable by the absence of the means of transport and communication from one part of the country to another. Corn, wool, wood, hay, and hides may be had in the interior at rates which would realize enormous profits at St Petersburg or Moscow, simply because there is no possibility of transporting the goods purchased. Railroads would quadruple the wealth of the country.*[3]

But by 1861 the country had only 2,232 miles of railway, one-fifth as much as France and one-sixth as much as Germany. The chief lines were the Baltic, from Warsaw to St Petersburg via Grodno, Vilno and Pskov, with a branch to Riga; the Nikolayevskaya, from St Petersburg to Moscow via Tver; and the line from Moscow to Nizhniy Novgorod, not completed until 1862. A line southwards from Moscow had reached Kolomna.

The Nikolayevskaya, which was so straight that it did not even go out of its way to serve Novgorod, was completed in 1851. It was built with French capital. Passenger trains, using wood fuel, performed the 400-mile journey, with 33 stations, in 20 hours, and foreigners found them very comfortable.[4] The slow speed was due to the poor state of the track. But it now took the traveller only 48 hours to reach St Petersburg from Berlin by the Baltic line. The Moscow-Nizhniy Novgorod journey took 18 hours.[5]

The St Petersburg-Moscow line was already carrying a heavy and varied freight: about 15 million puds (250,000 tons) in 1863. The chief items were as follows:

	puds
timber and wood products	*5,874,000*
groceries and chandlery	*2,261,000*
metals	*1,726,000*
hemp and flax	*1,542,000*
fish	*442,000*
tea	*304,000*

[1] *Felinska (1852), p. 46*
[2] *Atkinson (1858), p. 2*
[3] *Dicey (1867), p. 234*
[4] *Moor (1863), pp. 100-1; Heywood (1918), p. 22; Dicey (1867), pp. 90-1*
[5] *Moor (1863), pp. 115, 139*

I

But nearly 1 million tons, four times as much as by rail, arrived at St Petersburg by inland waterway. The new Moscow-Nizhniy Novgorod line carried about 6 million puds (100,000 tons). The freight carried eastwards from Moscow was more than double that brought from Nizhniy.[1] But goods brought in and out of the Volga town by water were ten times as much as the rail traffic.

An interesting addition to the railway system was the 45-mile long line linking the Volga navigation with that of the Don. This was completed before 1863.[2]

Population

The lethargy, stagnation and backwardness which characterized the economic geography of Russia were by no means to be found in the growth of population. Between 1800 and 1860 this rose from about 38 to 60 million. But, if the paralysing effect of the social system did not operate here, it did confine most of the increase to the already crowded lands of central and western Russia, while leaving the habitable lands of the south and south-east sparsely peopled. Although rates of increase were highest in the south and south-east, absolute increases were greatest in the south-centre or black-earth wooded steppe.[3] This intensification in the already densely peopled provinces is the most striking feature to come from a comparison of the population maps for 1795 and 1857 (figs. 47, 66), and even more impressive than the peopling of the outer steppes. Here settlement was concentrated along the river valleys and only occasionally pushed forward into the still empty grasslands in between.

Even in the most thickly inhabited provinces, the density of population was well below that for most European countries. The density for all 'Russia in Europe'—only 12 per square kilometre—was but an eighth of that of Italy or Britain, a sixth that of France, less than half that of Spain and well below that of Turkey.[4]

It was the social system, aided by the poverty of communications, that retained natural increase within the overpopulated mixed-forest podzol lands of the Industrial Centre and the wooded-steppe black-earth belt to the south of it. Here serfs were too valuable to let go: in the one area because of the *obrok* they paid and in the other for their agricultural labour. Yet a strong current of migration did set southwards and eastwards in spite of every obstacle. In 1862 it was possible to write that:

> *the centre of gravity of the Empire moves daily farther to the east and south-east. The district of Orenburg and the governments of Saratov,*

[1] *Semenov (1862-85), vol. 3, pp. 446-53*
[2] *Westwood (1964), p. 40; Ames (1947), p. 60*
[3] *Kabuzan (1963), pp. 159-65*
[4] *Block (1863), p. 216*

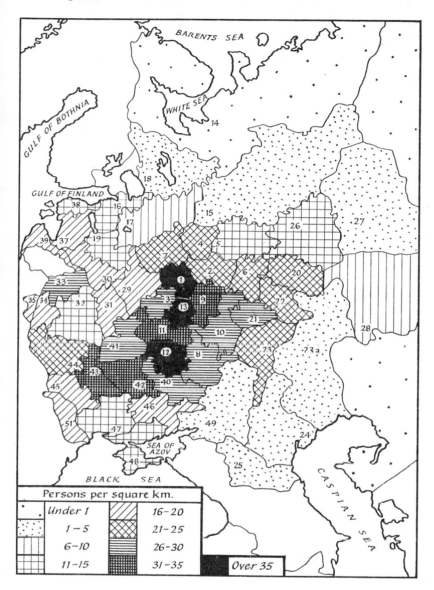

figure 66   Density of population according to the 1857 Revision
(data from Kabuzan). For key to provinces, see p. 395.

Samara and Caucasus are receiving a powerful impetus. It is towards
these regions that voluntary and forced colonization is directed.[1]

[1] Pauly (1862), p. 7

Military security sometimes necessitated the drafting of Cossacks—who became settlers—into the new lands, and some desultory attempts were also made to resettle state peasants on them.

The Uralian provinces of Vyatka, Perm and Orenburg all showed striking increases. Vyatka and Perm doubled their population between 1795 and 1857, while that of Orenburg multiplied by more than five times to 4½ million.

In Siberia, population continued to accumulate along the upper stretches of the great river valleys and especially round the towns of Tobolsk, Tomsk, Akmolinsk and Semipalatinsk. The settlement of the Far Eastern valleys of the Amur and the Ussuri had begun with the despatch thither of Transbaykalian Cossacks with their wives and families. The population of Siberia was becoming Russified as native tribes either declined through disease or adopted Russian ways. The chief exceptions were the nomadic Buryats, the cattle-rearing Yakuts of the Lena valley, and the distant Chukchi.[1] In all, the population of Siberia increased from 595,000 males at the fifth 'revision' in 1795 to 1,356,000 at the tenth in 1857.

The rural settlement landscape had undergone little change. Contemporary descriptions differ not at all from those of centuries before. When Wallace was first in Russia in the 1870s the typical village

> consisted of two long parallel rows of wooden houses. The road—if a stratum of deep mud can be called by that name—formed the intervening space. All the houses turned their gables to the passer-by, and some of them had pretensions to architectural decoration in the form of rude perforated woodwork. Between the houses, and in a line with them, were great wooden gates and the high wooden fences, separating the courtyards from the road.

Going into the drier south-eastern lands, he noticed that

> the ordinary wooden houses with their high sloping roofs gradually gave way to flat-roofed huts, built of a peculiar kind of unburnt bricks, composed of mud and straw. I noticed too that the population became less and less dense, and the amount of fallow land proportionately greater.[2]

The main alteration was to the homes of the gentry who, instead of 'the old Muscovite manor houses of logs or plaster-finished brick, with their rambling roofs, fantastic turrets and bulky ornaments', had begun to build

> colonnaded mansions, sometimes of considerable size, with a great columned reception hall and long, low wings half circling a broad forecourt of honour. With their stately porticos, their chapels and their theatres, their gardens, lakes and parks, their swarming retinues of servants, some of these mansions, in their borrowed European style, were very tolerable miniatures of Versailles.[3]

[1] *Nansen (1914), p. 357; Mirsky (1931), p. 248*
[2] *Wallace (1905), vol. 1, pp. 38, 252*
[3] *Robinson (1932), p. 53*

The towns, likewise, retained much of their former appearance. Wallace describes them thus:

However imposing they may look when seen from the outside, they will, with very few exceptions, be found on closer inspection, to be little more than villages in disguise. If they have not a positively rustic, they have at least a suburban appearance.

The houses are built of wood or brick, generally one-storeyed, and separated from each other by spacious yards. Many of them do not condescend to turn their facades to the street. The general impression produced is that the majority of the burghers have come from the country and have brought their country houses with them . . .

In the other parts of the town the air of solitude and languor is still conspicuous. In the great square, or by the side of the promenade—if the town is fortunate to have one—cows or horses may be seen grazing tranquilly, without being at all conscious of the incongruity of their position.[1]

But many of them had now begun to break away from their medieval sleep and to grow in population. The urban population has been variously estimated at 5·7 million (9·5 per cent of the whole in 1856), at 4·2 million (5·7 per cent of the whole) in 1858, and 6·1 million (9·9 per cent of the whole) in 1863, compared with 1¼ million (4 per cent) in 1800.[2] Both the total of urban population and the figures for individual towns defy realistic computation because of their large seasonal and floating components. Thus, although the 'permanent' population of the industrialized village of Ivanovo was put at 4,872, five of its factories alone employed between 6,000 and 7,000 workers, and it was said to have from 16,000 to 20,000 'temporary' inhabitants.[3]

An urban population of even 10 per cent would still have been small compared with France's 26 per cent and Britain's 55 per cent, especially as a quarter of the population of some Russian towns consisted of peasants.[4] The bulk of the industrial and much of the commercial population dwelt outside of the towns. The tsars had '*used their power so stupidly and so recklessly that the industrial and trading population, instead of fleeing to the towns to secure protection, fled from them to escape oppression*'. Or, as A. Bestuzhev wrote:

The bourgeois, a respected and influential class in all other countries, are with us contemptible, poor, tax-ridden and deprived of the means of existence. . . . In other countries they populate the cities, but our cities exist only on the map.[5]

In the following table the population of the leading Russian towns is given (in thousands) according to Rashin's estimates for 1863 and

[1] *Wallace (1905), vol. 2, pp. 224-5*
[2] *Lyashchenko (1956), vol. 2, pp. 115-16; Rashin (1956), p. 86*
[3] *Semenov (1862-85), vol. 2, p. 300*
[4] *Tegoborsky (1852-5), vol. 1, p. 143*
[5] *Wallace (1905), vol. 1, p. 229; Carr (1956), p. 364*

1811. Where Semenov's figures differ significantly, they are given as footnotes to the table.[1]

		1863	1811			1863	1811
1	St Petersburg	540	336	11 Tiflis	61	
2	Moscow	462*	270	12 Tula	57	52
3	Odessa	119	11	13 Berdichev	53	
4	Kishinev	94		14 Kharkov	52	10
5	Saratov	84**	27	15 Mogilev	48	6
6	Riga	78	32	16 Kronstadt	48***	
7	Vilno	70†	56	17 Astrakhan	43	38
8	Kiev	68	23	18 N. Novgorod	42	14
9	Nikolayev	65††	4	19 Taganrog	42	7
10	Kazan	63	54	20 Voronezh	41	22

      * Semenov 364 (1864)
    ** Semenov 70 (1859)
  *** Semenov (1863)
    † Semenov 60 (1860)
   †† Semenov 46 (1864)

Although no great accuracy can be claimed for these figures, certain observations can be safely made. St Petersburg, aided by a growth in maritime commerce; by railway communication with Europe, the Baltic provinces, the Industrial Centre and the Volga; and by the continued influx of the wealthy, had forged ahead and doubled its population since the beginning of the century. The rapid rise of Odessa, Nikolayev and Kherson, and of other southern ports such as Taganrog, was the urban expression of the opening up of the Black Sea steppes to settlement and cultivation, and of the development of the export trade in wheat, wool and linseed. The existence of these coastal outlets also stimulated traffic on the roads and rivers, and therefore commerce in the towns of the Ukraine. Hence the substantial expansion of Kiev, Kharkov, Berdichev and Zhitomir (fig. 67).

A third area of notable urban growth was the Volga-Ural region, again a zone of active settlement, agricultural expansion, and vigorous commerce, lying as it does between Old Russia on the one hand, Siberia and Central Asia on the other. Saratov, Nizhniy Novgorod, Samara (34,000), Orenburg (28,000), Yekaterinburg (24,000) and Perm (19,000) had all made marked progress. For the period of the great fair, Nizhniy Novgorod's population was swollen to 200,000 or more.[2]

There had been a change in the relative importance of Siberian towns, the population of the larger ones being:[3]

[1] *Rashin (1956), pp. 93-6; Semenov (1862-85)*, passim
[2] *Semenov (1862-5), vol. 3, pp. 446-53; Moor (1863), p. 151*
[3] *Semenov (1862-85)*

POPULATION OF TOWNS

- ● 500,000 – 750,000
- ● 250,000 – 500,000
- ● 100,000 – 250,000
- • 50,000 – 100,000
- • 20,000 – 50,000

figure 67   Russia in 1861: the larger towns (data from Semenov and Rashin).

Tomsk	25,605 (1870)	(7,772 in 1772)
Irkutsk	24,779 (1862)	
Omsk	19,467 (1862)	(1,186 in 1770)
Tobolsk	18,475 (1870)	(14,593 in 1772)
Tyumen	14,408 (1870)	
Barnaul	11,846 (1861)	
Semipalatinsk	9,633 (1863)	
Krasnoyarsk	8,776 (1861)	

Tobolsk has clearly lost its primacy. The towns on the Pacific coast were so small as scarcely to merit the name. Nikolayevsk, the new naval base, was the largest: its inhabitants worked with the fleet. Petropavlovsk, recently displaced as the Pacific naval base, though still an important post of the Russia-America company, had some 2,000 inhabitants, and its magnificent harbour was now to be used mainly by fishing vessels.[1] The older port of Okhotsk had but a couple of hundred residents.

Travellers still made the point that Moscow represented Asia, while St Petersburg stood for Europe. Dicey wrote (1866):

> *when you come back to St Petersburg from Moscow, you seem to have come back to a commonplace European city. A foretaste of the East hangs about in Moscow; you feel that you are standing on the extreme threshold of European civilization. In St Petersburg, Europe has conquered Asia; but in Moscow the struggle is still undecided.*[2]

Moscow had been rebuilt after the 1812 fire and, except for the inner Kremlin area, transformed. *'It was formerly the city of the Russian nobles; now it is a modern industrial town'.*[3]

The north-eastern and south-eastern suburbs, earlier settled by artisans and for long the refuge of the *raskolniki* or Old Believers, had become manufacturing areas crowded with factories and workers' dormitories. Industrialist raskolniks gave work and shelter to their coreligionaries and the proportion of Old Believers to the total population has been put as high as a half. The link between the long-persecuted, but shrewd and hard-working, members of the dissenting sects on the one hand and industrialization on the other, was very clearly seen in the Moscow of the mid-nineteenth century.[4]

Descriptions of the great Moscow market were substantially what they had been in Peter I's time:

> *There are yarns and cottons and Manchester goods, and Sheffield cutlery, and French silks, and German leather; and every article, in fact, which can possibly be smuggled across the frontiers. Then there are the Persian stalls, where Armenians in high dark fur caps sell Astrakhan wool and Persian silks and arms studded with stones. On other counters there are displayed all sorts of Circassian silver ornaments, cigarette cases, match-boxes . . .*[5]

Of the Baltic towns, Riga maintained a leading place amongst the cities of the Empire. Eckardt has left behind a picture of it as it was in the 1860s:

> *Through narrow streets, winding angularly in the old German fashion, upon which numerous gabled houses, immense granaries, and ancient cupolas, look down, a busy, lively commerce goes on; a never-ending stream of laden waggons rolls on to the banks of the majestic Düna, which is covered with numerous vessels.*
>
> *On the other side of the river, in the low Mitau suburb, chiefly built of wood, we see Jews, Poles, Russians, and Curland and Lithuanian peasants busily employed in landing ever fresh masses of flax, linseed*

[1] *Ditmar (1890), pp. 152-3*
[2] *Dicey (1867), p. 126*
[3] *Haxthausen (1847), vol. 1, p. 58*
[4] *Blackwell (1965), pp. 407-18*
[5] *Dicey (1867), p. 111*

and grain; for, all along the Baltic shores, until far into Lithuania, the cultivation of flax is the main income of the farmer.[1]
Dorpat was a university town and the intellectual home of the Baltic Germans, while Kurland's capital, Mittau, was a decaying market town with Jews in the ascendancy commercially. Revel still retained a medieval character with *'houses, workshops and warehouses intermingled'*.[2]

Odessa could be described thus in 1855, when only 60 years old:

the real capital of all Southern Russia—that is to say, the largest money centre, and the town to which all look up as the richest and most refined in the Empire after St Petersburg and Moscow.[3]

The town was *'neatly built of stone, the streets being wide and straight, and crossing each other at rightangles'*. It was occasionally *'visited by Polish families for sea-bathing'*.[4]

Several of the larger towns—Kishinev, Tiflis, Berdichev—were in non-Russian provinces which had been incorporated in the Empire only during the past century; these towns usually had large numbers of Jews among their inhabitants.

Social Geography

In 1875 the classes of the Russian Empire were subdivided numerically as follows:

	per cent
Nobles (hereditary and personal)	1·3
Clerical classes	0·9
Urban classes	9·3
Rural classes	82·2
Military classes	6·1
Foreigners	0·2

The numerical strength of the various classes of a society, taken together with the distribution of wealth (including land) among those classes, has important geographical consequences, since different classes make different uses of wealth and these often affect the landscape. Moreover, the transfer of wealth from productive to non-productive classes has important results for the transport pattern. In Russia the rural classes accounted for almost the whole production of the country's wealth, but retained very little of it. They had few legal rights, and none in practice. Landlords could still have corporal punishment inflicted on their serfs, who were liable to fifty strokes for merely lodging a complaint; they could have them banished to Siberia or conscribed into the army; peasant serfs could

[1] *Eckardt (1870), p. 356*
[2] *Eckardt (1870), p. 365*
[3] *Seymour (1855), p. 7*
[4] *Beeton (1872), under Odessa*

I*

be deprived of their land holdings by their status being changed to that of house serfs.[1] Serfs were thus defenceless against extortion from land-lords. State peasants were little better off, being at the mercy of corrupt and oppressive officials. The peasant villages continued, to reflect the poverty and squalor of their inhabitants. Only improvements in or the rebuilding of the manorial home, or possibly new machinery or farm buildings on the master's domain testified to the increased wealth of the country.

In consequence of the political and social systems, therefore, an over-whelming proportion of the country's wealth was concentrated in the hands of the monarchy and aristocracy. As in pre-Revolutionary France, where a somewhat similar situation prevailed, the Crown spent extrava-gantly in foreign adventures, the maintenance of a vast standing army, and in the embellishment of the seat of government and the maintenance there of a glittering court. To a greater degree even than eighteenth-century Paris, nineteenth-century St Petersburg was a city where wealth and luxury lived side by side with the direst poverty, an explosive mixture awaiting the revolutionary spark. Dicey observed in 1867:

> *In St Petersburg, however, poverty and wealth, luxury and misery, splendour and shabbiness, civilization and barbarism, go hand in hand, lie side by side together. It is a place which can only be described by superlatives. Everything is either superb or wretched; everybody is either wealthy or poor; Dives and Lazarus are the only two parts in the Russian life drama.*[2]

Only the richest nobles could maintain houses in the northern capital. Many more had town houses in Moscow which, because of its central situation, was a much more convenient place. The lesser gentry had to be content with lesser towns, but the same urban contrast between wealth and poverty was repeated all over the country. The growing habit of residence by the gentry in towns meant an intensification of traffic in and out of the urban centres. Most of the food and other produce of the estate needed to maintain the establishment in town was brought in by the land-lord's own peasants.

The higher ranks of the aristocracy were the most westernized and gallicized:

> *French is to a great extent a second language to educated Russians; you constantly hear them talking to each other in French; and till within the last few years it was almost unfashionable to speak Russian in good society at St Petersburg.*[3]

Residence in St Petersburg had for them the further advantage that it was the point of import for western goods. But, as in eighteenth-century France, most nobles lived beyond their means in an attempt to maintain a place in fashionable society, and had to choose between getting deeper and

[1] *Robinson (1932), pp. 42-3*
[2] *Dicey (1867), pp. 62-3*
[3] *Dicey (1867), p. 163*

deeper into debt or returning to their estates as discontented 'hobereaux'. By 1861 the nobility owed the State ½ billion roubles and more than two-thirds of their serfs were mortgaged. The growing relative poverty of the nobles enabled wealthy merchants to gain access to society. It also meant greater pressure upon the peasants from above and desperate attempts to exact more from the soil as well:

> *Being in pecuniary difficulties, and consequently impatient to make money, the proprietors increased inordinately the area of grain-producing land at the expense of pasturage and forests, with the result that the livestock and the manuring of the land were diminished, the fertility of the soil impaired, and the necessary quantity of moisture in the atmosphere greatly lessened.*[1]

Besides nobles and their households, the urban classes included a miscellaneous group coming to be known as the 'bourgeoisie', an important part of which was constituted by officials of the bureaucracy. Although most of the high and lucrative offices of state were held by nobles, in 1762 they had thrown off the burden of obligatory service imposed upon them by Peter I: an unwieldy and corrupt bureacracy and police had developed in their place. The bureaucracy had, since its inception, been largely staffed by Baltic Germans, as the social system with its educational backwardness made it difficult to recruit Russians with the necessary qualifications. Professional classes—growing in number, but still small by European standards—merchants, shopkeepers and master artisans, made up the rest of the bourgeoisie. Journeymen artisans, factory workers and labourers also contributed to the urban population.

A political and social phenomenon of the time was the growth of an intelligentsia, composed largely of the more thoughtful nobles and the growing number of university teachers and students. Just as the aristocracy was French in manners and language, so the intelligentsia derived their ideas mainly from German philosophy. Thus the government and the bureaucracy looked to Prussia because '*it was a kindred land of absolutism, militarism and bureaucracy*';[2] the aristocracy aspired to be French in civilization; the intellectuals borrowed their ideas from Germany. All three were thus divorced in manner and thought from the mass of the people to whom they were incapable of giving leadership.

The population of the Empire could be divided by nationality as well as by class. According to Pauly, about three-quarters were Slavs, between whom there existed:

> *a deeper sympathy than amongst the various latin and germanic peoples, and, correspondingly, a general antipathy to all foreigners, especially the Germans, an antipathy which goes back into the distant past.*[3]

There were about 1 million Germans, many of whom were in state

---

[1] *Wallace (1905), vol. 2, p. 194*
[2] *Mirsky (1931), p. 208*
[3] *Pauly (1862), p. 3; Haxthausen (1852), vol. 3, p. 14*

employment as soldiers, officials and policemen, and, as such, scattered throughout the Empire. Many more were skilled tradesmen in the towns. But most were either Baltic Germans, forming the landowning, professional and mercantile classes in the Baltic provinces (about 150,000), or they were inhabitants of new settlements: the Volga Germans, who lived in now flourishing colonies on both sides of the river between Samara and Saratov (about 300,000), and those settled on the steppes bordering the Black Sea and Sea of Azov (about 300,000).

The Volga Germans were still actively founding new colonies on the neighbouring steppe and also sending migrants to the Caucasus province.[1] The Azov Germans likewise were now multiplying fast and new settlements had been made near Mariupol.[2] The most flourishing colonies were those of the Mennonite religious sect. Those on the Moloshna

> *may well be compared to oases in the desert. Their neat cottages, with well-built barns and out-houses, surrounded by trees and gardens, and by highly cultivated fields, bear the signs of wealth and comfort, and of the care bestowed upon them by an industrious and intelligent population.*[3]

The southern steppes were still noteworthy for the diversity of peoples to be found settled on them. Besides Russians, Ukrainians and Germans, there were Greeks, Bulgarians, Serbs, Montenegrins, Armenians and Jews. Wallace, like Mary Holderness earlier in the century, found the Bulgarians second only to the Germans in '*agriculture and domestic civilization*':

> *Their houses are indeed small—so small that one of them might almost be put into a single room of a Mennonite's house; but there is an air of cleanliness and comfort about them that would do credit to a German housewife.*

The Jews, on the other hand, had failed to respond to attempts to make farmers of them:

> *Their houses are in a most delapidated condition, and their villages remind one of the abomination of desolation spoken of by Daniel the prophet. A great part of their land is left uncultivated or let to colonists of a different race. What little revenue they have is derived chiefly from trade of a more or less clandestine nature.*[4]

They took advantage of the relaxation of restrictions on their participation in trade to drift into the towns of southern Russia, where they soon came to form an important part of the urban population.

[1] *Bonwetsch (1919), pp. 88-93*
[2] *Klaus (1887), pp. 227-8*
[3] *Seymour (1855), p. 23*
[4] *Wallace (1905), vol. 1, pp. 311-12*

269

CHAPTER SIXTEEN
RUSSIA FROM THE LIBERATION OF THE SERFS
TO THE GREAT WAR, 1861-1914

The Anglo-French defeat of Russia in the Crimean War (1854-6) showed her strength to be illusory, and her power and prestige faded. Both in 1856 and 1878 the European powers combined to force their will upon her. Russia, so feared and admired during the forty years before the Crimea, found herself impotent and frustrated during the forty years afterwards. She was saved from isolation by France's need of her manpower to set against Germany's growing might; but only at the cost of participation in the 1914 war, which brought defeat, revolution, and the loss of most of the territory won by Peter I from Sweden and by Catherine II from Poland. As in 1853, so in 1877, a Russian defeat of Turkey led, at the Treaty of San Stefano, to the re-establishment of Russian domination of Turkey, but once again Britain, this time with Austria and Prussia, forced her to relinquish her gains at the Congress of Berlin in 1878.

The reversals of 1856 and 1878 had a profound and humiliating effect on Russian public opinion. This was passionately behind the government's policy in the Turkish question, where national, racial and religious feelings and commercial motives were all deeply involved. Traditional Russian friendship for Austria and Prussia was embittered into an enmity which made for a fresh alignment of powers between 1878 and 1914.

In 1879 the Austro-Prussian alliance isolated Russia. She was to find a new ally in France who, after her defeat by Prussia in 1870, and because of her low birthrate, needed a partner with abundant manpower. Another advantage to France of a Russian alliance was that Germany would have to fight on both fronts. The bait was money. In 1888 the first of many loans was floated in France. In 1890 joint staff talks took place, and in 1893 the Franco-Russian alliance was made. In 1907 Britain, also anxious at overweening German power and ambitions, joined Russia and France in the Triple Entente: agreed solutions were found in Persia and Afghanistan where hitherto the meeting of the Russian and British Empires had caused much friction.

Thus came about the alignment of power in the 1914-18 war. Russia and Austria could not allow each other to take Turkey's position in south-east Europe, and partition proved unworkable because of the strong patriotism of the Serbs. Behind Austria stood Germany, and behind Russia stood France, with a revanchist policy towards Germany. And associated with France was a Britain conscious that Germany must be checked.

The Congress of Berlin, 1878

It would be wrong to regard Russia's involvement in a Balkan crisis in the 1870s as an instance of imperialist, expansionist or aggressive intent on her part. Action was forced upon her by a series of spontaneous revolts of the Balkan Slavs against the Turks. That of the Bulgars (1876) was repressed with such appalling cruelty that Russian opinion was inflamed and the Tsar forced to act. Even had Russia intended eventual aggression, she was by no means ready at this time. Advantage had been taken of the Franco-Prussian War (1870-1) to repudiate those clauses of the Treaty of Paris (1856) which forbade her to maintain bases and fleets on the Black Sea, but the new fleet was not yet ready. Nor had the army reforms of 1874, intended to remedy the abuses and defects revealed by the Crimean War, had time to take effect. But, although Russia's hand was forced, Austria could not tolerate her intervention: '*once the Balkan Slavs were active, the Russian government dared not let them fail; Austro-Hungary dared not let them succeed*'.[1] Nevertheless, the Great Powers could have agreed on a mutually satisfactory formula but for the intransigence of the Turks.[2]

In April 1877 Russia declared war on Turkey and was joined by Rumania. Russia was handicapped by Turkish control of the Black Sea and by lack of a fleet on its waters. On land her armies crossed the Danube and entered Bulgaria but were unexpectedly held up for four months by vigorous Turkish resistance at Plevna. This delay allowed time for the memories of the Bulgarian atrocities to fade, and gave the powers hostile to Russia's moves an opportunity to organize counter-measures, military and diplomatic. Before the Russian armies had reached Constantinople, having liberated Turkey's Christian subjects, war fever was running high in Britain:

> We don't want to fight;
> But, by Jingo, if we do,
> We've got the ships, we've got the men,
> We've got the money too.
> We've fought the Bear before,
> And while we're Britons true:
> The Russians shall not have Constantinople!

The British Mediterranean fleet was ordered to pass through the Dardanelles, but war was avoided by Russia's promise not to occupy Gallipoli (February 1878). However, in March, the Russians imposed the Treaty of San Stefano on the Turks, according to the terms of which a large autonomous Bulgaria, stretching from the Danube to the Aegean, was to be set up under Russian protection and military occupation. Serbia and Montenegro were to be fully independent; Russia was to have Bessarabia and the Danube delta in return for which Rumania was to have the Dobruja.

Neither Britain nor Austria-Hungary would assent to these provisions, which meant Russian domination of south-eastern Europe, and they prepared for war. Bismarck, although he held that Germany should never quarrel with Russia, was yet bound to support Austria. At the Congress of Berlin (1878) a settlement, which replaced Russian by mainly Austrian and

[1] *Taylor (1954), p. 229*
[2] *Seton-Watson (1964), pp. 103-4*

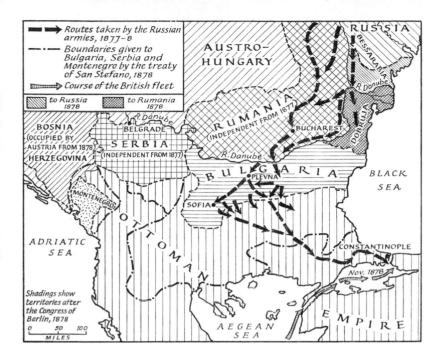

figure 68   South-east Europe, 1877-8.

Turkish control over much of the Balkans, was imposed upon a Russia already exhausted by her efforts and unable to continue the war against such opposition (fig. 68).

There was to be only a small Bulgaria, cut off from the Aegean, and therefore dependent on Austria for her communications; it was not to be a Russian protectorate. Austria was left free to take over Bosnia and Herzegovina. Britain took Cyprus. Russia was allowed to keep Batum, Kars and part of Bessarabia. Thus Russia, having at great cost fought what seemed to most Russians a thoroughly justifiable war, and having liberated fellow Slavs and coreligionaries from intolerable oppression, had to stand impotently by while the fruits of victory were either transferred to Austria or handed back to Turkey. Most of the resentment fell upon Germany who had failed to support Russia, and the determination grew that no further surrender to Austria could be brooked. No longer able to feel anything but bitterness for her Germanic neighbours, Russia was enticed into the snares of French diplomacy and irrevocably lined up with Germany's implacable and vengeful foe. Thwarted patriotism also turned against the Tsar, Alexander II, for his failure, and against the autocracy generally. The rebuff suffered by Russia at the Congress of Berlin in 1878 contributed to the 1914-18 war and to the overthrow of autocracy in 1917.

A menacing aspect to Russia of the Berlin settlement was that it left

Britain in a position to enter the Black Sea whenever she thought fit, provided she had the naval strength.[1] The willingness of Prussia and Austria to recognize the principle that the Straits should be closed in time of war was sufficient to bring Russia into the *Dreikaiserbund* in 1881, despite the resentment over Berlin. Likewise the Reinsurance Treaty between Russia and Germany in 1887 reaffirmed the principle of the closure of the Straits.[2] But early in the twentieth century, British antagonism to Russian policy in the Balkans and the Straits moderated. Germany's drive into the region and her increasing influence in Turkey were of more immediate concern. In Asia agreement was reached between Britain and Russia over other causes of discord between 1907 and 1910.

Asia

The conquest of the Caucasus (1859) left large Russian armies ready for further action. These were used to subdue Central Asia, consisting principally of the Uzbek khanates of Kokand, Bokhara and Khiva, between 1864 and 1884. These homes of ancient civilization, based on irrigation from the Syr and Amu rivers, were but shadows of their splendid past. Beyond the irrigated valleys were nomadic shepherds and mountaineers like the Turkmen, Tadzhiks and Kirghiz. One by one the settled districts with their ancient towns and the territories of the nomadic tribes were reduced to subjection. Krasnovodsk was founded on the east shore of the Caspian (1869) and the Trans-Caspian railway began to make its way eastwards from the new port in 1879, giving a water–rail route into the newly-acquired territory. Without modern weapons the khanates and nomads could offer no effective resistance and the waterless desert proved to be a more formidable enemy to the Russian armies than the inhabitants.

With the conquest of Turkestan and the building of the Trans-Caspian railway eastwards from Krasnovodsk (1873-85), Russian territory confronted the whole length of the northern frontier of Persia and made contact with Afghanistan. Beyond Persia lay the Gulf and beyond Afghanistan lay Britain's Indian Empire. Jealous suspicions of Russian motives were soon aroused. In Persia, although Russian influence prevailed in the north, British control was asserted in the south. The 1907 agreement accepted these two zones of influence, but interposed a neutral zone.

Russian influence was first established in Afghanistan (1878), but the second Anglo-Afghan War (1879-80) replaced it with British protection. A border incident between Russian and Afghan troops in 1885 caused a sudden flare-up of Anglo-Russian hostility which was, in the end, settled peacefully. Between 1900 and 1903 Russia failed to set up direct relations with Afghanistan, and was compelled to deal through British diplomatic channels as Britain insisted. In the 1907 Convention Russia

[1] *Taylor (1954), p. 251*
[2] *Seton-Watson (1964), p. 177*

accepted this exclusion, declaring Afghanistan to be outside her sphere of interest.

The Far East (fig. 69)

Russia's progress across Asia to the Pacific, and later into Kazakhstan, had been more the result of the inevitable expansion of a strong and relatively advanced power into lands sparsely inhabited by weak and backward tribes. There was little premeditation or policy in it. But during the second half of the nineteenth century further expansion, which could only take place at the expense of stronger and more populous states, viz the Central Asian khanates and China, had to be a matter of government policy, since it implied negotiations with other powers and necessitated planned campaigns involving the armed forces of the Tsar.

Apart from the motives of commercial expansion, strategic advance and the imperialistic ambitions of military commanders, Russian expansion eastwards had a philosophical basis in the beliefs propounded by a powerful group of Slavophils—the Easterners—that Russia had a civilizing mission in Asia. These views found wide acceptance after the humiliating retreat from south-eastern Europe forced upon Russia at Berlin in 1878, and they began to influence government policy.[1] Government circles saw a further advantage in an Eastern policy: that of distracting attention from Western ideas of constitutional reform:

This imperial advance of Russia was definitely adopted as a substitute for reform at home. Russia, in going eastward, was herself abandoning the West and trying to become more eastern; the last of the great medieval autocracies tried to forget Europe by plunging into Asia.[2]

The Treaties of Aigun (1858) and Pekin (1860) had brought the Russian frontier in the Far East south to the Amur and, in the coastal region, to south of Vladivostok. The exchange with Japan of the Kurile Islands for southern Sakhalin, making the whole of that island Russian, increased the security of this new Pacific territory. The northward projection of Manchuria, however, constituted an awkward interruption to the extent of Russian territory along the fiftieth parallel, an obstacle which became more serious once the trans-continental railway was planned. This Manchurian salient also made the frontier a larger, longer one, needing more troops to guard it. And this northern Chinese province barred the way to a warm water port: Vladivostok, founded in 1861, was ice-impeded in winter.

In 1895 Russia won the Chinese government's good will by persuading Germany and France to join her in demanding that Japan should abandon the foothold on the Chinese mainland which she had won in the Sino-Japanese war of 1894-5. By the Treaty of Alliance between China and Russia in 1896, the latter country guaranteed China against further attack.

[1] *Malozemoff (1958), pp. 90-3*
[2] *Pares (n.d.), p. 418*

In return a strip of land was conceded for the building of a Russian railway to Harbin in the heart of Manchuria.

Russia was interested in Korea as well as in Manchuria. The Korean peninsula lay immediately to the south of Vladivostok and might provide the desired warm-water port. If, however, that port were to be in the Yellow Sea, its value would be limited if Korea were in the hands of a foreign power. But Japan was prepared to connive at Russia's penetration of Manchuria if she herself were given a free hand in Korea.

Russia gained her Far Eastern warm-water port in 1898 when China was persuaded to lease Port Arthur and Dairen on the Liaotung peninsula and to grant a further railway concession enabling the Manchurian railway to be extended to these ports.

Meanwhile the building of the Trans-Siberian railway went ahead. Its easternmost section crossed Manchuria to terminate at Vladivostok. There were many arguments in favour of the project, despite its cost and the physical difficulties in its way. Without it a Far Eastern policy could not be pursued in face of the gathering military and naval power of Japan; without it Russian colonization of ex-Chinese territory would not be extensive enough to give substance to Russia's title; without it Russia's overland trade with China would suffer from sea-borne competition from maritime carriers. The course of the railway followed the discontinuous belt of rich black-earth soils which fringed the southern edge of the Siberian forest and along which towns and settlements founded by Russians had sprung up. It was opened as a single-track line in 1901, although passengers and goods had to detrain to cross lake Baykal.

Had wiser counsels prevailed, Russia would have been satisfied for the time being with her Manchurian gains and would have propitiated Japan over Korea, at least until the railway was completed. In 1902 Japan had strengthened her position by an alliance with Britain, who welcomed a partner able and willing to fight to arrest Russian expansion in the Far East. But influential speculators in St Petersburg were determined to pursue their plans to exploit Korea. The minister Pleve, who had the ear of the Tsar, thought '*a little victorious war to stop the revolutionary tide*' would not come amiss.[1] Emperor William II of Germany also did all he could to encourage the Tsar to embroil himself in the Far East so as to keep Russian attention diverted from the Balkans.

Accordingly Japan prepared for war, and a sudden attack on the Russian Pacific fleet gave her immediate command of the sea (February 1904). The Russian Baltic Sea fleet was eventually sent out to regain it (October 1904). After making the voyage round the Cape—use of the Suez canal was denied—it was destroyed on arrival in the Yellow Sea (May 1905). Meanwhile, Port Arthur had fallen (January 1905) and Japanese armies advanced into Manchuria. Japan had been able to bring 150,000 men into the war immediately, ferrying them across the seas she commanded, whereas the Russians had to bring their troops along the Trans-Siberian railway, 5,500

[1] *Seton-Watson (1964), p. 213*

figure 69   The Russian Far East and the Russo-Japanese War.

miles from Moscow. The journey took over a week, owing in part to the interruption at lake Baykal, where the line had not yet been carried through the mountainous country on the southern-side of the lake.

With revolution at home and defeat in Manchuria, Russia was forced to make peace, helped by American mediation, for the United States looked with suspicion on the Japanese victories. At the Treaty of Portsmouth (September 1905), Russia surrendered the Liaotung peninsula and Port Arthur to Japan and recognized a Japanese protectorate over Korea. Southern Sakhalin was ceded to Japan. Russia thus lost her only Pacific ice-free port after a tenure of less than seven years. She also lost the Trans-Siberian railway's short cut across Manchuria to Vladivostok. The line now had to be continued through all-Russian territory to the north. Although the obvious course was to build the new line along the Amur, through the well-populated districts of the valley, this would have placed it along the frontier and have left it exposed in case of war. It was therefore laid to the north of the river valley, involving a difficult course through hilly and uninhabited country.

The establishment of a virtual protectorate over Outer Mongolia, which had declared itself independent from China (1911-13), was some compensation for the defeat in the Far East. Valuable supplies of wool, hides and skins soon began to flow to Russian industry from Mongolia.

The last years of Tsarist Russia were filled with concern lest her Far Eastern territories should be overwhelmed by Chinese immigrants. Nansen asked in 1914,

> *Whence comes this great influx of the yellow race? In the first place it is due to the simple reason that there is a perceptible lack of labour in the East; the exploitation of its great natural wealth, its agriculture and its mines, demands a large supply of labour, which it is at present impossible to provide without the help of the yellow men.*
>
> *But there is the additional circumstance that the yellow labourer, Chinese or Korean, is superior in competition with the European, and one often hears it asserted by Russians that without him it would be impossible to live there.*[1]

Attempts were made to turn back this tide.

Russia and the West

Among those who have debated Russia's relationship to Europe there is general agreement that it was during this period that Russia was closest to Europe, and that in the decades immediately before the Great War the differences between Russia and western Europe were minimal: '*by 1900 Russia was perhaps more European than at any other time in her history*';[2] '*Russia was drawing rapidly nearer to western Europe*';[3] and

> *If we look back to the decade or two preceding the outbreak of the First World War, we have the impression that for a brief period the old debate over Russia's relationship to the west was losing its intensity and was perhaps beginning to appear irrelevant.*[4]

Superficially there is much evidence to support this view, some of it political but most of it economic. The local council (*zemstvo*) activities and the existence after 1905 of an elected assembly (the *Duma*) had clothed the nakedness of the autocracy in dress somewhat akin to the Western. The pursuit of imperialism, both political and economic, in Central Asia and the Far East, was certainly a European characteristic.

The old simple class structure inherited from Muscovy was rapidly evolving into a much more complex society. The liberation of the serfs in 1861 and, later, the loosening of communal bonds, enabled some peasants

---

[1] *Nansen (1914), p. 368*
[2] *Sumner (1951), p. 9*
[3] *Seton-Watson (1964), p. 299*
[4] *Roberts (1964), p. 11*

to become wealthy 'kulaks' while others degenerated into landless labourers, many of whom migrated into the towns to form an industrial working class. Large-scale industrial expansion, made possible for the first time by the fluidity of labour, the influx of foreign capital and the building of railways, gave rise to an influential class of financiers and industrialists. The abolition of serfdom in 1861, together with increased export opportunities arising from railway links with the ports and from expanding urban population abroad, gave agricultural land a value which led to a demand for it from wealthy merchants, industrialists and kulaks. The gentry ceased to be wholly a land-owning class engaged primarily in administering their estates and became increasingly urbanized. There was a rapid increase in the number of professional men. This new complexity of society was reflected in the formation of political groups, associations and parties, which reflected different views and interests.

In many ways, however, Russia continued to stand apart. The autocracy justified its continued existence on the ground that it was an integral part of Russia's past and an essential part of her independent future. It refused to compromise with Western liberalism and circumvented any forced concessions as best it could. And, if the institution itself was peculiarly Russian, the enormous and corrupt bureaucracy and the unbridled and brutal police forces upon which it relied could scarcely be called European in the context of late nineteenth and early twentieth-century Europe. Nicholas II's and his wife's strange relationship with the 'holy' but libidinous peasant Rasputin would have been inconceivable in any other European court.

Russia stood apart also in the nature of the gulf that divided the intelligentsia and the masses:

> The difference between the Russian intellectual and the Russian peasant was not the same as the difference between an educated and an uneducated person in a western country. Voltaire and a French agricultural labourer, Mr Gladstone and a British docker, lived on different cultural levels, but they belonged to the same culture . . .
> The Russian intellectual and the Russian peasant belonged to different cultures. The ideas of the Russian intellectual did not derive from Russian conditions, but were imported prefabricated from abroad.[1]

Yet Szeftel claims that, after 1905, 'Russian life aligned itself, until 1917, in all [my roman, W.H.P.] respects with the rest of Europe', and Beloff has written that at this time 'no one would have agreed to exclude from Europe the countrymen of Turgenev and Tolstoy, of Tchaikovsky or Paul Vinogradoff'.[2] But both Turgenev and Tolstoy are constantly contrasting Russians and Europeans. This is most evident in Turgenev's Smoke, where sarcasm is levelled at the behaviour of Russian 'barbarians' abroad, and their aping of European manners is ridiculed. It is apparent in the following paragraph of Anna Karenina:

[1] Seton-Watson (1956), pp. 398-9
[2] Szeftel (1964), p. 25; Beloff (1957), p. 213

> *The prince and princess had conflicting ideas in regard to living abroad. The princess thought that everything was lovely and, notwithstanding her assured position in Russian society, she put on the airs of a European lady while she was abroad, which was not becoming, for she was in every way a genuine Russian baruina. The prince, on the other hand, considered everything abroad detestable, and the European life unendurable; and he even exaggerated his Russian characteristics, and tried to be less of a European than he really was.*[1]

To draw this well-founded distinction between Russia and the West or Russia and Europe, even though it is merely to emphasize the distinctiveness of Russian civilization and carries no pejorative implication, occasionally provokes a rather tetchy reaction. Szeftel alleges that such contrasts offer '*excellent opportunities for the formulation of untested and self-gratifying hypotheses*', and Beloff complains that '*as soon as we shift away from the traditional divisions of geography, we risk sailing into an uncharted sea of personal whim and prejudice*'.[2] By '*traditional divisions of geography*' he presumably means the conventional Ural-Caucasus boundary of Europe which has been in vogue for little more than a century.[3] He apparently has in mind a Europe extending to the Urals when he refers to what he calls the '*geographers' Europe*', although, as has been shown in Chapter 1, if there is a geographers' Europe, it ends where many historians have limited historical Europe—in a zone extending from the Baltic to the Black Sea. An enquiry among European political geographers in 1935 revealed that more favoured the Polish-Russian frontier as the eastern boundary of Europe (thereby excluding Russia) than any alternative.[4] Those who accept a Ural boundary to Europe are merely adopting, unthinkingly, a line selected within eighteenth-century Russia for internal purposes. Assertions that historical Europe does not include Russia, even when put as bluntly as Marriott's, '*Russia is not, and never has been, a member of the European family*', do not conflict with a true geographical conception of Europe, however they may be impugned on other grounds.[5] Mirsky revealed a deeper perception of the true '*geographers' Europe*' when he wrote:

> *Geographers know only too well how artificial and unreal is the boundary of 'Europe' and 'Asia' as drawn on our maps. A line drawn from Murmansk to Galats, with the numerous climatic, botanic and cultural boundaries more or less closely superimposed on it, is a much more real boundary than the harmless little chain of the Urals.*[6]

Witte, who did more than anyone after Peter the Great to westernize Russia economically, emphasized her distance from the West:

[1] *Tolstoy (1887), p. 240*
[2] *Szeftel (1964), p. 27; Beloff (1957), p. 7*
[3] *Parker (1960)*
[4] *Coudenhove-Kalergi (1935), pp. 318-22*
[5] *Marriott (1944), p. 1*
[6] *Mirsky (1927), p. 313*

Russia . . . represents a world apart. Her independent place in the family of peoples and her special role in world history are determined both by her geographical position . . . and in particular, by the original character of her political and cultural development; a development which has been achieved through the living interaction and harmonious combination of three elements that have manifested their full creative power only in Russia.

And these elements are those fundamental to the doctrine of Official Nationality: Orthodoxy, Autocracy and the

Russian national spirit, as the basis of the internal cohesiveness of the state, a national spirit that creates a strong kernel, closely united yet free from nationalistic exclusiveness, possessed of a vast capacity for friendly companionship and cooperation with the most diverse races and peoples. It is on these bases that the whole edifice of Russian power has been built up, and it is therefore impossible for Russia to be fused with the West.[1]

These were the arguments by which the autocracy defended itself and in them there is no hint that

in standing against the nineteenth-century revolutionary, democratic, liberal or constitutional influences of the West, tsarism was standing not against Europe as such but against the new Europes in the name of the old Europe of the ancien régime.[2]

Although there may have been a grain of truth in this when applied to the earlier decades of the century, it is an argument difficult to sustain when applied to *fin de siècle* Russia.

Although the political concepts, upon which the intense political activity which developed in Russia were based, may have been Western in origin, their subsequent evolution and transmutation were Russian. The argument, for instance, as to whether it was desirable that Russia should go through the stage of capitalism or not, was inevitably peculiar to the realm of the tsars. Those who thought not, believed that socialism could be based on the Russian peasant commune and artisan artel, and were thus successors to the Slavophils, though without their mysticism:

Europe does not, and cannot, understand our social aspirations. She is not our teacher in economic questions. We believe that we are called to contribute to history a new principle, to say a word of our own, and not to repeat the traces of Europe.[3]

Nor could there be found anywhere in Europe the almost laughable paradox by which Marxists, capitalists and a government department (Finance) were united in advocating the advance of capitalism and, by implication, an intensification of the class struggle, while the Populists and the Ministry of the Interior were at one in their conservative approach to

---

[1] *Sumner (1951), p. 3*
[2] *Sumner (1951), p. 11*
[3] *Mihailov, quoted in Seton-Watson (1964), p. 61*

the ancient communal institutions of Russia.[1] The later differences that developed between the Social Revolutionaries and the Social Democrats, and between the Bolsheviks and the Mensheviks within the Social Democrat party, were the product of Russia's unique and non-Western class structure. The situation was further complicated by the exile of an increasing proportion of party propagandists in foreign countries, a result of growing repression at home. The endemic character of assassination and repression, the acts of terrorism against government and against the people that punctuated urban and rural life alike, were again scarcely European.

In the purely economic field, Russia was developing rather as a colony of the western and central European powers than as an independent nation. Mining and heavy industry were increasingly coming under foreign ownership. *'By 1914 Russia had gone a good part of the way towards becoming a semi-colonial possession of European capital'.*[2] Also, although the rapid industrial expansion of the thirty years before the Great War may appear as a late example of the industrial revolution experienced earlier in the West, it had distinct Russian characteristics; notably the preponderant role of the State:

> *State contracts played an enormous part in Russian production. It is estimated that in 1899 nearly two-thirds of Russian metallurgical production was taken by the State. Close links developed between officials and industrialists. Officials sat on many bodies supervising industrial activities.*[3]

Many Russians during this period sought relief from the isolation in which they found themselves in Europe by identifying themselves with other Orthodox or Slavic nations. Such Panslav sentiments were prominent in 'public opinion' whenever articulate Russians had a chance to express their feelings. In fact, Panslavism was one of the few attitudes which the wealthier or more educated classes—landowners, business men, merchants, officials, professional men, kulaks—had in common.

As there was one large and powerful Slav and Orthodox nation and many small and weak ones, the Panslav idea obviously had imperialistic attractions for the Russian government and it became an element in foreign policy. It was complicated by the fact that not all Orthodox nations were Slav and not all Slav nations were Orthodox. The inclusion of Slav peoples within the Austro-Hungarian and Turkish empires and the nature of the Russian autocracy presented difficulties. The tsarist government suppressed any manifestations of Polish, Ukrainian and White Russian nationalism. The Poles, in particular, were difficult to include in any broad Panslav view as, with few exceptions, they hated and despised the Russians, regarding them as Asiatic barbarians.[4] On the other hand, the

[1] *Seton-Watson (1964), pp. 142-3*
[2] *Mirsky (1952), p. 269*
[3] *Seton-Watson (1964), pp. 118-19; Miller (1926), p. 297*
[4] *Mirsky (1952), p. 240*

Ukrainians hated the Poles even more than they detested the Great Russian government.[1]

There was an upsurge of Panslav emotions following the rising of the Balkan Slavs in 1875-6. Panslav societies urged action upon the Tsar, contributions to help the Serbs flowed in, and volunteers left to fight in the Balkans.[2] But the frustrations of the Berlin agreement of 1878 offered a check to the movement. It was now the turn of those who advocated a Far Eastern imperialist policy. But when they too were brought to a halt —by Japan in 1905—there was a revival of Panslavism in so far as Russian opinion favoured the ideal of brotherhood among all Slavs, and supported intervention on their behalf when they were oppressed. But the chief oppressor of Slavs was the Tsar himself: his efforts to suppress Polish, Ukrainian and White Russian nationality were redoubled.

The effects of this policy were the reverse of those intended. Ukrainian nationalism was greatly strengthened. The movement, which at first adopted a cooperative Panslav attitude, was soon inspired with uncompromising hostility to the Great Russian autocracy. In fact, the Russian treatment of the Ukrainians within the Empire was so much harsher than that meted out to those in Austro-Hungary that it has been said that 'the majority of Ukrainians were pro-German by 1914'.[3]

[1] *Hoetzsch* (*1917*), *p. 403*
[2] *Mosse* (*1958*), *pp. 150-2*
[3] *Seton-Watson* (*1964*), *p. 322*

CHAPTER SEVENTEEN
THE RUSSIAN EMPIRE IN 1914

By 1914, a far-reaching transformation had taken place in the economy, the 1890s in particular having witnessed rapid industrialization. Although still well behind U.S.A., Britain, Germany, France, and even Belgium, in industrial production, Russia was making faster progress and well on the way to joining them in the front rank.

Yet, despite this progress, the Russian economy remained backward and its development uneven. The agricultural and industrial structure was riddled with medieval survivals. Many branches of engineering, such as machine tool production and motor car manufacture, and many aspects of the chemical industry, were entirely absent. To a far greater degree than elsewhere, State policy and foreign capital dominated industry, and the economy remained semi-colonial in relation to western Europe, with exports of primary commodities and imports of manufactured goods still characterizing external trade.

The importance of paternalistic state control and of foreign investment were both in part due to the fact that attitudes and conditions within Russia were unfavourable to the flowering of a spontaneous native industry. Among all classes, a belief prevailed that the improvement of agriculture should be Russia's main concern, and many saw her economic, social and political salvation only in an idealistic agrarian society with a feudal or communal organization. Industrial development should grow naturally from the home-based *kustar* handicrafts and the cooperative artisan artels. Witte's plans for westernization could make but limited headway in the teeth of such ideas.[1] Nevertheless, he succeeded in

> *encouraging the creation and extension of big factories, which must inevitably destroy the home industry, and even . . . undermining the rural Commune, and thereby adding to the ranks of the landless proletariat, in order to increase the amount of cheap labour for the benefit of the capitalists.*[2]

Having oscillated fitfully between these two opposing views of Russia's destiny, the autocracy had, by 1914, given the country the worst of both these mutually incompatible worlds.

Some idea of the relative importance of the various branches of the economy may be given by the tables opposite.

The data are for the whole Empire, within which there were considerable differences. Thus, the proportion of the population engaged in agriculture was over 80 per cent in Central Asia and Siberia, but only 56·6 per cent in Poland.

[1] *Laue (1963), pp. 277-87*
[2] *Wallace (1905), vol. 2, p. 373*

Source of National Income, 1913[1]

	per cent
Agriculture	51·4
Industry	28·0
Construction	4·1
Transportation	7·9
Commerce	8·6

Occupations of the People, 1897[2]

	per cent
Agriculture	74·6
Manufacturing industry	9·3
Private service	4·6
Commerce	3·8
Pensioners, rentiers	1·8
Transport	1·6
Public service	1·4
Military service	1·0
Mining	0·4
Clergy	0·6
others	0·9

Agriculture

Although serfdom had been abolished in 1861 and, although—more recently—the village commune had lost its hold, agriculture generally remained backward and the peasants impoverished. In many areas they were worse off than ever they had been before. The abolition of serfdom had meant yet another tax for them to bear in the form of redemption payments for land which they had always occupied and regarded as their own. Between 1861 and 1905, when payments ceased, they had paid almost £140 million and in so doing, beggared themselves beyond description. They continued to carry the full weight of heavy indirect taxation levied upon necessities—sugar, tea, cotton, iron, tobacco, vodka, etc.[3]

Many peasants, when they were freed, received smaller holdings than they had occupied under serfdom—on an average 4 per cent less.[4] Although as a class they subsequently purchased or leased land so as to increase their total holding, this was forced upon them by the stark choice between growing more food or starving. But in so doing they became further impoverished and indebted. Population growth soon outpaced this increase in peasant-held land so that the average holding decreased in size. A third

[1] *Lyashchenko (1956), vol. 2, p. 347*
[2] *Kennard (1913), p. 61*
[3] *Robinson (1932), p. 96; Alexinsky (1913), p. 141*
[4] *Robinson (1932), p. 87*

way in which Emancipation hurt the peasants was in its failure to grant them use of forest and meadow land to which they had previously had access. As firewood and pasture were essential, they were compelled to obtain them from the landowner in return for rent or work.[1]

Inevitably the impoverished peasant agriculture remained primitive, with at worst continual cropping of the soil to exhaustion, and at best the little relief afforded to the tired soil by the three-field system. Wooden implements still prevailed, and the total number of tractors and harvesting machines in the whole Empire could be counted in hundreds.[2] The misery of the peasants showed itself also in the squalor of their overcrowded underfurnished *izbas*, in the physical degeneration of men and women existing on potatoes and cabbage soup, in alcoholism, and in high mortality.[3] Driven in desperation by these conditions to revolt in 1905-6, they brought upon themselves the cruelties of a ferocious repression. After that they flocked in increasing numbers to seek work in the industrial areas and the towns.

Nevertheless, some peasants, more fortunate, more astute or more sober than their fellows, prospered to form the wealthy class of *kulaki*, who took advantage of the breakdown of the commune, of the poverty of the poorer peasants, and of the indebtedness of the gentry, to buy and consolidate land. These men acquired enough capital to hire labour, buy machinery and use fertilizers; their farms contrasted sharply with the squalid holdings of the poorer peasantry, and compared favourably with those of the more go-ahead landlords (*pomeschchiki*). And whereas the poorer peasants farmed mainly for their own subsistence, the *pomeshchiki* and *kulaki* had become to a large degree commercial farmers supplying the growing urban, industrial and export markets with agricultural produce.

The old class of landowning nobles was disposing of its land, mainly to peasants, and much of what was left was heavily mortgaged. '*The system of "free enterprise" which replaced the old forms of the economy was completely alien to the feudal mentality of the noble landlord*'.[4] Many were absentees and no longer had any interest whatever in their estates except as sources of revenue:

> *Absentee landlordism is the curse of this country, as it was in Ireland, and the profits of the crops are wasted in St Petersburg and Paris, in gambling and high living, and in all possible forms of extravagance. Very little of the money is left in the country; very little is used to improve the property or the conditions of the tenants, although there are commendable exceptions.*[5]

Only in the western (Baltic and Polish) provinces had the nobles succeeded in transforming themselves into successful commercial farmers. It was in

[1] *Baranskiy (1950), p. 126; Florinsky (1953), vol. 2, p. 926*
[2] *Lyashchenko (1956), vol. 2, p. 277*
[3] *Alexinsky (1913), pp. 147-50*
[4] *Alexinsky (1913), p. 143*
[5] *Curtis (1911), p. 253*

these regions that most of the increased purchases of machinery (valued at 28 million roubles in 1900, 61 million roubles in 1908, 109 million roubles in 1913) and fertilizer were made.[1]

As may be seen from the following table for 1904, average yields of grain per acre (in bushels), although well below those of north-western Europe, were of the same order as those in Mediterranean and New World countries:[2]

Germany	29·4	U.S.A.	12·5
U.K.	27·7	Argentina	12·1
France	18·6	Italy	11·8
Canada	16·8	Russia	11·4
Hungary	16·3	Spain	10·6
Rumania	12·6		

Although this low yield may be attributed '*partly to the system of land tenure and partly to the deficient methods of agriculture in use*',[3] when it is considered that so much of Russia's grain-growing land suffered from too little warmth, from drought, or from infertile and exhausted soils, it does not appear to be remarkably out of line with that of other countries with similar conditions.

It was a characteristic of Russian agriculture that increased production came rather from an increased acreage than from higher yields. This is not surprising in a country where overcropping, soil exhaustion, difficulty of climate, and lack of capital and technique made increased yields hard to obtain. But, as the map shows (fig. 70), the increase in sown area was not on the overcrowded central areas where it was most needed, but to the south and east, as well as in Siberia. Yet, had the capital and initiative been available, much could have been done by way of reclamation of swamp and other waste land. Travellers were struck by the contrast between Prussia and the Baltic provinces of the Empire, by no means its most backward region:

> *Anyone who has travelled by rail from Berlin to St Petersburg must have noticed how the landscape suddenly changes its character as soon as he has crossed the frontier. Leaving a prosperous agricultural country, he traverses for many weary hours a region in which there is hardly a sign of human habitation, though the soil and climate of that region resemble closely the soil and climate of East Prussia.*[4]

One of the worst aspects of peasant farming in Central Russia was the absence of sufficient pasture. Drainage would have done much to remedy this. Some progress was made in the 1870s and 1880s, but this laudable reclamation was not sustained.[5]

[1] *Lyashchenko (1956), vol. 2, p. 277*
[2] *Miller (1926), p. 56*
[3] *Miller (1926), p. 56*
[4] *Wallace (1905), vol. 2, p. 224*
[5] *French (1963), pp. 53-4*

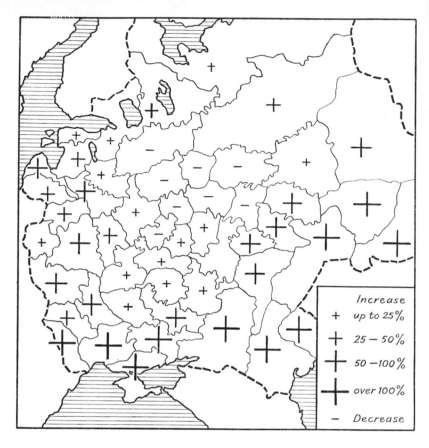

figure 70   Changes in the sown area, 1860-1913 (after Lyashchenko).

Although the production of grain had continued to increase since 1861, the output of dairy produce, vegetables and industrial crops had risen even faster, as a result of increased urbanization and industrialization. Much of this rise went to satisfy the export market. The principal increases were in cotton, sunflowers, sugar-beet, tobacco and potatoes, but flax and hemp had begun to decline.[1] Grain remained of overwhelming importance, although yields were falling on black-earth and non black-earth soils alike.

The acreage sown to *grain* and the total production seem to have grown steadily. The total annual harvest of all grains in 1906-10 was 68 million tons, distributed as follows:[2]

[1] *Lyashchenko (1956), vol. 2, pp. 275-80*
[2] *Kennard (1913), pp. 166-78*

	million tons
Russia	57
Poland	4
Siberia	4
Central Asia	2
Caucasus	1

The Russian figure of 57 million tons compared with 37 million tons in 1886-90 and 20 million tons in 1864-6, and its distribution amongst the various cereals is shown below (millions of puds). Earlier figures enable changes in relative importance to be seen.

	1886-90	1896-1900	1906-10
Rye	971	1,090	1,084
Wheat	352	501	892
Oats	519	595	705
Barley	183	275	485

Production of wheat had grown rapidly while that of rye had begun to decline. In 1886-90, the rye harvest had almost equalled that of the other three grains together, but in 1906-10 it was about half. This resulted from a sharp decline in rye growing in the central black-earth region and a more moderate decline in the industrial centre, while new wheat lands were opened up in the southern steppes and across the Volga.[1] Railways now linked these wheatlands with the densely populated central area and with the ports. The gap between the production of rye and wheat was even smaller in the Empire as a whole, since four times as much wheat as rye was grown east of the Urals. Forty-six per cent of total grain production was exported in 1911-13.[2]

The area actually sown in any one year was still between 60 and 70 per cent of the total arable, the remainder lying fallow but, while in 1875 the acreage in the Empire sown to wheat (12 million desyatins) was half that sown to rye (24 million desyatins), it was now almost as large (24:27). Grains took up about 90 per cent of the sown area, but industrial crops were fast increasing in production, especially in the black-earth centre, the west and north-west.

Potatoes, used not only for food, but as a source of starch and alcohol, now took up 3·8 million desyatins compared with 1·5 million in 1875, and annual production in 1906-10 averaged 32 million tons, distributed as follows:

	million tons
Russia	23·6
Poland	7·6
Siberia	0·7

[1] *Lyashchenko (1956), vol. 2, pp. 68-9*
[2] *Lyashchenko (1956), vol. 2, p. 280*

Over a quarter of the total output was exported in 1911-13.[1] The increased potato acreage in the north-western provinces had been mainly at the expense of flax and hemp, the production of which had begun to decline. Thus, the area of *flax*, having doubled from 800,000 desyatins in 1875 to 1,650,000 in 1902, fell sharply to 770,000 desyatins in 1910, when production was about 20 million puds, over three-quarters of which was exported. Likewise the *hemp* acreage, having risen from 200,000 desyatins in 1875 to 775,000 in 1897, had fallen back to 682,000 desyatins in 1906. Production was 19 million puds, of which a half was exported.[2]

The area under *sugar-beet* grew five times from 100,000 desyatins in the 1860s to 500,000 in 1900, but production of beet had risen twice as fast over the same period, from 41 million to 428 million puds or 7 million tons, yielding 1·7 million tons of sugar. Sixteen per cent was exported. Few crops were making more headway than *sunflowers*, grown mainly for their oil seeds. The acreage under this steppe plant rose by 61 per cent between 1901 and 1913. Even faster was the increase in *cotton* acreage (112 per cent). Production in Central Asia expanded rapidly after the introduction of American varieties in the 1880s and the coming of the railway. In 1911 cotton was grown on 486,000 irrigated desyatins (401,000 in Central Asia and 85,000 in the Caucasus) and the total production was 27·6 million puds (315,000 tons) of fibre. The area of most intensive cotton growing was the Ferghana valley, where 55 per cent of the acreage and production were concentrated, and where cotton was grown on 48 per cent of the irrigated land.[3] A little *tea*—about 200,000 lb.—was now being grown in the Empire, near Batumi.

Sown grass and fodder crops, almost unknown in 1861, were now spreading rapidly, and amounted in 1913 to about 2 per cent of the cultivated area. These, together with natural pasture, were most widespread in the northern, north-western and central industrial districts of Russia, and least extensive in the mixed-forest black-earth zone. Many northern and north-western areas were going over to dairy farming which had also made remarkable progress in Siberia. *Livestock* statistics for 1911 are given below (in millions):

	Cattle	Horses	Sheep & Goats	Pigs
Russia	32·2	17·6	39·1	10·9
Poland	2·2	1·0	1·0	0·6
Caucasus	5·9	1·4	11·6	1·2
Siberia	6·0	3·3	5·5	1·3
Central Asia	5·3	3·3	21·1	0·1

In ratio of cattle per 100 inhabitants, Siberia led with 76, followed by Central Asia with 60. For horses, the ratio was also highest in Siberia (59),

[1] *Lyashchenko (1956), vol. 2, p. 280*

[2] *Kennard (1913), p. 331; Lyashchenko (1956), vol. 2, p. 280*

[3] *Semenov (1899-1913), vol. 19, pp. 426, 458-63; Kennard (1913), pp. 136-8*

with Central Asia again second (54). Central Asia had 242 sheep and goats per 100 inhabitants, followed by the Caucasus with 110.[1] By and large, livestock were badly selected, poorly bred and, by the end of the winter, thin or half-starved. The proportion of horseless households had increased to almost a third and it could no longer be written, as it had been in 1801, that *'these animals are so common that it is rare to find a peasant, even among the poorest, who does not possess one or more horses'*. The reason for the decline was certainly not mechanization, but the extreme misery of many peasants.[2]

Agricultural Regions

The Industrial Centre. Here there had been a sharp falling off in the growth of grain which was now brought by rail from the steppes. The cultivation of industrial crops, of fodder crops for dairying, and of vegetables, especially potatoes, had largely taken its place, but there had been a decline in the cultivated area.

The wooded-steppe black-earth zone. This region, formerly the fertile and relatively prosperous granary of Russia, was now afflicted by the most appalling conditions of poverty and hunger among the peasants. The Emancipation had allowed them only very small allotments because these rich grain-growing lands were too valuable to the landlords (fig. 71). After years of overcropping, soils had everywhere deteriorated and yields declined. To make up for this deficiency there had been a continued encroachment upon pasture land which had become scarcer here than anywhere else in Russia (fig. 72). There was no room for sown grasses or fodder crops. Livestock were crowded onto ever smaller pastures, and overstocking and degeneration of what was left resulted. The number of cattle had perforce to diminish, leading to less manure for the arable, still more soil exhaustion and still lower yields. The railways had dealt the region a fatal blow, as it could not compete with wheat cheaply grown in the steppes, the Volga lands and the Kuban. The peasants were forced to abandon wheat as a cash crop and to replace it with dwindling yields of rye, buckwheat and spelt. Many could no longer afford to keep and feed their horses. Here the state could no longer extort its taxes and, because of physical degeneration, soldiers could not be recruited.

There were few industries, and the peasants, unlike those of the Industrial Centre, could not find work in the towns. Instead, those who were young and fit migrated seasonally to work for the landlords and kulaks of the new wheatlands. Others spent the summer in the large industrial towns of New Russia and the Ukraine where they picked up revolutionary ideas. The disturbances in Orel province in 1905 began with men who had

---

[1] *Kennard (1913), pp. 148-9*
[2] *Storch (1801B), vol. 2, p. 181; Lyashchenko (1956), vol. 2, p. 277;*
   Robinson (1932), pp. 103, 115

K

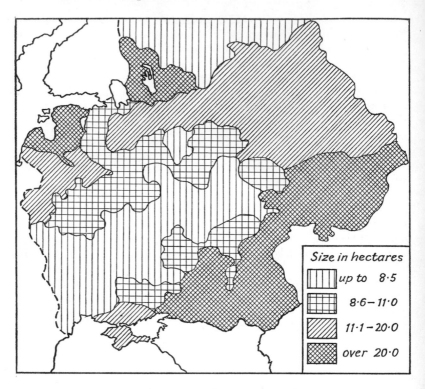

figure 71   Size of peasant holdings, 1905 (after Lyashchenko).

spent the summer working in Odessa, a centre of revolutionary ferment.[1] This migration amounted to $1\frac{1}{4}$ million persons a year or 25 per cent of the working population of the region. And, in the last twenty years before the Revolution, as soon as the commune's grip weakened and state restrictions were relaxed, 1 million people emigrated permanently from this afflicted region. They took their grievances with them to the labour-hungry towns where, plunged into conditions as abysmal as those they left behind in the country, they proved fertile material for revolutionary propaganda. They came into the towns in even greater numbers as a result of Stolypin's land enclosures; so that the policies of industrialization and land reform, calculated to preserve and strengthen the autocracy, ended by increasing the threat posed by the concentration of explosive potential in the cities. The peasants, having failed to redress their wrongs in the countryside in 1905, were to find their revenge in the towns.[2] (Fig. 73.)

Needless to say, peasant agriculture was at its most primitive in the

[1] *Schlesinger (1908), p. 51*

[2] *Haimson (1964), pp. 633-6; Laue (1965), pp. 44-5; Sinzheimer (1965), p. 219*

figure 72   The low-pasture belt in the 1890s (after Lyashchenko).

central black-earth region, where the wooden plough and harrow were in universal use.[1]

The West and North-West. These regions had made good progress and agriculture was flourishing. The rapid industrial development of Poland on the one side and of the Moscow region on the other, together with the building of railways between them, had stimulated farming, and the predominantly landlord agriculture had flourished as a result. When Mackenzie Wallace, who had been in the Smolensk area in the 1870s, returned there in 1903, he found that:

> *the houses were larger and better constructed than they used to be, and each of them had a chimney! That latter fact was important because formerly a large proportion of the peasants of this region had no such luxury, and allowed the smoke to find its exit by the open door. In vain I looked for a hut of the old type . . .*
>
> *Then I noticed a good many iron ploughs of the European model, and my yamstchik informed me that their predecessor, the sokha, with which I had been so familiar, had entirely disappeared from the district. Next I noticed that in the neighbourhood of the villages, flax was grown in large quantities. That was certainly not an indication of poverty, because flax is a valuable product which requires to be well manured, and plentiful manure implies a considerable quantity of livestock.*
>
> *Lastly, before arriving at my destination, I noticed clover being grown*

[1] *Baranskiy (1950), pp. 127-8*

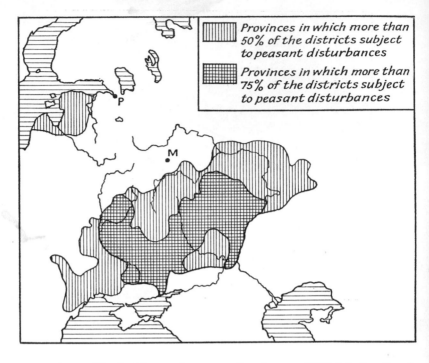

figure 73 Incidence of peasant disturbances, 1905-6 (after Lyash-chenko).

in the fields. This made me open my eyes with astonishment, because the introduction of artificial grasses into the traditional rotation of crops indicates the transition to a higher and more intensive system of agriculture. . . . I had never seen clover in Russia except on the estates of very advanced proprietors.[1]

The South-West: the Ukraine. In the westernmost governments a Polish minority owned much of the land: in Kiev province, Poles formed under 2 per cent of the population but owned 41 per cent of the land, while in Podolia they made up 2·3 per cent of the population and owned 53 per cent of the land. The landlords concentrated on growing sugar-beet, especially in Kiev province, and on producing grain for the distillery. Sheep became more numerous eastwards, especially in Poltava province whence wool was sent to the central industrial region. The growing network of railways, though designed mainly to serve mining and manufacturing, aided the prosperity of commercial agriculture. The landscape differed in many ways from that of Central Russia: in the largeness of the estates, where the plough was drawn by oxen; in the new steam mills that were appearing here and there; in the irregularly built villages with whitewashed cottages

[1] *Wallace (1905), vol. 2, pp. 202-3*

set in shaded fenced gardens; and in the more colourful garb of the peasants.[1]

The Caucasus. The northern area, or Kuban, was now the most prosperous wheat-growing region in the Empire, and its chief market for agricultural machinery. The farmers were Cossacks, Germans and efficient kulaks whose yields were normally high. This wheat specialization developed rapidly after the building across the region of the Rostov-Baku railway in 1876. In the mountains, transhumant livestock rearing was the chief occupation, but in Transcaucasia, a rich and varied agriculture and horticulture produced grain, fruit (including citrus), tobacco, rice, cotton and a little tea. The drier areas, notably the steppes of Azerbaydzhan, held large herds of sheep and cattle maintained on a nomadic or semi-nomadic basis.[2]

Crimea. The peninsula was a microcosm of the Caucasus region, with large-scale wheat on the steppes of the north, livestock rearing in the mountains, and orchards and vineyards in the valleys and along the south coast. According to an American journalist:

> *The Crimea is the hothouse, the conservatory of the empire, and supplies early vegetables to the tables of the rich residents of St Petersburg and Moscow, as the truck farms of Florida provide for those of our northern cities.*[3]

Central Asia and Kazakhstan. In Central Asia, agriculture and horticulture depended on irrigation, and by 1910 nearly 5 million desyatins, 2·6 per cent of the total area, were irrigated. Efficiency was hampered by the smallness of the peasant holdings, while the progress of Russian colonists growing American cotton was inhibited by difficulty in getting labour. Fruit and raw silk were important as well as cotton, especially after the opening in 1900 of the Orenburg-Tashkent railway. In Kazakhstan the traditional nomadic life of the Kazakhs had been disrupted. The northern steppes were now in the hands of Russian settlers growing wheat and barley and keeping sheep, and no longer served as summer pastures for the natives. Consequently the numbers of their livestock fell and the impoverished Kazakhs had retreated towards the desert.[4]

Siberia. As a result of the massive immigration of Russian peasants and the building of the Trans-Siberian railway, western Siberia was now sending vast quantities of food westwards to Russia and Europe. These consisted principally of a surplus of 80 million puds of grain (out of a total production of 235 million puds), 6 million puds of meat and 4½ million puds of butter. The production of the latter was the most valuable and had undergone a remarkable increase since the coming of the railway, as these figures show:

[1] *Hoetzsch (1913), p. 401; Schlesinger (1908), pp. 127-8*

[2] *Baranskiy (1950), p. 206; Lyashchenko (1956), vol. 2, p. 554*

[3] *Curtis (1911), p. 270*

[4] *Lyashchenko (1956), vol. 2, pp. 536-44; Baranskiy (1950), pp. 396-7*

	puds
1894	*400*
1898	*149,000*
1900	*1,050,000*
1906	*2,970,000*
1912	*4,459,000*

Every day a refrigerated butter-car train left Novo-Nikolayevsk (now Novosibirsk) for the Baltic. Siberia contained a high proportion of prosperous kulak peasant farmers who had combined in many instances to form butter-producing cooperatives. 1,318 of the 3,102 creameries in Siberia in 1911 were cooperatives.[1]

Siberian peasants, on an average, had many more livestock than those in Russia and their land holdings were much larger.[2] They did not use fertilizers or rotations, but sowed grain year after year until the land was exhausted, then left it fallow for ten years or more, while they tapped the wealth of freshly ploughed virgin land. The chief problem of the Siberian kulak was not land but labour; hence he was a relatively large user of machinery.

The Far East. The railway also brought about an increase of farming in the Amur and Ussuri basins. In the latter Nansen saw '*wide plains of arable land along the railway between the two mountain chains*'. In the central Amur plain it was

> *remarkable what the drainage for the railway has done here in a short time. Great stretches of what was formerly a complete swamp have now become good arable land, some of which is already in use, and this change has taken place since the winter of 1911-12.*[3]

The Forests

The assault on the forests continued unabated owing to the ever-increasing demand for firewood and timber. An estimate of 137 million desyatins of forest cover in Russia in 1875 had shrunk to one of 105 million in 1909. But the Empire as a whole still contained 347 million desyatins, mostly in Siberia.[4] Wood was still used for many domestic purposes, such as wooden pails, while tree bark was made into footwear and used for roofing.

The number of fur-bearing animals and, with it, the value of the fur trade continued to decline. Only 8,000 sables were reported killed in 1910 —compared with 160,000 ermine and 5 million squirrel—and their further hunting had been prohibited.[5]

[1] *Nansen (1914), pp. 293, 299; Lonsdale (1963), p. 491; Lyashchenko (1956), vol. 2, p. 525*

[2] *Treadgold (1957), pp. 206-15*

[3] *Nansen (1914), pp. 342, 384*

[4] *Kennard (1913), p. 104; French (1963), pp. 50-1*

[5] *Kennard (1913), p. 143*

Fisheries

The value of fish caught in and around Russia was now many times that of the fur trade. The principal fisheries were as follows:

Region	Weight of catch (millions of puds)	Value (millions of roubles)	Number employed
Caspian Sea	23·12	66·37	172,000
Black Sea	4·18	6·26	35,000
Baltic Sea	2·70	5·39	21,000
Far East	4·50	4·20	18,000
Central Asia	2·50	4·00	17,000
Northern Lakes	1·81	2·93	11,000
Upper Volga	2·92	2·28	10,000
White Sea-Murmansk	0·90	2·00	14,000

The above table shows the overwhelming importance of the Caspian sturgeon fishery. Millions of these fish were caught each year, largely to feed the caviar and isinglass industries.[1] About 200 whales a year were caught off the Murman coast.

Mining and Metallurgy (fig. 74)

Mineral production in 1913 was as follows:

	million tons		tons
Coal	30·4	Manganese (1910)	720,000
Petroleum	9·0	Copper	33,000
Iron ore	9·6		puds
Pig iron	4·5	Gold	3,886
Steel	4·6	Silver	906
Salt	2·0	Platinum	335

Coal. Russia now stood fifth in world production after U.S.A. (571 million tons), United Kingdom (290 million tons), Germany (190 million tons), and France (41 million tons), and in recent years her production had soared: it had quadrupled in twenty years. Nevertheless, a quarter of total consumption was imported because foreign coal could compete successfully at Petersburg with the home product. Two-thirds of the Russian output came from the Donets basin as may be seen from the regional figures for 1910 given below:

[1] *Kennard (1913), pp. 151-2*

	Output (*million puds*)	Labour force
Donets	1,019	133,402
Poland	341	25,109
East Siberia	67	4,038
Urals	43	6,517
Kuznets	32	1,726
Moscow	14	2,402
others	28	
	1,544	

The large number of workers in the Donets basin reflects in part the difficulty of working the thin and broken seams and in part the number of small peasant kustar and artel workings.[1]

Russian coal was consumed in the following ways (1910):

	per cent
Railways	27·8
Metallurgy	21·0
Manufacturing	10·5
Sugar refining	6·8
Steam vessels	5·5
Salt works	0·8
Gas works	0·7
other uses	26·9

Petroleum. Oil production had reached a peak in 1901 (706 million puds) but had since declined, partly through labour troubles and partly through loss of markets, to 588 million puds in 1910 and to 561 million puds in 1913.[2] The Russian Empire had been overtaken by U.S.A. and now stood second in world output. Through superior salesmanship and the paralysis of the Russian industry during the troubles of 1905-6, the Standard Oil Company of America had captured the western markets, and those of the East had been lost to Dutch East Indies and Burmah oil. In 1914 production was distributed regionally as follows:

	million puds
Baku	425
Grosny	75
Surukhany	20
Cheleken Island	10
Maykop	7
others	13
	550

[1] *Lyashchenko (1956), vol. 2, pp. 400, 413; Kennard (1913), pp. 189-93*

[2] *Lyashchenko (1956), vol. 2, p. 401*

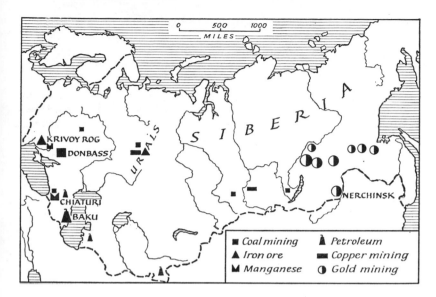

figure 74   The Russian Empire, 1914: mining.

The Baku field was a curious blend of ancient and modern methods. While a pipeline carried 10 per cent of the annual production to the Black Sea coast at Batumi, one could also see 'camels loaded with cans of refined petroleum plodding through the sands'.[1]

The oil industry was in a chaotic condition. There had been an uncontrolled 'oil rush' in the late 1870s and there were now 100 companies on the Baku field with 736 wells within ten miles of the city. The refineries were situated in a suburb known as Chernygorod or Black Town, and the most advanced were those owned by the Nobel company.[2] Labour unrest was rife and there was also constant trouble between the Persians and Armenians who together constituted the labour force.

Iron Ore. The Urals had ceased to be the main source and in 1913 their production of 105 million puds was well below a quarter of the total. The western Ukraine, principally the mines at Krivoy Rog, now dominated output with 420 million puds or 75 per cent of the total for the Empire. Working on a large scale had begun here in 1885.

Pig Iron. Of the 1913 production of 283 million puds, 67 per cent came from the Ukraine (Lugansk, Kharkov, etc.), 20 per cent from the Urals (as against 83 per cent in 1861), and 10 per cent from Poland. The Ukrainian industry had begun with the opening in 1884 of a railway linking the Krivoy Rog ironfield and the Donets coalfield; its rise during the subsequent thirty years had been remarkable. An average annual production of

[1] *Curtis (1911), p. 217*
[2] *Curtis (1911), pp. 225-7*

K*

672,000 puds in 1874-8 had become 89,000,000 puds in 1899-1901, and 190,000,000 by 1913[1]. This rapid expansion was associated with the demand created by railway building, and was dominated by nine large modern works which together produced $2\frac{1}{2}$ million tons or nearly 80 per cent of Ukrainian production.

The Urals area was handicapped by the absence of coking coal, the growing of wood for charcoal making, the difficulty of attracting labour to an inhospitable region, and the obsolete equipment. But for the artificial maintenance of high prices in a protected market, the Urals industry would have registered a sharp decline instead of a gradual increase in total production. A fourth metallurgical area, after the Ukraine, Urals and Poland, was St Petersburg where imported British or German coal was used with Swedish ore.[2]

Steel. Russia ranked fifth, after U.S.A., Germany, U.K. and France. In 1911, when production was 4 million tons, the principal regions were:[3]

	tons
Ukraine	*2,096,000*
Urals	*771,000*
Poland	*448,000*
Baltic	*217,000*
Moscow	*179,000*

Steel in the Moscow area was made from iron and coke brought from the Ukraine. Metallurgical skills had long been established here and the Moscow industry owed its existence to this factor in the absence of local raw materials. The total quantity of iron and steel goods made in Russia from her iron and steel production in 1913 was 247 million puds (4 million tons), with 57 per cent coming from the Ukraine and 17 per cent from the Urals.[4]

Manganese. The Russian steel industry was aided by the possession of two large and accessible deposits of high-grade manganese ore which enabled the Empire to claim half the total world production. Nearly 70 per cent came from Chiaturi in Georgia, the rest from Nikopol on the Dnieper.[5]

Manufacturing Industry

An index to the growth of all industry during the years immediately preceding 1914 is given by the following figures for the value of industrial production (millions of roubles):

[1] *Semenov (1899-1913), p. 377; Lyashchenko (1956), vol. 2, pp. 400, 412*

[2] *Lyashchenko (1956), vol. 2, pp. 400, 412*

[3] *Kennard (1913), p. 201*

[4] *Lyashchenko (1956), vol. 2, pp. 400, 413*

[5] *Lyashchenko (1956), vol. 2, p. 559*

1896   2,645
1899   3,503
1904   4,917
1909   4,982
1913   6,882

They show a marked plateau in the period 1904-9 separating steep rises before and after.[1] Although an industrial revolution had taken place during the thirty years before 1913, Russia still stood well behind the advanced nations of the western world, and in many ways her industrialization had developed on different lines. It was dominated by foreign capital and much of its direction and management lay in foreign hands. Large enterprises played a bigger part than in any European country, and syndicates, cartels, trusts and monopolies were more widespread and powerful.[2] These throve more on government orders than on satisfying the ordinary consumer, and this gave a one-sided development to industry which has persisted in the Soviet period. The fantastic contrasts between the new and the western on the one hand, and the traditional and the Russian on the other, were found in this as in other aspects of the Russian economy and society. Old peasant *kustar* industries survived alongside the great capitalist concerns, and a large proportion of industry, including factory industry, shunned the towns. Factory workers were housed in large barracks attached to the works, or even in the factory itself, and often lived in the most appallingly disgusting conditions.[3]

Lyashchenko gives the following tables showing the source of foreign capital in Russian industry in 1916 and the type of activity in which it was most important:[4]

Nationality	Millions of roubles	Percentage
French	731·7	32·6
British	507·5	22·6
German	441·6	19·7
Belgian	321·6	14·3
American	117·8	5·2
others	122·8	5·6
	2,243·0	100·0

[1] *Lyashchenko (1956), vol. 2, pp. 412-13*
[2] *Alexinsky (1913), p. 115; Lyashchenko (1956), vol. 2, pp. 324-5*
[3] *Troyat (1961), pp. 90-4; Robinson (1932), p. 109; Wallace (1905), vol. 1, p. 138*
[4] *Lyashchenko (1956), vol. 2, p. 380*

Industry	Total capital	Foreign capital	Percentage
	(*Millions of roubles*)		
Mining	917·8	834·3	91
Metallurgy	937·8	392·7	42
Textiles	685·4	192·5	28
Chemicals	166·9	83·6	50
Woodworking	68·8	25·7	37

According to the *Russian Year Book* for 1913, 196 foreign companies operated in Russia with a capital of over 410 million roubles in 1911, a relatively small proportion of the total foreign capital invested in Russia. A statistical summary is given below:

Industry	Nationality of Company			
	Belgian	French	British	German
Mining	18	21	22	6
Public utilities	22	5	1	5
Engineering	6	3	3	2
Metallurgy	7	1	1	2
Chemicals	1	3	2	5
Textiles	4	6	0	0
Ceramics and glass	7	2	0	0
Commercial	1	2	3	2
Building, public works	1	4	1	1
others	3	2	1	0
	70	49	34	23

In addition there were 6 Swiss, 3 Dutch, 3 Austrian, 3 Swedish, 3 American, 1 Italian and 1 Turkish company. Two of the Swedish companies ran the telephone systems of Moscow and Warsaw, and one of the American companies sold and repaired automobiles and ran taxi services in the towns. Belgian companies ran almost all the urban tramways. If these foreign companies are classified on the basis of capital employed in Russia, the following table results:

Industry	Capital (*millions of roubles*)			
	French	Belgian	British	German
Mining	83·5	44·7	90·7	15·3
Metallurgy	2·0	4·8	0·2	2·0
Engineering	12·4	14·6	1·3	1·0
Ceramics and glass	2·0	6·9	—	—
Chemicals	3·3	0·8	0·2	3·3
Textiles	18·6	6·4	—	—
Public utilities	11·0	32·6	0·2	2·9
others	9·1	4·3	4·7	0·6
	141·9	115·1	97·3	25·1

Also: U.S.A. 15·7 (engineering), Swiss 6·7 (chiefly textiles), Dutch 2·4, Swedish 6·5 (telephones), Austria 0·6, Turkish 1·0, Italian 1·1.

The shortage of industrial labour caused by the Emancipation of 1861 was short-lived. As peasant poverty and population increased, so did the numbers seeking work. Without this process, the industrial revolution could not have happened. At first, when the commune was still strong, the new factory workers retained a share in village life and returned periodically to the village where their families remained. But, as time went on, the rural connection lessened, the visits ceased, wives and children were brought to the factory, and the ranks of the landless proletariat were further swollen.[1] The Stolypin legislation of 1906-11, by dissolving the communal ties, hastened this process. Nevertheless, by 1914 there may still have been as many as 5 million urban workers whose homes were in the village. And 30 per cent of the larger factories and works and 70 per cent of all factory workers, according to Alexinsky, were permanently outside the towns: '*Russian capitalism goes from the town to the country, and there builds its palatial factories beside the humble* izba *of the* mujik'.[2]

Also mainly—but not wholly—outside the towns were the numerous *kustar* craftsmen and *artel* artisans who, because of the lopsided nature of Russian factory industry, with its bias towards producer's goods and State requirements, were enabled to survive, whether they worked independently and sold in the village and town markets, or whether they dealt with a wholesaler. A wide range of goods made from locally procurable raw materials was turned out by these craftsmen: felt boots, linen clothing, silks, lace, sheepskin coats, leather goods, pottery, wooden pails and spoons, brooms and shovels, toys, stoves, samovars, nails, knives, forks, harmonicas, ikons, jewellery, silver ornaments, etc.[3] Such domestic crafts were concentrated in the central industrial region round Moscow. But in the 'colonial' areas of the Empire, the Russian factory product was more effective in killing the local handicraft industries.[4]

Owing to the great growth of the cotton manufacturing industry, textiles now took the leading place among Russian industries, with about one-third of the total value of production, as may be seen from the table below:[5]

Industry	Value of Production (*millions of roubles*)	per cent
Textiles	818	32
Food processing	722	28
Mining, metallurgy and metal working	614	23
Livestock-products processing	117	4

[1] *Rashin* (*1958*), *p. 8; Robinson* (*1932*), *pp. 108-9*
[2] *Alexinsky* (*1913*), *p. 133*
[3] *Robinson* (*1932*), *p. 104; Troyat* (*1961*), *pp. 205-6; Schlesinger* (*1908*), *pp. 60-4*
[4] *Baranskiy* (*1950*), *p. 336*
[5] *Krassnow* (*1907*), *p. 233*

	Value of Production	
Industry	(*millions of roubles*)	per cent
Timber working	91	3
Leather working	57	2
others	226	8

The ancient livestock-products industry, with its emphasis on tallow, soap, grease and candles, had not only lost its pristine dominance but suffered an absolute decline. Leather working also, largely a peasant *kustar* occupation, had made little progress.

The Russian cotton textile industry was now fourth in world order. Situated mainly in the densely populated central industrial area it enjoyed the advantages of cheap, abundant and skilled labour and a large home market. It was wholly a modern factory industry protected by high tariffs. Between 1900 and 1913, the number of spindles increased from below 7,000 to over 9,000 and the amount of cotton consumed, from 16 million to 26 million puds. The linen industry also recorded growth, and the amount of flax processed increased from just over 3 million puds in 1900 to nearly 5 million in 1913.[1]

Sugar refining underwent continued rapid expansion among the food processing industries, and the production of sugar in 1913 was 108 million puds compared with 1·5 million in 1861 and 49 million in 1900.

The Geographical Distribution of Industry. There were, by the end of the nineteenth century, six regions which could be said to be, to a degree, industrialized, and these areas produced, in 1908, 82·5 per cent of Russia's total industrial output (including minerals) by value (fig. 75). They also contained 85·6 per cent of the country's industrial labour force.[2] They are listed below and illustrated diagrammatically (fig. 76).

	per cent	per cent
1 Central Industrial Provinces	27·2	
a Moscow province		13·0
2 Ukrainian Provinces	18·3	
a Mining and metallurgical provinces		10·5
b South-western sugar-beet provinces		7·2
3 The Baltic Provinces	15·3	
a St Petersburg province		9·8
4 Poland	11·4	
5 Trans-Caucasian Provinces	5·2	
a Baku province		4·8
6 Urals	5·1	

The Central Industrial Region was mainly concerned with textiles although chemicals and metal working were significant. For Moscow province alone, industrial production in 1908 subdivided thus:

[1] *Lyashchenko (1956), vol. 2, pp. 401-2*
[2] *Lyashchenko (1956), vol. 2, p. 429*

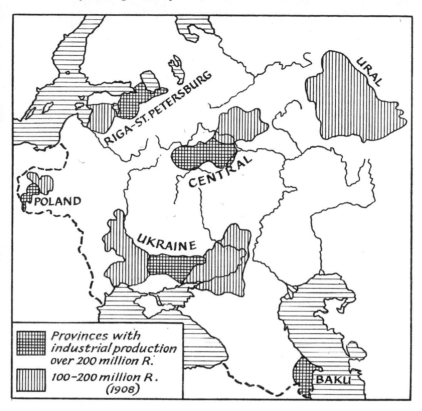

figure 75   Russia in 1914: industrial regions.

	per cent	per cent
Textiles	*61*	
of which cottons		*44*
woollens		*12*
silks		*5*
Metal Working	*10*	
Chemicals	*10*	
Food processing	*10*	
others	*9*	

The leading position of the cotton industry is apparent. The linen industry, although insignificant in Moscow province, was very important elsewhere in the central industrial region, notably in the 'governments' of Kostroma, Vladimir and Yaroslavl.[1] The metal working was chiefly on the eastern margins of the region and a large-scale works at Sormovo near Nizhniy Novgorod manufactured locomotives, rolling stock, traction engines and steam rollers.

[1] *Kennard (1913), p. 133*

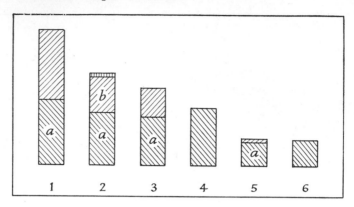

figure 76   Industrial regions: relative industrial output by value,
1908.

The concentration of railways on Moscow had greatly enhanced the position of the central region, enabling it to employ its large reserves of skilled labour on raw materials brought from farther afield than previously, such as cotton, silk, coal, iron and salt.

At St Petersburg, metal working, engineering and cotton textiles were important. Just as Moscow relied increasingly on rail-brought raw materials, so St Petersburg used materials brought by sea. Here, more than elsewhere, industry was urban, and almost wholly located in and about the capital. Even faster than the industrial growth of St Petersburg had been that of Riga, where similar industries based on imported raw materials had developed. Among its products were steam engines, agricultural machinery, wire and gramophones.

The two industrial areas of the Ukraine were the mining and metallurgical Krivoy Rog–Donets area, and the sugar-refining area of which Kiev was the centre. There were metallurgical works at Lugansk, Yuzovo and Druzhkov, and engineering works at Odessa, Kherson, Alexandrovsk and Nikolayev.

The Urals and the Caucasus regions were concerned mainly with the extraction and treatment of minerals: iron ore, copper, platinum, petroleum and manganese.

Trade and Transport

Subject to the qualification '*that Russian trade statistics can only be taken as affording useful indications as to general tendencies*',[1] the following conclusions may be drawn. Firstly, foreign trade doubled in value during the first years of the twentieth century, but imports were rising faster than exports:

[1] *Miller (1926), p. 45*

	Total trade (*million roubles*)	Exports *per cent*	Imports *per cent*
1901-5	*1,573*	*60*	*40*
1906-10	*2,113*	*57*	*43*
1911-13	*2,779*	*55*	*45*
1913	*2,895*	*52*	*48*

Germany had displaced Britain as Russia's main trading partner. She took in 1913 a third of Russia's exports as against a fifth by Britain, and she sent almost a half of Russia's imports whereas Britain now supplied only 12 per cent. This change is connected with another—the fall in the proportion of overseas trade to about 65 per cent and a corresponding increase in the proportion of trade across land frontiers. The railway was a main cause of this shift. But in absolute terms overseas trade was very much greater than in 1861 and continuing to expand.

The general nature of the trade, according to commodities is summarized below. The corresponding percentages for 1802 are added in brackets for comparison:

Russian Trade by Commodity Groups, 1911 (percentages)

	Imports	Exports
Raw materials	35% *(18%)* (*cotton, wool, silk, hides and skins, rubber, tallow*)	22% *(57%)* (*timber, flax, hides and skins, linseed, hemp*)
Metals and minerals	7% *(20%)* (*coal, tin, lead, copper, zinc*)	4% *(8%)* (*petroleum, platinum, manganese*)
Food and drink	12% *(28%)* (*tea, fish, wines and spirits*)	65% *(20%)* (*cereals, eggs, butter, sugar, peas, beans, potatoes*)
Manufactures	34% *(31%)* (*machinery, textiles, paper, chemicals*)	2% *(12%)*
Others	12% *(3%)*	7% *(3%)*

The importance of raw materials among the imports is testimony to the degree of industrial progress within Russia, but the insignificance of manufactured goods among the exports shows how far Russian manufactures were confined to the highly protected home market.

There follows a list of the twelve leading imported commodities by value (millions of roubles), along with a similar list for 1802:

1911		1802	
Machinery and parts	133·6	Woollens	5·8
Raw cotton	105·9	Refined sugar	4·8
Hides and skins	47·5	Silver	3·4
Wool	43·1	Cottons	3·3
Coal and coke	39·0	Dyestuffs	2·5
Fish	30·0	Wine	2·4
Tea	29·3	Salt	1·3
Raw rubber	27·8	Coffee	1·0
Woollen yarn	25·3	Fruit	1·0
Raw silk	24·8	Gold	0·8
Paper	24·4	Live animals	0·7
Chemicals	20·4	Fish	0·6

These figures show that Russia had developed her textile, leather and rubber industries to such an extent that she now imported the raw materials for them rather than the finished products, but that she remained heavily dependent upon the foreigner for machinery of all kinds and especially agricultural machinery.

Exports continued to consist mainly of primary commodities, but their nature had changed greatly during the past century, as a comparison of the leading export commodities for 1911 and 1802 shows (millions of roubles):

1911		1802	
Wheat	258·7*	Tallow	9·7
Barley	214·4	Raw hemp	9·3
Timber	141·6	Raw flax	5·8
Eggs	80·7	Rye	5·6
Oats	73·2	Iron	4·6
Butter	70·9	Wheat	4·1
Raw flax	63·9	Leather and leather goods	3·1
Maize	57·5	Linseed and hempseed	2·5
Sugar	48·3†	Sailcloth and canvas	2·3
Rye	42·6	Hempseed and linseed oils	1·6
Hides and skins	35·5	Live animals	1·4
Petroleum	29·0	Timber	1·4

* much less than normal owing to bad harvest
† much more than normal owing to bad harvest in Europe

Foodstuffs now preponderate and, in a normal year, cereals alone made up half the value of all exports. This change resulted from two main causes: the growth of markets for foodstuffs in industrialized Europe, and the opening up of new Russian lands by the railway.

RAILWAYS

The building of railways lay behind almost every one of the great changes that had taken place in the Empire's economic geography since 1861. By

1912 there were over 46,000 miles of railway built upon a broad gauge of 1·524 metres. Although unfavourable comparisons are often made with the degree of progress in western countries, this was a great achievement in view of the late start and the extreme poverty and backwardness of the country as a whole. The geographical factor was generally favourable, the uniformity of relief presenting few problems. Badly drained land and the necessity for bridging innumerable streams gave most difficulty. Most bridges were wooden and had to be crossed at slow speed. Farther afield, lack of water in Central Asia, and the mountains of eastern Siberia and the Far East, were formidable obstacles.[1]

There had been two periods of maximum growth: 1866-76 and 1891-1901. Up to about 1870, most lines were built to bring the foodstuffs and raw materials of the agricultural areas to Moscow and the Central Industrial Region, a stage largely complete by 1876. The 1870s were principally devoted to linking these same agricultural areas to the seaports, while the 1880s witnessed the construction of important connecting lines.[2] During the 1890s and after, railways were continued out to frontier regions, partly for military reasons; many branch lines were built; and the Ukrainian network was filled to a density more comparable with that achieved in advanced western countries. The table below shows how the extent and the regional emphasis of railway building changed in successive five-year periods (bold type indicates over 2,000 km added during the period; roman type, 2,000-1,000 km; italics, 1,000-500 km).[3]

1864-8	3,265 km	Centre, *Ukraine, West—North-West*
1869-73	9,419 km	**Centre, Ukraine,** West—North-West, *Lower Volga, Caucasus*
1874-8	6,156 km	Ukraine, Lower Volga, *Centre, Caucasus Urals*
1879-83	1,774 km	*Caucasus*
1884-8	5,283 km	*Central Asia, Ukraine, West—North-West*
1889-93	3,442 km	*Ukraine, Lower Volga*
1894-8	11,533 km	**Lower Volga, Centre,** West Siberia, Ukraine, *Urals, East Siberia, Caucasus, North and Upper Volga, West—North-Wes*
1899-03	13,739 km	**West Siberia, Centre,** Ukraine, Caucasus, West—North-West, Central Asia, *North and Upper Volga, Lower Volga*
1904-8	7,922 km	Kazakhstan, West—North-West, *Ukraine, North and Upper Volga, Centre, Lower Volga*
1909-13	4,174 km	Ural, *Centre, Ukraine, Caucasus*

[1] *Buslepp (1926), p. 12*
[2] *Lyashchenko (1956), vol. 2, pp. 118-21*
[3] *Ames (1947), p. 60*

The Trans-Siberian was built in 1891-1901 to further the colonization of Siberia and to bring Russian power to bear in the Far East. The line was originally brought to Vladivostok across Manchuria, but with the loss of control of that province after the 1904-5 war, a longer but all-Russian route was built along the Amur and Ussuri valleys. The Amur stretch was still under construction in 1914, but other sections of the Trans-Siberian were already being double-tracked.[1]

Grain formed the preponderant rail freight, especially in Russia proper, but cotton was of increasing importance in Central Asia, as were butter and eggs in Siberia. Coal, iron and manganese dominated the traffic of some lines in the Ukraine as did manganese and petroleum in the Caucasus. Timber continued to move mostly by water. In 1911 the railways carried 208 million tons of freight. Thus waterways, which carried about 30 million tons at the turn of the century, had been displaced as Russia's main means of transport. Waterway freight consisted primarily of timber (52 per cent), grain (14 per cent), petroleum (11 per cent) and salt (2·5 per cent), and about half the total traffic was carried on the Volga, where the upstream movement was greater than the downstream.[2]

Population

Between 1861 and 1914 the population of the Empire rose from 73 million to 170 million. The following table shows the distribution among various parts of the Empire in 1910, at the census of 1897, and at the tenth revision of 1857 (in millions):

	Russia	*Poland*	*Siberia*	*Caucasus*	*Central Asia*	*Total*
1857	*59·3*	*4·8*	*4·3*	*4·3*	—	*72·7*
1897	*94·2*	*9·4*	*5·7*	*9·2*	*5·7*	*124·2*
1910	*118·7*	*12·1*	*8·2*	*11·7*	*10·0*	*160·8*

Population was rising at the impressive rate of 3¼ million a year for, although the death rate was high (31 per thousand, or twice as high as in Britain), the birth rate was much higher (47 per thousand).

A comparison of figs. 77 and 66 shows that, while an axis running across Russia from south-west to north-east remained the most densely populated zone, it was now the south-western end of this axis, rather than its north-eastern part, that had the densest population. The western Ukrainian 'governments' of Podolia, Kiev and Poltava now held the greatest concentration of rural population. When rate of increase is considered (fig. 78), it is clear that the central areas have had the smallest and peripheral areas the greatest. It is particularly noteworthy how almost all the western provinces, Baltic, Lithuanian, White Russian, Ukrainian and Bessarabian,

[1] *Nansen (1914), pp. 280, 387*
[2] *Gille (1949), p. 174*

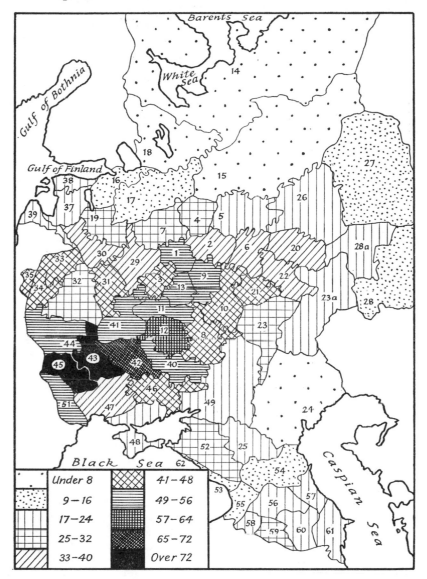

figure 77 Density of rural population in 1910 (persons per sq. km). For key to provinces, see p. 395.

have shared in this high proportional increase. Throughout this border zone agriculture had improved sufficiently to sustain this rise.

Since 1861 Russian settlers had crossed the middle and lower Volga in great numbers, and a prosperous kulak agriculture had been established there, yielding large harvests of grain, except when afflicted by drought.

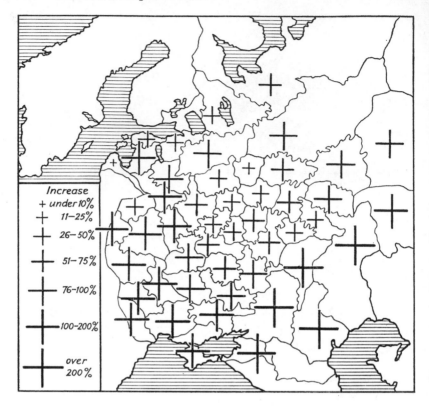

Increase
+ under 10%
+ 11–25%
+ 26–50%
+ 51–75%
+ 76–100%
+ 100–200%
+ over 200%

figure 78   Percentage increase in rural population, 1857–1910.

Railways now crossed this region from Ufa and Orenburg to Samara, and from Uralsk to Saratov. The flood of Russian settlers continued eastwards into Bashkiria and resulted in the further dispossession of the native people.

The higher rates of increase in the peripheral areas of Russia should not obscure the fact that substantial absolute increases had taken place in the already overcrowded and poverty-stricken central areas, especially in the Central Black-Earth region (fig. 79). All the regions shown in the diagram are approximately equal in area, except Siberia. Yet the increase in rural population of the Central Black-Earth region is exceeded substantially only by the Ukraine, it is almost as large as that which took place on the fertile steppes of New Russia, and it is greater than that for the whole of Siberia.

Mobility was a striking feature of the Russian population. Apart from those permanently leaving in search of new lands, there were the peasants who migrated to the towns for winter work, and those who invaded the areas of prosperous landlord and kulak farms in the Ukraine and the Volga region for summer work. It has been estimated that 6 million peasants migrated annually, including $1\frac{1}{4}$ million men and boys from the Black-

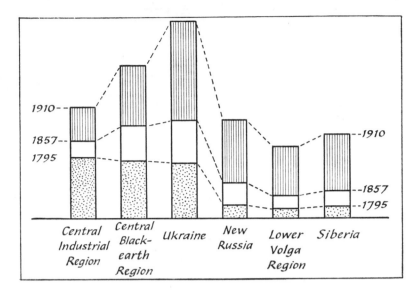

figure 79   Population: regional increases, 1795-1857, and 1857-1910.

Earth Centre.[1] There were, besides, countless exiles, pilgrims, itinerant pedlars and 'holy men'.

The official figures for emigration to the Asiatic provinces of the Empire are shown in fig. 80 along with emigration to the U.S.A. But while the latter was mostly of Jews from the towns of western Russia, that to Siberia was mainly of Russian and Ukrainian peasants. Cossacks had been the chief element earlier, and political exiles and convicts were continually arriving. The two main factors in the sharp increase of eastward movement after 1906 were the Trans-Siberian railway and the 1906 Edict relaxing restrictions on colonization. But many settlers returned to Russia in proportions varying from 5 per cent to 36 per cent of the annual total emigrating.

The main exodus was to western Siberia, and in 1910 over 60 per cent of the total population of Siberia was in the provinces of Tomsk and Tobolsk. But an increasing number were finding their way farther east into Transbaykalia (population in 1911: 869,000), the Amur province (where population rose from 120,000 in 1897 to 286,000 in 1911) and to the Maritime province, whose 1911 population was 524,000. In these easterly regions a large minority was non-Russian: this did not consist of native tribesmen but of Koreans and Chinese whose cheap and efficient labour was sought after by mining companies, farmers, etc. In Transbaykalia and in the Maritime province the proportion of Russian inhabitants was below 70 per cent. (Fig. 81.)

[1] *Baranskiy (1950), p. 127; Troyat (1961), p. 207*

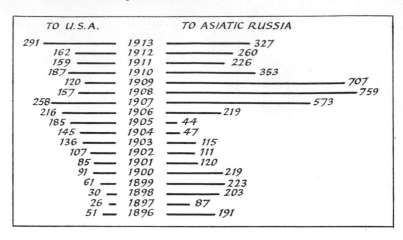

figure 80   Emigration from European Russia, 1896-1913 (the figures show the annual total in thousands).

The population of Central Asia had increased even faster than that of Siberia, but this was mainly due to the natural increase of the native inhabitants who still formed 90 per cent of the population:

	1897	1910
Siberia	5,699,000	8,220,100
Central Asia	5,721,700	9,973,340

The chief areas of Russian settlement were the Kazakh steppes (wheat), and the irrigated valleys of Ferghana and the Syr Darya (cotton).

The great Northland, with its vast expanses of tundra and tayga, remained an empty wilderness. The southern boundary of this area, as defined by Armstrong, follows the Arctic Circle in Russia, the 60th parallel in Siberia, and, in the Far East, a line trending southward to 55°N on the Pacific coast. Yet this enormous extent of land, comprising little less than half the territory of the Empire, supported a population which can have been little more than 150,000 and of whom about 40,000 or 50,000 were Russians.[1]

According to the 1897 census, two-thirds of the population of the Empire belonged to the three main divisions of the Russian people. The great majority of these lived in Russia proper, with 4 million members of the Baltic peoples (Lithuanian, Latvian and Estonian) to the north-west of them, 8 million Poles to the west, and 1 million Rumanians to the south-west, all within the bounds of the Empire. In the western and south-western towns were 5 million Jews; and 1¾ million Germans lived in the Baltic provinces, or along the Volga, or by the Azov Sea. Only 57 per cent

[1] *Armstrong (1965), pp. 44-94*

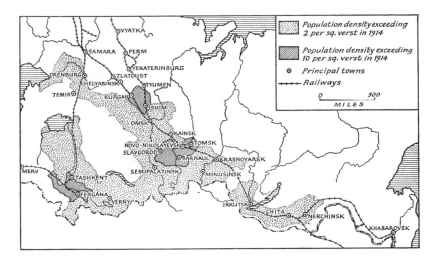

figure 81   The Russian Empire in 1914: population density in Siberia and Central Asia. Based, with permission, upon the map on pages 208-9 of D. W. Treadgold, The Great Siberian Migration, *published by Princeton University Press, copyright Princeton University Press.*

of these Germans practised agriculture. The rest worked in industry and various services, as did a much smaller number of English, French and Italians. Also in the southern provinces lived nearly 200,000 Greeks and slightly fewer Bulgarians, mostly farmers and fishermen.[1]

To the north and east of the main mass of Great Russians were 2½ million representatives of various Finnic peoples such as the Cheremisi, Chuvashi and Mordva of the Middle Volga, and the Bashkirs of the southern Urals. In the Caucasus region were 4½ million Georgians, Armenians, Azerbaydzhanians, and mountaineer Circassians. Scattered in a broad belt from the Crimea across southern Russia, up into the southern Urals, were nearly 4 million Tartars. In Siberia and Central Asia lived nearly 10 million Turkish peoples such as Kazakhs, Kirghiz, Turkmen and Uzbeks.

In 1914 there were about 10 million Russians and Ukrainians in Asiatic Russia. In Central Asia they were a minority, but in Siberia they formed the vast majority. Most of them were concentrated in a narrowing belt eastwards along the Trans-Siberian railway, but some of them—exiles, released or escaped convicts, miners, fur traders—lived amongst the native peoples of tayga and tundra. These included the Chukchi, Koryaks, Kamchadales and Ostyaks, none of which numbered more than a few thousand. More numerous were the 75,000 Tungusy, the 250,000 Turkic

[1] *Juraschek (1906), pp. 101-2; Ischanian (1913), pp. 74-5; Lyash-chenko (1956), vol. 2, pp. 530-1*

Yakuts, the 200,000 Tartars of western Siberia, and the 332,000 Mongol Buryats of eastern Siberia.

Despite army reform and the government's drive for the russification of subject nationalities, the Cossacks retained their privileged position. They continued to serve the Tsar as a special cavalry, providing their own horses and weapons in return for their land and an autonomous local administration. There were now eleven Cossack armies, their names an index to their progressive use as garrisons eastwards to the Pacific: Don, Kuban, Terek, Astrakhan, Ural, Orenburg, Siberia, Semirechye, Transbaykal, Amur and Ussuri.[1]

> *By a combination of generosity and compulsion the government had disciplined the whirlwind; these fighters on horseback who were once the terror of the landlords had now become the scourge of a discontented peasantry.*[2]

Rural Settlement

Stolypin's legislation (1906-11) was, in Riasanovsky's words *'the most important factor of all in the changing rural situation, because it tried to transform the Russian countryside'*.[3] But it is difficult to ascertain how far the reform, which was aimed at converting communally administered medieval strips into large enclosed 'freehold' farms, affected the pattern of rural settlement and altered the appearance of the landscape. When holdings were consolidated, the new farmer sometimes—but not always— left the village and built himself a new 'isolated' homestead or *khutor*. Although earlier authorities have mentioned 24 per cent of communal households withdrawing from the commune, Mosse has claimed recently that significant results from the reform were confined to peripheral areas, where the commune had never been well established, and that it made little impact in the central regions. There was certainly opposition from the women, who were unwilling to forego the social life of the village for the loneliness of the farmstead, and from moneylending merchants who thought the new farmers would be more difficult to exploit than the village peasants.[4]

The Towns

The urban population of Russia proper was over three times as large in 1914 (18·6 million) as in 1863 (6·1 million). It had grown faster than the rate of increase of the population as a whole, so that its share of the total

[1] *Troyat (1961), p. 124*
[2] *Robinson (1932), p. 92*
[3] *Riasanovsky (1963), p. 480*
[4] *Mosse (1965), pp. 267-73*

increased from under 10 per cent in 1863 to about 15 per cent in 1914. For the Empire (excluding Poland and Finland) the urban population had increased to 23·3 million or 13·8 per cent of the total.

There were in 1914 29 towns with a population of over 100,000 compared with 16 in 1897 and only 3 in 1863.[1] They were as follows:

Population of Leading Russian Towns in 1897 and 1914 (thousands)

	1897	1914
St Petersburg (Petrograd)	1,264·9	2,118·5
Moscow	1,038·6	1,762·7
Riga	282·2	558·0
Kiev	247·7	520·5
Odessa	403·8	499·5
Tashkent	156·0	
Tiflis	159·6	307·3
Kharkov	174·0	244·7
Saratov	137·1	235·7
Baku	111·9	232·2
Yekaterinoslav	112·8	211·1
Vilno	154·5	203·8
Kazan	130·0	194·2
Rostov-on-Don	119·5	172·3
Astrakhan	112·9	151·5
Ivanovo-Voznesensk	54·2	147·4
Samara	90·0	143·8
Tula	114·7	139·7
Omsk	37·3	134·8
Kishinev	108·5	128·2
Minsk	90·9	116·7
Tomsk	52·2	114·7
Nizhniy Novgorod	90·1	111·2
Yaroslavl	71·6	111·2
Vitebsk	65·9	108·2
Nikolayev	65·6	102·2
Yekaterinodar	65·6	102·2
Tsaritsyn	55·2	100·8
Orenburg	72·4	100·1

It is worth noting that the two major cities contained nearly 30 per cent of the urban population in 1914, compared with 20 per cent in 1897 and only 16 per cent in 1863. The railways had done much to concentrate population in the two capitals. (Fig. 82.)

Riga, after a period of fantastic growth, had displaced Odessa from the third position held by the Black Sea port in 1897. The meteoric rise of Odessa had continued throughout the nineteenth century (119,000 in 1863;

[1] *Rashin (1956), p. 93*

figure 82   Russia in 1914: the larger towns (data from Rashin).

404,000 in 1897), but its growth slackened in the twentieth. To some extent, the changed position of the two ports reflects a revival of the supremacy of Baltic trade relative to that of the Black Sea. It is, besides, a result of the greatly enlarged hinterland Riga had gained from her excellent rail communications which reached beyond the Volga, and of the industrialization of the town.

Kiev, as an administrative, commercial and industrial centre for that part of Russia with the fastest growing population, had also overtaken Odessa. Both *Tashkent* and *Tiflis* had been medium-sized towns before the Russian conquest and both had grown rapidly after becoming the military and administrative capitals for Central Asia and Caucasia respectively. Connected by rail with Russia, they became centres of greatly expanded agricultural, industrial and commercial activity. The mixed population of

Tiflis was made up of Russian soldiers and officials, German tradesmen, Persian shopkeepers, Armenian dealers, Tartar labourers and many others. *Baku* had more than doubled its population since 1897 as a result of oilfield development and the expanding commercial activity of its port and railways. These latter had enabled it to oust Astrakhan from the position of chief recipient of trans-Caspian trade. Curtis wrote (1911):

> *The quays along the seashore in front of the city for a mile or more are occupied by steamers and sailing vessels discharging and receiving cargoes, which lie in great stacks upon the wharves. Long processions of carts and wagons are constantly coming and going between the docks and the railway stations. Nearly all the commerce of Central Asia is handled there and it is brought or carried away by the two railways, one running to Batoum and the other to Odessa and Moscow.*[1]

The population consisted mainly of Persians, Armenians and Tartars.

6 of these 29 larger towns were on the Volga. Most of them had benefited from the agricultural expansion of the region and the coming of railways. They all collected grain from their hinterlands and sent it to Moscow, St Petersburg or Riga by rail or water. *Nizhniy Novgorod*, whose prosperity was based on river transport, had made the least progress. The railways had broken the hold it once held on trade in many goods, and the opening of the Suez canal, by lessening the volume of overland traffic, had likewise lessened the importance of its fair. The trade in tea and raw cotton, formerly very valuable here, had now vanished. The fast growth of *Kharkov* (52,000 in 1863) and *Yekaterinoslav* (20,000 in 1863) had resulted from the mining and industrial revolution that had taken place in the Ukraine and New Russia.

Over the period 1863-1914, the fastest-growing Russian towns were Tsaritsyn (12-fold increase), Yekaterinoslav (10·6-fold), Kiev (7·6-fold), Riga (7·2-fold) and Ufa (6·1-fold). The towns whose progress was slowest over the same period were Mogilev (1·1-fold), Berdichev (1·4-fold), Petrozavodsk (1·4-fold), Nikolayev, Taganrog, Novgorod and Kaluga (all 1·6-fold).[2]

By 1897, the leading *Siberian* towns were:

Tomsk	52,000	Tyumen	30,000
Irkutsk	51,000	Vladivostok	29,000
Omsk	37,000	Krasnoyarsk	27,000
Blagoveshchensk	33,000	Tobolsk	20,000

The first three had been in the same order back in the 1860s. Tobolsk had continued to stagnate. Blagoveschensk and Vladivostok owed their position to the settlement and development of the Amur valley and Maritime province. By 1914, four towns had raced ahead of the rest: Omsk (135,000 in 1914), Tomsk (115,000 in 1914), Novo-Nikolayevsk (85,000 in 1914)

[1] *Curtis (1911), p. 218*
[2] *Rashin (1956), pp. 89-91*

and Vladivostok (89,000 in 1910). The first three owed their growth to the flood of immigrants into west Siberia, and subsequent industrial and commercial development which followed the building of the railway, although *Tomsk* itself was not on the main line. As an established town, however, and as administrative capital of the most densely populated and fastest developing Siberian province, it had an initial advantage over the new and better placed railway town of *Novo-Nikolayevsk* on the Ob, which was destined, under the name of Novosibirsk, to become Siberia's leading city. It was already its fastest growing town.

Vladivostok, which had temporarily ceased to be Russia's primary Far Eastern port and naval base, grew very rapidly after the loss of its rival, Port Arthur, during the war with Japan. Its 1910 population of 89,000 consisted of 53,000 Russians, 29,000 Chinese, 3,200 Koreans and 2,300 Japanese.[1] Also growing fast was the railway and garrison town of *Khabarovsk* (1910: 52,000), well placed at the junction of the Amur and the Ussuri.

---

[1] *Nansen (1914), pp. 338-9*

CHAPTER EIGHTEEN
THE GREAT WAR (1914-18)
AND THE SOVIET PERIOD (1917-60)

After 1892 Germany realized that, having incurred Russian enmity, she would have to fight the next war on two fronts. With Napoleon's experience in mind it was decided that, as the war with Russia would necessarily be a long drawn-out affair, every effort should be made to strike a quick and decisive blow in the west; hence a swift drive through Belgium and southern France was planned. As it turned out, however, a decision was to be reached first on the eastern front where the plan had been defensive only. In retrospect it is clear that a knock-out blow could have been aimed at Russia, giving the Central Powers freedom to concentrate on the western front where maximum strength was needed.

The war began on the Russian front with a massive invasion of East Prussia which came disastrously to an end at Tannenberg (August 1914). The land was difficult, glaciated country with lakes, marshes and sandy ridges; the German commander and his men knew its geography perfectly; the Russians floundered in a frontier zone which had been deliberately left unreclaimed by the Prussians as a defensive measure.

Failure in East Prussia was more than balanced by driving the Germans out of Poland and the successful invasion of Austrian Galicia where the Slavonic population was not hostile to the Russian troops. Soon they were fighting their way through the Carpathians. In 1916 there were massive desertions of Slav troops, principally Czech, from the Austrian side. This was the sum of Russian success, however. Strategic and economic difficulties of supply, aggravated by corruption and incompetence in high places, began rapidly to undermine Russian fighting power.

Russia was the least developed industrially of the belligerents and therefore heavily dependent on imports for carrying on the war. But her geographical isolation made it impossible to keep up a sufficient flow of imports. The German navy was supreme in the Baltic, and the Turks held the Straits for the Central Powers, despite the offer of extravagant concessions by Russia. German cruisers entered the Black Sea and bombarded Odessa (October 1914). The British landings at Gallipoli were a desperate attempt to force this way open—an essential measure if Russia was to play an effective part in the war. With this route closed, Russia, dependent as she was on supplies from the West, had only the bravery of her poorly armed troops, almost wholly unsupported by artillery, to rely on. She could hope for nothing but to survive on the defensive until her allies won the war.

The only way Russia could be supplied was from the ice-impeded port of Archangel, or from Vladivostok by way of the single-track Trans-Siberian railway, a distance of thousands of miles. These alternatives were hopelessly insufficient and the building in 1916 of a railway from ice-free Murmansk to Petrograd (St Petersburg was thus renamed in 1914) came too late. Meanwhile the internal Russian railway system, at the best of times starved of capital and overstrained by the vast area it had to serve, broke down under the enormous demands made upon it by war. After Nicholas II made his ill-judged decision to go to the front as Commander in Chief, the Empress and the filthy hypnotic peasant Rasputin, under whose spell she moved, were left behind to wield the awesome powers of the Russian autocracy. Able men were dismissed to make way for favourites, sycophants and the merely corrupt. The rot spread downwards. The mining of coal, the smelting of iron, the production of munitions, and the manufacture of woollens all declined to levels well below those of peace-time. Not even supplies of food could be maintained: the peasants were in the army and transport was breaking down. Confusion spread from the civilian centres to the rear and from the rear to the battle front. The Germans allowed Lenin into this situation and a Bolshevik dictatorship was established under his brilliant leadership (November 1917), amid the chaos that followed the abdication of Nicholas II (March 1917).

The Treaty of Brest Litovsk, March 1918

Despite the misgivings of colleagues, Lenin sought peace at any price from the Germans. Promises of peace had helped to seat him in power, and he knew that Russia was in no state to fight on; he saw clearly that the Bolsheviks must have a breathing space in which to consolidate their position; he realized that if the Allies won the war, the peace imposed by Germany would cease to mean anything while, if they lost, Russia would probably have to accept even more disadvantageous terms than those accepted at Brest Litovsk in 1918 (March). Russia lost almost all the territory she had gained since the accession of Peter I and the Germans made a separate treaty with the Ukraine (fig. 83). But the real loss to Russia was that she forfeited the long-coveted control of the Straits and Constantinople which had been promised by her allies in a secret treaty (1915). The Germans also had offered her Constantinople if she made a separate peace with them (1915). As it was, Russia failed to get the prize and not even her victory in 1944-5 enabled her to achieve this particular ambition.

The Treaties of Versailles and Riga (1919-20)

As the military power of first Russia and then Germany collapsed, the various nations that lay between them declared their independence (1917-18). The Versailles treaties sanctioned the formation of newly independent states from the territory of the old Russian Empire: Finland, Lithuania, Latvia, Estonia and Poland. Of these, only Poland and Lithuania had been fully independent in the past. The Allies intended to surround Germany with states owing their existence to and dependent for their

figure 83   The western boundary of Russia, 1914-21.

survival upon the West, and also to insulate Russia from Germany, lest these two war-ruined giants should come together. Poland was not satisfied with the frontiers the Allies would have given her, but fought her own war with the Soviets: at the Treaty of Riga (1920) she succeeded in taking back much of the old Russian territory lost under Catherine II. This overgrasping policy was unwise because it ensured the future hostility of Russia as well as of Germany. Apart from the new states, the

L

Soviets had to deal with the assertion of local independence by many of the non-Great Russian nationalities who remained within Russia's boundaries: White Russians, Ukrainians, Armenians, Georgians, Azerbaydzhanis, Crimean Tartars, Bashkirs and Kirghiz all declared their independence (1917-19).

The Intervention and the Civil War (1918-20)

In 1918 the Allies landed troops on various Russian coasts to watch over the arms dumps that had been landed there and to bring comfort to anti-Bolshevik forces. The British seized Murmansk and Archangel, and also Batum, the oil port on the Black Sea. French troops were landed at Odessa and the Japanese occupied the Vladivostok area; American troops followed to keep an eye on the Japanese. At these and other peripheral points anti-Soviet or White armies were organized. These laboured under many handicaps: allied assistance was lukewarm; much of their strength came from local malcontents who were satisfied to keep the Bolsheviks from their own lands, but who were unwilling to leave their home districts to fight the centrally-placed Reds; they were situated in the outer corners of the country so that they could not join forces, but could be dealt with by the central Red Army one by one; they lacked unity of command and purpose, having nothing in common but hatred of the Bolsheviks: their motley forces included army officers, gentry, professional men, intellectuals, revolutionaries opposed to the Bolsheviks, students, peasants, and, most important militarily, Cossacks. On the whole, the peasant population detested both sides, for both armies raided, requisitioned and terrorized; generally, they were more hostile to the Whites who, if victorious might attempt to re-establish the old order and take back the land which had been seized from the gentry at the Revolution.

Lenin's Bolsheviks had many advantages. Above all they held the central area with its good communications and its great and populous towns: these included Petrograd, the former capital (renamed Leningrad in 1924), and Moscow which had become capital once more in March 1918 (fig. 84). Here were the main industries and quantities of stores intended for the German war. The large population of urban workers was permeated by revolutionary ideas: working in factories, they had not become sickened and tired by several years campaigning on the front. Many of them proved willing recruits of the Red Army which also contained a large proportion of seasoned troops who provided leadership, discipline and training. Added to these advantages were superb command, skilful propaganda and unity of purpose—a combination which the White armies could not match.

Yudenich threatened Petrograd from Estonia in 1919 but failed, as did a southward drive from Archangel. In the south, Denikin established his authority in the Donets region and in the Ukraine, before advancing on Moscow late in 1919 and reaching Orel, 200 miles away; but the Poles,

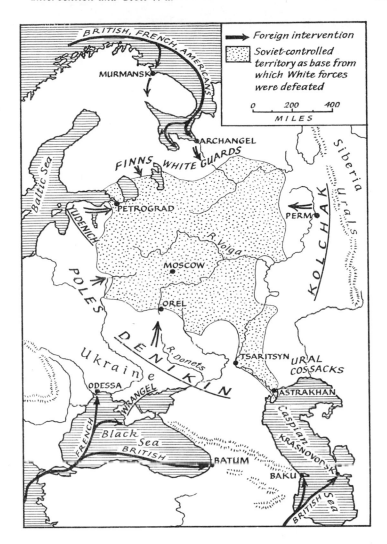

figure 84 Intervention and Civil War, 1918-20.

upon whose help he was relying, were not anxious to see this strong and
ambitious leader established as Russian ruler; he was abandoned not only
by them but by the Cossacks, who formed most of his army and who went
back to their homes in the south. Denikin collapsed early in 1920. The most
formidable threat of all came from Siberia, where the Whites were rein-
forced by Czech prisoners of war. Kolchak advanced from Omsk across the
Urals to the Volga, but he too was finally routed in 1920. There remained
Wrangel who held out in the Crimea till November 1920. The year 1920
was not only the end of the Civil War but of the foreign intervention,

except for the Japanese who were loath to abandon their foothold on the Soviet Pacific coast. But, under American pressure, they evacuated Vladivostok in 1922 and Russian Sakhalin in 1925.

The U.S.S.R.: 1923-41

The tsarist autocracy had suppressed nationalist aspirations in all parts of the Empire, but many of the leading Bolsheviks were not Great Russian: Trotsky was a Jew, Stalin a Georgian. This enabled them to frame their new state in such a way as to give scope to nationalist aspirations without detracting from the power of Communist dictatorship. In 1923 the Bolshevik territory was reorganized as the Union of Soviet Socialist Republics. The name 'Russia' was absent from the title of the state, although the Russian republic was by far the largest and included Siberia. The more important nationalities were given self-governing republics of their own, linked together indissolubly by the fact that the Communist party provided the government in each. Nevertheless, it appeared that Ukrainians were ruling in the Ukraine, Georgians in Georgia, and so forth, and this appearance was not altogether without reality.

The Soviet Union, although a pariah among the nations in the 1920s, was henceforth left unmolested by the war-wearied victor powers. Many expected it to collapse of its own accord. The main cause of hostility towards it was the propaganda with which it tried to promote revolutionary ideas. Its motive was as much self-protective as ideological. As Trotsky said:

If the peoples of Europe do not arise and crush imperialism, we shall be crushed—that is beyond doubt. Either the Russian revolution will raise the whirlwind of struggle in the West, or the capitalists of all countries will stifle our struggle.[1]

When these fears were seen to be exaggerated and Stalin had triumphed over Trotsky, improved relations with the West became possible. In the 1930s a successful diplomatic offensive won recognition by the United States (1933), a place in the League of Nations (1934) and an alliance with France (1935): once again the rising power of Germany was to be confronted with war on two fronts. Yet, when war did come in 1939, the Soviet Union, contemptuously isolated by the Munich agreement of 1938, made its separate pact with Germany, whereby Hitler had to fight only on his western front. The parallel between the temporary accommodation between Napoleon and Alexander I in 1807 and that between Hitler and Stalin in 1939 is obvious: in both instances the pact was broken by invasion of Russia, the failure of which resulted in Russian armies pursuing the defeated aggressors far west into Europe.

The Moscow pact of August 1939, followed by Hitler's destruction of the Polish state in the following month, enabled Stalin to advance the western frontier of the Soviet Union. Control over the Baltic states was

[1] *Carr (1956), pp. 17-18*

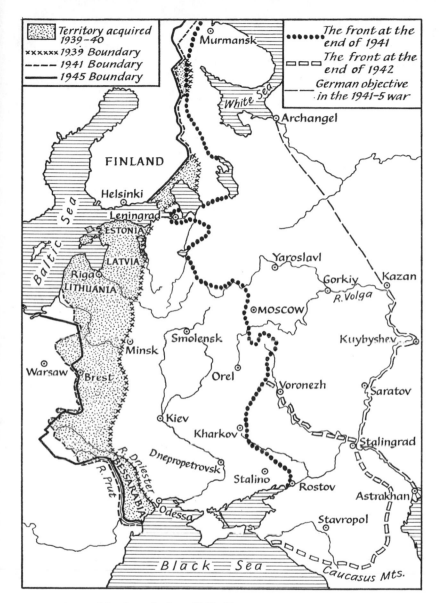

figure 85   Boundaries, 1939-45.

established, and Bessarabia and the eastern provinces of Poland were
annexed. As most of the Polish territory so acquired had formed part of
ancient Russia and as its population was Orthodox in religion and White
Russian in nationality, there was some truth in the Soviet claim that their
share in the 1939 partition was 'the liberation of western White Russia

and western Ukraine', although some areas, such as that round Lvov, had never before been Russian. The seizure of Bessarabia in 1940 alarmed Hitler because he was dependent on Rumanian oil and did not wish to see the Russians so close to it. His obsession with the safety of this oil led him to seek the domination of the whole Balkan region, even though this meant undermining the agreement with Russia. (Fig. 85.)

The new frontier was similar to that of 1914, and gave Russia the protection of its greater distance from Moscow and the Ukraine, should invasion come from the west. But Leningrad and Murmansk remained uncomfortably close to the fortified Finnish border in view of the close relationship between Finland and Germany. In October 1939 the Soviets went to war with Finland to rectify this position, and in March 1940 Finland ceded the territory demanded.

The Soviet Union was excluded entirely from the Balkans by successful German military and diplomatic moves, and this strained the Soviet-German understanding to the utmost. When, in March 1941, the Yugoslavs overthrew their German-dominated government, Stalin at once made a friendship pact with the new patriotic regime. The Germans thereupon forced Yugoslavia back into the fold and, at the same time, seized Greece. Turkey added to the completeness of the German domination of the whole of south-eastern Europe with a treaty of friendship with Germany.[1]

The German Invasion, 1941

Early on the morning of 22 June 1941, the German armies crossed Russia's new frontier. The target set for them by Hitler was a line from Archangel to Astrakhan. This would have given him immense agricultural, mineral and industrial resources to balance the likely intervention of the United States against him. The target line was nowhere reached. Instead, after a rapid initial advance in 1941 to a line running from near Leningrad past Moscow to Rostov-on-Don, and its extension to Stalingrad (formerly Tsaritsyn) in 1942, the exhausted Germans were driven back in 1943 and 1944.

As in the Napoleonic invasion, the vast size of the country and its extreme climate were decisive in the German defeat. Size meant a choice of objectives separated by great distances; this destroyed German unity of purpose. The army chiefs were for an all-out drive on Moscow as the administrative and political capital, but Hitler was tempted by the economic wealth of the Ukraine and the oil of the Caucasus. In consequence, the initial all-out drive against Moscow, amazingly swift and successful owing to Guderian's matchless skill in mechanized warfare, was suspended in August 1941.

The immense distances involved also created supply problems. As the line advanced, the territory to the rear fell pray to partisans, and supply

[1] *Chambers* (1963), pp. 523-5

convoys suffered heavily from ambush as well as breakdown. The frequency of forested areas gave the Russian regulars and guerrillas many opportunities.

Climate operated in conjunction with the Russian roads. There was no system of surfaced roads comparable to that of western Europe. In summer they were rutted dusty tracks whose loose grit and sand wrought havoc among the engines of armoured vehicles. One Panzer division lost the bulk of its heavy tanks in this way.[1] Worst of all was the mud into which the autumn rains converted these same dusty roads of summer. When, at the end of September, Hitler ordered the resumption of the offensive against Moscow, everything depended on how long a rainy season would intervene before frost hardened the roads. At first the resumed advance went well, but by mid-October the mud was having its effect. The speed of the advance, which had averaged 28 miles a day in the summer, had now dropped to barely a single mile and never more than three.[2] By the end of October the Germans were completely immobilized.

The frost came on the night of 6 November 1941, but the delay had given the Russians time to destroy bridges, lay minefields, build anti-tank obstacles, and bring in reinforcements from Siberia. The Germans were not ready for the frost: they had no winter clothing and no anti-freeze. And the temperature dropped rapidly to unprecedented levels: in late November it was −40°C or F. Once more the Germans were immobilized, this time because their vehicles would not function in such low temperatures. The German air force was grounded for the same reason and control of the skies passed to the Russians. Unlike the Russians, with their big boots stuffed with paper and rags, the Germans wore tight-fitting hob-nailed jackboots; these were conducive to frost-bite from which the men suffered cruelly. Frost-bite was soon claiming more casualties than enemy action.[3] Neither Russian aircraft, vehicles nor men were affected in the same way, as both were well prepared for winter's worst. On 5 December 1941 the attempt to take Moscow was abandoned.

Although the Germans were to fight on through 1942, win more victories and make further advances, the war was probably already lost: German resources would no longer suffice to win it on a front so long and so far from supply bases, and in conditions so adverse. Already ¾ million men had been lost. Equally serious was the number of tanks and guns destroyed. '*Russia so conducted her resistance that, even if she lost the war, the Teutonic race would never recover from its victory.*'[4] Russian casualties were even heavier than the German but their reserves were far greater and they were fighting the war on one front only. Failure by the Germans to win a decisive victory in 1941 also meant that Allied help—first British and later American—had time to take effect. As soon as Russia was

[1] *Carell (1964), p. 93*
[2] *Carell (1964), p. 149*
[3] *Carell (1964), p. 183*
[4] *Chambers (1963), p. 531*

attacked, Britain offered assistance, and by August 1941, supplies were arriving at Murmansk. Foreign aid, though small in 1941, grew rapidly throughout 1942 as American production of armaments increased.

This situation was reminiscent of the mid-sixteenth century when England first made friendly contact with an isolated and beleaguered Muscovy. Now, as then, assistance could only be given by rounding the North Cape. But in 1941, Murmansk, a large ice-free port connected by rail with Leningrad and Moscow, was available to receive outside help, as well as the White Sea port of Archangel. Carell writes that the flow of supplies that came in via Murmansk was '*an endless stream*'. He asserts that more aircraft and tanks entered Russia during the first year of the war than the Germans began the campaign with.[1] But the quality of much of the aid was poor and its value less than its bulk suggests.

Murmansk was listed among the main objectives of the German invasion. Hitler was at first more concerned in safeguarding Narvik, from which Swedish ore was shipped in winter when the Bothnian Gulf was frozen, and the nearby Petsamo nickel mines upon which his steel industry depended, than with the Allied use of Murmansk. Despite enormous exertions, operation 'Platinum Fox', which was intended to take the Germans the sixty miles from the Finnish border to Murmansk, could not be accomplished: the Russians were better able to cope with the rock and scree, the lakes and torrents, the winter ice and snow of the awful tundra waste. The Germans had expected roads, but none existed (one of the many surprising failures in German intelligence on the Soviet Union). Not even mules could negotiate much of the rocky, slippery terrain. Supplies failed the Germans at critical periods, while the Murmansk railway continued to assure the Soviet troops—Siberians for the most part—adequate reinforcements and stores. The Germans could not spare the aircraft to break this lifeline by bombing, as their air force was already overstrained on other sectors of the front.

Although they failed to take Murmansk, in 1942 the Germans began to inflict heavy losses upon the convoys making for it, using aircraft and submarines operating from northern Norway, and in June of that year the port was almost wiped out in an air raid. Archangel thereafter took its place, but so dangerous had the northern route become that British shipments by way of it were suspended and the Persian Gulf used instead.

The Germans had not only been unprepared for the trials of Russian roads and the Russian winter, but they had underestimated the Soviet Union's military and industrial strength. In this they were not alone, as it was widely believed throughout the West that Russia would be quickly defeated.[2] Russian secrecy had played its part in creating the illusion of Russian weakness, and this had been strengthened by the poor equipment used by the Soviets in the Finnish war. The achievements of the Stalinist Five-Year Plans had not been properly appreciated in the West. As

[1] *Carell (1964), p. 424*
[2] *Werth (1964), pp. 145, 279*

recently as 1928 the economy barely exceeded the level of 1913. Despite Soviet boasts, what could this nation of backward peasants, afflicted in succession by war, revolution, civil strife, foreign invasion, famine, terror and purge, and torn by inner dissension and intrigue, echoing with accusations of traitor and saboteur, have achieved in a brief decade? Had not almost all the higher echelons of administrative and financial command been destroyed by the 1937 purges? But, as Mackinder had written in 1935, '*a new map of Scythia*' was evolving: '*Whatever our reserves of scepticism, it will be at our peril that we neglect to take account of it.*'[1]

The U.S.S.R. in 1941

Mackinder's '*new map of Scythia*' was the result of a transformation affected by Stalin's three Five-Year Plans (1928-32, 1933-7, 1938-41). The first two of these coincided with a period of severe economic depression in Western countries. This crisis of capitalism helped Stalin in his revolutionary programmes as it meant that machinery and skilled labour which would normally have been kept busy in the West were available for service in Russia.

AGRICULTURE

The programme of industrialization envisaged by Stalin required an agricultural revolution before it could be put into effect. The post-revolutionary system of peasant proprietorship was no less primitive and inefficient than that of tsarist days, and less productive, yet it employed the great majority of the population. The merging of the peasant plots into large collectives would, it was hoped, make possible surpluses of farm produce which would serve both to feed the towns and provide exports to pay for imports of machinery. Mechanization would free enough labour to satisfy the needs of industrial expansion. So, in the early 1930s the land of the wealthy peasants (*kulaki*) was confiscated, mechanized collective farms were established from which compulsory deliveries of produce were extorted, and the kulaks, together with uncooperative and unreliable peasants, were deported to labour camps for the building of new towns, factories, railways and canals. Of the 1,600 people who arrived in the new saw-milling town of Igarka, on the lower Yenisey, in 1931, 40 per cent were kulaks. The proportion was not higher '*because the* kulaks *had to be watched at work, and hurried on by us class-conscious workers*'.[2]

There were by 1939 about ¼ million collective farms (*kolkhozy*) with an average size of 1,000 acres. They were served by about 7,000 machine-tractor stations where the machinery was maintained. The cultivated area had been expanded from 113 million hectares in 1928 to about 140 million, by drainage in the swampy districts of the north-west, irrigation

1 *Mikhaylov (1937), p. vi*
2 *Smolka (1937), p. 187*

L*

in the arid areas of the Ukraine, southern Russia and Central Asia, and by the ploughing up of new land in southern Siberia and Kazakhstan. Poor scrub-covered land in central Russia was cleared mechanically and fertilized with peat. Land newly brought into cultivation was organized into state farms (*sovkhozy*) of which, in 1939, there were about 4,000 with an average area of 10,000 acres.

The collectivization and mechanization of agriculture may be looked upon as a war waged by the towns for the control of the countryside, a war the object of which was to obtain supplies of food and labour. The Soviet state had been established by the workers of the towns led by urban revolutionaries. The peasants, having seized gentry land, stood aside in self-sufficient independence. The mechanization of agriculture made them dependent on the towns for oil and machinery. Each machine-tractor station (MTS) was a unit of urban control over the countryside, both economic and political. The mechanical section held the fate of each *kolkhoz* in its hands, since it could allocate machinery when and where it chose; the political section looked after plan fulfilment, propaganda, purges and other Party matters, and exercised a general surveillance over the farms.[1]

Many changes had taken place in the distribution of crops. Wheat replaced rye as the chief cereal on the non-black-earth lands of central and north-western Russia. Sugar-beet cultivation was extended into western Siberia, Central Asia and Transcaucasia. The area under cotton doubled as a result of expanded irrigation in Central Asia and of new plantings in Transcaucasia, northern Caucasus and southern Ukraine. Land growing tea rose from a mere 1,000 hectares in 1913 to 50,000 hectares. New plants which were introduced and widely cultivated included sorghum, soya bean, koksagyz (a dandelion-like plant from whose roots rubber is obtained) and tung.

The aims of the agricultural revolution were only partly achieved. A supply of forced labour for industrialization was forthcoming and the expansion of cotton production was particularly satisfactory, enabling Russia almost to dispense with foreign supplies of a commodity which had topped the list of imports in 1913. But the collective farms perpetuated much of the old inefficiency to which were added abuses of all kinds. The better farmers had been carried off to labour camps; those who remained suffered from unjust extortion and bitterly resented their return to serfdom: they had become serfs of the state instead of serfs of the landlords.[2]

Such was the hostility to the Party in the countryside that Stalin had to abandon the idea of full collectivization and allow the *kolkhozniki* to retain a private plot of their own, just as they had under landlord serfdom. This concession had two consequences: firstly, there remained a large element of subsistence farming in Soviet agriculture, since the private plot was used primarily to support the peasant and his family; secondly, it proved

[1] *Fainsod (1959), pp. 280-93*
[2] *Fainsod (1959), pp. 265-79*

difficult to get the peasant off his plot and on to the collective, thus jeopardizing the success of the latter. Although the private allotment system was regarded by the Communists as '*a temporary compromise*',[1] they dared not tamper with it, especially when the German menace arose. The private ownership of land gave some hope that the peasant would be willing to fight to defend it.

MINING AND METALLURGY

Although before 1914 chance finds had already revealed that the Russian Empire possessed great mineral wealth, many valuable deposits known to exist were not worked. But less than 1 per cent of the country was geologically mapped. By the time of the German invasion the Soviet government had mapped about half the country geologically and large areas had been intensively prospected.[2] As a result, the extent and workability of many known deposits was more closely estimated while several new ones were discovered. As early as 1935 first place was claimed in reserves of petroleum, iron ore, manganese, gold, phosphorus and platinum, and second place in coal.[3]

In actual output remarkable progress was made, as the table shows (millions of tons):

	1913	*1928*	*1940*
Coal	*30*	*36*	*166*
Petroleum	*9*	*12*	*31*
Electricity	*2*	*5*	*48 (billions of kwh)*
Iron ore	*9*		*27 (1938)*
Pig iron	*4*	*3*	*15*
Steel	*5*	*4*	*18*

In both coal and oil the older producing areas (Donbass and Baku) were modernized and new areas developed. Less than 60 per cent of coal now came from the Donbass, most of the rest coming from the Kuznetsk basin (Kuzbass). Karaganda—4½ million tons in 1940—was rapidly growing in production, as were the East Siberian fields. In the North, mining began at Vorkuta in 1933 on the Pechora field. Although most petroleum still came from the Caucasus, the great riches of the Volga-Ural region had been discovered and had begun to be exploited, though as yet on a small scale. (Fig. 86.)

In 1928 the country possessed an obsolescent and run-down iron and steel industry in the Ukraine and an obsolete one scattered across the central Urals. By 1940 the Ukrainian industry had been strengthened and modernized. New works were built at Krivoy Rog on the ironfield, at Stalino (formerly Donetsk) on the coalfield, and at Zaporozhe near the

[1] *Treadgold (1957), p. 271*
[2] *Leimbach (1950), p. 28*
[3] *Mikhaylov (1937), p. 39*

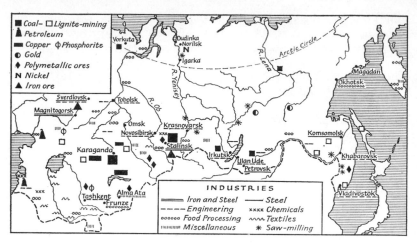

figure 86   Central Asia and Siberia: new economic developments, 1928-40

Dnieper power station, as well as at Kerch and Mariupol on the Sea of Azov. Two new integrated iron and steel bases had been established. One of these was sited near a massive deposit of magnetite in the southern Urals at Magnitogorsk, and the other on the Kuzbass coalfield at Stalinsk (formerly Novokuznetsk). The Magnitogorsk plant used coke brought by rail from the Kuzbass, while Stalinsk used iron ore brought back in return by rail from the Urals. Thus rail transport was fully utilized and costs were low in consequence. Magnitogorsk alone was producing in 1940 more iron and steel than the whole country in 1928. Six of the old works in the Urals were modernized to produce the highest grade charcoal steel.[1] Many steelworks, using pig produced elsewhere, were established in Russia— at Moscow and older centres such as Tula and Lipetsk, in the Urals (Chelyabinsk, Nizhniy Tagil), and in Siberia (Petrovsk, Komsomolsk).

A modern steel industry needs supplies of ferro-alloys—metals such as manganese, nickel, tungsten and chromium—to impart special qualities to the steel. Whereas before the Soviet period Russia was a producer of manganese only, by 1940 deposits of all the important ferro-alloys were being worked in areas which the Germans were not to reach—principally in the Urals. Non-ferrous mining and metallurgy likewise made striking progress, notably copper: new mines in Kazakhstan were producing three times the total pre-Five-Year Plan production. Output of aluminium, lead, zinc and tin, almost non-existent previously, was also expanding.

Several new mining centres were established in the Northland. The mining of nickel, copper and apatite in the Kola peninsula gave rise to the new towns of Kirovsk (1929) and Monchegorsk (1935). The Pechora coalfield was developed around Vorkuta after 1933. Nickel began to be

[1] *Mikhaylov (1937), pp. 84-5*

mined at Norilsk in 1940 and sent by rail to the lower Yenisey at Dudinka. New goldfields were opened up in north-east Siberia. Forced labour was used in these new ventures.[1]

ELECTRIFICATION

Lenin was a powerful advocate of electrification and this was the only branch of the economy which made significant progress in the 1920s before the Stalinist Five-Year Plans. Its great advantage was that it enabled low-grade fuels to be used locally, thus saving the transport of high-grade coal. The Industrial Centre, hitherto a large importer of Donbass coal, which took urgently needed rail car space, came to depend for much of its light, heat and power needs upon electricity generated from local resources of lignite and peat. The largest users of mechanically extracted and dried peat were the Gorkiy (1925: installed capacity 204,000 kw) and Shatura (1925: 180,000 kw) stations. Peat was also used at Sverdlovsk in the Urals. The chief lignite-consuming station was Kashira (1922: 186,000 kw), south of Moscow.

Later, large lignite-fired stations were erected in the Urals at Chelyabinsk (1930), Berezniki (1931) and Sredneuralsk, near Sverdlovsk (1935). For the first time electric power was generated in Siberia, using Kuznets and Cheremkhovo coal. Many large stations were built in the Ukraine to work with coal dust, and oil was used at Baku, Grosniy and Kuybyshev. Several small hydro-electric stations were built in Georgia, at Archangel, on the Volkhov (1926) and Svir (1933) rivers in the north-west near Leningrad, and, largest of all, at Dnepropetrovsk (1932: 558,000 kw). The output of electricity, which had been 2 billion kwh in 1913 and had fallen to 0·5 billion kwh in 1921, had risen to 26 billion in 1935 and to 48 billion in 1940. (Fig. 87.)

MANUFACTURING

Just as the collectivization and mechanization of agriculture were essential if the new industrialization was to have the labour and food it needed, so an engineering (machine-building) industry capable of providing the farm equipment was a prerequisite of the new agriculture. Hence tractor factories had first priority in the first Five-Year Plan. Although much machinery had at first to be imported, the country was soon able to rely upon the tractors, etc., which poured forth from the new works at Kharkhov, Rostov, Saratov, Stalingrad, Semipalatinsk, Chelyabinsk and Tashkent.

This initial emphasis on tractors not only made possible the successful introduction of the new order, but it contributed towards its survival. For the tractor factories were easily converted to the production of tanks. The Soviet Union was soon able to give the Germans a very unpleasant surprise in the tank-power it was able to put into the field against them. Hitler in 1942 confirmed this: '*If anyone had told me before the war began that the Russians could mobilize 35,000 armoured vehicles, I should have said*

[1] *Armstrong (1965), pp. 128-35*

figure 87   Russia: new economic developments, 1928-40 (electricity generation, 1921-40).

he was mad. But in fact they have up to now put 35,000 of them into battle'.[1] Most of the Soviet tractor/tank manufacturing capacity remained in Russian hands throughout the war, and equipment in centres that fell into German hands—e.g. Kharkov and Rostov—was removed beyond their reach.

[1] *Carell (1964), p. 59*

More difficult to introduce, but vital if self-sufficiency were to be achieved, was the capacity to make machine tools, ball bearings and precision instruments requiring the highest qualities both of skill and raw materials. Yet, with much foreign help, this branch of industry was successfully established in Moscow, Leningrad and Gorkiy.

Soviet resistance in the war would have been short-lived had not a large chemical industry been built up by 1940. Its peacetime production of fertilizers was convertible to that of explosives in war, and its output of synthetic rubber was probably greater even than that of Germany.[1] Potato alcohol was the chief raw material and much of the plant was built in the Urals, Transcaucasia and Siberia, out of enemy reach.

Aims of Soviet industrial planning—although the emphasis shifted from time to time—were in the main to locate industry near raw materials and energy sources, to achieve regional self-sufficiency, and to save transport. The Soviets had inherited a transport system that was hopelessly inadequate. To have made good this deficiency to the full would have delayed advance in other directions for a decade or more. Hence it was essential to plan in such a way as to minimize transport requirements. In tsarist Russia, manufactured goods were either imported or made at St Petersburg and in the Moscow area, whence they were distributed all over the Empire in return for raw materials and semi-finished goods. Even the Ukraine sent coal, iron and steel to the Industrial Centre for working up. Under the Five-Year Plans, the Ukraine developed engineering (agricultural and mining machinery, transport equipment) and chemical industries, so that it consumed far more of its own primary output. The Volga cities— Kazan, Kuybyshev, Saratov, Stalingrad—developed automotive and railway rolling stock engineering as well as tractor/tank manufacture. The Urals witnessed the creation of many new chemical and engineering works as did many Siberian towns: Novosibirsk (mining machinery), Stalinsk (locomotives and rolling stock), Irkutsk (mining machinery), Ulan Ude (railway repair shops), Khabarovsk (oil refining), Komsomolsk (riverboat building). In Transcaucasia, engineering, chemical, textile and food processing industries spread rapidly, and in Soviet Central Asia many towns became textile centres.

Thus, many regions beyond the reach of the invader had an industrial base capable of continued expansion and production, even if cut off from those western parts of the country to which they had previously looked for supplies.

TRANSPORT

As so much emphasis was placed on heavy industry before 1940, and as economic development was tailored as far as possible to make the best use of the existing means of transport, progress in this field was less impressive than in industry. Tables 7 and 8 summarize the changes:

[1] *Dobb (1948), p. 296*

Table 7
Freight Turnover by Mode of Transport (billions of tons-km)

	1913	1928	1940
Railway	65·7	93·4	415·0
Sea	19·9	9·3	23·8
Waterway	28·5	15·9	35·9
Motor vehicle*	0·1	0·2	8·9
Pipe line	0·3	0·7	3·8

* see footnote to Table 8

Table 8
Total Freight Carried by Mode of Transport (millions of tons)

	1913	1928	1940
Railway	132·4	156·2	592·6
Sea	13·9	8·0	31·2
Waterway	32·7	18·3	72·9
Motor vehicle*	10·0	20·0	858·6
Air	0·0		0·04
Pipeline	0·4	1·1	7·9

* much motor vehicle movement took place off main roads, e.g. on farms, desert tracks, etc. The increase in road transport was much less.

Railway milage had been almost doubled since 1913 (58,500 km to 106,100 km). Freight turnover increased more than six-fold, a striking testimony to the intensive use of the available lines. Yet with rapid industrialization, traffic soon outstripped capacity, and there were transport crises when the waterways were frozen. Shortage of goods waggons was the chief bottleneck[1]. (Fig. 88.)

The great achievement of the first Five-Year Plan (1928-32) was the Turksib, a 900-mile line linking Central Asia with western Siberia, making possible irrigated farming and mining at points along its course which otherwise could not have been developed for lack of transport. The new coalmining town of Karaganda and the new metallurgical centre of Mangitogorsk were linked to the railway system by new lines. Under the second Five-Year Plan (1933-7) only 3,000 km of new line were laid, but almost twice that length of existing track was double-tracked. Novosibirsk was joined to the Kuzbass at Leninsk. The third Plan (1938-41) saw the building of only a few short lines.[2] Electrification was introduced in the mountainous areas of the Caucasus and on the Murmansk railway, both in regions without coal. Diesels began to be used in the arid areas where water was scarce. (Fig. 89.)

The length of navigable inland waterways doubled also (59,400 km to 107,300 km), but freight turnover on them increased by only a quarter.[3]

[1] *Westwood (1964), pp. 228-9*
[2] Chemins de Fer (*1946*), *pp. 27-9, 46*
[3] Forty Years (*1958*), *p. 214*

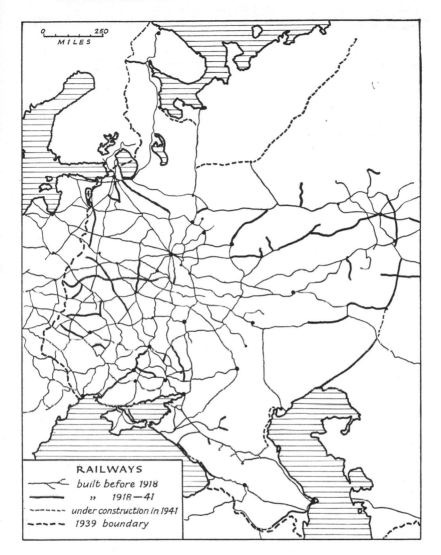

figure 88   Russia: railways, 1918-41.

Yet two important links had been constructed. The Baltic-White Sea canal (1933) gave Leningrad waterway connection with the new Arctic mining areas of the Kola peninsula and with the Northern Sea Route and its timber trade. It helped to relieve the overburdened Murmansk railway. The Moscow-Volga canal (1937) joined the capital to the northern part of the Russian waterway network. Bulky goods such as timber, building stone and cement, destined for Moscow, could now move by water instead of rail. In the Ukraine, the flooding of the Dnieper rapids for the hydro-

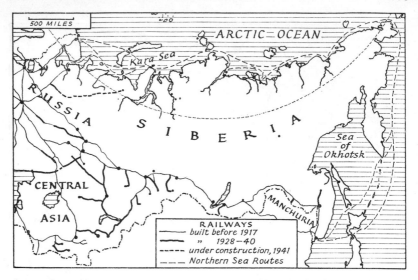

figure 89   Central Asia and Siberia: railways, 1918-41.

electric power station made the Dnieper navigable without interruption for the first time. Traffic on the Ob, Yenisey and Lena, the three great rivers of Siberia, increased substantially with Arctic development, but was hindered by the lack of wharves and other port facilities at landing points.[1]

THE NORTHERN SEA ROUTE

The desperate transport situation in the U.S.S.R. deepened Soviet interest in the commercial exploitation of the north-east passage along the northern coast of Asia. This would have the double advantage of improving access to northern resources and of providing an alternative west-east route to the Trans-Siberian railway. The north-east passage was negotiated for the first time in a single summer in 1932; freighters were convoyed along part of the route in 1933 and 1934, and throughout the passage in 1935. The use of aircraft to reconnoitre possible channels through the ice was the main factor in this success, and the warming up of northern waters, which has taken place during the last hundred years, probably facilitated it. The building of stations along the coast, with wireless, meteorological, aeronautical and hydrographical services, where hydrological and sea ice research could be carried on, accompanied the development of the route. There seem to have been 24 of these stations in 1932, 55 in 1937 and about 60 or 70 during and after the War.[2]

The new route did not prove as helpful as was hoped, partly for physical reasons, such as great variations in the length of the open season and the

---

[1] *Krypton (1956), pp. 129-30*
[2] *Armstrong (1952), pp. 35, 91; Krypton (1956), p. 113*

frequency of fog, and partly for lack of ice-breakers, whose assistance was essential for convoys navigating the route. As late as 1940 the head of the Northern Sea Route administration (*Glavsevmorput*) could complain that operations were still more like expeditions than normal voyages. '*There can be no doubt at all that the economic results of the working of the Northern Sea Route during the first eight years (1933-40) were so small as to be out of all proportion to the effort and money expended.*'[1]

The total annual cargo carried averaged about 200,000 tons. Most of this was timber exported from the lower Yenisey westwards to Britain by way of the Kara Sea. The industrial development of southern Siberia meant that supplies for the Arctic were more conveniently sent down the great rivers than despatched from Russia by way of the Northern Sea Route. When the Norilsk nickel and copper mining and smelting enterprise was established in the 1930s, 60 per cent of the supplies came by way of the Yenisey and 40 per cent from the west by the sea route.[2]

Although they remained far less important than railways, increased use was made of roads: old ones were surfaced and new ones made. A new road was cut, for instance, from Magadan on the Sea of Okhotsk coast to supply the Kolyma goldfields. But the great increase in the number of motor vehicles consisted chiefly of lorries used to take produce from farm, mine and factory to the railway, rather than for interurban transport. Because of the preponderance of short hauls, the enormous increase in the amount of freight carried by motor vehicles was not marked by an increase in turnover of anything like the same order.

Faced with an inadequate system of surface transport and with great difficulties of distance and terrain, the Soviet government inevitably turned to aircraft to move an increasing proportion of the passenger traffic and for the supply of remote districts. The first regular airline was opened in 1923 between Moscow and Gorkiy.[3] The development of aviation by 1940 was such that the U.S.S.R. was able to confront Germany with a large aircraft industry and numerous pilots experienced in operating in Russian conditions.

Marine transport by Soviet ships made little progress over 1913, because the degree of self-sufficiency and self-denial achieved through the use of local resources sharply reduced overseas trade. That there was, none the less a modest increase, is attributable to increased traffic on the Black, Azov and Caspian Seas, and on the northern sea route.

TRADE

The volume of Russian trade was much reduced compared with late tsarist times. In 1910-11, trade by volume amounted to about 32 million tons, to which imports contributed 8 million tons and exports 24 million tons. In 1938 overseas trade was less than 11 million tons, of which imports

[1] *Armstrong (1952), pp. 48, 112*
[2] *Krypton (1956), p. 151*
[3] Forty Years (*1958*), *p. 220*

were 1·1 million tons and exports 9·7 million tons. But, in value, imports at 1,387 million roubles were slightly above exports at 1,329 million roubles. There were several reasons for this reduced volume of trade. War, revolution, civil war, and the subsequent chaos, had removed the country from world commerce for a decade, so that old connections were broken and markets lost; hostility to the Soviet regime, arising from the excesses of Bolshevism and the confiscation of foreign investments, discouraged many western merchants from resuming commercial relations; the Soviet Union in any case no longer had great surpluses of primary commodities, as she needed them to feed her own cities and factories; and now that she made her own machinery, grew her own cotton and tea, mined her own coal, caught her own fish and produced her own rubber, those items that dominated imports in 1914 shrank in importance. Her reduced foreign trade was an index of the degree of self-sufficiency she had achieved.

Such trade as existed was viewed not so much as a normal relationship with the outside world, to be encouraged as far as possible, but as a temporary evil to be eliminated as soon as full economic independence was reached. As certain metals and items of machinery had to be imported, pending their expanded production at home, such commodities had to be exported as would sell abroad: timber, grain, petroleum and furs. Exports of timber meant forced-labour lumber camps in the tayga zone; exports of grain meant consumer shortage within the country itself.

The lesser importance of foreign trade meant that seaports like Leningrad and Odessa, that had flourished on foreign commerce, were now overtaken by ports whose trade was mainly internal. In 1938 the three leading ports of the Soviet Union by tonnage of goods handled were not seaports but the three Caspian lake ports of Baku, Astrakhan and Makhach Kala. Leningrad and Odessa were fifth and sixth in order respectively and, while the trade of the former was still almost wholly foreign, that of Odessa was now 75 per cent internal. The geographical position of the leading ports in foreign overseas trade—Leningrad, Batumi, Archangel and Mariupol—reflects the importance of the main items of export: Karelian timber, Caucasus oil and steppe grain.

POPULATION

The 1926 census gave the U.S.S.R. a population of 147 million, or 23 million less than the total for the Russian Empire in 1914. But considerable loss of territory, notably in Poland and the Baltic states, had occurred since 1914. Within the territory of the U.S.S.R. there had been a small increase of about 5 million. This negligible increase was the result of a series of calamities: war, revolution, civil war, famine and epidemic. But for these disasters, the population would have been between 20 and 30 million more.[1]

The economic and military weakness of the new state demanded that these losses be made good as fast as possible, but the early Bolshevik

[1] *Lorimer (1946), pp. 29-30*

attitudes to marriage and the family as bourgeois institutions, and their declared intention to relieve women of a life of successive pregnancies, resulted in a reverse tendency. The Divorce decree of 19 December 1917 stated that '*a marriage is to be annulled when either both parties or one at least appeal for its annullment*'. The Abortion decree of 18 November 1920 declared that abortions were '*to be performed freely and without any charge in Soviet hospitals*'.[1] Abortions sharply reduced the birth rate in towns and began to have an effect in the countryside. In Moscow by 1926 there were half as many abortions as live births, and by 1934 nearly three times as many.[2]

In 1936 Stalin, no doubt for economic and military as well as for social reasons, called a halt. Abortion was prohibited and a series of measures was introduce to encourage large families: allowances were introduced for mothers of large families, and the provision of maternity homes, nurseries and kindergartens was increased. As a result, the Moscow birth rate doubled (*1934:* 14·7 per 1,000; *1938*, 28·5) while that for the country as a whole rose from 30·1 in 1935 to 38·3 in 1938.[3] Divorce was made harder. Improved medical services, reducing the mortality rate at all ages, also played a growing part in increasing the population. The census of 1939 gave a total population for the U.S.S.R. of 170 million, an increase of 23 million in just over 12 years. Territorial changes following the German invasion of Poland and the war with Finland, as well as a year's natural increase, brought the total for 1940 up to 196 million and it cannot have been much short of 200 million when war broke out in 1941.

The composition of the 1939 population differed in many ways from that of 1926 and tsarist times. The urban population proportion had increased from 17·9 per cent in 1926 to 32·8 per cent. In absolute terms it had doubled while the rural population was slightly less than it had been in 1926. By occupation also there had been significant changes in this brief period:

Proportion of the population engaged in:	1926 per cent	1939 per cent
Agriculture	77·6	53·8
Industry, trade and social service	18·2	41·9

By age distribution there were marked deficits in the age groups 5-9 (reflecting the period of terror and famine associated with the agricultural upheaval of the 1930s) and 15-24 (due to the catastrophes of 1914-23). As a result of the war period, there was still a large excess of females: 7 million in 1939.

In nationality, the proportion of Russians increased from 53 to 58 per cent, but that of Ukrainians, whom the agricultural changes of the early 1930s had hit hardest, fell sharply from 21 to 16 per cent. The non-

---

[1] *Schlesinger (1949), pp. 30-44*
[2] *Lorimer (1946), p. 127*
[3] *Lorimer (1946), p. 130; Schlesinger (1949), pp. 269-79*

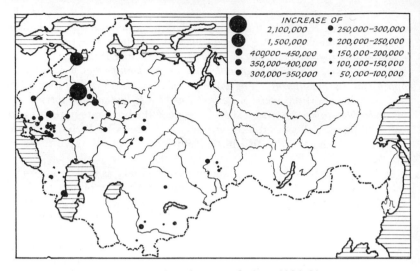

figure 90   Increases in urban population, 1926-39.

Russian peoples of the Caucasus, Central Asia and Siberia, for whom the Soviet period meant a release from the harsher conditions of colonial exploitation and oppression, showed a strong natural increase, but the Kazakhs, whose nomadic economy had been disrupted by enforced settlement and collectivization, and who had been reduced to misery and starvation, suffered a marked decline.

The main aspect of the geographical distribution of population change was undoubtedly the movement from country to town, rather than from one part of the country to another. And the influx into the two great western cities of Moscow and Leningrad—their combined population increased by 3·6 million in 1926-39—was the greatest migration of all: their natural increase was among the lowest in the country. Preoccupation with percentage increases obscures the fact that the main increase of population took place in the older centres. (Fig. 90.)

Nevertheless there were also important migrations into the Urals, the Northland, Central Asia, Caucasia and Siberia, associated with the transfer of labour for industrial development (fig. 91). By percentage increase of urban population, the fastest-growing regions were:[1]

	per cent
Karelia-Murmansk	458
East Siberia	284
Far East	229
Kazakhstan	229
Central Siberia	212
Turkmenistan	204

[1] *Lorimer (1946), p. 154*

But absolute increases were greatest in:

Ukraine	*5,822,000*
Industrial Centre	*5,756,000*
Urals	*2,472,000*
North West	*2,021,000*
West Siberia	*1,664,000*
Kazakhstan	*1,187,000*

The combined absolute increase of the six leading regions by percentage was a mere two-thirds of the absolute increase of the Industrial Centre or the Ukraine alone. On the other hand, the Ukraine, Industrial Centre, West Siberia and Turkmenistan all lost rural population in varying degrees, whereas Karelia, East Siberia, the Far East and Central Siberia all gained it—as did Caucasia and Central Asia (apart from Turkmenistan). The leading Soviet towns by population in 1939 and 1926 are listed in Table 9:

Table 9
Population in Soviet Cities in 1939 and 1926 (thousands)

		1939	1926	Position in 1926
1	*Moscow*	*4,137*	*2,029*	*(1st)*
2	*Leningrad*	*3,191*	*1,690*	*(2nd)*
3	*Kiev**	*846*	*514*	*(3rd)*
4	*Kharkov**	*833*	*417*	*(6th)*
5	*Baku*	*809*	*453*	*(4th)*
6	*Gorkiy*	*644*	*222*	*(11th)*
7	*Odessa**	*604*	*421*	*(5th)*
8	*Tashkent*	*585*	*324*	*(7th)*
9	*Tbilisi*	*519*	*294*	*(9th)*
10	*Rostov-on-Don**	*510*	*308*	*(8th)*
11	*Dnepropetrovsk**	*501*	*237*	*(10th)*
12	*Stalino**	*462*	*174*	*(16th)*
13	*Stalingrad**	*445*	*151*	*(20th)*
14	*Sverdlovsk*	*426*	*140*	*(21st)*
15	*Novosibirsk*	*406*	*120*	*(25th)*
16	*Kazan*	*402*	*179*	*(14th)*
17	*Kuybyshev*	*390*	*176*	*(15th)*
18	*Saratov*	*376*	*220*	*(12th)*
19	*Voronezh**	*327*	*122*	*(24th)*
20	*Yaroslavl*	*298*	*114*	*(27th)*
21	*Zaporozhye**	*289*	*56*	*(78th)*
22	*Ivanovo*	*285*	*111*	*(28th)*
23	*Archangelsk*	*281*	*77*	*(47th)*
24	*Omsk*	*281*	*162*	*(18th)*
25	*Chelyabinsk*	*273*	*59*	*(69th)*

* *towns taken by the Germans*

The towns with the *highest percentage increases* were (1939 as percentage of 1926):

1	*Karaganda (Kazakhstan)*	*New*
2	*Magnitogorsk (Urals)*	*New*
3	*Stalinogorsk (Central Russia)*	*New*
4	*Komsomolsk (Far East)*	*New*
5	*Stalinsk (Kuzbass)*	*4353·8*
6	*Stalinabad (Tadzhikstan)*	*1472·1*
7	*Murmansk (Kola peninsula)*	*1333·6*
8	*Dzerzhinsk (Central Russia)*	*1160·7*
9	*Prokopyevsk (West Siberia)*	*1000·5*
10	*Kamensk-Uralskiy (Urals)*	*948·3*

The highest absolute increases are given in *Table 10* which indicates the region in which they were found and the industries, the establishment or extension of which contributed towards the expansion of the town:

Table 10
Soviet Towns in 1939 with an increase of Population of 150,000 or more over 1926 (increases in thousands)
Abbreviations used in the table:

Regions		Industries	
C	— *Central Russia*	*chem.*	— *chemicals*
Ca	— *Central Asia*	*eng.*	— *engineering*
Cc	— *Caucasus*	*ag.*	— *agricultural machinery*
ES	— *East Siberia*	*air.*	— *aircraft manufacture*
FE	— *Far East*	*auto.*—	*automotive*
K	— *Kazakhstan*	*el.*	— *electrical machinery*
N	— *North*	*min.* —	*mining machinery*
NW	— *North West Russia*	*misc.*—	*miscellaneous*
WR	— *White Russia*	*m.t.*	— *machine tools*
WS	— *West Siberia*	*ship*	— *ship and boat building*
Uk	— *Ukraine and Lower Don*	*text.*	— *textile machinery*
Ul	— *Urals*	*rwy.*	— *railway workshops*
V	— *Volga*	*fert.*	— *fertilizers*
		food	— *food processing*
		i.s.	— *iron and/or steel*
		nfm.	— *non-ferrous metallurgy*
		oil	— *oil refining*
		syn. r.	— *synthetic rubber*
		text.	— *textile machinery*
		wood	— *woodworking*

1	Moscow	2,108	C	i.s., eng. (m.t., auto., misc.), chem., food, text.
2	Leningrad	1,501	NW	eng. (ship, misc.), i.s., text., food
3	Gorkiy	422	C	eng. (auto., misc.), food
4	Kharkov	416	Uk	eng. (ag.)
5	Baku	356	Cc	eng. (min.), text.
6	Kiev	333	Uk	eng. (ship, el., misc.), text., food
7	Stalingrad	294	V	eng. (ag., auto)
8	Stalino	288	Uk	coal, i.s.
9	Novosibirsk	285	WS	eng., food
10	Sverdlovsk	285	Ul	eng. (min.), food
11	Ivanovo	274	C	text.
12	Dnepropetrovsk	264	Uk	i.s., eng. (rwy)
13	Tashkent	262	CA	eng. (text.), text.
14	Zaporozhe	234	Uk	i.s.
15	Tbilisi	225	Cc	text., wood, paper
16	Kazan	222	V	eng. (ship, rwy)
17	Kuybyshev	215	V	eng. (auto), cement, food
18	Chelyabinsk	214	Ul	eng. (ag.)
19	Voronezh	205	C	eng. (ag., text.), syn. r.
20	Archangelsk	205	NW	wood, chem., eng. (ship), food
21	Rostov-on-Don	202	Uk	eng. (ag.)
22	Alma Ata	185	K	text.
23	Odessa	184	Uk	eng. (misc.)
24	Yaroslavl	184	C	eng. (auto), syn. r., tyres
25	Stalinsk	166	WS	i.s.
26	Karaganda	166	K	coal
27	Makayevka	161	Uk	coal, i.s.
28	Mariupol	159	Uk	i.s.
29	Krivoy Rog	159	Uk	i.s.
30	Saratov	156	V	eng. (ag.), food

The growth of towns in the 1926-39 intercensal period is a good guide to the distribution and degree of industrialization accomplished in the first two Five-Year Plans. As soon as the illusion created by the percentage approach is dispelled, it becomes clear that the Moscow area, Leningrad and the Ukraine, with their inherited skills and equipment, and their superior communications, have been the main foundations upon which the new edifice has been built.

The Immediate Results of the 1941-5 War

The occupied territory had been devastated. The Russians had removed everything, including even heavy machinery, that they had time to carry off, and destroyed what they could of the remainder. Much else was

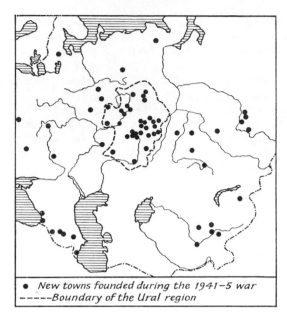

figure 91   New towns, 1941-5 (after Baranskiy).

destroyed in the actual fighting, and the Germans also blew up or burned everything they could before leaving. The most serious loss of all was that of housing, and at the end of the War, not only those returning, but the survivors already in the area, had no adequate shelter apart from what they could find in ruins and dug-outs.

That the war could be carried on was a result mainly of the development of eastern regions beyond the enemy's reach and the transfer thither of industrial equipment from the threatened zone, and secondarily of foreign aid. But extreme difficulties and shortages had been caused during the period of initial dislocation, especially as some products of the occupied area—certain high-grade steels, manganese—could not be produced in sufficient quantity elsewhere in the country.

The transfer of machinery and plant from the west, and the frantic wartime expansion of the east, did more to change the distribution of Soviet industrial production than either the pre-war or the post-war plans. Over 1,500 industrial enterprises were moved between July and November 1941, most of them going to the Urals (667), followed by Kazakhstan and Central Asia (308), West Siberia (244), the Volga region (226), and East Siberia (78).[1] Nevertheless, in most branches of production, output in 1945 was well below the 1940 level. Coal was down from 166 to 149 million tons, petroleum from 31 to 19 million tons, and steel from 18 to 12 million tons.

[1] *Werth (1964), p. 216*

The substantial gains of territory made by the U.S.S.R. as a result of the war were not of outstanding economic value. They included many regions of poor, swampy soil in White Russia, and of rocky tundra and forest in Karelia. But the lands added to western Ukraine possessed much good wheat land, and the Baltic states brought a large production of potatoes and hemp. Apart from oil and gas in the western Ukraine, the Pechenga nickel deposits and the coal of southern Sakhalin, mineral gains were small. Heavy industry was almost wholly absent from the acquisitions, but light industry was more widespread, textiles having some importance in the Baltic states. Vyborg, Riga and Lvov were established centres of miscellaneous industry, including engineering, textiles, woodworking and food processing. However, these lands also had been ravaged by war and were initially more of a liability than an asset to the U.S.S.R.

POPULATION

Not until the census figures for 1959 appeared was it fully realized how heavy had been the losses due to the war. The 1941 population of about 200 million for the enlarged territory of the U.S.S.R. may well have dropped to about 170 million by 1945. About 25 million people died as a direct result of the war, and the birth rate fell sharply because of the separation of the sexes; among those born, the adverse conditions produced an extremely high mortality.

It was to offset this heavy wartime loss of population that the new family law of 1944 gave very considerable inducements towards having large families. Under this law it was possible for a woman who had many children, depending on their number and age, to receive up to 12,200 roubles in a year—over three times the average annual wage. Unmarried mothers were included. Furthermore, motherhood medals were awarded to women who had borne five children and more, and the gold star of the Order of Mother Heroine to those who gave birth to a tenth.[1] In Lorimer's words, the law's provisions 'constitute in effect one of the most decisive pro-natalist programs ever inaugurated in any country'.[2]

The war produced important migrations. At its beginning about 85 million people (43 per cent) of the population lived in territory that was to come under the German occupation. It was, of course, in this area that the heaviest loss of life took place. But large numbers fled or were moved from it, both eastwards by the Russians and westwards by the Germans. The population of the Ukraine appears to have fallen by a half between 1939 and 1943.[3] The population from the evacuated areas was resettled in areas where new mining and manufacturing ventures had been begun in the 1930s—in the North, in West Siberia, in Kazakhstan and, above all, in the Urals.

[1] *Schlesinger (1949), pp. 367-77*
[2] *Lorimer (1946), p. 179*
[3] *Lorimer (1946), p. 196*

For political reasons the Volga Germans were transferred to the Altay region of West Siberia. At the end of the war, other peoples with whom Stalin was dissatisfied were uprooted and sent to labour camps or resettled in developing parts of the country. These included the Crimean Tartars, the Kalmyks, and the Chechens from the Caucasus.

All these wartime and post-war movements had a permanent effect in increasing the population and economic activity of the receiving areas, even though the old evacuated regions filled up again after the war. At the end of the war, many Poles were moved from the western territories of the Soviet union for resettlement in East Prussia.

Post-War Trends

The first five years after the war were years of reconstruction during which the Stalinist tyranny continued to exact sacrifice and self-denial from the war-wearied population. From 1950 onwards, the industrial expansion of the country and the development of its eastern and northern frontiers was resumed after a decade of interruption.

In agriculture, farms grew larger and were supplied with improved machinery and, after Stalin's death in 1953, the peasants were wooed with incentives to cooperate more wholeheartedly and efficiently in socialist agriculture. Punitive taxes imposed by Stalin on private plots after the war were lowered, and the machine-tractor stations abolished (1958). Rapid population growth outran grain production and Khrushchev launched the 'Virgin and Idle Lands Scheme' on the steppes of Kazakhstan to remedy this; he also promoted the cultivation of maize. Both campaigns were ill-conceived and worse executed. They failed to take account of climatic and soil conditions and they diverted men and equipment from established areas and crops, but losses incurred in this way were not made good by corresponding gains from the innovations. The Virgin Lands scheme was at first very successful. Grain production rose remarkably from 82 million tons in 1953 to 140 million tons in 1958, but by 1963 had fallen back to 107 million tons. An investment of 30 billion roubles, which could have achieved much in drainage in the west or irrigation in the south-east, had been largely dissipated. Furthermore, in 1963 nearly $2\frac{1}{2}$ million tons of wheat had to be imported from Canada alone at a cost of 143 million roubles.[1] Maize acreage rose from only 3·5 million hectares in 1953 to 37·1 million in 1962, but in the latter year only 7 million hectares were producing grain.[2] '*Much of the green fodder corn appears to have been sown simply to fulfil a sowing norm and then ignored.*'[3]

In mining, great new resources continued to be discovered and exploited. The 1950s witnessed the development of the Volga-Ural oilfield as one of

[1] *Torgovlya (1964), p. 255*
[2] S.S.S.R. v tsifrakh *(1962), pp. 139-41*
[3] *Anderson in Laird (1963), p. 260*

the world's largest, while the 1960s saw the addition of the West Siberian field, leaving the metal-rich Urals rising from a veritable sea of oil. Pipelines were laid to eastern Europe and from its plethora of petroleum the U.S.S.R. offered to supply the West as well. Natural gas became for the first time an important source of energy. In the production of coal and iron ore, the U.S.S.R. passed the U.S.A. to take first place in the world. One after the other, giant hydro-electric power stations, many of them of greater capacity than any in the U.S.A., came into production. These were mainly on the Volga, which the dams have converted into a succession of reservoir lakes, and where the great rivers of northern Asia leave the mountainous country of the south. Nuclear power stations have also been built.

Some increases in Production, 1950-60

	1950	1960
Coal (millions of tons)	261	513
Petroleum (millions of tons)	38	148
Iron ore (millions of tons)	40	107
Steel (millions of tons)	27	65
Electricity (billions kwh)	90	292
Cement (millions of tons)	10	46

Upon this expanding energy and mineral base, heavy industry has gone from strength to strength: developments include new integrated iron and steel works at Novotroitsk (southern Urals), Temir Tau (Kazakhstan near Karaganda) and at Rustavi in Uzbekistan, as well as expansion in the older metallurgical areas. Stalin's death in 1953 was important because his conservatism had held up the introduction of new techniques. Now, at last, attention could be given to the introduction of up-to-date technology and new products. Foreign help was enlisted in the establishment of modern chemical works. Breathtaking progress occurred in rocketry and electronics. Transport was modernized and overseas trade revived.[1] The huge gold reserve, accumulated as a result of an estimated annual production of 10 million ounces (second only to South Africa) and careful hoarding during the Stalinist era, has been freely drawn upon to make purchases abroad.[2] All this happened under Khrushchev, but it is significant that Kosygin, the man who was to succeed him, was rising in the Soviet hierarchy as an expert on light industry. Whereas even Khrushchev (1954-64) had refused to consider the possibility of widespread private ownership of motor cars, Kosygin invited Italian and French help in their mass production.

During the early 1960s the Soviet economy appeared to be increasingly beset by troubles which led, in 1964, to Khrushchev's dismissal. The ambitious Seven-Year Plan (1959-65), which he had forecast might well be overfulfilled,[3] had, in fact, to be virtually abandoned in 1963, and much

[1] *Westwood (1966), p. 186*
[2] Comparisons *(1959), p. 440*
[3] *Khrushchev (1959), p. 43*

lower targets substituted. Enough capital was not available for the many projects envisaged, especially as military spending could not be reduced, as Khrushchev had hoped: the Americans rebuffed every suggestion for relaxation of tension except for a limited nuclear-weapon testing agreement. The crude methods which had been effective in heavy industry in Stalin's day were applicable neither to agriculture nor to light industry. The crisis in agriculture continued because the government refused to take local variations of soil and climate into account, planning according to its needs rather than to the physical possibilities.

The state of light industry was exemplified by the following quotation from Khrushchev in 1959:

> *It has become the tradition to produce not beautiful chandeliers to adorn homes, but the heaviest chandeliers possible. This is because the heavier the chandeliers produced, the more a factory gets since its output is calculated in tons. So the factories make chandeliers weighing hundreds of kilograms and fulfil the plan. But who needs such a plan?*[1]

A machine-tool factory in Minsk supplied an engineering works in the Urals with 2 million roubles-worth of machinery so defective that none of it would work, yet the Minsk factory had received bonuses for surpassing the quota.[2] *'Few periods of Soviet economic history have been—on balance— so full of disappointments for the Soviet leaders and the Soviet people as the years since 1958.'*[3]

Population distribution is the key to how far the regional emphasis of industrial development in the U.S.S.R. has changed since the War. As the 1939 census did not give adequate regional data, a full comparison with 1959 census information is not possible, but the degree of urban expansion gives a good guide. Urban population increased from 33 per cent of the whole in 1939 to 48 per cent in 1959. From the incidence of this growth it is clear that, whereas in the 1926-39 period, the bulk of absolute increase took place in Russia and the Ukraine, in 1939-59 other areas of the country, notably the Urals, West Siberia and Kazakhstan, have taken a much greater share. This was primarily a result of the war, but also of the planned development of eastern and northern regions. (Fig. 92.)

The North (as defined on page 312) in 1959 held 2 million people, about 80 per cent of whom were Russians, compared with about 460,000 in 1926 (22 per cent Russian).[4] Much of this increase took place during and after the war. There were now many towns which, though not large, had come to exist where there had been no significant urban development before. The larger ones are listed below, with their 1959 population in thousands, the economic activity which gave rise to them, and—where available—the date of their foundation:[5]

[1] *quoted in Schwartz (1965), p. 141*
[2] Many Crises *(1964), p. vii*
[3] *Schwartz (1965), pp. 121-2*
[4] *Armstrong (1965), pp. 125-6*
[5] *Armstrong (1965), pp. 128 et seq*

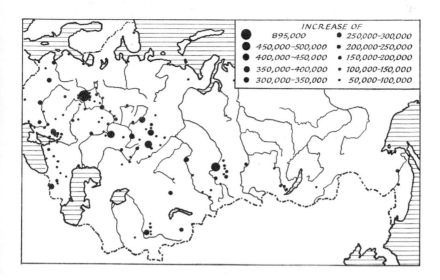

figure 92   Increases in urban population, 1939-59.

Murmansk, (222), seaport, fish processing, 1916
Kirovsk (39), apatite mining, fertilizers, 1934
Monchegorsk (46), nickel and copper mining, 1939
Kandalaksha (37), aluminium refining, paper mill
Vorkuta (55), coal mining, 1933
Norilsk (109), nickel and copper mining and refining, 1940
Dudinka (16), mineral river port
Igarka (14), timber river port, 1927
Bodaybo (18), gold mining
Aldan (12), gold mining, 1923
Ege-Khaya-Batagay-Deputatskiy (11), tin mining, 1941
Mirniy (6), diamond mining, 1956

There has been no comparable development in the Canadian North where population can still be counted in tens of thousands, not in millions; but the Canadian North has also been free of forced labour.

The largest absolute increases were made by the towns listed below. These give a more realistic picture of actual progress than percentage increases. Towns occupied by the Germans are given in italics and, naturally, they are relatively few compared with those appearing in the similar list for 1926-39.

Soviet Towns in 1959 with an Increase of Population of 150,000 or more over 1939
(increases in thousands; for abbreviations of regions, see p. 344)

1	Moscow	895	C	17 Alma Ata	224	K
2	Novosibirsk	481	WS	18 Krasnoyarsk	219	ES
3	Kuybyshev	416	V	19 *Riga*	212	NW
4	Chelyabinsk	415	Ul	20 Novokuznetsk	207	WS
5	Perm	373	Ul	21 Saratov	205	V
6	Sverdlovsk	351	Ul	22 *Krivoy Rog*	188	Uk
7	*Donetsk*	329	Uk	23 Orenburg	187	Ul
8	Tashkent	326	CA	24 *Gorlovka*	184	Uk
9	Yerevan	309	Cc	25 Nizhniy Tagil	178	Ul
10	Ufa	300	Ul	26 Komsomolsk	176	FE
11	Gorkiy	298	C	27 Tbilisi	175	Cc
12	Omsk	298	WS	28 Prokopyevsk	175	WS
13	*Minsk*	270	WR	29 Barnaul	172	WS
14	*Kiev*	256	Uk	30 Magnitogorsk	165	Ul
15	Kazan	241	V	31 Baku	159	Cc
16	Karaganda	232	K	32 Dnepropetrovsk	152	Uk

In the 1926-39 list of absolute urban increase (Table 10 on p. 345), only 6 of 30 towns were to be found in and east of the Urals. In the 1939-59 list, the number is 17. The towns to grow fastest percentagewise are given in Table 11, with the economic activity that has been the main cause of growth. They provide some indication of the more important new enterprises established in developing areas since the war:

Table 11
Soviet Towns with the Fastest Rate of Growth 1939-59

Name of Town	*Population 1959 (thousands)*	*As % of 1939*	*Region**	*Activity**
Angarsk	134	*new*	*ES*	*h.e.p., chem., wood*
Volzhskiy	67	*new*	*V*	*h.e.p., syn. r.*
Oktyabrskiy	65	*new*	*V*	*oil mining*
Novokuybyshevsk	63	*new*	*V*	*suburb of Kuybyshev*
Nakhodka	63	*new*	*FE*	*outport of Vladivostok*
Rustavi	62	*new*	*CA*	*i.s.*
Vorkuta	55	*new*	*N*	*Pechora coal mining*
Angren	55	*new*	*CA*	*Uzbek coal mining*
Mezhduretchensk	55	*new*	*WS*	*Kuzbass coal mining*

Table 11—continued

Name of Town	Population 1959 (thousands)	As % of 1939	Region*	Activity*
Bratsk	51	new	ES	h.e.p., nfm., wood
Novotroitsk	57	22,000	Ul	i.s.
Temir Tau	54	11,000	K	i.s.
Sumgait	52	822	Cc	steel tubes, chem.
Norilsk	108	778	N	nfm. and mining
Korkino	85	739	Ul	lignite mining
Krasnoturinsk	62	647	Ul	nfm.
Gukovo	53	598	Uk	Donbass coal mining
Ust-Kamenogorsk	117	580	K	h.e.p., nfm.
Chirchik	65	444	CA	h.e.p., chem.
Severodvinsk	79	368	NW	outport of Archangelsk

* see key on p. 344.

Although agglomerations, conurbations or 'metropolitan areas' have been less developed in the U.S.S.R. than in Western Europe and North America, some of the larger towns underwent enough suburban development in 1939-59 to give the total built-up area a much larger population than that of the leading individual city. This is shown in Table 12.

Table 12
The Ten Largest Agglomerations According to the 1959 Census[1]

	Population of agglomeration (thousands)	Population of main city (thousands)
Moscow	7,884	5,032
Leningrad	3,579	2,888
Donetsk	1,409	701
Gorkiy	1,372	942
Kharkov	1,322	930
Kiev	1,281	1,102
Kuybyshev	1,134	806
Tashkent	1,070	911
Baku	1,025	636
Dnepropetrovsk	1,001	658

The above table emphasizes the strength of the pull of western centres,

[1] *Perevedentsev (1965), pp. 31-9*

M

with good communications, services and skilled labour. The absolute increase in the population of the Moscow agglomeration alone ($2\frac{1}{4}$ million) was much larger than that of all the twenty towns making the biggest percentage increase put together.

The age structure of the population had changed markedly between 1939 and 1959, chiefly as a result of the war. There were now two age groups in pronounced deficit to disturb the regularity of the pyramid: 34-45, the generation which had borne the brunt of the war, and which was, in any case, smaller from the reduced birth rate of the 1914-23 period; and 10-20, shrunken because of the very low war-time birth rate. Such irregularities make for all kinds of difficulty in government and administration. The disproportion among the sexes was now much greater even than in 1939 and 1926, with a surplus of 21 million women.

CHAPTER NINETEEN
THE RUSSIAN RELATIONSHIP
TO EUROPE, AMERICA AND CHINA

Whatever we may think about the more or less European character of the Empire which lasted from Peter I to Nicholas II, the 'Red Tsardom' created in November 1917 was and remained non-European if not anti-European.[1]

The character of the Communism of the Bolsheviks who seized power in 1917 must be judged by its actions, not by its origins. That these were in nineteenth-century Europe is irrelevant to the nature of a movement that had developed in twentieth-century Russia in response to peculiarly Russian conditions. Bolshevism, in its initial behaviour in power, was a strong reaction against the European values introduced from the West; it was directed against monarchy, aristocracy, middle-class liberalism and parliamentary democracy; against capitalism, trade unionism, private enterprise and peasant proprietorship; against all theistic religion and bourgeois morality; against freedom of expression in the arts. When all of these are taken away, little of Europe is left in Russia. The westernized elements of society—aristocracy and bourgeoisie—were scattered to the four corners of the earth, and the new leaders came from the masses whom Europeanization had scarcely touched, although some of them had been influenced by periods of exile in the West. Their aim was to establish a new civilization altogether and, although they themselves saw it was potentially international, it none the less gratified Russia's yearning for a culture of her own. It gave her pride in a creative destiny rather than the ashamed confusion she had felt in her imitative past. Nearly a thousand years of fulmination by the Orthodox Church against the corrupt individualism, materialism and greed of the West, meant that the new regime's similar denunciations of capitalist and bourgeois society did not sound strange. The emphasis on communal activity and organization would have satisfied many nineteenth-century Slavophils as a laudable return to the path prescribed by Russia's unique past. But, whereas the nineteenth-century thinkers, Slavophil and Westerner alike, failed to grasp the necessity for Russia to keep on equal terms with the West in industrial and military techniques, the Communists, because of the economic materialism which Marx had taught them, were able to combine a distinctive non-Western culture with an advanced Western technology. Previously a choice had to be made between rejecting Western technology, thus exposing Russia to foreign domination, or accepting it, thereby denying her separate identity. Thus the schism between nineteenth-century Slavophil and Westerner was to some extent closed.[2]

Although the change of capital from St Petersburg—renamed Petrograd

[1] *Halecki (1950), p. 97*
[2] *Toynbee (1954), pp. 132-3; Sinzheimer (1965), p. 218*

to get away from its German name—to Moscow was made in 1918 for practical reasons, it was inevitable sooner or later as an affirmation of the new attitude of self-sufficiency. It was symbolic of the substitution of a policy of isolated continental development for one of close overseas relationship. A denunciation of Petrograd, written in 1917 by an Englishman, Nevill Forbes, powerfully expresses the emotions many Russians must have felt:

> *Majestic, spacious, even beautiful, cold, sunless, tragic, mysterious, dank and gloomy like the forests which surround it, and unhealthy, it has had a sinister and unwholesome influence on Russian history. It has warped Russia with its damp breath . . .*
>
> *But the creation of a purely political capital has brought its own nemesis. Now that its population has risen and has destroyed the chains which riveted it there, the sooner the horrible place is abandoned and Moscow is once more made the capital, the better for everybody. A cross between Byzantium and Stockholm, it never was anything but foreign, as its founder wished it to be, and it never will be anything else, in spite of its absurd, neo-Slavonic, pseudo-Russian name of Petrograd.*[1]

The point has often been made that Russia from time to time made strenuous efforts to westernize herself so as to be able to resist Western encroachment. Ivan IV had this in mind when he encouraged new contacts with England. Peter I, by a whirlwind of terror and compulsion, accomplished a technical revolution which enabled Russia to emerge as a power in eighteenth-century Europe. She brought first Sweden and then Prussia to their knees, vanquished Turkey, and repelled a French-led invasion by a European army, although geographical factors predominated in the latter victory.

The Crimean defeat of the mid-nineteenth century revealed that she had again fallen behind. Alexander II thereupon reopened the country to Western ideas, instituted administrative, social and military reforms, and a belated and limited industrial revolution took place. This progress, however, bedevilled as it was by the political and social chaos into which the country was falling, was no match for the incomparably superior advances made by German technology.

Russia was saved in 1917-19 by Germany's defeat at the hands of the Western allies. It was essential that the breathing space thus gained should be used to rehabilitate the country's industrial and military strength, a task made all the more difficult by the destruction and dislocation caused by the second Troublous Times (1914-23). In a country where the mass of the population were peasants who had been able, for the first time, to appropriate the land for themselves, and who were content to live upon what they had, in ease or penury, without undue exertion beyond what was needed for their primitive mode of life, only a complete, ruthless and rapid transformation of society, brought about through relentless compulsion, could achieve success. Stalin saw this need:

[1] *Beazley (1918), p. 245*

One feature of the history of old Russia was the continual beating she suffered for falling behind, for her backwardness. She was beaten by the Mongol khans. She was beaten by the Turkish beys. She was beaten by the Swedish feudal kings. She was beaten by the Polish and Lithuanian gentry. She was beaten by the British and French capitalists. She was beaten by the Japanese barons. All beat her—for her backwardness: for military backwardness, for cultural backwardness, for industrial backwardness, for agricultural backwardness . . .

Do you want our socialist fatherland to be beaten and to lose its independence? If you do not want this, you must put an end to its backwardness in the shortest possible time and develop genuine Bolshevik tempo in building up its socialist system of economy . . .

We are fifty or a hundred years behind the advanced countries. We must make good this distance in ten years. Either we do it or they crush us.[1]

Stalin's forced modernization enabled the country to survive conquest and brought it power and glory in 1945. But no sooner had this been achieved than further progress by the West was signalled by the dropping of A-bombs on Japan. Immediately the U.S.S.R. became a second-class power again, her victory had become hollow and she stood, like the rest of the world, defenceless against the new weapon. There could therefore be no post-war respite for the weary and afflicted peoples who now had to assume the added and costly burden of nuclear research. Again party and people responded. Not only was the immense material damage done by the war made good, but in 1949 the Soviets produced an atomic explosion, and in the 1950s even moved ahead of the Western world in some aspects of rocketry.

The 1941-5 war left the Soviet Union as a close-knit political unit, covering one-sixth of the land surface of the earth, and with enough geographical cohesion and unity to justify its being regarded as a distinct subcontinental division of the 'world island'. To the west of it lay Europe, distinguished by its geological, geographical, linguistic and political variety (fig. 93). But it was doubtful now whether Europe had survived as a cultural entity: it had obviously forfeited its world dominance:

The diversity of Europe proved stronger than its unity. Coming after countless other wars, some of which had involved most of the countries of Europe, the war of 1914-18, the greatest and last 'European War', had such consequences that European civilization obviously could not stand another. When, nevertheless, such a war started in 1939, it necessarily became a real World War, decided by non-European forces and ending in catastrophe for the whole of Europe.[2]

What is commonly called the 'historic Europe' is dead and beyond resurrection.[3]

[1] *Quoted in Toynbee (1954), pp. 139-40*
[2] *Halecki (1950), p. 52*
[3] *Holborn (1951), p. x*

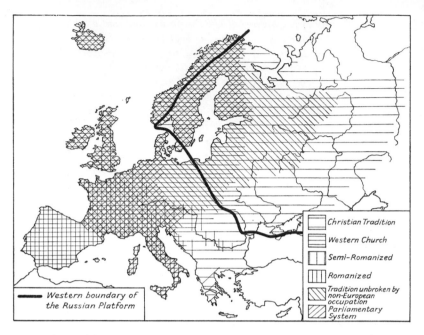

figure 93   An historical attempt to show degrees of Europeanization.

. . . *the traditional Europe—the Europe of our history books, the Europe of Louis XIV and Napoleon and Bismarck—is dead and beyond resurrection.*[4]

As a result of the war, the relationship between Russia and Europe became overshadowed by that between Russia and America. Before 1914 both the Russian Empire and America were subordinate to Europe in many ways. Economically they were indebted to European creditors and culturally they accepted European standards. The 1914-18 war weakened Europe to such an extent that, for the first time for many centuries, it ceased to emit cultural impulses and began to receive them. While a new American civilization began to penetrate Europe from across the Atlantic, powerfully aided by the new motion pictures, militant socialist ideas from Moscow began to be accepted by the European working classes and some intellectuals. The 1941-5 war had resulted in the military invasion of Europe by vast non-European forces from the west and the east, and ended in partition along the line of the Iron Curtain. While in the eastern, Soviet, sphere, de-Europeanization was forcibly carried out in the face of opposition from the Catholic church and occasional physical resistance, western European countries voluntarily accepted Americanization and the presence of American troops. (Fig. 94.)

[4] *Barraclough (1955), pp. 216-17*

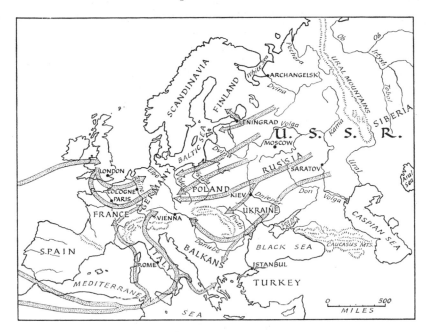

figure 91   Europe: the American and Soviet 'invasions', 1943-5.

THE U.S.S.R. AND EASTERN EUROPE

The end of the war with Germany found the Soviets in possession of all eastern Europe except much of Yugoslavia, Greece and Turkey. Yugoslavia was liberated by its own Communists. Although the Western Allies hoped to see democratically elected governments in the countries of eastern Europe, especially in Poland, the Soviet Union was determined that regimes amenable to itself should prevail and, between 1946 and 1948, Communist dictatorships were set up in all of them except Greece, which was not in the agreed Soviet sphere, and Turkey, which lay beyond it.

The Soviets could not seriously have been expected to abandon lightly their hard-won control over these bordering lands which had been used more than once as springboards for an attack upon Russia. In view of the strong anti-Russian feeling which existed to some extent in all of them, the Russians could not afford to allow democratic choice if they were to retain control; they knew too that the Americans had the wealth to draw 'free' governments into their own orbit. The Soviets were helped by the flight of many who feared and hated Communism, and by the leading part Communists had taken in active resistance to the Germans; this meant that they had the prestige of national heroes and the strength which military experience and arms in their hands gave them. They were thus able to seize power without much help from the Red Army, although its mere presence made for submission and compliance.

This formation, by a state that had repeatedly suffered aggression from the West, of a 'cordon sanitaire' in countries that had, through weakness or compliance, helped to make such aggression possible, was misrepresented by the United States as a threat to the whole of Europe, justifying continued American presence in western Europe, and even excusing the rearmament of the Germans. It is true that the Soviets also intrigued against the pro-Western government imposed upon Greece in the teeth of opposition from those resistance groups who had fought the Germans, and had tried to bully Turkey; but in view of the traditional but still frustrated aims of Russia in south-east Europe, this proved an irresistible temptation and bore no relation to any plan to enslave all Europe. They even refrained from force when Yugoslavia rejected Stalinist control.

THE U.S.S.R. AND GERMANY

The same consideration that led the U.S.S.R. to the enforced maintenance of communist dictatorship in eastern Europe compelled it to establish similar control over its share of occupied Germany: a democratic Germany would even more certainly be anti-Russian; it would again grow strong with Western aid, and would once more menace Soviet control of eastern Europe.

The war ended with stronger and more unanimous hostility to Russia in Germany than anywhere else. For many centuries the Germans had extended their influence eastwards at the expense of Slavic peoples whom they regarded as their inferiors. This attitude had been intensified by Nazi propaganda that the Russians were bestial subhumans. The initial atrocities, not unnaturally committed by the angry Soviet troops on their first incursion into Germany, were aggravated by the fact that many of these troops came from Asia (Kazakhs, Siberians, etc.). The Russians immediately and systematically stripped their zone of Germany of everything that could be used as 'reparations' for their own devastated territory, and a migration of refugees to western Germany began. These were eventually to form a minority 3 million strong and their hatred for Russia became a strong political factor making against any move towards reconciliation between West Germany and the Soviet Union. Resentment against the state that had stripped them of territory and deprived them of unity was allied to the humiliation of having, in one calamitous defeat, surrendered all the achievements of a long history of progress in the East.

The German problem presented Russia with a dilemma. To give freedom and acquiesce in unity would mean a hostile power ranged against her. But continued occupation and division ensured perpetual hostility and resulted in the German Communist party becoming one of the weakest in a country where, before the Nazi period, it had been one of the strongest. Matters were made worse by the ill-conceived arrangement whereby all occupation powers had a share in Berlin which was itself imprisoned within the Soviet zone. West Berlin was to become a beacon of liberty in a sea of East German discontent and therefore a standing provocation to the Soviets.

There are advantages from the Soviet viewpoint to be set against the perpetuation of German ill-will: Germany is rendered less dangerous potentially by division and Poland is tied to Russia by her possession of such a large extent of former German territory. Furthermore, if Germany is ever to be peacefully united or to recover her lost lands, this can only be done peacefully by turning to the Soviet Union. The West can do nothing to help in this way. Against this must be set the danger that Germany might hope to reach these goals in war, and there the cooperation of the West would be essential. Be that as it may, the German attitude is undoubtedly an obstacle in the way of any major improvement in Soviet relations with the West.[1]

THE U.S.S.R. AND FRANCE

Russia's relationship with France has always been more indirect than that with Germany, with whom she came into actual physical contact whenever the thin screen of weaker East European peoples was penetrated. Yet it was French culture that was established in St Petersburg during the eighteenth century and a French general who came uninvited to Moscow in the nineteenth; and very soon afterwards a Russian tsar rode triumphantly in Paris. The French again took part in the invasion of the Crimea. But the Russians never held the French in the same strange mixture of admiration and dislike, awe and contempt with which they regarded the Germans. The French, perhaps, seemed more human and less formidable, and eventually they and the Russians drew together, in fear of the common enemy, because of their position on either side of him. Just as it was French culture that was adopted in the eighteenth century, so it was French capitalism that predominated in the industrial revolution of the late nineteenth.

Although the military alliance between France and the Russian Empire ended in the defeat and destruction of the latter in 1917, and French troops subsequently aided the anti-Bolshevik Whites, this did not prevent the formation of a Franco-Soviet alliance in 1935. Again, despite the failure of this pact in the 1938 and 1939 crises, the fall of France in 1940, and de Gaulle's fruitless visit to Moscow in 1944, it seemed in 1966 as if it were to Russia that Gaulliste France was turning, seeking a counterweight, not this time to Germany, but to the power of the United States in Europe.

De Gaulle's old-fashioned idea of a Europe that extends to the Urals was as pleasing to the Soviet government as his determination to resist the American domination of western Europe. For although the division between Europe and Asia has no real significance whatever in the U.S.S.R., it is obviously convenient for the Soviet Union to claim to be a European power entitled to a voice in purely European matters and also to urge the exclusion of the U.S.A. from them. Just as Stalin had said to Matsuoka, the Japanese foreign minister in 1941, 'We are Asiatics too',[2] so could Kosygin propose in 1966 a pan-European conference on European security in which the U.S.S.R. would participate as a European power.

[1] *For an examination of the relationship between Russia and Germany, see Laqueur (1965), pp. 252, 266-87*
[2] *Werth (1964), p. 121*

M*

THE U.S.S.R. AND BRITAIN

Although relations between Britain and Russia were good, though mainly on a commercial basis, for over two hundred years after Chancellor's arrival in Moscow in 1553, Britain in the nineteenth century conceived an unreasonable fear of Russian expansion towards the sea and undertook to resist it at every point. Except for the brief periods 1905-17 and 1941-5, when both were motivated by hostility to Germany, relations between the two countries have been unfriendly. British public opinion took kindly neither to tsarist autocracy nor to communist dictatorship. Yet the Russians have suffered tyranny not from choice but from necessity.

Since the war, British policy towards the U.S.S.R. has been merely an echo of that of Washington. Possibly an independent Britain would have continued the wartime alliance. But by 1945 'the Anglo-American relationship had become that of patron and client'.[1] By acting as host to American bases and weapons directed against the U.S.S.R., British governments have compelled the Soviets to train nuclear missiles upon Britain, thereby ensuring the island's destruction in case of major war, a situation hardly conducive to good relations between the two countries.

An alternative policy for Britain would have been to have rejected dependence on American financial assistance, and the military alliance and bases that went with it, and instead, with parsimony and austerity, to have steered a course free of entanglement with either great power, in the manner of Queen Elizabeth I in a similar world situation. Certainly, for countries such as Britain, the U.S.S.R. has much to offer. She has a surplus of many of the commodities Britain needs, notably petroleum, and she is likely to be a market for both producers' and consumers' goods for a very long time to come.

Were it not for the suspicions of governments, it is likely that the British and Russians, as peoples, might have developed a more fruitful and permanent friendship than either has succeeded in keeping with any other European people. The author of an illuminating wartime book on 'Russia and Britain' wrote:

> *There is in these two disparate countries, one immense, the other little, situated at the farthest extremities of the European mass, a spirit of humanity and kindness which is distilled from the same ingredients, and which is found nowhere else.*[2]

However that may be, it is certainly true that both peoples are less geographically introverted than other Europeans, the British looking overseas and the Russians eastwards. Both built great empires, the possession of which had profound influences upon their life and outlook. But, whereas a continental empire can be bound and assimilated to the mother country, a scattered overseas empire inevitably develops break-away tendencies.

[1] *Taylor (1965), p. 598*
[2] *Crankshaw (n.d.), p. 104*

THE U.S.S.R. AND THE UNITED STATES

Both the Russian and American empires resulted from expansion over a whole continental area at the expense of less advanced peoples. The 'metropolitan' Muscovite state which developed between Europe and the Urals during the fifteenth and sixteenth centuries obtained dominion throughout northern Asia during the eighteenth. The 'metropolitan' American power which developed between the sea and the Appalachians during the seventeenth and eighteenth centuries spread rapidly across the North American continent to the Pacific in the nineteenth.

It was to be some time before the appearance of these two powers on opposite sides of the Pacific and Arctic oceans was to become a hostile confrontation. Japanese sea power intervened in the Pacific and was of more concern to both powers until the 1940s. Not until British influence in Canada was replaced by American, and not until aircraft and rockets made the Arctic ice surmountable, did the northern ocean acquire strategic significance.

During the nineteenth century tsarist Russia accommodated the United States by relinquishing her claim to territory in Oregon and California south of 54°40' in 1824-5 and by the sale of Alaska in 1867. Nicholas II's Far Eastern policy was not so disturbing to the United States, with its eyes on Japan as a potential rival in the Pacific, as it was to Great Britain. Even during the Intervention, American forces were in the Russian Far East more as a counterbalance to the Japanese than to assist the Whites. American pressure secured the withdrawal of the Japanese from the Soviet mainland in 1922.[1]

There was much more popular sympathy in the United States with the Russian Revolution than in Europe, and the Americans had stepped in to relieve famine in 1921-2. But 'big business' in America did not look kindly upon communism, the danger of which was heightened by the onset of the Great Depression. Nevertheless, the United States recognized the Soviet Union in 1933, partly to obtain cessation of communist propaganda in the U.S.A. Fear of Japan's aggressive intentions also played its part in improving relations, especially in the U.S.S.R., alarmed by the Japanese seizure of Manchuria.

Franklin D. Roosevelt, America's powerful president from 1932 to 1945, remained sympathetic to the U.S.S.R., a sympathy strengthened by the collision of American and Japanese power in the Pacific. During the war he formed an admiration for Stalin with whom he readily cooperated. His death and replacement by Truman abruptly changed this cordial relationship. But circumstances had changed as well as men: Japan had been defeated; the new atomic bomb gave the United States irresistible power; American and Russian forces faced each other across the prostrate body of Europe. A new world political pattern had developed, with the U.S.S.R. representing the centre and the United States dominant amongst the peripheral powers.

[1] *Treadgold (1964), p. 233*

The effect of the war on the relative strengths of the U.S.S.R. and the U.S.A. was far-reaching. Before 1939, America was stagnating in economic depression while the Soviet Union was undergoing rapid industrialization. But war preparations and war itself had pulled the United States out of an economic slough into an unprecedented boom. It now had an industrial capacity developed far beyond the pre-war level and a technology of the most advanced kind. The problem was how, in peace time, to employ this immense industrial capacity. But the effect on the U.S.S.R. was a loss of 25 million or more lives, the destruction of the industrial potential of the most developed parts of the country, and an indescribable degree of suffering and weariness. Although Russian troops occupied half Europe, their presence was urgently needed back in Russia: for agricultural revival, for industrial reconstruction, and for social well-being. Families had long been divided and the sexes separated. Even when all the men were back in Russia, there would still be a surplus of several million women.

Yet, despite all her sacrifices, Russia again found herself plunged suddenly into technological backwardness and military defencelessness. The U.S.A. at the end of the war, was not only strengthened and enriched, but sole possessor of the ultimate weapon. Her will could be enforced upon Russia by the mere threat of its use. The Cuban crisis of 1962 showed that even the fully nuclear-armed U.S.S.R. of the 1960s would withdraw before an American ultimatum rather than risk atomic war. The relatively weak Russia of the late 1940s and early 1950s would have had no choice.

Economically, however, America could not admit this. Her economy was so geared to the production of a vast flow of weapons that it was economically and politically difficult to halt it. Therefore, despite possession of weapons which the U.S.S.R. did not have and against which she had no defence, and despite the appalling and crippling losses which the Soviet Union had suffered, it suited the U.S.A. to brand the U.S.S.R. as a potential aggressor. It also suited those countries of western Europe which had come to rely upon American aid, and which could not or would not stand upon their own feet, to pay lip service to this myth and to subscribe to the American-dominated anti-Soviet North Atlantic Treaty Alliance.

The Russians knew that the dropping of the atomic bombs on Japan was unnecessary because they had themselves received intimations of Japanese readiness to surrender. They believed that '*their real purpose was, first and foremost, to intimidate Russia*'. Actually, the effect was to produce:

> on the Russian side a feeling of anger and acute distrust vis à vis the West. Far from becoming more amenable, the Soviet Government became more stubborn. Inside Russia, too, the regime became much harder after the war instead of becoming softer, as many had hoped it would be.[1]

THE ARMS RACE

The Soviet Union entered the arms race of the 1950s reluctantly. Because it was striving with insufficient industrial capacity to achieve goals of

[1] *Werth (1964), p. 1,004*

expanding production, increased armaments expenditure delayed the time when it would achieve its aim of becoming the leading industrial nation with the highest standard of living. But American productive capacity and labour were not fully utilized; the steel industry was working at under 70 per cent of capacity and unemployment was high. In such circumstances disarmament was as impracticable for the United States as it was urgent for the U.S.S.R. As the American Senate was told in 1960:

> *We, in this country, have such an involvement of military spending in our domestic economy that it is politically risky even to talk of cutting back defense spending, even if it be a waste that we are cutting out.*[1]

Although the press and politicians of the U.S.A. and other western countries fostered the myth of a peace-loving America frustrated in its desire for disarmament by the intransigence of an aggressive Russia, there was no such picture in the official reports and industrial magazines. In these the Soviet desire for a relaxation of tension and disarmament was admitted, but it was argued that America could not afford to respond. Soviet overtures were at first regarded as signs that Russia could not stand the pace, which therefore should be quickened:

> *What the Russians have been shooting for at the disarmament conferences in London is quite clear. They are caught up in an economic crisis. . . . They want to slow down the arms race because the U.S. pace is too stiff for their existing technical resources to match.*[2]

When, however, the 'sputnik' showed that, far from being dismayed, the Soviet response had been to outdistance the United States, it was said that the Russians needed a period of 'peaceful coexistence' to enable them to overtake the United States economically. Should they be allowed this respite, *'the gap between our two economies by 1970 will be dangerously narrowed'*.[3]

Military production had become an integral part of the American economy, with the Department of Defense

> the largest organization known to man. At the time of the Commission's studies, its expenditures consumed one-seventh of the national income. The Department employed 4,300,000 people, which was twice the combined manpower of the ten largest corporations of the Nation. Its assets, real and personal, approximated to $140 billion, which equalled the value of all privately owned land in the United States.[4]

From every part of the country came incessant demands from senators, representatives, unions, chambers of commerce, etc., for more 'defense' spending. A member of a U.S. Senate committee quoted from a newspaper article that *'in view of the slight downturn in business the Government was going to pump prime by putting out more defense contracts'*.[5] After another

[1] Defense Procurement (*1960*), p. 186
[2] Fortune (*August 1957*)
[3] Comparisons (*1960*), p. 11
[4] Defense Procurement (*1960*), p. 397
[5] Defense Procurement (*1960*), p. 188

downturn in the United States economy, *Business Week* reported (15 October 1960):

> *A quiet boost to the economy—Faster rate of defense spending. . . . Large new contracts are being announced almost daily at the Pentagon and at defense procurement offices around the country. . . . Some degree of political motivation is widely assumed among Pentagon career employees.*

It is no secret that big business corporations have great influence over the policies of the U.S. Government. For them huge million-dollar 'defense' contracts on a cost-plus basis are much preferable to touting domestic appliances to reluctant housewives.

When a country is economically and politically committed to such heavy military spending, and when a preponderant part of the sales of many of the largest industrial companies in the country are to the Defense Department, the taxation and waste involved have to be plausibly justified, and to this end an enemy has to be created in the public mind. Hence there was constant and hysterical abuse of the Soviet Union, its system and its leaders on television and radio, and in the press and magazines, organs of opinion controlled by the big corporations through their advertising. But by the mid-1960s there was a possibility that China would take Russia's place as bogeyman and pretext.

THE U.S.S.R. AND CHINA

Although Russia's relationship with the old China was imperialistic, her geographical position as a land neighbour ensured that it was different from that of the European powers whose approach was by sea. Whereas they established themselves in the most densely populated parts of China proper, Russian encroachment was marginal and in regions not heavily populated and not part of metropolitan China. As a result, Russian territorial gains at China's expense have been more permanent and more tolerable than the privileged positions which other foreigners seized for themselves in the Chinese ports.

Russia's position between Asia and Europe produced, in the late tsarist period, a distinctive attitude towards China. In this attitude conflicting elements of repulsion and attraction were present:[1] the distant memory of the Mongol terror was revived as a 'yellow peril'; yet some felt that Russia's destiny was to bring civilization to the East and others believed that economic and territorial expansion there would solve her political problems.

As it was the fur trade that drew the Russians eastwards into Siberia, they were at first kept busy in the northern forests, out of China's way. It was the desire to establish overland trade relationships that eventually attracted their attention southwards, a motive that did not involve them in serious territorial dispute or military conflict. Manchu China was strong enough to deter Cossack incursions into her Empire. Consequently the boundary established by the Treaties of Nerchinsk (1689) and Kiakhta

[1] *Stepin (1962), pp. 251-2*

(1727) was not disturbed until 1858. The caravan trade with China contributed to Russia's commercial wealth during that period, gave her a stronger position in dealing with her European trading partners, and contributed to the prosperity and fame of Nizhniy Novgorod and Astrakhan.

By the mid-nineteenth century, China's strength was so much reduced and Russia's position in Siberia so much stronger, that some pressure on the old boundary between the two was inevitable. The flow of settlers into Siberia was growing and, unlike the fur traders, they wanted to settle as far south as the mountainous nature of the borderland would allow: this meant the Amur valley and, farther east, the Ussuri valley. And, as Russia became more conscious of her potential role in the Pacific, a naval base as far south as possible, so as to minimize the hindrance of winter ice, became a motive. Annexations, bringing the Empire in the east south to the Amur and to Vladivostok, were made in 1858-60. Farther west, adjustments to Russian advantage were made on the Tyan Shan boundary between 1864 and 1881, but the upper Ili valley was returned to China in the latter year. The Ili flows into lake Balkhash and the Russians have since argued that the whole valley should come under their jurisdiction.

During the 1880s, partly as a reaction to rebuffs in south-eastern Europe, and partly because of the growing influence of 'Easterners' in the making of policy, renewed government interest was shown in the Far East, and Korea came at times under Russian protection, a status questioned by Japan in the 1890s. But in the 1890s Russia's position was strengthened by the building of the Trans-Siberian railway, one reason for which was to have closer economic ties with China. Russia joined with the European powers in forcing Japan to surrender Korea in 1895, while she herself obtained from China a concession to carry the Trans-Siberian through Manchuria to the coast at Vladivostok, and this railway was to be policed by Russians. As a result Russian influence in Manchuria grew greatly and Harbin became a Russian town.

In 1898 Nicholas II could not resist the temptation of joining in the exploitation of China's weakness, although Russia had guaranteed China's territorial integrity. When the Germans forced the Chinese to give them a 99-year lease of Kiao-Chow, he in turn exacted the lease of Port Arthur. The Trans-Siberian railway was joined to Port Arthur, and the Tsar could claim that his Empire now had an ice-free outlet on to the Pacific. But if Port Arthur was to be secure, control of Korea was necessary and this the Japanese were prepared to fight to resist. Port Arthur's acquisition thus led on to the disastrous war with Japan. It also meant that the Russians forfeited Chinese good will and shared in the odium that attached to other foreign exploiters of China's weakness. Feelings against Russia became even stronger when the Russians played—with the Japanese—the leading part in the capture of Peking in 1900, during the Boxer rebellion. The Soviet Union today, in its relations with China, suffers still from Nicholas II's part in the rape of China.

The Bolshevik revolution and subsequent ostracism of the new Soviet state by the Western world, evoked much sympathy amongst those Asians who resented Imperialism, and relations between the new nationalist government in Nanking of Sun Yat-sen and Chiang Kai-shek and Moscow were at first warm and close. But when the Nationalists extended their control northwards and questioned the rights which the Russians had resumed over the Chinese Eastern railway, their friendship vanished and Russian advisers were expelled (1928-9). The Soviets, however, could find compensation in the growing strength of Mao-Tse-tung's communist movement in the eastern uplands. When Japan invaded China in 1937, the Soviet Union aided both Nationalists and Communists.

In 1945, the Soviet Union's war aims were unashamedly to bring back the situation of 45 years before, after Nicholas II had seized Port Arthur. Roosevelt sympathized with them, particularly with the need for a warm-water port on the Yellow Sea, and promised to secure Chiang Kai-shek's acquiescence on the part of China. At Yalta it was agreed that Outer Mongolia should remain independent of China under Soviet protection, that the U.S.S.R. should have the use of the port of Dairen and the naval base of Port Arthur, and that the Manchurian railways should be jointly operated by the Soviet Union and China in such a way as to protect '*the pre-eminent interests of the Soviet Union*'.[1]

The Soviet Union had thus, unlike all the Western powers, carried the old Imperialism towards China into the new era. But the situation was to change dramatically between 1946 and 1950 with the defeat of Chiang Kai-shek's Nationalists by Mao Tse-tung's Communists. In the Sino-Soviet Treaty of 1950, the U.S.S.R. promised to help build up the economy and military strength of Communist China and to surrender Port Arthur, Dairen and control of the Manchurian railways. Doubtless it was thought that, although China could in no sense be a satellite, she would long be dependent on the Soviet Union for technical advice and equipment, if not grateful for the stocks of Japanese arms which, handed over to Mao, were largely instrumental in his success.

Korea had, in 1945, been divided along the 38th parallel into two zones, the northern under Soviet and the southern under American control. When the Russian and American troops went, they left behind a communist régime in the north which proceeded with land reforms, and an American-backed government in the south which preserved the old social order. When, in 1950, the North Koreans invaded the South, their army met with little resistance until the United States intervened in strength. If the Soviet Union was behind the northern invasion, the motive may have been the same as that behind the intervention in Korea of half a century before, which provoked the war with Japan. For the newly-gained possession of Port Arthur meant little if the Yellow Sea was to be dominated by the presence of a foreign power in Korea. On the other hand, the discontent of the peasantry in the south may have been enough to tempt the communist zeal of the northerners, without outside instigation, although it

[1] *Treadgold* (1964), *p. 396*

is unlikely that they would have undertaken such an adventure without Soviet consent at least.

Soviet economic and military assistance to China were at first on a very large scale, enabling China to participate in the Korean War and to begin the process of modernization. In return for machinery, equipment and petroleum, the U.S.S.R. imported tungsten and other metals, and textiles. Early in the 1950s more than 70,000 Russian military and civilian advisers were stationed in China. Possibly resentment at this dependence, Soviet refusal to help with nuclear weapons, and a Russian willingness to compromise with the capitalist world, all played a part in the deterioration of relations after Stalin's death. In 1960 the Soviet advisers began to go home.[1] China has questioned the Soviet Union's title to lands once part of the Chinese Empire and has accused her of complicity with the United States. In consequence of this split, trade between the two countries has shrunk, to the disadvantage of both. In 1956 Soviet trade with China was greater than that with any other country and amounted to 27 per cent of the whole; by 1958 its share had dropped to 17 per cent and in 1963 it was only 4 per cent.[2]

Seen on a political map, the U.S.S.R. and China seem to share the 'heartland' of the world island between them. But maps of population and development show that China proper is maritime rather than continental and, therefore, part of the world periphery.[3] China's eastern continental or 'heartland' areas are empty, except where they border upon developing Soviet regions. Here the peoples are non-Chinese and have more in common with those across the border in the U.S.S.R. Many of them do not take kindly to Chinese rule. The peoples of Outer Mongolia have several times reaffirmed their preference to remain in the Soviet orbit. Pro-Soviet revolts have occurred in the Ili valley region. Had the Soviet-Chinese alliance proved more lasting, it is likely that, with the building of railways into outer China from the U.S.S.R. and with increased help from Russia, the more remote or 'heartland' areas of both countries would have developed faster economically.[4]

THE U.S.S.R. AND JAPAN

The relationship with Japan has been briefer and less complex than with China. Both became interested in extending their influence in the Far East at the same time—the 1880s and 1890s—and some degree of hostility was present throughout the first half of the twentieth century. The U.S.S.R. regained in 1945 more than she had lost in 1905, but Japan had caused her much anxiety during the interwar period and during the last war itself.

[1] *Freeborn (1966), p. 263*
[2] *Torgovlya (1964), pp. 11-15*
[3] *See the next chapter, pp. 371-380*
[4] *For a recent account of Chinese activity and policy in Sinkiang, see Freeberne (1966), pp. 103-24*

In 1966 a new economic deal was being negotiated between the two countries whereby Russia would buy Japanese textiles and consumer goods in return for oil and minerals, in the extraction and transport of which, Japanese interests would take part. But the Japanese claim to the southern Kurile Islands and Russian refusal to consider it, were obstacles to better relationships, as were constant quarrels over fishing rights.

THE GLOBAL POSITION OF THE U.S.S.R.

In 1904, and again in 1918, Sir Halford Mackinder, the man responsible for a renaissance in British geography, drew attention to what he called a 'pivot area' or 'heartland' which, because it was inaccessible to sea power, was potentially in a strong strategic position. If it were developed economically, it could threaten the supremacy of established powers whose strength lay in naval and commercial command of the seas. This 'heartland' corresponded to the bulk of the territory of the Russian Empire.[1]

In showing that there was potential conflict between the inaccessible heart of the 'world island' and its margins, Mackinder was but applying to the future a principle of political geography which had often operated, though on a smaller scale, in the past. Many nations had taken shape only

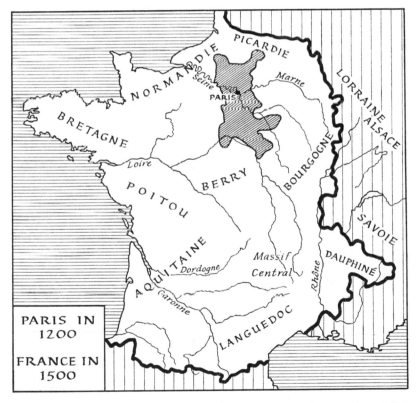

figure 95   The 'core' of France and its eventual expansion, 1200 1500: the 'heartland' principle on a national scale.

[1] *Mackinder* (1904); *Mackinder* (1919)

after a long struggle between a centrally-placed 'core' and peripheral areas (figs. 95, 96). In Europe the same process was at work on a continental scale. France, centrally placed in the old European system—which did not include Russia—continually disturbed the seventeenth and eighteenth centuries with her attempts to dominate the states around her. But peripheral alliances delayed her success until 1810, by which time it was too late (fig. 97). For Russia had become part of the European political and military system. France now lay too far to the west to reach Moscow without courting disaster. As Leibnitz was the first to observe, it was Germany which was central to this greater Europe.[1] No sooner was she unified by the railway and strengthened by industrialization, than she too embarked on the same course. By 1942, the Third Reich commanded the European periphery. But again it was too late: Russia had moved her power into and beyond the Urals. (Fig. 98.)

Mackinder foresaw that the principle of potential conflict between central and marginal powers would apply to the world as a unit as soon as Russia became strong. And he lived to see the heartland '*manned by a garrison sufficient both in number and quality*'.[2] The strategic aspect of his concept has been weakened by the coming of air power and nuclear weapons, and it will doubtless be affected—though in a way not easy to judge—by the nuclear-armed submarine. Yet, air power has still but limited capacity to move men and equipment in great quantities, and nuclear weapons are being relegated increasingly by strategists to the ultimate step of a lengthy stairway of 'escalation'.[3] Apart from the military aspect, there is also much evidence to support a contention that, where a vigorous and united central power exists, it exercises a strong centripetal pull upon weaker outlying heterogenous areas. The unifying of old Muscovy, of Napoleonic France and of Hitlerite Germany did not depend on military force alone: in each instance there were 'fifth columns' or 'fellow travellers' in most of the threatened peripheral areas. A strong central power emits a political, cultural or ideological flame which proves irresistible to many moths outside. On the other hand, the efforts of the stronger or more immune of the peripheral powers to unite the others, by persuasion or by force, are bitterly resented.

Post-war history cannot be fully understood except in terms of tension between the centre and the circumference of the world island. The 1939–45 war consisted essentially of two separate continental struggles, one in Europe and North Africa, the other in South-East Asia. Since then, the strengthening of the heartland by Russia and the determination of the U.S.A. to resist the expansion of the 'Communist bloc' at all points round its circumference, have produced—for the first time—a global strategy. A future war arising from and fought according to this strategy would be the first *World* War. The so-called World Wars I and II were continental, not

---

[1] *Fritzemeyer (1931), p. 148*
[2] *Mackinder (1943), p. 601*
[3] Fortune *(1965), pp. 110-12, 246-54*

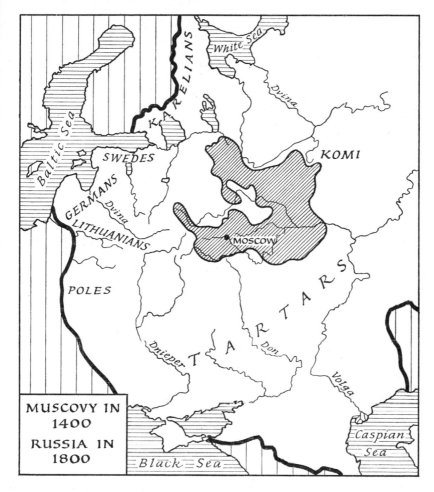

figure 96   The 'core' of Russia and its eventual expansion, 1400-1800.

global, in their conception and execution. If a world war is one fought in many parts of the world, then the Seven Years' and Napoleonic Wars, fought in North America, the West Indies, India, the East Indies and South Africa, as well as Europe, better deserve the name.

Mackinder would thus seem to have been justified in claiming in 1943 that his concept of the heartland was *'more valid and useful today than it was either twenty or fifty years ago'.*[1] Attempts to suggest that it depended upon looking at the world on a Mercator projection, whereas actually two similarly-placed super-powers confront each other across the 'icy sea', fail to convince. A map showing the land hemisphere serves only to reinforce the

[1] *Mackinder (1943), p. 603*

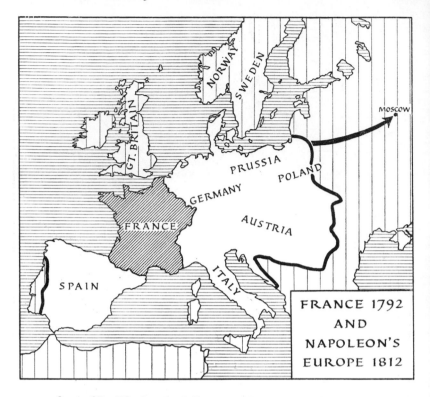

figure 97 The 'core' of Europe and its expansion, 1792-1812: the 'heartland' principle on a continental scale.

'heartland' position of the U.S.S.R. and to confirm the distinction between it, as a central power, and the U.S.A. as the leading circumferential state. In the centre is a 'heartland' consisting of the communist bloc. Around it are islands and peninsulas of varying size and power, but all peripheral to the heartland (fig. 99). The two great powers are not comparable in world position. This is clear from the fact that, whereas North America is entirely surrounded by oceans, the Soviet Union is land and ice locked. Whereas the U.S.A. has no land neighbours except Canada and Mexico, the U.S.S.R. is in actual contact with fourteen countries and within short reach of many more. Economically, the U.S.A. draws widely upon other peripheral states for human skills and raw materials, while the U.S.S.R. is almost completely self-sufficient.

As the economic development of the Volga-Baykal zone of the U.S.S.R. progresses, so the strength and applicability to global strategy of the heartland concept increases. This development of a continental interior— brilliantly described by Hooson in *A New Soviet Heartland?* (1964)—has been strengthened further by the discovery of the great West Siberian oilfield and the beginning of the second Trans-Siberian railway. This

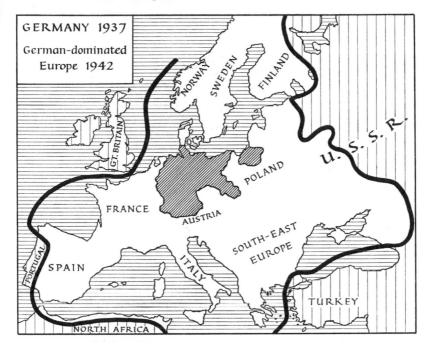

figure 98   The 'core' of greater Europe and its expansion, 1937-42.

building of a self-sufficient industrial zone, far from any ocean and independent of overseas trade, is unique. Here, for the first time, is truly continental development. Elsewhere, continents have not evolved as independent units, but rather their coastlands have developed in conjunction with overseas trade. This is clear and obvious in the southern continents with their great seaports and empty interiors. But, even in North America, industrial and commercial activity is concentrated in coastal zones in response to overseas and coastwise trade and transport. The chief apparent exception—the Great Lakes industrial area—found that it needed a seaway link with the ocean if it were to continue to prosper. While population is moving into the Soviet continental heartland from other parts of the U.S.S.R., most states of the interior of the U.S.A. are losing population to the coastal and lakeside regions.

Urban development strikingly demonstrates this difference between the Soviet Union and the rest of the world. The Soviet territory contains 30 cities whose population is over ½ million and 13 of them (43 per cent) are over 600 miles from the sea. In the rest of the world there are about 200 cities of similar size, but only 5 of them (2½ per cent) are so far from the sea.[1] The Arctic Ocean and Hudson Bay have not been regarded as 'sea' in these counts. If land-locked seas, such as the Baltic, were also excluded,

[1] *Buslepp (1926), pp. 13-20*

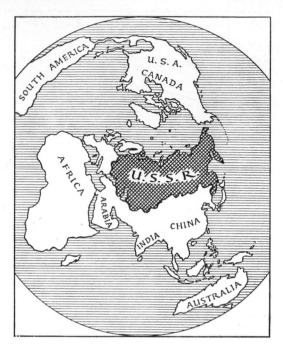

*figure 99   The U.S.S.R. and the peripheral lands: the 'heartland'
principle on a world scale.*

and distance from the ice-free and open ocean alone considered, then the
contrast between the U.S.S.R. and the rest of the world would be even
greater.

The reason for this striking difference between the continental development of the U.S.S.R. and the coastal development of all other continents,
lies partly in Russia's history of vain struggle for free and open outlet to the
ocean, and partly in the application of Marxist doctrine which supposedly
belittled the environment as a factor. Russia welcomed Marxism in part
because it promised that, if a country was ahead in historical development
of its social structure, i.e., if it had replaced capitalism by socialism, then
Man's triumph over Nature would follow.[1] As Nature—or the physical-
geographical environment—was harsh in Russia, it became all the more
desirable to establish the kind of society which could so order the means of
production as to triumph over it. Various ambitious Stalinist schemes were
entitled *'great plans for the transformation of Nature'*. Such ideas and
terminology were doubtless of great value at first in giving the Soviet
people the courage and confidence to tackle their unfavourable geographical
position and physical environment in a bold and imaginative way, and in
making them readier to undergo hardship. But they also led to difficulties

[1] *See Burke (1956), pp. 1035-51; Cole & German (1961), pp. 20-31*

through underrating the environmental factor which, because of the capital needed to deal with it when hostile, becomes an economic factor. The difficulties have been most apparent and have come quickest to the fore in agriculture, because here the environmental factor is the strongest. But they are also present in every aspect of the Soviet economy and of Soviet society—and they have led, not only to a greater sophistication in Soviet economics and the appraisal of alternative investment projects, but to much controversy among Soviet geographers about the role of geography.[1] This has led to the abandonment of the extreme Stalinist view, which is regarded as a distortion of true Marxist-Leninist principles.[2]

Stalinist Marxists have not been alone in their contemptuous attitude to the geographical factors of position, climate, etc. L. S. Amery commented on Mackinder's 'heartland' concept that it

> *would not matter whether they [great powers] are in the centre of a continent or on an island; those people who have the industrial power and the power of invention and science will be able to defeat all the others.*[3]

More recently, Gottmann has written:

> *Once we admit that no climatic regime is an obstacle that could not be overcome by a stubborn and organized national endeavour, then the eventual part of the environment in international affairs is reduced to a small lot indeed.*[4]

There is a modern tendency thus to minimize the environmental factor, a tendency which leads to serious errors of judgment.[5] Though it may be true that Man is now able to develop a continental interior with modern technology, despite distance from the sea and a harsh climate, the fact remains that it is more costly economically and more difficult socially. Therefore, a state which pursues such a capital-demanding policy, at once places itself in a disadvantageous position in competing with states better placed geographically. For this reason the success of the Soviet economic heartland is not assured. It remains true that the carriage of goods by sea is very much cheaper than by land and that a continental interior can be developed only at much greater cost than a coastal region.[6] Pipelines may mitigate this disadvantage to some extent, and the new airship centres at Novosibirsk and Nizhniy Tagil in the Urals point to the hope that dirigibles may also help.

The following table of index costs of moving one ton over one kilometre

---

[1] *Kalesnik (1965); Anuchin (1960); Anuchin (1965); Saushkin (1965); Ryabchikov (1964)*
[2] *Saushkin (1964), p. 10*
[3] *Quoted in Jackson (1964), p. 45*
[4] *Gottmann in Jackson (1964), p. 22*
[5] *Fisher (1965), pp. 13-19*
[6] *Weigert (1957), p. 261*

from Irkutsk to Deputatskiy in East Siberia, is informative in this respect:[1]

Dirigible airship	*100*
Aircraft	*443*
Road—Rail	*384*
River—Rail	*75*
River—road—northern sea route	*53*

But the last two combinations are available for only brief seasons each year. So that, although transport of heavy machinery by dirigible is much cheaper than other all-season alternatives, it is still considerably dearer than methods available all the year round to more favoured countries, but only for two or three months to the Soviet Union.

Quite apart from transport, the physical environment of much of the Soviet interior is such as to add formidably to the costs of constructing and operating industrial plant and housing population. Each time these difficulties are overcome, and a new enterprise is established in swamp, on permafrost, in the mountains or the desert, a great triumph for Soviet technology and ingenuity is hailed. Yet the cost is enormous and, although it can be minimized by planning industrial complexes that make the most of expensive installations with the minimum of labour,[2] it remains a fact that it would have been much cheaper to import by sea. This is true of the wheat so dearly purchased by the Virgin Lands scheme and of many other commodities abundantly available on the world market. Where capital is desperately short and so much needs to be done, the temptation to yield to economic expediency by concentrating growth in the west must be great. But to give way to this temptation would be to become, once more, a country whose industrial development was highly and dangerously concentrated in the margins of Europe within reach of the great seaports. Such a Russia would no longer be the heartland of the land hemisphere, but back again on the eastern fringe of Europe in an east-west Atlantic-centred Mercator-projected world. Soviet difficulties in industrializing the continental heartland are not limited to the economic liabilities of un-favourable physical geography and distance from the sea. There are human problems as well. A modern industrial state depends upon the cooperation of able management and skilled labour. The newly developed eastern areas are desperately short of these, because Soviet citizens show just as marked a preference for living in Moscow, Leningrad and the west as Americans do for California, Florida and Arizona. This problem is aggravated because the local ethnic groups fail, for various reasons, to provide the labour required for industrial development. This therefore is normally Russian and has to be enticed from Russia.[3] Siberian industrial development has been slowed down because the migration of labour to new areas has not kept pace with the installation of capital equipment. There has even been a

[1] *Alexeyeva (1965), p. 206*
[2] *Pomus (1964), p. 376; Krotov (1964), pp. 50-6*
[3] *Perevedentsev (1965), pp. 31-9*

migration away from some parts of Siberia, mainly because of the harsh conditions there.[1]

To persuade skilled men to leave Russia and endure the hardships of the Siberian heartland, something more substantial than propaganda is required. Higher pay, longer leave, earlier retirement—these and other inducements add still further to the great cost of developing the continental interior. The burden falls upon the whole nation in terms of deprivation and sacrifice. The unpopularity these cause may constitute a threat to the security and permanence of the authoritative government upon whose existence such plans for conquering Nature depend. For competing political parties would be unlikely to succeed with policies involving austerity and hardship.

One is forced to conclude that the Russian's struggle with an unkind geographical position, which for a thousand years involved him in fighting for access to the ocean, which he could never satisfactorily gain, is no less severe now that he is grappling with the development of a continental interior. The word 'problems' appears more and more often in the titles of contributions to Soviet economic geography: it appears in 17 of the 50 titles of periodical articles listed in *Soviet Geography* for March 1965 and is implicit in several others.

There has been a traditional conflict between those who, seeing themselves as Europeans, held that Russia must keep contact with Europe and the world overseas, and those who considered they were a people apart Eurasians some would say—destined to develop their own civilization in isolation, or at the most as a bridge between Europe and Asia.[2] This division of opinion or allegiance is also found amongst Russian emigrés.[3] This conflict has a geographical foundation because it arises from two different ways of looking at Russia's global position—the first sees this as being on the eastern march of Europe in a rectangularly conceived world stretching from west to east with the Atlantic in the centre; the seco nd, as the heartland of the world island. A history shaped by the former vi ew brought Russia little but conflict, frustration, disillusion and backwardness. The second promises much in the way of independence and world power, but only at a very high price economically, socially and politically.

Stalin chose the second path and the Soviet Union has made impressive progress along it. Yet increasingly the westward pull of old Russia is being felt and the wisdom of much investment in Siberia and elsewhere is being questioned. As Hooson remarks, *'the forces favouring concentration in the west . . . have recently been gathering strength'*.[4] It is admitted that many experts would have preferred to spend the money invested in the Virgin Lands of Kazakhstan on draining the marshes of White Russia, and western industrial areas continue to grow rapidly because of the

[1] *Pokshishevskiy (1964), p. 7*
[2] *Stepin (1962), pp. 251-2*
[3] *Mirsky (1927), pp. 311-12*
[4] *Hooson (1966), p. 345*

availability of skilled labour, while Siberian factories remain unmanned. Spherical though the earth may be, it rotates towards the east: the Sun draws the torrid zone across its middle, neglecting the frigid regions around the poles; between them it allows—in the northern hemisphere—temperate situations where alternating land and sea masses meet, but away from such favoured margins extreme climates make life difficult even for modern Man. Whatever strategic value there may be in polar and land-hemisphere views of the globe, the traditional east-west rectangular one, old-fashioned though it may be, is by no means obsolete. It retains great economic significance and therein—and in China—lies the threat to Russia's future as the 'heartland' of the World Island.

ADELUNG, F. (1846). *Kritisch-Literarische Ubersicht der Reisenden in Russland bis 1700*. St Petersburg & Leipzig.
ALEKSEYEVA, T. I. (1965). 'Dirizhabl na Severe', *Problemy Severa*, Vol. 9, pp. 201-6.
ALEXINSKY, G. (1913). *Modern Russia*. London, Fisher Unwin.
AMES, E. (1947). 'A Century of Russian Railroad Construction, 1837-1936', *American Slavic and East European Review*, Vol. VI, pp. 57-74.
ANDERSON, J. (1963). Commentary on 'Low and High-Yielding Crops in the U.S.S.R.' by Norman Jasny, *Soviet Agricultural and Peasant Affairs* (ed. R. D. Laird). Lawrence, Kansas, University of Kansas Press.
ANDERSON, M. S. (1954). 'English Views of Russia in the Seventeenth Century', *The Slavonic and East European Review*. London, Vol. 39, pp. 143-53.
ANUCHIN, V. A. (1960). *Teoreticheskie Problemy Geografii Metody geograficheskikh issledovaniy*. Moscow.
ANUCHIN, V. A. (1965). 'A Sad Tale About Geography' (trans.), *Soviet Geography*, Vol. 6, No. 7, pp. 27-31.
ARMSTRONG, T. (1952). *The Northern Sea Route: Soviet Exploration of the North East Passage*. Cambridge, Cambridge University Press.
ARMSTRONG, T. (1965). *Russian Settlement in the North*. Cambridge, Cambridge University Press.
ATKINSON, J. A. & WALKER, J. (1812). *A Picturesque Representation of the Manners, Customs and Amusements of the Russians*. London, 3 vols.
ATKINSON, T. W. (1858). *Oriental and Western Siberia*. London.
BAIN, R. N. (1908). *Slavonic Europe: 1447-1796*. Cambridge, Cambridge University Press.
BARANSKIY, N. (1950). *Ekonomicheskaya Geografiya SSSR*. Moscow.
BARRACLOUGH, G. (1955). *History in a Changing World*. Oxford, Blackwell.
BARSOV, N. P. (1885). *Ocherki Russkoi istoricheskoi geografii*. Warsaw.
BAUMGARTEN, N. DE (1927). *Généalogies et marriages occidentaux des Rurikides russes du xe au xiiie siècle*. Rome, Institutum Orientalum Studiorum.
BEAZLEY, C. R. (1949). *The Dawn of Modern Geography*. New York, Peter Smith, 3 vols.
BEAZLEY, R. et al. (1918). *Russia from the Varangians to the Bolsheviks*. Oxford, Clarendon Press.
BEETON, SAMUEL (1868). *Dictionary of Geography*. London.
BELL, J. (1763). *Travels from St Petersburg to Diverse Parts of Asia: 1715-18 & 1719-22*. Glasgow, 2 vols.
BELOFF, M. (1957). *Europe and the Europeans*. London, Chatto and Windus.
BLACKWELL, W. L. (1965). 'The Old Believers and the Rise of Private Enterprise in Early Nineteenth-Century Moscow,' *Slavic Review*, vol. 24, pp. 407-18.
BLANCHARD, R. (1936). *La Géographie de l'Europe*, Paris, Alcan.

BLOCK, M. (1863). 'Tableau comparé de la puissance des divers Etats de l'Europe', *Revue des deux Mondes*, Vol. 2, p. 216-24.

BLUM, J. (1961). *Lord and Peasant in Russia from the Ninth to the Nineteenth Century*. Princeton, Princeton University Press.

BOND, E. H. (ed.) (1856). *Russia at the Close of the Sixteenth Century*. London, Hakluyt Society.

BONWETSCH, G. (1919). *Geschichte der deutschen Kolonien an dem Volga*. Stuttgart, Deutsches Ausland-Museums.

BRIDGE, C. A. G. (ed.) (1899). *History of the Russian Fleet during the reign of Peter the Great by a contemporary Englishman* (1724). London, Navy Record Society.

BRUCE, P. H. (1782). *Memoirs of Peter Henry Bruce Esq*. London.

BURKE, A. E. (1956). Influence of Man upon Nature—the Russian View: a Case Study. *See* THOMAS, W. L. (ed.) (1956).

BUSLEPP, W. (1926). *Die Entwicklung der russischen Eisenbahnen in der Vergangenheit und Gegenwart*. Wurzburg, Becker.

BUSSOW, C. (1617). Verwirter Zustand des Russischen Reiches. *See* ADELUNG, F. (1846).

CARPINI, P. (1598). *See* HAKLUYT, R. (1598).

CARELL, P. (1964). *Hitler's War on Russia*. Trans. from German by E. Osers. London, Harrap.

CARR, E. H. (1953). *The Bolshevik Revolution*, Vol. III. London, Macmillan.

CARR, E. H. (1956). Russia and Europe. *See* PARES, R. & TAYLOR, A. J. P. (ed.) (1956).

CARR, J. (1805). *A Northern Summer* (1804). London.

CHADWICK, N. K. (1946). *The Beginnings of Russian History*. Cambridge, Cambridge University Press.

CHAMBERS, F. P. (1963). *This Age of Conflict: The Western World—1914 to the Present*. London, Hart-Davis.

CHAPPE D'AUTEROCHE. M. l'ABBÉ J. (1770). *A Journey into Siberia, made by order of the King of France . . . in 1761, containing an account of the manners and customs of the Russians, the present state of their empire, etc.* London.

CHEMINS DE FER. (1946). *Les Chemins de Fer en U.R.S.S.* Paris, Presses Universitaires de France.

CLARK, J. G. D. (1952). *Prehistoric Europe*. London, Methuen.

CLARKE, E. D. (1810). *Travels in Various Countries*, Vol. I. Russia, Tartary and Turkey (1800). London.

CLARKSON, J. D. (1962). *A History of Russia*. London, Longmans.

CLAUSEWITZ, C. VON (1843). *The Campaign of 1812 in Russia*. London.

COCHRANE, J. D. (1824). *Narrative of a Pedestrian Journey through Russia and Siberian Tartary . . . during the years 1820-23*. London.

COLE, J. P. & GERMAN, F. C. (1961). *A Geography of the U.S.S.R.: the background to a planned economy*. London, Butterworths.

COMPARISONS (1960). *Comparisons of the United States and Soviet Economies: Hearings before the Joint Economic Committee, Congress of the United States*. Washington, D.C., U.S. Government Printing Office.

CONSTANTINE PORPHYROGENITUS. *De administrando imperio*. See MORAVCSIK (1949).

COUDENHOVE-KALERGI, R. N. (1935). 'Wo liegt die Ostgrenze Europas?' *Paneuropa*, vol. 11, pp. 318-22.

COXE, W. (1780). *An Account of the Russian Discoveries between Asia and America*. London.

COXE, W. (1784). *Travels into Poland, Russia, Sweden & Denmark*, 2 vols. London.

COXE, W. (1790). *Travels into Poland, Russia, Sweden & Denmark*, Vol. 3. London.

CRANKSHAW, E. (n.d.). *Russia and Britain*. London, Collins.

CRAVEN, LADY E. (1789). *A Journey through the Crimea to Constantinople in a series of letters*. London.

CRESSEY, G. (1951). *Asia's Lands and Peoples*. 2nd ed. New York, McGraw-Hill.

CROSS, S. H. (1930). *The Russian Primary Chronicle*. Cambridge, Mass., Harvard University Press.

CROSS, S. H. & SHERBOWITZ-WETZOR, O. P. (1953). *The Russian Primary Chronicle: Laurentian Text*. Cambridge, Mass., The Medieval Academy of America.

CURTIS, W. E. (1911). *Around the Black Sea*. London, Hodder & Stoughton.

CUSTINE, A. DE (1843). *La Russie en 1839*, 4 vols. 2nd ed. Paris.

DALLIN, D. J. (1964). *The Real Soviet Union*. New Haven, Yale University Press.

DANILEVSKI, N. (1920). *Russland und Europa*, trans. K. Nötzel. Stuttgart, Deutsche Verlags-Anstadt.

DEFENSE PROCUREMENT (1960). *Hearings before the Sub-committee on Defense Procurement*. Washington, U.S. Government Printing Office.

DICEY, E. (1867). *A Month in Russia during the Marriage of the Czarevitch*. London.

DITMAR, K. VON (1890). *Reisen und Aufenthalt in Kamschatka in den Jahren 1851-1855*, Vol. I. St Petersburg.

DOBB, M. (1948). *Soviet Economic Development since 1917*. London, Routledge & Kegan Paul.

DOSTOYEVSKIY, F. M. (1911). *Polnoye sobraniye sochineniye*, vol. 11. St Petersburg.

DVORNIK, F. (1949). *The Making of Central and Eastern Europe*. London, Polish Research Centre.

ECKARDT, J. (1870). *Modern Russia*. London, Smith, Elder.

EDE, C. (1951). *The War Speeches of the Rt Hon. Winston S. Churchill*. London, Cassell.

EFIMOV, A. V. (1950). *Iz istorii russkikh expeditsii*. Moscow.

ERICSSON, K. (1966). 'The Earliest Conversion of Rus to Christianity', *The Slavonic and East European Review*, Vol. 44, pp. 78-121.

FAINSOD, M. (1959). *Smolensk under Soviet Rule*. London, Macmillan.

FELINSKA, E. (1852). *Revelations of Siberia by a Banished Lady*, 2 vols. London.

FENNELL, J. F. I. (1961). *Ivan the Great of Moscow.* London, Macmillan.

FISHER, C. A. (1965). *The Reality of Place.* London, School of Oriental and African Studies.

FISHER, R. H. (1943). *The Russian Fur Trade, 1550-1700.* Berkeley & Los Angeles, University of California Press.

FLETCHER, G. (1591). *Of the Russe Commonwealth. See* BOND, E. H. (1856).

FLORINSKY, M. T. (1953). *Russia, a History and an Interpretation,* 2 vols. New York, Macmillan.

FORSTER, G. (1798). *A Journey from Bengal to England,* 2 vols. London.

FORTY YEARS (1958). *Forty Years of Soviet Power.* Moscow.

FREEBERNE, M. (1966). 'Demographic and Economic Changes in the Sinkiang Uighur Autonomous Region', *Population Studies,* vol. XX, pp. 103-24.

FREEBORN, R. (1966). *A Short History of Modern Russia.* London, Hodder & Stoughton.

FRENCH, R. A. (1963). 'The Making of the Russian Landscape', *Advancement of Science,* vol. 20, pp. 44-56.

FRITZEMEYER, W. (1931). 'Christenheit und Europa', *Historische Zeitschrift,* beiheft 23.

GEORGEL, J. F. (1818). *Voyage à St Pétersbourg en 1799-1800.* Paris.

GERSCHENKRON, A. (1962). *Economic Backwardness in Historical Perspective.* Cambridge, Mass., Harvard University Press.

GILLE, B. (1949). *Histoire économique et sociale de la Russie.* Paris, Payot.

GREKOV, B. D. (1949). *Kievskaya Rus.* Moscow.

GUTHRIE, M. (1802). *A Tour performed in the years 1795-96 through the Tauride or Crimea . . .* London.

HAIMSON, L. (1964). 'The Problem of Social Stability in Urban Russia', 1905-17. *Slavic Review,* vol. 23, pp. 619-42.

HAKLUYT, R. (ed.) (1598). *The Principal Navigations. . . .* London.

HALECKI, O. (1950). *The Limits and Divisions of European History.* London, Sheed & Ward.

HAXTHAUSEN, A. VON. (1847). *Studien über die innern Zustande, das Volksleben und insbesondere die ländlichen Einrichtungen Russlands,* vols. 1 & 2. Hannover.

HAXTHAUSEN, A. VON. (1852). *Studien . . .* Vol. 3. Berlin.

HERMANN, B. F. J. (1810). *Die Wichtigkeit des russischen Bergbaues.* St Petersburg.

HERMANN, B. F. J. (1790). *Statistische Schilderung von Russland.* St Petersburg.

HERODOTUS. *History. See* POWELL, (1949).

HEYWOOD, R. (1918). *A Journey in Russia in 1858.* Manchester (private).

HOETZSCH, O. (1913). *Russland.* Berlin, Reimer.

HOLDERNESS, M. (1823). *New Russia: A Journey from Riga to the Crimea . . .* London.

HOOSON, D. J. M. (1964). *A New Soviet Heartland?* Princeton, N.J., Van Nostrand.

HOOSON, D. J. M. (1966). *The Soviet Union.* London, University of London Press.

HORSEY, J. *Travels. See* BOND, E. H. (1856).

HRUSHEVSKY, M. S. (1941). *A History of the Ukraine.* New Haven, Yale University Press.

IDES, E. Y. (1706). *Three Years' Travels from Moscow overland to China . . .* London.

ISCHANIAN, B. (1913). *Die auslandischen Elemente in der russischen Volkwirtschaft.* Berlin, Siemenroth.

JACKSON, W. A. D. (1964). *Politics and Geographical Relationships.* New York, Prentice Hall.

JENKINS, R. J. H. (ed.) (1962). Commentary on Constantine Porphyrogenitus *De Administrando Imperio.* London, Athlone Press.

JENKINSON, A. (1558). *The Voyage of . . . See* HAKLUYT, R. (1598). London.

JURASCHEK, F. VON (1906). *Otto Hübners Geographisch-statistische Tabellen aller Länder der Erde.* Frankfurt-am-Main, Keller.

KABUZAN, V. M. (1963). *Narodonaseleniye Rossii v xviii—pervoy polovine xix v.* Moscow.

KALESNIK, S. V. (1965). 'Some results of the new discussion about a "unified" Geography' (trans.), *Soviet Geography,* vol. 6, no. 7, pp. 11-16.

KARAMZIN, M. (1820). *Histoire de l'Empire de Russie,* trans. St Thomas & Jauffret, vol. 5. Paris.

KENDREW, W. G. (1953). *The Climates of the Continents,* 4th ed. Oxford, Clarendon Press.

KENDRICK, T. D. (1930). *A History of the Vikings.* London, Methuen.

KENNARD, H. P. (1913). *The Russian Year Book for 1913.* London, Eyre & Spottiswoode.

KERNER, R. J. (1946). *The Urge to the Sea: the course of Russian History.* Berkeley and Los Angeles, University of California Press.

KHITROWO, B. DE (1889). *Itinéraires Russes en Orient.* Geneva.

KHOZYAYSTVENNO-STATISTICHESKIY ATLAS (1857). *Khozyaistvenno-statisticheskiy atlas Yevropeiskoy Rossii,* 3rd ed. St Petersburg.

KHRUSHCHEV, N. S. (1959). *Control Figures for the Economic Development of the U.S.S.R. for 1959-1965.* Ottawa, U.S.S.R. Embassy.

KLAUS, A. A. (1887). *Unsere Kolonien: Studien und Materialen zur Geschichte und Statistik der auslandischen Kolonisation in Russland.* Odessa.

KLYUCHEVSKIY, V. O. K. (1956-8). *Kurs Russkoy Istorii,* 5 vols. Moscow.

KOCHAN, L. (1962). *The Making of Modern Russia.* London, Jonathan Cape.

KOROBOV, A. V. (1964). 'Geografiya i khozyaystvo', *Izvestiya Akademii Nauk SSSR, seriya geograficheskaya,* vol. 4, pp. 3-11.

KOTOSHIKHIN. (1906). *O Rossii v tsarstvovaniye Alekseya Mikhailovicha.* St Petersburg, Tipografiya Glavnogo Upravleniya Udelov.

KRASSNOW, A. VON & WOEIKOW, A. (1907). *Russland.* Leipzig, Freytag.

KRIZHANICH, Y. I. (1859-60). *Russkoye gosudarstvo v polovine xvii v,* 2 vols. Moscow.

KROTOV, V. A. (1964). 'Geographical Aspects and Problems of the Industrialization of Siberia', *Soviet Geography*, vol. 5, no. 9, pp. 50-6.

KRYPTON, C. (1956). *The Northern Sea Route and the Economy of the Soviet North*. London, Methuen.

KULISCHER, J. M. (1922). *Ocherk istorii russkoy promyshlennosti*. Petrograd.

KULISCHER, J. (1925). *Russische Wirtschaftsgeschichte*, 2 vols. Jena, Fischer.

LAIRD, R. D. (1963). *Soviet Agricultural and Peasant Affairs*. Lawrence, Kansas, University of Kansas Press.

LAQUEUR, W. (1965). *Russia and Germany*. London, Weidenfeld & Nicolson.

LAUE, T. H. VON (1963). *Sergei Witte and the Industrialization of Russia*. New York, Columbia University Press.

LAUE, T. H. VON (1965). 'The Chances for Liberal Constitutionalism', *Slavic Review*, Vol. 24, pp. 34-46.

LE BRUN, C. (1759). *A new and more correct translation of Mr Cornelius le Brun's Travels*. London.

LEIB, B. (1924). *Rome, Kiev et Byzance à la fin de xie siècle*. Paris, Picard.

LEIMBACH, W. (1950). *Die Sowyetunion*. Stuttgart, Franckh'sche Verlagshandlung.

LENSEN, G. A. (1964). *Russia's Eastward Expansion*. Englewood Cliffs, N.J., Prentice Hall.

LESSEPS, F. DE. (1790). *Journal historique du voyage de M. de Lesseps du Kamtschatka jusqu'à son arrivée en France* (1788), 2 vols. Paris.

LONSDALE, R. E. (1963). 'Siberian Industry before 1917,' *Annals of the Association of American Geographers*, Vol. 53, pp. 479-93.

LORIMER, F. (1946). *The Population of the Soviet Union: History and Prospects*. Geneva, League of Nations.

LYALL, R. (1823). *The Character of the Russians and a detailed History of Moscow* . . . London.

LYASHCHENKO, P. I. (1956). *Istoriya narodnovo khozyaystva SSSR*, 2 vols. Moscow.

MACARTNEY, C. A. (1930). *The Magyars in the Ninth Century*. Cambridge, Cambridge University Press.

MACKINDER, H. J. (1904). 'The Geographical Pivot of History', *Geographical Journal*, vol. 23, pp. 424-31.

MACKINDER, H. J. (1919). *Democratic Ideals and Reality*. London, Constable.

MACKINDER, H. J. (1943). 'The Round World and the Winning of the Peace', *Foreign Affairs*, vol. 21, pp. 595-605.

MALOZEMOFF, A. (1958). *Russian Far Eastern Policy*, 1881-1904. See LENSEN, G. A. (1964).

MANY CRISES (1964). *The Many Crises of the Soviet Economy*. Washington, D.C., U.S. Government Printing Office.

MARRIOTT, J. A. (1944). *Anglo-Russian Relations, 1689-1943*, 2nd ed. London, Methuen.

MARSDEN, C. (1942). *Palmyra of the North: the first days of St Petersburg*. London, Faber & Faber.

MATTHAEI, F. (1883-5). *Die wirthschaftlichen Hülfsquellen Russlands und deren Bedeutung fur die Gegenwart und die Zukunft*, 2 vols. Dresden.

MAZOUR, A. G. (1958). *Russian Historiography*. Princeton, N.J., Van Nostrand.

McNEILL, W. H. (1964). *Europe's Steppe Frontier, 1500-1800*. Chicago, University of Chicago Press.

MIKHAYLOV, N. (1937). *Soviet Geography*, 2nd ed. London, Methuen.

MILLER, M. (1926). *The Economic Development of Russia, 1905-14*. London, King.

MIRSKY, D. (1927). 'The Eurasian Movement', *The Slavonic and East European Review*, vols. 5, pp. 311-12.

MIRSKY, D. (1952). *Russia, A Social History*. London, The Cressett Press.

MOOR, H. (1863). *A Visit to Russia in the Autumn of 1862*. London.

MORAVCSIK, G. (ed.) (1949). Constantine Portphyrogenitus *De Administrando Imperio*. Budapest, Peter Tudomanyeqyetemi.

MORRISON, J. A. (1952). 'Russia and Warm Water', *United States Naval Proceedings*, vol. 78, pp. 1169-79.

MOSSE, W. E. (1958). *Alexander II and the Modernization of Russia*. London, English Universities Press.

MOSSE, W. E. (1965). 'Stolypin's villages', *The Slavonic and East European Review*, vol. 43, pp. 257-74

NANSEN, F. (1914). *Through Siberia, the Land of the Future*, trans. by A. G. Chater. London, Heinemann.

OBOLENSKY, D. (1950). 'Russia's Byzantine Heritage', *Oxford Slavonic Papers*, vol. 1, pp. 37-63

OBOLENSKY, D. (1962). Commentary on Chapter 9 of Constantine Porphyrogenitus *De Administrando Imperio. See* JENKINS, R. J. H. (1962).

ODDY, J. J. (1805). *European Commerce*. London.

ODERBORNIUS, P. (1582). *De Russorum religione, ritibus nuptiarum, funerum, victu, vestitute, etc.*

PAINTER, G. D. ET AL. (eds.) (1965). *The Vinland Map and the Tartar Relation*. New Haven, Yale University Press.

PARES, B. (n.d.). *A History of Russia*, 3rd ed. London, Jonathan Cape.

PARES, R. & TAYLOR, A. J. P. (eds.) (1956). *Essays Presented to Sir Lewis Namier*. London, Macmillan.

PARKER, W. H. (1960), 'Europe: how far?' *Geographical Journal*, vol. 126, pp. 278-97.

PAULY, T. (1862). *Description ethnographique des peuples de la Russie*. St Petersburg.

PEREVEDENTSEV, V. I. (1965). 'Obliyanii etnicheskikh faktorov na territorialnoe pereraspredeleniye naseleniya', *Izvestiya Akademii Nauk SSSR, seriya geograficheskaya*, no. 4, pp. 31-9.

PERRY, J. (1716). *The State of Russia under the present Czar*. London.

PINKERTON, J. (1802). *Modern Geography*, 2 vols. London.

PINKERTON, R. (1833). *Russia, or Miscellaneous Observations on the Past and Present State of that Country and its Inhabitants*. London.

PLATONOV, S. F. (1929). *Histoire de la Russie*. Paris, Payot.

POKSHISHEVSKIY, V. V. (1956). 'Nekotoryye Voprosy ekonomiko-geograficheskogo Polozheniya Leningrada', *Voprosy Geografii*, 1956, pp. 104-29.

POKSHISHEVSKIY, V. V. ET AL. (1964). 'On Basic Migration Patterns', *Soviet Geography*, Vol. 5, no. 10, pp. 3-18.

POMUS, M. I. (1964). 'Vostochnaya Sibir', *Geograficheskiye Problemy Krupnykh Rayonov SSSR*. Moscow.

PORTAL, R. (1950). *L'Oural au xviiie siècle: étude d'histoire économique et sociale*. Paris, Institut d'Etudes Slaves.

PORTER, R. K. (1809). *Travelling Sketches in Russia and Sweden, 1805-1808*. London.

POWELL, J. (1949). Trans. Herodotus *History*, 2 vols. Oxford, Clarendon Press.

PURCHAS, S. (1613). 'His Pilgrimes', *Hakluyt Society Extra Series*, vol. 1 (1905).

PUSHKAREV, S. G. (1965). 'Russia and the West', *The Russian Review*, vol. 24, p. 138.

PUTNAM, P. (ed.) (1952). *Seven Britons in Imperial Russia, 1698-1812*. Princeton, Princeton University Press.

RAEFF, M. (1964). 'Russia's Perception of her Relationship with the West', *Slavic Review*, vol. 23, pp. 13-19.

RANKE, F. VON (1824). *Geschichte der romanischen und germanischen Völker von 1494 bis 1535*. Leipzig.

RASHIN, A. G. (1956). *Naseleniye Rossii za 100 let, 1811-1913*. Moscow.

RASHIN, A. G. (1958). *Formirovaniye rabochego klassa Rossii*. Moscow.

RECHBERG, C. DE, & DENNING, G. B. (1812-13). *Les Peuples de la Russie*. Paris.

RECLUS, E. (1875). *Nouvelle Géographie Universelle*, vol. 1. Paris.

REINEGG, J. (1796). *Allgemeine historisch-geographische Beschreibung des Kaukasus*. Gotha & St Petersburg.

REUILLY, J. (1806). *Voyage en Crimée et sur les bords de la Mer Noire, 1803 . . . Notes sur les principaux ports commercants*. Paris.

REYNOLD, G. DE. (1950). *La Formation de l'Europe*, Vol. VI, Le Monde Russe. Paris, Plon.

RIASANOVSKY, N. V. (1963). *A History of Russia*. London, Oxford University Press.

ROBERTS, H. L. (1964). 'Russia and the West: A Comparison and Contrast', *Slavic Review*, vol. 23, pp. 1-12.

ROBERTS, L. (1638). *The Merchant's Mappe of Commerce*. London.

ROBINSON, G. T. (1932). *Rural Russia under the Old Regime*. New York, Macmillan.

ROOS, H. U. L. VON (1911). *Mit Napoleon in Russland*. Stuttgart, Lutz.

ROUSSEAU, J. J. (1826). 'Considérations sur le gouvernment de Pologne', *Oeuvres*, ed. M. Mussay Pathay, vol. 5. Paris, Werdet.

RYBAKOV, B. A. (1948). *Remeslo drevnei Rusi*. Moscow.

RYBAKOV, B. A. (ed.) (1966). *Istoriya SSSR*, Vol. 1. Moscow.

RYABCHIKOV, A. M. (1964). 'O vzaimodeystvii geograficheskikh nauk', *Vestnik Moskovskogo Universiteta, seriya geografiya*, 1964, no. 3, pp. 7-19.

SAUSHKIN, Y. G. (1964). 'Vzaimodeystviye prirody obshestva', *Geografiya v shkole*, 1964, pp. 10-13.

SAUSHKIN, Y. G. (1965). 'Po povody odnoy polemiki', *Vestnik Moskovskogo Universiteta, seriya geografiya*, 1965, no. 6, pp. 79-82.

SCENES (1814). *Scenes in Russia: describing the manners, customs, diversions, modes of travelling*, etc. London.

SCHELTING, A. VON. (1948). *Russland und Europa*. Berne, Francke.

SCHLESINGER, M. L. (1908). *Russland in XX Jahrhundert*. Berlin, Reimer.

SCHLESINGER, R. (1949). *Changing Attitudes in Soviet Russia: the Family*. London, Routledge & Kegan Paul.

SCHWARTZ, H. (1965). *The Soviet Economy since Stalin*. London, Gollancz.

SEGUR, COMTE PHILIPPE-PAUL, DE. (1825). *Histoire de Napoléon et de la Grande Armée pendant l'année 1812*, 2 vols. 4th ed. Brussels.

SEMENOV, P. (1862-85). *Geografichesko-Statisticheski Slovar Rossiyskoy Imperii*, 5 vols. St Petersburg.

SEMENOV, V. P. (ed.) (1899-1913). *Rossiya: polnoye geograficheskoye opisaniye nashego otechestvo*, 19 vols. St Petersburg.

SEREDONIN, S. M. (1916). *Istoricheskaya geografiya, lektsii*. Petrograd, Typografiya Glavnogo Upravleniya.

SETON-WATSON, H. (1956). The Intellectuals and Revolution: Social Forces in Eastern Europe since 1848. See PARES & TAYLOR (1956).

SETON-WATSON, H. (1964). *The Decline of Imperial Russia*. London, Methuen.

SEYMOUR, H. D. (1855). *Russia on the Black Sea and Sea of Azov*. London.

SINZHEIMER, G. P. G. (1965). 'Russian Backwardness and Economic Development', *Soviet Studies*, vol. 17, pp. 209-25.

SMOLKA, H. P. (1937). *Forty Thousand Against the Arctic: Russia's Polar Empire*, revised ed. London, Hutchinson.

SORLIN, I. (1965). 'Le témoignage de Constantin VII Porphyrogenète sur l'état ethnique et politique de la Russie au début du xe siècle'. *Cahiers du Monde Russe et Sovietique*, vol. 6, pp. 147-88.

S.S.S.R. V TSIFRAKH (annual). Moscow.

STEPIN, F. (1962). 'Rossiya mezhdu Evropoy i Aziey', *Noviy Zhurnal*, no. 69, pp. 251-76.

STEWART, E. H. & HYDE, H. M. (ed.) (1934). *The Russian Journals of Martha and Catherine Wilmot*. London, Macmillan.

STORCH, H. (1801 A). *The Picture of Petersburg*. London.

STORCH, H. (1801 B). *Tableau historique et statistique de L'Empire de Russie à la fin du xviiie siècle*. Paris.

STRAHLENBERG, P. J. (1730). *Das Nord und Ostliche Theil von Europa und Asia*. Stockholm.

SUMNER, B. H. (1944). *Survey of Russian History*. London, Duckworth.

SUMNER, B. H. (1950). *Peter the Great and the Emergence of Russia*. London, English Universities Press.

SUMNER, B. H. (1951). 'Russia and Europe'. *Oxford Slavonic Papers*, vol. 2, pp. 1-16.

SVININE, P. (1814). *Sketches of Russia*. London.

SWINTON, A. (1792). *Travels into Norway, Denmark and Russia in 1788, 1789, 1790 & 1791*. London.

SZEFTEL, M. (1964). 'The Historical Limits of the Question of Russia and the West', *Slavic Review*, vol. 23, pp. 20-7.

TACITUS, *Germania*.

TAYLOR, A. J. P. (1954). *The Struggle for Mastery in Europe: 1848-1918*. Oxford, the Clarendon Press.

TAYLOR, A. J. P. (1965). *English History: 1914-1945*. Oxford, Clarendon Press.

TEGOBORSKY L. (1852-55) *Etudes sur les forces productives de la Russie*, 3 vols. Paris.

THOMAS, W. L. (ed.) (1956). *Man's Role in Changing the Face of the Earth*. Chicago, University of Chicago Press.

TOLSTOY, L. (1887). *Anna Karenina*. London.

TOOKE, W. (1799). *View of the Russian Empire during the reign of Catherine II and to the close of the present century*, 3 vols. London.

TORGOVLYA (1964). *Vneshnyaya Torgovlya za 1963*. Moscow.

TOYNBEE, A. J. (1954). *A Study of History*, Vol. 8. Oxford, Clarendon Press.

TREADGOLD, D. W. (1957). *The Great Siberian Migration*. Princeton, Princeton University Press.

TREADGOLD, D. W. (1964). *Twentieth Century Russia*, 2nd ed. Chicago, Rand McNally.

TROYAT, H. (1961). *Daily Life in Russia under the last Tsar*, trans. from French by M. Barnes, London, Allen & Unwin.

TUGAN-BARANOVSKY, M. (1900). 'Geschichte des russischen Fabrik-gewerbes', *Zeitschrift fur Social- und Wirthschaftsgeschichte*, Ergänzun-sheft 6. Berlin, Felber.

TURGENEV, N. (1847). *La Russie et les Russes*, Vol. 3. Grimma.

USCOMBE, R. (1571). 'Letter written . . . the 5th day of August 1571', R. HAKLUYT's *The Principal Navigations*. Glasgow, James Maclehose (1903).

VAMBERY, H. (1864). *Travels in Central Asia*. London.

VERNADSKY, G. (1948). *Kievan Russia*. New Haven, Yale University Press.

VERNADSKY, G. (1953). *The Mongols and Russia*. New Haven, Yale University Press.

VERNADSKY, G. (1959A). *The Origins of Russia*. Oxford, Clarendon Press.

VERNADSKY, (G.) (1959B). *Russia at the Dawn of the Modern Age*. New Haven, Yale University Press.

VIGEL, F. F. (1891). *Zapiski*. Moscow.

WALLACE, D. M. (1905). *Russia*, 2 vols. London, Cassell.

WATSON, J. S. (1960). *The Reign of George III: 1760-1815*. Oxford, Clarendon Press.

WAWILOW, S. I. ET AL. (1952). *Grosse Sowjet-Enzyklopädie*, 2 vols. Berlin, Verlag Kultur & Fortschritt.

WEBER, F. C. (1721). *Das Veranderte Russland*. Frankfurt.

WEIDLÉ, W. (1949). *La Russie absente et présente*. Paris, Gallimard.

WEIGERT, H. W. ET AL. (1957). *Principles of Political Geography*. New York, Appleton-Century-Crofts.

WERTH, A. (1964). *Russia at War: 1941-45*. London, Barrie & Rockliff.

WESTWOOD, J. N. (1964). *A History of Russian Railways*. London, Allen & Unwin.

WESTWOOD, J. N. (1966). *Russia, 1917-1964*. London, Batsford.

WHITWORTH, C. (1758). 'An Account of Russia as it was in the year 1710', *Fugitive Pieces*, vol. 2. London.

WILMOT, M. & C. (1803-8). The Russian Journals of Martha and Catherine Wilmot. *See* STEWART, E. H. & HYDE, H. M. (1934).

WILSON, R. T. (1861). *Private Diary of Travels, Personal Services and Public Events . . . 1812, 1813 and 1814*. London.

WITTFOGEL, K. A. (1956). The Hydraulic Civilizations. *See* THOMAS, W. L. (ed.) (1956).

WOODWARD, E. L. (1938). *The Age of Reform: 1815-70*. Oxford, Clarendon Press.

ZLOTNIKOV, M. (1946). 'Ot manufaktury k fabrike', *Voprosy istorii*, No. 11-12, pp. 36-9.

GLOSSARY

arsheen: a unit of measurement, equal to 28 inches.
artel: a partnership of artisans.
barshchina: labour dues owed by peasants to landlords.
boyarin, boyar: baron of Old Russia.
chernozem: black earth (soil).
chetvert: capacity measure of 5¾ bushels.
desyatina, desyatin: about 2·7 acres.
dvoryanin, dvorian: nobleman.
guberniya: 'government', province.
izba: traditional Russian house built of logs.
kolkhoz: collective farm.
kulak: wealthy peasant.
kustar: domestic (cottage) industry.
mir: peasant commune.
obrok: money payment or rent due to landlord.
oprichnina: royal domain created by Ivan IV from boyar lands.
podzol: thin, poor, leached, grey soil.
pomeshchik: landlord, noble.
pud: measure of weight: 36 English pounds (61 puds=1 ton).
slavophil(e): preferring national or traditional Russian usages.
smerd: free peasant in Kievan Russia.
sokha: a light plough.
streltsy: semi-professional troops stationed mainly in Moscow and other
    towns from the reign of Ivan IV to that of Peter I.
tayga: northern coniferous forest.
uezd: administrative district.
versta, verst: two-thirds of a mile (1,167 yards).
zolotnik: about 4·25 gms.

LIST OF PROVINCES
referred to by numbers in figures 33, 47, 48, 49, 66, 77

1	Moscow	31	Mogilev
2	Vladimir	32	Minsk
3	Kaluga	33	Vilno
4	Yaroslavl	34	Grodno
5	Kostroma	35	Belostok
6	Nizhniy Novgorod	36	Vyborg
7	Tver	37	Lifland (Livonia)
8	Voronezh	38	Estland
9	Ryazan	39	Kurland
10	Tambov	40	Kharkov
11	Orel	41	Chernigov
12	Kursk	42	Poltava
13	Tula	43	Kiev
14	Archangel	44	Volynia
15	Volodka	45	Podolsk
16	Petersburg	46	Yekaterinoslav
17	Novgorod	47	Kherson
18	Olonets	48	Tauria
19	Pskov	49	Cossacks of the Don
20	Kazan	50	Cossacks of the Black Sea
21	Penza	51	Bessarabia
22	Simbirsk	52	Yekaterinodar
23	Saratov	53	Sukhum
23(a)	Samara	54	Vladikavkaz
24	Astrakhan	55	Batum
25	Caucasus	56	Tiflis
26	Vyatka	57	Temir-Khan-Shura
27	Perm	58	Kars
28	Orenburg	59	Yerevan
28(a)	Ufa	60	Yelizavetpol
29	Smolensk	61	Baku
30	Vitebsk	62	Novorossiysk

INDEX

N.B. Sub-entries are arranged in chronological order.

RUSSIA, WEST SIBERIA AND CENTRAL ASIA

•••••••• Boundary of Kievan
Russia at its maximum extent.
1054

▬▬▬▬ Boundary of Muscovy,
1533

·—·—·— Boundary of Russian
Empire, 1801